ORCHESTRATION

STEPHEN DOUGLAS BURTON

Associate Professor, George Mason University

Prentice-Hall, Inc., Englewood Cliffs, N.J. 07632

Library of Congress Cataloging in Publication Data

Burton, Stephen Douglas.
  Orchestration.

  Bibliography
  Includes index.
  1. Instrumentation and orchestration. I. Title.
MT70.B95   785′.028   82–381
ISBN 0–13–639500–7   AACR2

Dedicated to Christopher and Sara Keene

Printed in the United States of America

10   9   8   7   6   5   4   3   2   1

Editorial supervision/production and interior design by Diane Lange
Cover design by Janet Schmid
Manufacturing buyer: Harry P. Baisley

ISBN: 0-13-639500-7

PRENTICE-HALL INTERNATIONAL, INC., LONDON
PRENTICE-HALL OF AUSTRALIA PTY. LIMITED, SYDNEY
PRENTICE-HALL OF CANADA, LTD., TORONTO
PRENTICE-HALL OF INDIA PRIVATE LIMITED, NEW DELHI
PRENTICE-HALL OF JAPAN, INC., TOKYO
PRENTICE-HALL OF SOUTHEAST ASIA PTE. LTD., SINGAPORE
WHITEHALL BOOKS LIMITED, WELLINGTON, NEW ZEALAND

Contents

Preface

This book is meant both as a general reference for the professional or amateur musician interested in the study of orchestral scores and as a textbook for the student interested in composition or arranging. Each chapter is clearly divided into sections so that it can be adapted to individual needs. In the case of the violin, for example, the sections on description, tuning, range, and positions could be included while the sections on the origin of the instrument and the more complicated techniques of harmonics, special effects, and so on could be omitted. The chapter on the harp, Parts III and IV (which include chapters on writing for band, jazz band, and films, and on new techniques and instruments), and the appendices on unusual instruments could be reserved for more advanced courses. The chapter on writing for school ensembles and choruses might be useful only for students of music education. The table of instrumental ranges and the glossary should be useful to students at all levels.

Part II, Writing for Orchestra, is cross-referenced to excerpts from orchestral scores of all periods. Thus, concepts of orchestration are illustrated with substantial sections of music, and their interrelations are shown rather than each example's being used to illustrate a single concept. In addition, orchestration is not approached from the viewpoint of one particular period or aesthetic, but rather scoring is discussed in terms of individual lines (melody) and harmonic structure (chords) as they occur in music of all periods. The chapters on arranging preexisting music for orchestra, on the human voice, on notation, on rehearsal and performance (including writing and copying of score and parts), and on scoring for other ensembles expand the scope of this book beyond that of the usual orchestration text. The *Orchestration Workbook* and *Instructor's Manual in Orchestration,* also published by Prentice-Hall, Inc., are keyed to chapters in this volume. A reasonable knowledge of harmony and literature on the part of the student is presumed.

New York City, October 19, 1979

ABOUT THE AUTHOR

Stephen Douglas Burton was born in Whittier, California, on February 24, 1943. His music has been commissioned and performed by orchestras such as the Berlin Philharmonic, Berlin Radio (SFB), National Orchestra of Paris (ORTF), Israel Philharmonic, Chicago Symphony, National Symphony, Pittsburgh Symphony, and others under such conductors as Sir Georg Solti and Antal Dorati. Other works have been commissioned by the American Dance Festival and the Chamber Music Society of Lincoln Center. He has transcribed music for the Joffrey Ballet and composed music for film. His opera, *The Duchess of Malfi,* was premiered by the Wolf Trap Opera Company, performed at *Artpark* with the composer as stage director, and nationally broadcast on NPR. Burton's *Songs of the Tulpehocken* is recorded on Louisville First Edition Records (LS757) with Kenneth Riegel, tenor, and the composer conducting the Louisville Orchestra. His Symphony No. 2, *Ariel,* has been recorded by Peters International (PLE128) with Diane Curry, mezzo-soprano, Stephen Dickson, baritone, and the Syracuse Symphony under the direction of Christopher Keene. Burton's music is published by B. Schott's Söhne, Mainz & London; Bote & Bock, Berlin & Wiesbaden; Editions Salabert, Paris; and Belwin-Mills, New York.

Mr. Burton has been a Guggenheim Fellow, has received grants from the National Endowment for the Arts and the National Opera Institute, and has awards from the American Society of Composers, Authors, and Publishers. He has contributed to music journals in the United States, Germany, and Brazil and appears on the National Educational Television series, "Music." He has served on the American Council on Germany, the C. Michael Paul Chamber Music Residency Program Selection Panel, and the advisory panel to the Virginia Commission on the Arts. He has also been Music Director of the Munich Kammerspiele.

Mr. Burton studied at the Oberlin Conservatory, the Peabody Institute, and the Mozarteum Academy in Salzburg, Austria. He has taught at Catholic University and is presently Associate Professor of Composition at George Mason University.

ACKNOWLEDGMENTS

The author wishes to thank Richard Graef and Walter Horban of the Chicago Symphony, Miran Kojian, Virginia Harpham, Richard Parnas, John Martin, Loren Kitt, Truman Harris, and David Flowers, all of the National Symphony, for their assistance in proofreading the chapters on the instruments. Sam di Bonaventura, Joseph Kanyan, Glenn Smith, Julie Lambdin, and Vera Heuser of George Mason University, Roy Gunther of George Washington University, and Donald Hefner of Catholic University were also of great help. Thanks also to Anita Lambkin of the Fairfax County Library in Virginia, Wayne Shirley and Michael Donaldson of the Library of Congress, and Henry Grossi and Rick Crouch of Dale Music Company. Most special thanks to Norwell F. Therien, Executive Editor of Humanities and others at Prentice-Hall and the pre-publication reviewers of this volume. Thanks also to Max Schlaefer and James Mosher.

Finally, special thanks to my wife, Louise, who bore with me through many difficult months and who made many helpful suggestions.

PART I

THE INSTRUMENTS
OF
THE ORCHESTRA

1

Classification
of
Musical Instruments

Traditionally, musical instruments in the Western world are classified as *strings, winds,* or *percussion.* Orchestral strings include the violin, viola, cello, bass, and harp. Orchestral winds are divided into *woodwinds* (originally all made of wood, the flute, oboe, clarinet, bassoon) and *brass* (trumpet, horn, trombone, tuba). *Percussion* includes a wide variety of instruments of definite and indefinite pitch. A fourth classification, *keyboard* instruments, is sometimes used in the orchestra. They include the piano and the celesta, both also classified as percussion, and the organ, which is also classified as a wind instrument.

This is a satisfactory, and in fact desirable, means of classifying musical instruments from a musician's standpoint, since the classification relates to the use of those instruments in most music. This system will be used throughout this text. There is, however, another, scientific classification which is more descriptive of exactly how sound is produced by each instrument. This classification is especially useful for the study of non-Western instruments:

1. *Idiophones.* Instruments in which the vibrating material is any elastic substance such as metal or wood. These instruments can be further classified according to the method of setting them in vibration: struck together, struck with beaters, stamped on the ground, shaken, scraped, plucked, or rubbed (friction idiophones).

2. *Membranophones.* Instruments in which the vibrating material is a membrane, such as the drums.
3. *Aerophones.* Instruments in which vibrations are created directly in the air, such as the wind instruments.
4. *Chordophones.* Instruments in which vibrating strings produce the sound.
5. *Electrophones.* Instruments in which the sound is generated electronically.

A knowledge of acoustics, the nature of sound, and the way various instruments produce sound is extremely important for an understanding of string harmonics, the role of overtones in orchestral combinations, and other such practical considerations. Therefore, Appendix B, "Acoustics and How Instruments Work" should be studied if the student lacks a background in this area.

Figure 1–1 shows various methods of referring to the octave register of any pitch. This text uses the more common system, Number 5, which the reader should memorize before proceeding with Chapter 2.

Figure 1-1

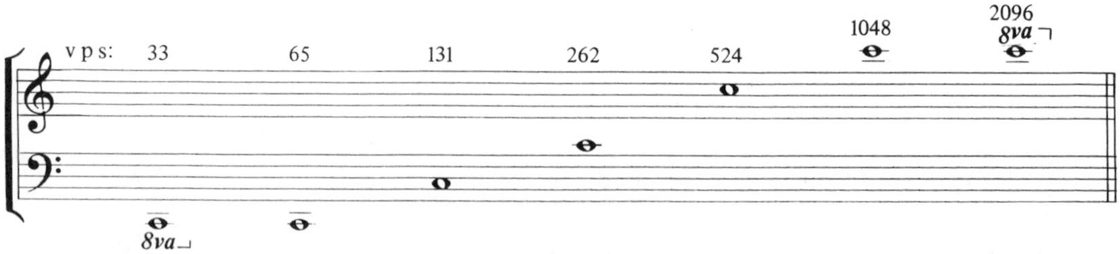

v p s:	33	65	131	262	524	1048	2096
1.	Contra	Great	Small	One-line	Two-line	Three-line	Four-line
2. Wavelength:	32'	16'	8'	4'	2'	1'	6"
3. Organ terminology*	64'	32'	16'	8'	4'	2'	1'
4.	CCC	CC	C	c	c'	c''	c'''
5.	CC	C	c	c¹	c²	c³	c⁴
6.	C₂	C₁	C	c	c¹	c²	c³

*see Appendix A

2

The Violin

Ital. *violino(i)*   **Ger.** *Geige(n), Violine(n)*   **Fr.** *violon(s)*

1. ORIGIN

The violin descended from the medieval fiddle through the *lira da braccio* and the rebec, appearing in its present form in the latter half of the sixteenth century. The bow, which probably originated in India, was introduced to Spain in the eighth century by the Moors and was in use throughout most of Europe by the twelfth century.[1]

Violin making reached its peak with three great craftsmen of the seventeenth and early eighteenth centuries, Nicolo Amati, his pupil Antonio Stradivari, and Giuseppe Guarnieri "dé Gesù." No modern instrument maker has been able to equal the beauty of tone of these instruments, which were made over two centuries ago and today are valued at hundreds of thousands of dollars each.

---

[1] See Bibliography for books which deal with the origin of instruments.

2. DESCRIPTION

The overall length of the violin is about 23½ inches (60 cm). The effective sounding length of the strings (from nut to bridge) is a little less than 13 inches (33 cm). The arched belly (top, table, or soundboard) is usually of pine or spruce, the back of maple or sycamore. The fingerboard (see Figure 2–1) is made of ebony. The belly is reinforced by a strip of wood called the *bass bar*. A wooden soundpost transmits vibrations from the belly to the back of the instrument. Stylized *f*-holes are cut in the belly at either side of the bridge. The strings used to be made exclusively of the entrails of sheep or pigs (not catgut, although the term is still used). Today the E string is made of metal and the other strings are wound with a metal such as aluminum or silver. They are attached to the stringholder and drawn over the bridge, a piece of wood which is supported on the belly by the tension of the strings. The strings continue over the nut at the end of the fingerboard and finally are wound around pegs with which they can be tuned. The violin is held under the chin with the aid of the chin rest. The four fingers of the left hand vary the length of each string by pressing the string against the fingerboard in order to play different pitches.

The bow is held in the right hand near the heel (frog) and is drawn across the strings so that the horsehair comes in contact with them and sets them in vibration. The tension of the hair is adjusted by use of the screw in the heel of the bow.

Figure 2-1

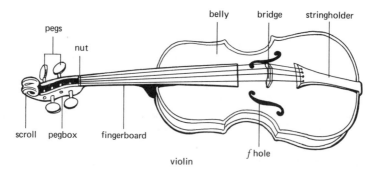

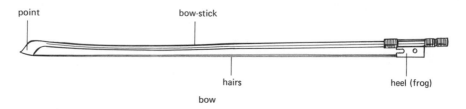

3. TUNING

The strings of the violin are tuned to the notes g, d¹, a¹, and e² and are numbered, as in all bowed instruments, from the highest string in descending order of pitch:

Figure 2–2

e²—I, a¹—II, d¹—III, g—IV

In orchestral scores one sometimes encounters directions to play on a certain string. The following terminology is common:

English	**Italian**
on the A string	sulla La corda
II.	sulla IIᵃ (2ᵃ) C. (corda)
A————————	

German	**French**
auf der A-Saite	sur la II. (2ᵉ) corde
II.	sur (le) A (La)

Numerous abbreviations of these directions are to be met with. Foreign terms for the strings of the violin are as follows:

	Italian	**German**	**French**
I	mi	E	mi (E)
II	la	A	la (A)
III	re	D	ré (D)
IV	sol	G	sol (G)

Scordatura is an unusual tuning of the strings to facilitate performance or change the tone color of the instrument. Berlioz tells us that, when playing in flat keys, the famous nineteenth-century virtuoso Niccolo Paganini sometimes tuned the strings of his violin up a half step and transposed the music at sight in order to utilize the more brilliant sound of *open* strings (strings not stopped with the fingers of the left hand), his open strings then being a♭, e♭¹, b♭¹, and f², notes common in flat keys. Today *scordatura* is generally used only at the direction of the composer. In his Fourth Symphony Mahler calls for a violin with its strings tuned up a whole step to imitate the tone of a cheap street fiddle. Saint-Saëns in *Danse Macabre* and Stravinsky in the 1919 version of the

Firebird Suite call for E strings tuned down a half and whole step respectively. Strauss, in *Ein Heldenleben,* has the player tune the G string down a half step, and Bartók in *Contrasts* calls for the tuning g$\sharp$, d¹, a¹, e$\flat$² so that the tritones can be played on open strings.

4. RANGE

The whole notes in the violin range shown in Figure 2–3 represent the practical limits of writing for violin in a professional symphony orchestra. The solid note represents a safe upper limit in most nonprofessional ensembles. The entire range can be extended a third higher to b⁴ by the use of *harmonics,* which will be treated in section 10 of this chapter. The use of *pizzicato* (see section 16), *trills* (section 8), or *multiple stops* (section 9) limit the practical range of the instrument.

Figure 2–3

It must be stressed that even in professional orchestras the notes above a³ become increasingly difficult to execute and problems of intonation become greater with each step higher in pitch. Therefore, passages in this altitude should be carefully considered. Obviously, the slower and simpler the passage the more time the player has to be sure the finger is placed on just the right spot to play the note in tune. Certain doublings, which will be treated in Part II of the text, can also aid the effectiveness of passages in the extreme upper reaches of the violin range. Solo violinists, who are usually virtuoso players, are often asked to perform much more complex music than members of a section who must play precisely together. Unprepared high notes, that is, notes not taken by step or small intervals, are relatively secure in a professional orchestra up to about c⁴ provided they are preceded by a beat or two rest so that the player can fix his position.

5. POSITIONS

The violin technique is essentially one of hand position. If the fingers of the left hand are placed over the strings near the nut, they naturally fall over the strings at the points where a series of four ascending steps will be produced if the fingers press the string against the fingerboard and the string is set in vibration by the bow. As Figure 2–4 shows, this series of four ascending steps can be produced above *any* of the four open strings of the violin by the player's merely moving the fingers of the left hand *across* the strings, which involves only a slight movement, without moving the hand up and down the fingerboard at all. In *first position*, therefore, all the pitches from g to b² are available to the player (Figure 2–4a).

Successively higher positions (up to seventh) are found by merely moving the left hand up the fingerboard toward the bridge. In each higher position, the hand moves one step higher.

The fingers of the left hand are numbered from 1 (index finger) to 4 (little finger). 0 indicates an open string. In third position, for example, the index finger of the left hand is placed over a² on the E string, d² on the A string, and so on (Figure 2–4c). Higher positions are generally used only on the E string, where each step up in pitch requires a higher position, except when one is playing across the strings or playing an ascending melodic passage on one string in order to maintain consistent tone color. For this reason, a composer will sometimes indicate a specific string.

Figure 2–4

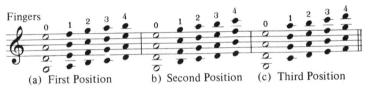

(a) First Position   b) Second Position   (c) Third Position

All sharps and flats within the violin's compass are available by a slight alteration of finger position. It should be noted that no matter how high the position in which the violinist is playing, all four open string pitches are always available simply by lifting the finger from the string. Passages exploiting the violin's ability to play across the strings and to alternate an open string with an adjacent stopped string are common, especially in the repertoire for solo violin (see Figure 2–5).

Figure 2–5   Vivaldi, *Concerto grosso, Op. 3, No. 11*

Naturally, the technique of the violin involves frequent shifts from one position to another. In addition, the extension of the fourth finger to encompass intervals larger than the fourth in any one position on any one string and the use of *half positions* in between the normal positions to facilitate certain passages are common practice.

Since the strings of the violin are tuned to the tonics of the first four sharp keys on the circle of fifths, one might rightly assume that the violinist is most comfortable playing in those keys. Also, sympathetic vibration of the open strings makes for greater resonance. Although professional players are called upon to play extraordinarily complex music, it will well repay the composer/ arranger to keep some general rules in mind. First, in arranging for nonprofessional ensembles, it is wise to keep to keys of no more than three or four sharps or flats. Second, avoid enharmonic keys (D♭ and C♯, for example) involving many flats (write in E major, an easy key for the violin, not F♭ major, a difficult one). The Beethoven, Brahms, and Tchaikovsky violin concerti are all in the key of D major. Half (23) of Mozart's 47 (not 41) symphonies are in the key of G, D, or A, and none is in a key that goes beyond three sharps or flats.

Finally, when writing highly chromatic or atonal music for strings, avoid as much as possible mixing sharps and flats in any one passage. Use enharmonic equivalents for double sharps and double flats. The saving of time and tempers in rehearsal and the increased effectiveness in performance will be more than adequate compensation for the extra trouble.

6. TONE

The tone of the violin is extremely rich in overtones, lending the instrument its characteristic poignancy or warmth. Shifting from one string to another while playing a melody can be done quite evenly so that no perceptible break occurs (although violinists tend to avoid open strings in the middle of lyrical melodies both because of their brighter tone and because they must be played without *vibrato;* see section 7). Nevertheless, each string has its own characteristic tone. The E string, being made of metal, is particularly brilliant, having strong upper partials. Most of the lyrical melodies one associates with the "singing" tone of the violin are played on this string. The A string is softer in tone and especially appropriate for quieter melodies. The D string has a quiet, sweet tone well suited for soft, gentle passages. The G string, with its strong lower overtones, is full and resonant, even rasping in quality and is often used for sonorous melodies either in *forte* or in *piano.* Positions up to the seventh are possible on the lower strings, although usually only the lower ones are used, higher passages being played in a correspondingly lower position on the E string. The examples in Figure 2–6 illustrate passages which exploit the tone qualities of the individual strings.

Figure 2–6

a) G-string   Beethoven, *Symphony No. 3*

Figure 2–6 (cont.)

b) D-string   Mahler, *Symphony No. 3*

Stravinsky, *Symphony in Three Movements*

c) A-string

Copyright © 1946 by Schott & Co., Ltd., London. Copyright © renewed.
Used by permission of European American Distributors Corp., Sole U.S. agent for Schott & Co.

d) E-string   Bartók, *Concerto for Orchestra*

7. VIBRATO

Vibrato is a technique used to increase the resonance of a tone on a string instrument. It is produced by shaking the wrist, thereby creating a slight oscillation of the fingertip on the stopped string and causing a small fluctuation in the pitch. A slight overindulgence in vibrato can produce a result considered in bad taste in many styles of music. Leopold Mozart vehemently warned players against its abuse. Today it is universal in most styles of music. Conductors may ask players for the speed or intensity of vibrato they think is appropriate for a particular passage. Occasionally, composers will indicate that a particular passage is to be played with no vibrato for a particularly cold or "white" tone:

English	**Italian**
without vibrato	*senza vibrato*
German	**French**
nicht vibrierend	*sans vibrer*

Contemporary scores will sometimes indicate the intensity of the vibrato as well ("slow vibrato," "rapid vibrato").

8. PORTAMENTO, GLISSANDO, TRILLS, FINGERED TREMOLO

Portamento is a normal part of violin technique. It simply means that the finger slides from one note to another on the same string when shifting posi-

11

tions or when playing certain passages. In passages such as the one in Figure 2–7, the portamento is stylistic. The finger slides up the string each time to the second eighth note. Where the portamento is not stylistically appropriate, it can be made hardly audible by subtleties of technique. The choice is left to the player, the section leader, or the conductor unless the composer specifically indicates its use.

Figure 2–7   R. Strauss, *Der Rosenkavlier*

Portamento is also used in fingering certain chromatic passages, though in a passage such as Figure 2–8, alternate fingerings would be used to enable each note to be played with a different finger. It should be noted that we are referring here only to *legato* passages. Using separate bows on each note (see section 14) completely alters the picture and such passages can be performed quite distinctly. The above should not deter one from writing legato chromatic passages for the violin, however. They can be quite effective.

Figure 2–8   Stravinsky, *The Rite of Spring*

The *glissando* (slide) means exactly the same as the portamento but is usually used to refer to portamenti that are indicated in the score and usually to those which cover a wide interval (a sixth or more) and are used for a special effect. Glissandi can be "faked" across the strings by the player's finger sliding on one string and then crossing to an adjacent string for the last note; the break as the bow switches from one string to another is perceptible, however. Figure 2–9 shows a glissando used for a special effect. Solo technique includes a

Figure 2–9   Mahler, *Symphony No. 4*

glissando combined with vibrato in which individual notes are heard in the course of the slide.

Trills are performed on a string instrument simply by stopping the lower note of the trill with one finger and rapidly bringing the next higher finger on and off the string. In a string section this produces a shimmering sound of extraordinary effectiveness. There are two limitations to be borne in mind.

First, trills performed on open strings are not as even or effective as trills performed on stopped strings. This need not prevent the student from writing trills on the notes e^2, a^1, and d^1, since those trills can all be performed on the next lower string as stopped notes. The half-step trill on the low g, however, should be avoided if possible, unless a particularly harsh effect is desired.

Second, the note g^3 should be taken as a reasonable upper limit for the lower note of a trill. Above this the tension of the string and the difficulty of execution combine to make trills on higher notes better avoided. Figure 2–10 shows a famous passage which exploits the ethereal quality of a trill in the upper range of the violin.

Figure 2–10   Wagner, *Siegfried, Act III*

The *fingered tremolo* is merely a trill performed on one string encompassing an interval greater than a second. Regarding, for a moment, the position technique of the violin, it should be clear that major and minor thirds and perfect fourths can be performed in this way. The augmented fourth or even the perfect fifth are possible with a fourth-finger extension but are better avoided.

These tremoli can be either *measured* or *unmeasured*. In the first case it is best always to write out at least one beat in tempo and then use the musical shorthand shown in Figure 2–11 for the rest of the passage.

Figure 2–11

When the tremolo is performed unmeasured, all the players alternate the notes as rapidly as possible. In this case, it is a good idea to write note values faster than could reasonably be performed as a measured tremolo (32nd notes at $\quarternote = 120$, for instance) and, in addition, add the word "tremolo," just to be certain. Figure 2–12 shows the shorthand.

The rule for notation of tremoli is to make each note the total duration of the sound and add at least three beams between the stems. In the case of whole notes, the beams are placed above or below the notes. The beams are placed between the stems of quarter notes but do not connect the stems. With half notes, the first eighth-note beam may or may not connect the stems, though there is increasing preference for the connected beam. With eighth notes, the first beam connects the stems, the rest do not. These passages must be slurred for reasons which are explained in section 11.

Figure 2–12

Although it is often done by beginning students of orchestration, there is no point in writing tremoli in two parts to secure the homogeneous sounding of both upper and lower notes at the same time (see Figure 2–13). The tremolo will be performed the same way and sound just as smooth if notated as in Figure 2–12. (Other tremoli are treated in section 15.)

Figure 2–13

9. CHORDS

Although the technique of the violin is predominantly that of playing single melodic lines, it is possible for two notes to be played simultaneously on adjacent strings (*double stops*). In the normal method of playing, the bow is brought into contact with one string at a time, but, as can be seen in Figure 2–14, by merely slightly altering the angle of the bow with relation to the strings, the

Figure 2–14

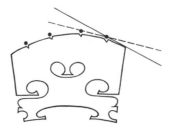

player can set two strings in vibration at once. With a certain amount of pressure, three strings can be brought into the same plane, the bow hair curves, and *triple stops* result. The bow can also be rapidly drawn over all four strings producing *quadruple stops*. The term *double stop* is often used to refer in general to playing on more than one string at a time, even though its precise meaning is limited to the simultaneous sounding of only two strings.

The use of chords was much more common during the baroque era, when music was more contrapuntal than during subsequent periods of music history. The classic examples of the extensive use of chords are the unaccompanied works for solo strings by J.S. Bach (see Figure 2–15). In music written from the classical era to the present day, extensive use of multiple stops is encountered only in occasional passages in the virtuoso solo repertoire and even more rarely in the orchestra, where they can, however, be extremely effective if used judiciously.

Figure 2–15   J. S. Bach, *Violin Sonata No. 3*

There are two considerations to be borne in mind in writing for the orchestral string section as opposed to the soloist. First, the orchestral parts should be simpler since such players are usually (though not always) not of solo caliber. They play an enormous amount of music of various kinds and do not have time to practice a difficult passage over and over until they have perfected it. Second, it is possible to divide a string section in the orchestra and have two or more notes played by different groups of instruments (see section 20).

The reasons for writing chords for a solo instrument are obvious. First, there is no other way to play more than one note at a time on a string instrument. Second, the technique of playing chords is quite "showy" and this fact has been exploited by almost all composers of solo violin music (see Figure 2–16).

Writing multiple stops instead of dividing the section in the orchestra is generally done when the resultant increased resonance of tone is desired.

Figure 2–16   Mendelssohn, *Violin Concerto*

DOUBLE STOPS

Figure 2-17   Beethoven, *Symphony No. 9*

Figure 2–17 illustrates how effective the double stop on open strings can be (here played with a *bowed tremolo;* see section 15). Obviously, any pair of *adjacent* open strings can be played as a double stop by a slight adjustment of the angle of the bow. Any open string can also be combined with any stopped note on an adjacent string. One must keep in mind that the resonant tone of the open string combined with a stopped note very high on an adjacent string may sound "pinched" in tone quality because of the shortness of the stopped string. Also, double stops in which the upper note is not at least d¹ (Figure 2–18) are clearly impossible since both notes would be available only on one string (g).

Figure 2-18

Unisons of an open string with a stopped string can be used for increased resonance, as shown in Figure 2–19.

Figure 2-19

Passages involving an open string and a series of notes on an adjacent string are possible but are better written for divided strings in the orchestra (Figure 2–20).

Figure 2-20

Any open string can be combined with any stopped string up to about fourth position with good results. (The E string, of course, can be used up to seventh position or higher with the open A string.) Clearly, a higher open string can be the lower of two pitches if a high position is being employed on the next lower, stopped string, as in Figure 2–21.

Figure 2–21

played on
stopped
G-string
open D-string

The fingering for double stops in which both notes are stopped can be seen in Figure 2–22. Intervals from the second to the octave in all forms (major and minor, perfect, augmented, and diminished) are possible. The perfect fifth is played by placing one finger directly across two strings. By means of a fourth-finger extension, ninths and even tenths are possible (Brahms and Bruch concerti), as are double-stopped unisons (when the lower note is an open string, ninths and larger intervals are, of course, quite easy).

Figure 2–22

Fingers

In effectiveness and ease of execution, sixths are the most useful and common double stop, with thirds a close second. Because the perfect intervals are more closely related in the overtone series than the imperfect consonances, the intonation of fourths, fifths, and octaves is somewhat more dangerous than that of thirds and sixths. A slight imprecision in intonation is much more audible in the perfect intervals. Any major or minor third or sixth is relatively easy as long as the lower note of the interval does not rise above g^2. After that, they become increasingly difficult, though not impossible, to execute. Double trills in thirds are also possible but are best written for divided strings in the orchestra. Sequences of thirds and sixths in a moderate tempo can be written, especially for solo instruments, but are best if they stay on the same two strings. Obviously, there are often two ways to perform a double stop (see Figure 2–23); the player will choose the most convenient.

Figure 2–23

a) on G on D   b) on D on G

Seconds and fourths are also playable, although they become more difficult after the lower note rises above g^2. Of course, seconds whose upper or lower note is an open string are easy.

Sevenths and octaves are possible so long as the lower note does not rise above e^2. The easy octaves are those whose lower note is an open string, a major or minor second above the open string, or a perfect fourth above the open string (see Figure 2–24 for the easy octaves).

Figure 2-24

Figure 2–25 shows all the relatively easy double stops.

Figure 2-25

TRIPLE STOPS

Whereas double stops are effective in either *piano* or *forte*, triple and quadruple stops are generally used only in the *forte*. Since a triple stop can be performed simultaneously only with some degree of pressure from the bow, and therefore volume, and since the quadruple stop must be arpeggiated, their normal use is for increased resonance and volume. Again, those chords in which the higher numbered fingers are on the higher strings are somewhat more convenient (Figure 2–26).

Figure 2-26

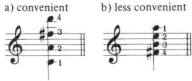

Triple stops in which two notes are open are easy. They can be written for any two open strings and an adjacent string stopped anywhere within its range. Triple stops in which one note is open can be played by combining any open string with two adjacent strings stopped to produce any playable double stop (see Figure 2–25), or an open string in the middle with stopped strings on either side.

Triple stops with no open notes are best built on one of the models shown in Figure 2–27. In Figure 2–27a, the chord consists of a fifth above a sixth; at b, a sixth above a fifth; and at c, two sixths. These chords are playable, in both their major and minor forms, as long as their lower note does not rise above a¹. Also,

Figure 2–27

augmented triads built on pattern b, with the third and fifth of the chord raised by a half step, are playable within this range (see Figure 2–28). Diminished triads built on pattern c, with raised root and third, also are quite playable (see Figure 2–28). In fact, a sequence of these chords is not out of the question for the solo player since they are made entirely of major sixths and so the fingers can move up and down the fingerboard, transposing the chord higher or lower, without changing their position relative to each other (see Figure 2–28).

Figure 2–28

QUADRUPLE STOPS

Quadruple stops are possible with three open strings and a string stopped anywhere within its range. The two open lower strings can be combined with any playable double stop on the two upper strings and, although the possibilities are more limited, the two open upper strings can be combined with

Figure 2–29

any playable double stop on the two lower strings (see Figure 2–29). The combination of the open D and A strings with stopped E and G strings is somewhat awkward but occurs (Bach solo sonatas). Clearly, any triple stop possible on the upper three strings can be combined with the open G string. Likewise, any triple stop playable on the lower three strings can be combined with the open E string.

Although quadruple stops with at least one open string sound best (in general, the more open strings, the more resonant the chord), quadruple stops with all four notes stopped are possible. They are best built on a pattern of two sixths and a fifth or three sixths as in Figure 2–30. In no case should the lowest note rise above d¹.

Figure 2–30

A few rules should be kept in mind when one is writing chords:

1. Use open strings whenever possible.
2. Triple stops are generally more effective than quadruple stops unless the quadruple stop includes an open string.
3. Do not try to write complete chords. Ease of fingering takes precedence (multiple stops or single notes in the other sections can supply any needed notes).
4. Unless the passage is extraordinarily exposed (lightly accompanied), voice-leading from one chord to the next in a sequence should not be considered more important than writing easily playable parts.
5. Stick to the simpler keys (see section 5).
6. Triple and quadruple stops are possible as broken chords (see section 12).
7. A series of chords require a certain amount of time for the player to "set" his fingering. Give at least a beat or two of moderate time for the more difficult chords.
8. Avoid skipping over strings. A noticeable break will occur as the player raises the bow from the string so as not to engage the string in between. In Figure 2–31, although the player *could* play the third in seventh position on the D and A strings, it would be normal to play it in third position on the A and E strings, which would require a leap of the bow over the D string from the G string.

Figure 2–31

9. Generally, avoid wide leaps from one double stop to another unless they could be part of one quadruple stop and therefore require no change of hand position on the strings. See Figure 2–32.

Figure 2–32

10. In writing for nonprofessional ensembles, it is prudent to avoid multiple stops as much as possible except those double stops containing an open string.

10. HARMONICS

Italian	**German**	**French**
armonico(i)	*Flageolett(en)*	*harmonique(s)*

Harmonics (see Appendix B) are produced on string instruments by lightly touching a string at one of the points (*nodes*) along its length which divide it into simple ratios, so that the string vibrates in segments of its overall length ($\frac{1}{2}$, $\frac{1}{3}$, $\frac{1}{4}$, $\frac{1}{5}$, etc.) and produces overtones. For instance, if the G string is stopped (pressed against the fingerboard) at the point exactly halfway between the bridge and the nut, the note g^1, an octave above the open string results: the string has been halved in length, doubling the frequency of the sound and thereby producing the pitch an octave higher.

If, however, the string is merely lightly touched at the same point, the string will be forced to vibrate in two equal segments each producing the note an octave higher than the open string (g^1). As one ascends the overtone series, obtaining successively higher harmonics by dividing the string into thirds, fourths, fifths, and so on by touching the string at any point that produces one of these ratios, the sound of the harmonic becomes more distinct from that of a stopped string. The stopped note has all the rich overtones associated with the tone of the violin whereas the harmonic is a much purer note, being an overtone itself. It has a flute-like quality which is immediately recognizable.

Figure 2–33 shows those *natural* harmonics (harmonics on open strings) possible on the G string. Not all are of equal quality nor do they "sound" with equal ease. The harmonics obtainable at three-fifths and five-eighths of the string length, for example, are not good on the E and A strings. The last three harmonics on the list are also best on the lower two strings.

As Figure 2–34 shows, some harmonics are available at several points along the string. The fourth overtone (fifth harmonic), for example, is available at one-fifth, two-fifths, three-fifths, and four-fifths of the string length. The player will usually choose the harmonic nearest to where he is playing at the moment. Figure 2–33 also illustrates the difficulty of playing in higher positions on

Figure 2–33

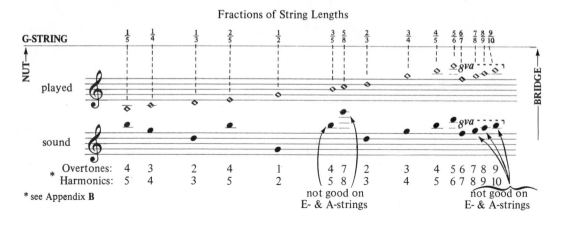

Figure 2–34

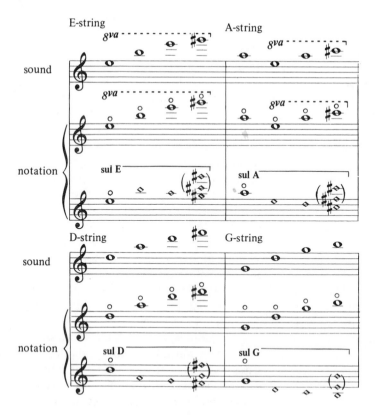

the violin. The first third of the string length from the nut encompasses the notes g to d¹, a perfect fifth. The second third encompasses an entire octave, and yet another octave occurs in just the next one-sixth of the string length. Figure 2–34 shows the practical natural harmonics available on all four strings as well as both methods of notation encountered in scores. The first method shows the sound produced by the harmonic but the second is more practical as it shows the player exactly where to finger the string. One should indicate on what string the harmonic is to be played; otherwise, confusion could result above d¹.

As can be seen from Figure 2–34, some notes are available on more than one string as harmonics (for example, d¹, the first overtone on the D-string or the second overtone on the G string). The context of the passage determines which is chosen.

It should be mentioned that players commonly utilize the first overtone (the octave above the open string) as part of their normal technique in passages where no harmonic is indicated.

Rarely, one sees examples of doubled-stopped harmonics (Paganini). The only practical ones are the first overtone on adjacent strings (see Figure 2–35).

Figure 2–35

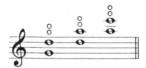

Even more infrequently, one finds harmonics played as a broken chord, the fingers of the left hand lightly touching the four strings as the bow is drawn rapidly from one string to another, producing an arpeggio in harmonics (see Figure 2–36). Only a few such chords are practical (see Figure 2–37).

Figure 2–36   Ravel, *Quartet in F*

Figure 2-37

sound

played

Stravinsky originated a much more effective use of natural harmonics: the harmonic glissando on one string. This is performed by simply running the finger up and down the string near the end of the fingerboard while the string is being bowed as for a sustained note. Figure 2–38 shows the notation. Since harmonics sound on a string only at the nodes shown in Figure 2–34, only the notes of the overtone series will sound, no notes in between. Therefore, paradoxically, an arpeggio is created by a glissando.

Figure 2-38

Artificial harmonics are those played on a stopped string. They are produced in exactly the same way as natural harmonics, limited by the possible stretch from the first finger, which must stop the string, to the fourth finger, which must lightly touch it at one of the nodes which produces a harmonic. The sound is the same as, if somewhat less resonant than, the natural harmonics played on the open string. Also, vibrato is possible with artificial harmonics, unlike natural harmonics which are on an open string. Since the normal stretch from first to fourth finger is a perfect fourth, this is the surest and by far the most common artificial harmonic in use. Since the fourth above the open string produces a harmonic two octaves above the pitch of the open string, it follows that the fourth above the pitch of the stopped string will produce a harmonic two octaves above that. The notation is shown in Figure 2–39. Notation 2–39a is the best, since it shows the player exactly what note to stop and what note to touch. Figure 2–39b also shows the note which results in actual sound, but this

Figure 2-39

is clumsy. Figure 2–39c merely shows the resultant pitch and is not to be recommended (although so great an orchestrator and conductor as Richard Strauss[2] condones it). The truth is that even in the best orchestras, in many cases string players are not able to decide at a glance how a particular harmonic can be produced. Much time in rehearsal may be wasted as a result.

The lowest artificial harmonic produced by the fourth is a^{b2}, the first note above the open G string. Occasionally the harmonic produced by stretching a perfect fifth from the first finger on the stopped note to the fourth finger touching the string is used. This extends the range in artificial harmonics of the violin down to e^{b2} (see Figure 2–40).

Figure 2–40

Artificial harmonics of the major or minor third, producing the fourth and fifth overtones, are possible but of poor quality and almost never used. Berlioz[3] writes of artificial harmonics of the major sixth (producing the fourth overtone) and the octave (producing the octave), but since most players could finger these only by holding the violin in the lap, bowing it like a cello, and using the thumb of the left hand as a movable nut in order to be able to stretch the sixth and octave, they need hardly be considered practical. The use of scordatura (section 3) to extend the harmonic range of the G string downward is also possible, but since these notes are available on the lower string instruments as harmonics of much better quality and ease of execution, it is hard to think of a reason one would employ them.

The ethereal, crystalline quality of harmonics have made them one of the favorite orchestral effects since they were first used in the early nineteenth century. If anything, they have been overused by many composers in this century. Like any striking musical effect, they can be startlingly effective at their first appearance, still welcome at their second, but by their third are like the guest who stays too long at dinner.

High, sustained harmonics, as well as chords of harmonics in a string section divided into several parts (see section 20), often combined with tremoli (section 15) or with mutes (section 17), are common orchestral fare.

Melodic passages in harmonics are less characteristic either of their sound or of the technique involved in playing them (which, in the case of artificial harmonics, requires two fingers of the left hand for each note). If they are written, they should be kept stepwise and not too fast; remember that they require

---

[2] Berlioz-Strauss, *Treatise on Instrumentation* (New York: Belwin-Mills, 1904 [date of Strauss's revision]), p. 38.

[3] Berlioz-Strauss, p. 35.

continual shifting of position for the left hand. Use natural harmonics rather than artificial wherever possible, because of both their easier execution and their slightly more resonant sound.

Figure 2–41 shows the range, in both natural and artificial harmonics, of the violin.

Figure 2–41

* quindicesima or quindecima = a fifteenth (two octaves) above

Figure 2–42 gives some representative examples of the use of harmonics.

Figure 2–42

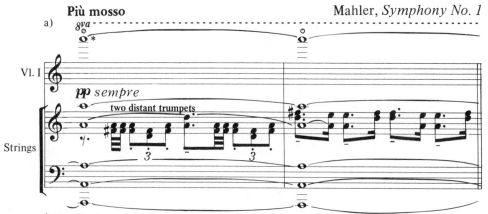

Mahler, *Symphony No. 1*

Più mosso

a)

Vl. I

pp sempre

two distant trumpets

Strings

*although written as a natural harmonic, would be played as an artificial harmonic.

Stravinsky, *L'Histoire du Soldat*

b) ♩ = 120

Solo Vl.

p

Copland, *Symphony No. 3*

c) ♩ = 144

Vl. I

f

11. THE BOW

Italian	German	French
archetto	*Bogen*	*archet*

The bow is brought into contact with the strings halfway between the end of the fingerboard and the bridge. It can be drawn over the strings either from the frog to the point (downbow) or from the point to the frog (upbow).

⊓   ∨

English *downbow*   *upbow*
Italian *arcata in giù*   *arcata in su*
German *Abstrich*   *Aufstrich*
French *tiré*   *poussé*

The musical symbols for downbow and upbow above are used only when there is some special reason for indicating an unusual bowing. Beginning orchestrators tend to write them much more frequently than is necessary.

The slur (⌒) is used to indicate a group of notes taken on one bow (*legato*). It is important, in writing for strings, to understand that the slur should be used to indicate bowings, *not* musical phrases, although the two sometimes coincide and some composers indicate only phrasing without regard to bowing technique (such as Wagner). There is no way to give a hard and fast rule as to how many notes can be taken on one bow. The rate at which the bow is drawn across the strings depends primarily on how loud the passage is. Figure 2–43 shows both a loud passage where the bow is drawn almost its full length in a

Figure 2–43

a) **Allegro vivo** (♩ = 144)   Tchaikovsky, *Symphony No. 6*

b) **Allegro molto**   Mozart, *Symphony No. 41, K. 551*

c) incorrect:

relatively short time and a soft passage where the bow takes somewhat longer to traverse the strings. These two passages represent the normal limits in time of notes taken under one bow. Slurs connect different *groups* of notes and should never connect to the same note (Figure 2–43c). The upbow stroke is best for crescendo since it moves from the weakest part of the bow to the strongest (the frog, where the bow is held).

It is important to slur trills and fingered tremoli or the players may mistake them for bowed tremoli (section 15). Long, sustained notes in a string section can be tied as long as desired. The players will change bows at will, and the overall effect will be of a sustained tone. *Staggered* bowing means that different parts of a string section will change bows at different times for a continuous legato. Finally, the string player can change from one bow direction to another with no perceptible break in the phrasing. Therefore, even if a string passage contains many changes of bow direction, the effect can be of a continuous legato.

It should be noted that in scores of the baroque era, bowing indications are sporadic and inconsistent. Also, the bowing technique was quite different in that time. In any case, bowings do not seem to have been needed since, in most cases, the style of the music left little doubt as to the character of the passage. The classical composer was content with slurs and occasional staccato marks to show what he wanted. Not until the nineteenth century did composers begin to indicate in more detail how their string parts should be played.

12. ELEVATIONS

Elevation refers to the various angles at which the bow can come into contact with the strings. Figure 2–14 shows how the bridge holds the strings in an arc rather than a plane, so that the bow can touch one string at a time. Double stops, of course, are played by holding the bow in between these elevations so that it can come into contact with two adjacent strings at once. If the bow is rapidly lifted from the lowest elevation (touching the E string) to the highest (touching the G string) and back again, chords can be played across the strings, as in Figure 2–44.

Figure 2–44

13. AT THE BRIDGE OR FINGERBOARD, AT THE POINT OR FROG (HEEL)

English	Italian
at the bridge	*sul ponticello*
at the fingerboard	*sul tasto (flautando)*
at the point	*alla punta*
at the frog	*al tallone*
German	**French**
auf dem Steg	*près du chevalet*
am Griffbrett	*sur la touche*
an der Spitze	*a la pointe*
am Frosch	*du talon*

The bow is sometimes brought into play partly on or near the bridge to create a hard, glassy tone. This is often combined with bowed tremoli (section 15) and harmonics, which are somewhat easier to produce in this fashion. When the bow plays over the end of the fingerboard, the tone becomes light and feathery. Occasionally conductors will ask for this effect whether it is indicated or not.

The bow has most force where it is being held, at the frog, and this placement is sometimes indicated in passages of extreme force, especially those involving successive downbows. The point, or lightest part of the bow is sometimes indicated, especially in light, high bowed tremoli, often combined with bowing at the bridge. Figure 2–45 gives some examples of these effects.

Figure 2–45

a) At the bridge   Stravinsky, *Rite of Spring*

Figure 2-45 (cont.)

b) On the fingerboard   Mahler, *Songs of a Wayfarer*

c) At the point   Berlioz, *Symphonie Fantastique*

plus vite   *animez*

a punta d'arco

Vl. I

pp

d) At the frog   Mahler, *Das Lied von der Erde*

schwer am Frosch

Vl. I

Copyright © 1912 by Universal Edition, A.G., Vienna. Copyright renewed.
Revised Edition copyright © 1962 by Universal Edition, Vienna and London.
Used by permission of European American Music Distributors Corp., Sole U.S. agent for Universal Edition.

At the end of any section of music involving unusual bowings or other procedures, one of the following indications should be used:

English	**Italian**
normal	in modo ordinario
ordinary	normale
natural	
German	**French**
Normal	jeu ordinaire
Gewoehnlich	naturel

14. BOWINGS

Various types of bowing (Fr. *coups d'archet*) other than legato are commonly used on the violin. Although there is some disagreement as to terminology, the main categories are generally agreed on.

1. *Détaché* (separate bows) means simply that the bow changes direction with each note. The notes are not, in fact, perceptibly detached from one another, but merely articulated more strongly than in legato bowing. No indication is necessary for this type of bowing; the absence of slurs is sufficient indication. Sometimes *détaché* is indicated by dashes over the note indicating much bow is to be used on each note. An exceptionally long stroke is called *le grand détaché*.

2. *Martelé, marqué* (Ital. *martellato, marcato*) is an even more strongly articulated, "hammered" bow stroke. It can be indicated by accents, arrowheads, or even dots or dashes. It differs from the *détaché* only in that the bow is stopped on the string between each stroke, creating a strongly accented note followed by a distinct break. A combination of *martellato* bowing and playing at the frog creates even greater force. Most forceful and distinct of all are separate downbows at the frog. Since the bow must be lifted from the strings to attack them again, this bowing is of great force and effect. It should not be kept up too long and is of use only in loud, strongly accented passages. Mahler occasionally asks the player actually to hit the strings with the bow (Ger. *mit dem Bogen geschlagen*).

3. The combination of legato bowing with a separate "push" on each note produces an expressive bowing known as *louré* (Ital. *portato*). The throbbing sound which results is especially suited to certain slow, lyric melodies. The indication is a slur with a dash over or under each note.

4. *Staccato* is a term which has caused confusion among players, conductors, and composers because it means several things in string technique. There is a true violin staccato in which several notes are taken with a single upbow but a distinct stop is made between each note. Although some virtuoso solo music exploits staccato bowing (*staccato volante*, flying staccato), the only examples found in the orchestra consist of two or three notes taken on an upbow before a downbeat, as in Figure 2–46. This technique is often referred to a *group staccato*. It also occurs in the notation shown in Figure 2–47. This notation seems to mean that the second note is to be played staccato, but what it means to a string player is that the first note is shortened as well. Otherwise there would be no way to articulate the two notes under one bow.

Figure 2–46

Figure 2-47

The preceding bowings are all *on the string.* There is another class of bow-ings in which the bow, taking advantage of its natural resiliency, literally bounces on the string. These are called *off-the-string* bowings.

5. *Sautillé* (Ital. *saltando, saltato;* Ger. *Springbogen, gestossen*) is a short, rapid, bouncing stroke in the middle of the bow, indicated by dots. The same indica-tion is used for (Ital.) *spiccato,* in which the bow is dropped on the string and lifted again after each note.

6. *Jeté* or *ricochet* means the upper third of the bow is thrust against the string on a downbow, bouncing over a series of two or three notes. Soloists can obtain ten or more separate notes on one *jeté* stroke. The notation is a slur with dots over or under each note head.

By now the reader must be quite confused as to how to indicate the bowing of any particular passage. Nothing can substitute for the study of a multitude of scores if the composer wishes to obtain a mastery of writing for strings. The im-portant thing is for the composer to indicate as clearly as possible the sound that he wants by judicious use of slurs, staccato marks, accents, and so forth. In performance, the solo player will choose that bowing which best fits his own technique in order to best realize the passage. In the orchestra, the *concert-master,* leader of the first violins, or the *principals,* leaders of the other sec-tions, determine exactly which bowing is to be used unless otherwise instructed by the conductor. Any one passage may have several correct bowings, depend-ing on such matters as individual interpretation, and no two players will use exactly the same bowings at all times. This makes it even more crucial, however, that the composer indicate what he wants in his score even if its realization may have several solutions.

It should be noted that the *names* of the bowings are seldom written in the score, the markings being sufficient to communicate to the player the bowing to be used.

Different bowings are compared in the examples in Figure 2–48. Example f shows an upbow used on a strong beat to articulate a particular rhythm. A rare bowing is the *Viotti* stroke, a short bow on an upbeat, a longer bow in the same direction on the beat. *Bariolage, arpeggio,* or *arpeggiando* is sometimes used to describe bowing broken chords across the strings. *Saccade* is the technique of applying pressure to the bow in order to play triple stops.

Figure 2-48

a) détaché

Allegro ma non troppo (♩ = 66)   Beethoven, *Symphony No. 6*

b) martelé

R. Strauss, *Death and Transfiguration*

etwas breiter

ff marcato

c) louré

Larghetto   Händel, *The Messiah*

dolce

d) sautillé

Allegro di molto   Mendelssohn, *Overture to A Midsummer Night's Dream*

pp   *sempre stacc.*

e) jeté

Con fuoco   Stravinsky, *Fireworks*

jeté   *jeté*

mf   *p poco a poco cresc.*

f)

15. BOWED TREMOLO

The bowed tremolo is performed not by a rapid alternation of the fingers of the left hand on different notes on the same string, but by the rapid alternation of the bow in different directions over the string. Obviously, the two effects are quite different. While the fingered tremolo has a floating, airy sound, the bowed tremolo can have a threatening, stormy sound on the lower strings and an ethereal, brilliant quality in the upper range. In any case, the effect is nearly always dramatic and can easily be overused.

The oldest type of bowed tremolo is the *measured tremolo* which has been in use since the seventeenth century. The bow simply performs a rapid *détaché* stroke. The notational shorthand for this is simply to write out each change of pitch in normal notation and add slashes *through* the stems (not between, as with the fingered tremolo) to indicate the value of the repeated notes. It is wise always to write out a beat or two in their strict rhythmic values at the beginning of such a section to distinguish it from an unmeasured tremolo (see Figure 2–49). The measured tremolo is used primarily to gain added rhythmic excitement at climaxes.

Figure 2–49

measured tremolo:

Unmeasured tremoli* occur when the bow moves as fast as possible back and forth over the strings. This is not particularly effective on a solo instrument (although it occurs in the Debussy Sonata), but in an orchestral string section it can have great impact. The notation is simply to write at least three (in a slow tempo, four) slashes through the stem (or, in the case of whole notes, above or below the note head). It is wise to add the word *tremolo* to avoid any confusion with a measured tremolo.

Anything which can be fingered normally on the violin can also be played tremolo, including double stops, which are particularly resonant and effective. *Sforzandi*, divided chords, and tremoli played at the bridge and with the tip of the bow are all common effects. It is also possible to combine fingered tremoli in one section with bowed tremoli in another. Tremoli can be used in an inner part as accompaniment as well. The only restriction is that after a while the bow arm tires and the tremoli are likely to become less rapid and intense and lose their effectiveness. The old rule of too much of a good thing applies here too.

Figure 2–50 shows both high and low tremoli. The first example, a measured tremolo, is the famous storm at the opening of *Die Walküre*. For increased sonority, the violins are directed to play on both G and D strings in unison.

Much less common are (1) tremoli, usually measured, produced by alternating the bow between two strings, a device which is not often useful or effective, (2) simultaneous fingered and bowed tremoli on the same instrument, which can be very effective, and (3) the extinct "undulating tremolo" (Ital.

Figure 2–50

a) **Stormy** Wagner, *Die Walküre*
(immer auf doppelten Saiten)

Vl. II

lower
strings

b) **Andante** Liadov, *The Enchanted Lake*

div. a 3

Vl. I

ondeggiando, Fr. *ondulé*) used by Gluck. There is some disagreement as to whether this was performed as a sort of unmeasured *louré,* was a series of *jeté* strokes performed by each player out of tempo to create an overall tremolo effect, or was simply an indication for vibrato. Another form of the tremolo alternating two strings is the tremolo on the unison produced by two adjacent strings (Figure 2–51d). Tremoli can also be combined with glissandi and harmonics. A dotted tie can be used to indicate that no new accent is to be made over the bar line.

Figure 2–51

a) Tremolo between strings Brahms, *Symphony No. 1*
Più andante

Vl. I

b) Bowed and fingered tremolo Brahms, *Symphony No. 2*
Allegro con spirito

c) Obsolete undulating tremolo Gluck, *Alceste*
tremolando or *tremolo*

35

□

Figure 2–51 (cont.)

d) tremolo on two strings

e) tremolo with glissando   Mahler, *Das Lied von der Erde*

f) tremolo with harmonics

16. PIZZICATO

When the string is plucked with the fingers, the indication *pizz.* is used. The return to normal bowing is indicated by the word *arco*. A note or short series of notes played pizzicato can be interpolated into a bowed passage. In this case, the bow remains in the hand and the right index finger is used to pluck the string. The change from arco to pizzicato can be made almost instantaneously after an upbow, when the right hand is close to the strings, but requires a bit more time after a downbow. A beat of moderate time should be allowed for the return to arco.

Pizzicati become more resonant at lower pitches. Above the note d^3, the E string becomes so tight as to reduce the effectiveness of the sound. The tone becomes dry and pinched.

It is not necessary to write pizzicato notes as short rhythmic values since the sound almost immediately disappears no matter what notation is used. The only difference between the two notations in Figure 2–52 is visual.

Figure 2-52

For longer passages in pizzicato, the player will lay the bow on the music stand so that the right hand is free. More time must be given between pizzicato and arco in this case. Although soloists have developed refined pizzicato techniques, the average orchestral player should not be called on for complex passage work, especially left-hand pizzicato (see the list below).

Figure 2–53 shows several examples of the uses of pizzicato in the orchestra.

Figure 2-53

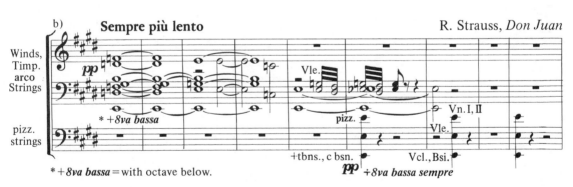

Following are several other kinds of pizzicato that are occasionally found. They are illustrated in Figure 2–54.

1. Multiple stops (a).
2. With vibrato (b). For purposes of added resonance, it is often played with vibrato even when not so indicated.
3. Left-hand pizzicato, played with a free finger of the left hand (c). Left-hand and right-hand pizzicato can also be alternated.
4. Snap pizzicato (d). The string is plucked with such force that it "snaps" against the fingerboard.
5. Tremolando, the fingers strumming rapidly back and forth over the strings (e). Sometimes the words *quasi guitara* are added.
6. Glissandi from a plucked note (f). This is practical only for ascending pitch.

Rarer effects include plucking the string with the fingernail (g), and pizzicato harmonics (h).

Figure 2–54

One should remember that the volume of sound possible with pizzicato is much less than with arco.

17. THE MUTE

English	Italian
with mute(s)	*con sordino(i) (c.s.)*
without mute(s)	*senza sordino(i) (senza sord.)*

German	French
mit Daempfer(n)	*avec sourdine(s)*
ohne Daempfer(n)	*sans sourdine(s)*

Mutes have been known since at least the baroque period but are rarely indicated in scores before the nineteenth century. Most players today have mutes attached to the strings below the bridge so they can be slipped up to the bridge within a bar of moderate time. Therefore, a bar rest should be given both before and after muted passages to enable the player to take the mute on or off. The next passage the instruments play after a muted passage must be marked *without mutes,* or, more commonly, in Italian, *senza sord.* It is also helpful to mark the end of a muted passage *mutes off* (*via sord.*) in order to give the player plenty of time to remove the mute. Otherwise he may suddenly come to the next passage marked *senza sord.* only to discover the mute is still on and there is no time to take it off.

It is important to realize that the primary reason for using the mute is to veil the tone color of the instrument, not lessen the volume; a fine *pp* is possible without mutes. Similarly, muted pizzicati, although used, are less resonant than unmuted pizzicati, which can sound just as quiet.

When there is no possibility of a rest in the string parts before a passage calling for mutes, an indication is on rare occasions given for the players to put mutes on "by stand" (*poco a poco con sord.*): each stand successively stops playing for a moment to put on the mutes. So brief a disappearance of the sound of two violins is unnoticeable. The effect is gradually to veil the string tone. Mutes can also be taken off gradually (*poco a poco senze sord.*). The combination of muted strings and tremoli is used to great effect in the famous opening of the *Liebestod,* (Figure 2–55).

Figure 2–55   Wagner, *Tristan und Isolde*

18. OTHER EFFECTS

Col legno means that the strings are set in vibration by the wood of the bow rather than the horsehairs. There are two types of col legno, (1) *col legno bat-*

tuto (Ger. *geschlagen*) and (2) *col legno tratto* (Ger. *gestrichen*). The strings are struck percussively with the bow in the *battuto* and drawn across the strings like the horsehairs in the *tratto*. Berlioz was the first to use *col legno* in a symphony in the well-known *Songe d'une nuit du sabbat* ("Dream of a Witches' Sabbath") from his *Symphonie Fantastique* (Figure 2–56), though it was first used in the orchestra in Tobias Hume's *Musical Humors* of 1605. It is effective only in a large body of strings upon rare occasions. The effect, as might be expected, is woody and lacking in a strong feeling of definite pitch. The *col legno tratto* is often performed with the edge of the hair of the bow as well, since the wood alone hardly sets the string in vibration very efficiently. This effect was introduced by Schoenberg and his pupil Berg and is sometimes found in contemporary scores. The effect is not very satisfactory except for sound effects and players do not like to employ the technique for very long because it can ruin the finish on their bows, which can cost hundreds or even thousands of dollars. A player performing such a passage has often been seen to take up a second, inferior bow to save wear and tear on his good one. Glissandi, tremoli, and harmonics are all possible with *col legno*.

Figure 2–56   Berlioz, *Symphonie Fantastique*

a) col legno battuto

b) col legno tratto

Other techniques which have been used include the glissando up to any node on the string which can produce a natural harmonic, a glissando along the entire string length as high as the player can play, and left-hand pizzicato played simultaneously with a bowed note on another string (Figure 2–57).

Figure 2–57

a) gliss. to harmonic b) gliss. up string.   c) l. h. pizz. & arco

The strings, unlike the more penetrating brass instruments, have only rarely been used for offstage effects. The gavotte in Act II of *Tosca* is the example that comes to mind. They have been used this way even less often in the concert hall, Berlioz's *Harold en Italie* being an example.

Chapter 37 describes additional string techniques.

19. THE SOLO VIOLIN

Examples of the literature for solo violin and piano are, of course, multitudinous. Nothing particular need be said about writing for this combination of instruments since they compete well with each other in terms of contrasting tone colors and dynamic range.

There are also many examples of the violin playing with a small group of instruments. The particular form of the string quartet will be considered in Chapter 7. Although the literature for small groups of violins alone is scarce outside of violin method books, the limitations of writing for an ensemble of instruments played by the students in the classroom, even a group of two or three violins, can be a spur to the imagination of the student arranger. There is nothing that can replace the experience gained from hearing one's arrangements, preferably of one's own compositions, actually performed. Several assignments of this type will be found in the workbook which is available with this text. Another aid is to have student players demonstrate individual instruments as they are being studied in class.

20. THE ORCHESTRAL VIOLIN
SECTIONS

In the orchestra, the violins are divided into two groups, first and second violins (I and II). This is historically a convention from the string quartet (two violins, a viola, and a cello), but remains standard today. At each music stand (desk) there are two players. In a major orchestra there are usually eight or more desks of first violins and eight desks of seconds (32 or more violins all together). Smaller orchestras make do with fewer strings.

Traditionally, the bulk of the melodic material is entrusted to the first violins. In fact, the famous fiasco at the rehearsal of the "Great" C Major Symphony of Schubert, conducted by Mendelssohn, was not, as is commonly supposed, due to the piece's being so difficult, but rather due to a rebellion of the violinists. They were piqued at having to play mostly accompaniment figures instead of the melody. Often the seconds double the firsts at the octave below, thus strengthening the part, the first overtone of the seconds reinforcing the notes played by the firsts. Of particularly emphatic character is a doubling of the firsts and seconds in unison (Figure 2–58).

Figure 2-58 Beethoven, *Symphony No. 5*

Divided string sections are used when a passage is so difficult that a more secure reading might be obtained by dividing it between two or more parts of the section, or when a section is called upon to play more than one part. The indication for this is *divisi* (Ger., *geteilt*). With more than two parts, it is best to add the number of divisions required (*div. in 3, in 4,* etc.). These parts should be written on separate staves and bracketed together, and each part should be numbered (1, 2, etc.). If the two parts are quite simple and no confusion would result in reading them on the same staff, they may be so written with stems up on the upper part and down on the lower part.

It is also possible to call for only half the section to play in order to achieve a lighter tone. This is indicated by the words *la metà* (Ger. *die Hälfte*). Individual desks can be indicated as well.

English	Italian	German	French
desk(s)	leggio(i)	Pult(Pülte)	pupitre(s)

The obvious extreme toward which this is tending is to write a separate part for each player in the section. This has been done in certain contemporary scores to obtain a special effect.

It must be remembered that at each division of the section the number of strings on any one part is fewer and that they therefore have less power. Divisions in two, three, or four parts are common. At the end of a divided section one should indicate the return to unison playing within the section by the word *unisono* (*unis.*). The word *tutti* is also used, though incorrectly; *tutti* means the entire orchestra playing together. Various examples of *divisi* writing are shown in Fig. 2-59 including the well-known *Feuerzauber* (Magic Fire) music. Here Wagner intentionally wrote a passage of such difficulty for the violins that it is impossible to be played with precision by a group of violinists in the orchestra. This, however, is exactly the shimmering, firelike effect he wanted.

Figure 2-59

Divisi passages have been common only since the nineteenth century. One exception that comes to mind is the "Farewell" symphony of Haydn in which the court musicians pack up their instruments and leave desk by desk in order to make clear to Count Esterházy that their vacations are long overdue.

Solo violins have been used with the orchestra from earliest times in the concerto. An occasional violin solo, played by the concertmaster, is often interpolated into orchestral works. It is almost obligatory in the Adagio section of a classical ballet *pas de deux,* for instance. The part is written on a separate staff above the rest of the section and marked *solo.* More than one solo can be written (*2 soli, 3 soli,* etc.). Strauss writes for twelve in *Don Quixote.* It should be mentioned that there is a danger of writing for a small number of strings in unison. Beats (see Appendix B) and slight differences of intonation are much more noticeable in a group of two or three strings playing the same notes than in an entire section, where the overtones of the instruments interact and create the beautiful "shimmering" quality of a large number of strings playing together. Anyone who has ever listened closely to the cello parts of Villa-Lobos's *Bachianas Brasileiras No. 5* for soprano and eight cellos (with the justly famous hummed aria) knows that two string players, even exceptionally good ones, playing the same line are never quite in tune with each other. This problem disappears when there are a large number of strings and the individual differences merge to create the characteristic tone color of a string section. Therefore, it is wise to write either for solo instruments or for at least four on one part.

The reinforcement of overtones within a string section also accounts for the fact that sixteen violins playing together are not sixteen times as loud as one violin playing alone. Therefore a solo violin, with a judicious lightening of the orchestral accompaniment, can hold its own against the orchestra so long as the solo instrument is kept higher in pitch than the rest of the strings and given a rhythmically independent part. The more brilliant tone color of the soloist distinguishes it from the mellow sound of the violin section. Of course, there are sections, especially in violin concerti, where the composer wants a climax in the orchestra, and no amount of ingenuity will allow the solo instrument to play above the din. On the other hand, it would make no sense for the soloist to cease playing just at the musical climax. The best thing to do in this case is give the soloist a rapidly moving, high-pitched, subsidiary part, keep the main melodic material in the orchestra, and hope for the best.

It is well to mark passages where each player is expected to play double stops as *non div.* Otherwise, confusion can result. In older scores (before the nineteenth century) divided passages were seldom marked. Presumably it was left up to the player whether to play a passage of two notes at a time as *divisi* or as double stops.

It seems prudent to end this chapter with a word of caution. Many of the special effects on the violin described above (multiple stops, harmonics, tremoli, *col legno,* etc.) are necessarily discussed at length. Since they are special techniques, some space must be given to their explanation. It must be borne in mind, however, that a special effect, on the violin as on any other instrument, is effective in inverse proportion to how often it is used. At least 90 percent of violin writing involves straightforward passages of single notes bowed in one of the ways described in section 14.

3

The Viola

Ital. *viola(e)*   **Ger.** *Bratsche(n), Viole(n)*   **Fr.** *alto(s)*

1. ORIGIN

The viola probably preceded the violin, since *violino* is merely the Italian masculine diminutive of *viola*. Note that in Italian, the plural of *viola* is *viole*, not *viola* as often appears, incorrectly, in scores.

2. DESCRIPTION

Although violas differ slightly in size, they are, on the average, some 4 inches (10 cm) longer than the violin. The sounding length of the strings is a little more than 2 inches (5 cm) longer than on the violin.

3. TUNING

The viola is tuned a fifth below the violin to the notes c, g, d¹ and a¹. The three upper strings are tuned to the same notes as the three lower strings of the violin. The strings are numbered from I to IV in descending order. The C string is *do* in Italian and French.

Figure 3–1

4. RANGE

The viola is written in the alto clef (the third line is middle C) and, for occasional passages that stay in the high range, the treble clef. The primary reason for using the treble clef for high passages is to avoid using many leger lines. Frequent changes of clef should be avoided, however, as they make the music more difficult to read. Most viola parts lie comfortably in the alto clef most of the time. The range (Figure 3–2) can be extended an octave by the use of harmonics. The solid note in the illustration represents a safe upper limit for non-professional ensembles. Playing above third position is somewhat more awkward for the violist than for the violinist.

Figure 3–2

5. POSITIONS

The technique of the viola is the same as that of the violin. Because of the viola's size, the distance between notes is slightly greater than on the violin, making chromatic passages a bit easier to perform. It should be pointed out that the viola is too small to properly resonate the low C. The difficulty is that if the instrument were made to the proper size for its tuning, it would be too large to be played under the chin and too small to be played between the legs like the cello. Human limitations, then, are responsible for the viola's being scientifically a mongrel instrument. It is probably due to this fact, however, that we can enjoy its highly distinctive and beautiful tone color.

6. TONE

The top string of the viola has a quite distinct "nasal" quality which has often been exploited by composers for short passages of plaintive melody. The lowest two strings have a particularly austere, dark sound. It is important not to think of the viola as just a lower-pitched violin. It is most useful playing in its lower two and one-half octaves, where its unique timbre is most evident.

7. VIBRATO

The vibrato technique is the same as on the violin, though somewhat slower and wider in the lower register.

8. PORTAMENTO, GLISSANDO, TRILLS, FINGERED TREMOLO

These techniques are also the same as on the violin except that the fingered tremolo is best limited to no more than a perfect fourth on one string and the octave on two adjacent strings. The fourth finger cannot be extended to intervals as large as those on the violin because of the greater length of the viola's strings.

9. CHORDS

Again, the technique is the same as on the violin except, of course, transposed down a perfect fifth. Quadruple stops are particularly heavy-sounding on the viola; triple stops are usually preferable. Avoid quadruple stops above third position, where they are more awkward than the corresponding stops on the violin. As with the violins, use as many open strings as possible.

10. HARMONICS

Artificial harmonics on the viola should be limited to those produced by touching the string a perfect fourth above the stopped note, although occasional perfect fifth harmonics are encountered. They should not extend above third position on the A string (Figure 3–3). The complete harmonic range of the viola in both natural and artificial harmonics is shown in Figure 3–4.

Figure 3–3

Figure 3–4

11. THE BOW

The viola bow is a bit thicker and heavier than that of the violin.

12. ELEVATIONS

The technique is the same as on the violin.

13. AT THE BRIDGE OR FINGER-BOARD, AT THE POINT OR FROG

The technique is the same as on the violin.

14. BOWING

The technique is the same as on the violin.

15. BOWED TREMOLO

This is quite effective on the viola. It has a sharp, biting effect in forte and a silken effect in piano, due to the tone color of the instrument.

16. PIZZICATO

Pizzicati are more resonant than on the violin but become dry above the note e^2, though this very quality has been exploited by such composers as Berg (in his violin concerto). As with harmonics, the higher pizzicati are usually best left to the violins.

17. THE MUTE

The muted viola is very effective. The mute seems to enhance the unique timbre of the instrument.

18. OTHER EFFECTS

These are the same as for the violin, though altered in tone on the viola.

19. THE SOLA VIOLA

Adjectives in Italian applied to the viola must agree with it in gender (*sola* or *sole,* not *solo* or *soli*). Although it is the only instrument of the violin family in the feminine gender, it has probably the most "masculine" tone. Occasional short solo passages for the viola can be of telling effect in the orchestra, although the solo repertory is scanty before the twentieth century, Berlioz's *Harold in Italy* being a rare example. William Walton and Walter Piston have written concertos for the instrument.

One must beware of orchestrating too heavily; the viola is easily covered. Also, the striking tone color of the instrument, while pleasantly different at first, can soon become cloying. A few examples are shown in Figure 3–5.

Figure 3–5

Wagner, *Tristan und Isolde*

*as is usually the case in Wagner, the slurs denote general phrasing, not bowings.

Figure 3–5 (cont.)

R. Strauss, *Don Quixote*

Henze, *Compases para Preguntas Ensimismadas*

20. THE ORCHESTRAL VIOLA SECTION

There are usually from eight to twelve violas in a symphony orchestra, several less than in a violin section. They usually sit on the conductor's right, upstage of the cellos, though occasionally downstage. The latter seating seems less effective because the *f*-holes of the instruments are then in the least efficient position for directing the sound out to the audience.

The violas lend a richness to the middle voices in the string ensemble. They are often called upon to play figurations, repeated notes, throbbing figures, broken chords, and so forth. They are frequently divided into two or more sections or asked to play double stops. They are also a good bass for the upper strings in high-pitched harmony. They can function as the upper voice in low-pitched string writing as well. Their unison doubling with the cellos adds a noticeable edge to the tone and, although it takes away some of the brilliance of the cellos, it adds weight (See Figure 2–57).

Violas doubling the violins usually take away some brilliance from the violin and add weight. Although the unison doubling of violas with cellos can be excellent, the continual doubling of the bass line an octave higher by the violas (primarily because the orchestrator can't think of anything else to do with them) is to be avoided. The interest which can be given to these inner parts is evident on almost every page of the works of Wagner, Strauss, Mahler, Stravinsky, Berg, Bartók, and composers of similar stature.

On occasion, the viola section is taken into ranges higher than normal, such as in Strauss's *Ein Heldenleben* ($g^{\sharp 3}$), but this usually occurs in a unison passage with the violins and many winds as well. The beginning of Shostakovich's Symphony No. 5 where the violas enter on $e^{\flat 3}$ in an exposed passage is unusual. The fact that the tempo is slow and the note values long lessens its difficulty.

Finally, a word must be said about the status of the viola in relation to the other strings of the orchestra. Over the last hundred years or so, no instrument except perhaps the contrabassoon has suffered such merciless invective. Berlioz, in 1844, referred to violists as "the refuse of violinists" and wistfully yearned for a time in the dim future when violists would be as proficient on their instrument as violinists and not choose to play the viola because they were not very good violinists. Forsyth roguishly observes that players were put on the viola because they were "too wicked or senile" to play the violin.

In defense of violists it must be said that Mozart preferred playing the viola in string quartets so that he could listen to the outer parts and Beethoven played the viola in the opera house in Bonn before he moved to Vienna. Nevertheless, it must be admitted that if one has virtuoso pretentions and leans

Figure 3-6

a)   Brahms, *Symphony No. 2*

Violas in sixths with the first violins.

Figure 3-6 (cont.)

b) **Adagio** (♩= 54)   Tchaikovsky, *Symphony No. 6*

Viols take the last figure of the melody from the bassoon, adding their distinctive timbre.

c) **Adagio**   Bruckner, *Symphony No. 4*

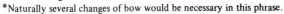

*Naturally several changes of bow would be necessary in this phrase.

                                 Elgar, *Enigma Variations*

d) **Andantino**

Figure 3-6 (cont.)

Hoiby, *Suite from "Summer and Smoke"*

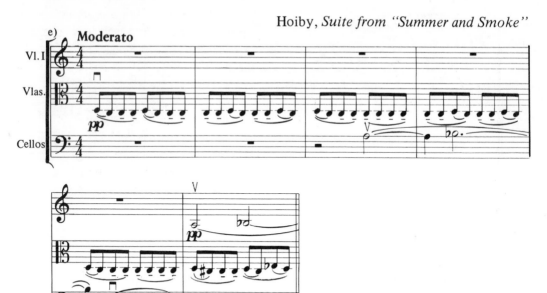

Wm. Schuman, *Symphony No. 8*

* At the discretion of the conductor, Glock. I may be played one octave lower than written, as in some halls the written sounds may be too predominant.

toward the string instruments, he is unlikely to choose the viola as his instrument. Also, there seems to be a psychological conditioning after playing inner parts in an orchestra for years, so that in many orchestras the violas are likely to be timid about playing parts clearly marked as solos. This, combined with their fewer numbers compared to the violins, makes it difficult to achieve the volume or intensity from the viola section that can be asked of the violins. Nevertheless, in our best orchestras, the viola section matches the violins in technique and virtuosity. If one keeps these points in mind when orchestrating viola parts, and keeps the accompaniment light and transparent when the violas are in the forefront, the effort will be well repaid.

4

The Cello

Ital. *violoncello(i)*   **Ger.** *Violoncello(i)*   **Fr.** *violoncelle(s)*

1. ORIGIN

Another member of the violin family, the violoncello is almost universally abbreviated to "cello" in English today.

2. DESCRIPTION

The instrument is placed between the legs and held off the floor by an adjustable peg attached below the tailpiece. The neck is held against the left shoulder. As with the viola, the cello's length, 48 inches (122 cm) is not great enough for its pitch to resonate properly. In the cello, however, this is compensated for by its much greater depth of $4\frac{1}{2}$ inches (11 cm). The effective string length is 27 inches (68 cm) and the bridge is $3\frac{5}{8}$ inches high (9 cm), compared to about 1 inch ($2\frac{1}{2}$ cm) for the violin.

3. TUNING

The cello is tuned an octave below the viola (see Figure 4–1).

Figure 4–1

4. RANGE

The range of the cello extends up to g^2 and above for soloists, although the cello section is best kept to c^2 and below. Nevertheless, the cello is much more facile in its extreme upper range than the viola, partly because of the greater length between notes on the longer string and partly because the playing position alleviates the awkwardness of reaching around the body of the instrument for high positions. Britten, in *Peter Grimes*, takes the cello section up to d^3. These stratospheric altitudes are not uncommon in contemporary scores. Harmonics can extend the range up to g^3 (see section 10). Nonprofessional orchestras are best kept below a^1.

Figure 4–2

The cello uses the bass clef, the tenor clef (indicating fourth line middle C) for moderately high passages, and the treble clef for very high passages. As with all instruments, use whichever clef keeps the part on the staff but avoid changing clefs too often. Until the beginning of the twentieth century, notes in the treble clef were always written an octave higher than concert pitch (see Figure 4–3). No one is quite sure why such an inefficient notation was used.

Figure 4–3   Beethoven, *Quartet in E♭ , Op. 127*

a) notation

Adagio molto espressivo

Figure 4–3 (cont.)

b) Sound:

5. POSITIONS

Because of the greater length of the cello strings, the distance from the first to the fourth finger of the left hand is normally a minor third in the lower positions, but it can be extended to a major third. (Figure 4–4 shows some typical cello fingerings.) Cello technique, therefore, involves more shifting of position

Figure 4–4

than that of the violin or viola, especially in passages made up of intervals larger than a third and scale passages not utilizing open strings (that is, in those keys with more than three sharps or two flats). These disadvantages are more than compensated for by the cello's more agile chromatic technique in the lower positions (where each half step is played by an individual finger) and by the possibility, because of the way the cello is held, of bringing the thumb into play as a "movable nut" to extend the stretch of the left hand in the higher positions. Also, as on the violin and viola, the distance between the notes becomes less the higher one plays on the string, so that above a^1 the cellist is essentially fingering the same way a violinist would in the lower positions. Figure 4–5 shows the notation for *thumb positions*. (These are not usually written in scores; the player will automatically use the thumb position to facilitate execution of a difficult passage.)

Figure 4–5

6. TONE

The striking tone one associates with high-pitched cello melodies is due to the vibrant, singing tone of the cello A string, rich in upper *partials* (overtones). This characteristic of the instrument has been much exploited by composers (see Figure 4–6). The D string is warm and pure in tone, and the two lower strings have a rich, mellow tone color.

Figure 4–6

a) the A-string.   Brahms, *Symphony No. 2*

b) the D-string.   Beethoven, *Symphony No. 9*

Figure 4–6 (cont.)

c)   The lower strings   Wagner, *Lohengrin*

*played, naturally, on the open C-string.

7. VIBRATO

The vibrato technique is the same as on the violin but wider and often somewhat slower.

8. PORTAMENTO, GLISSANDO, TRILLS, FINGERED TREMOLO

Because of the greater string length, in the lower positions the fingered tremolo should be limited to no more than a major third on one string and a minor seventh on two adjacent strings.

9. CHORDS

Again, because of the greater stretch on the cello, avoid sevenths and octaves in the lower positions. Triple and quadruple stops are good on the patterns shown in Figure 4–7 so long as the top note does not extend beyond g^1. The frequent use of broken chords in the cello as accompaniment is illustrated in Figure 4–12a.

Figure 4–7

10. HARMONICS

Because of the longer string, harmonics "sound" easily on the cello. Natural harmonics up to the seventh overtone (eighth harmonic) are common, although the seventh harmonic is somewhat flat in relation to tempered tuning. Harmonic glissandi can be made to sound up to the twelfth harmonic (see Figure 4–8). The most common artificial harmonic is that touched a perfect fourth above the stopped string, as on the violin, except that the thumb is used to stop the string to enable the third finger to stretch the perfect fourth. Figure 4–8 shows the range, in natural and artificial harmonics, of the cello. This range can include the notes a♭ to b by the use of the artificial harmonic at the perfect fifth, producing a twelfth above the stopped note, but this extension is somewhat less sure on the cello than on the violin. The minor third artificial harmonic (producing a tone two octaves and a fifth above the stopped note) is possible but seldom used.

Figure 4–8

11. THE BOW

Although the cello bow is somewhat shorter, heavier, and less elastic than the violin bow, all the bowings possible on the violin are effective on the cello.

12. ELEVATIONS

Although the strings are bowed from the opposite side of the instrument than the violin and although slightly greater elevations are needed to change from one string to another, this in no way affects writing for the instrument.

13. AT THE BRIDGE OR FINGER-BOARD, AT THE POINT OR FROG

These techniques are the same as on the violin.

14. BOWINGS

As stated in section 11, cello bowings are the same as for the violin. Because of the shorter bow and the longer, and therefore less responsive strings, more force must be exerted over a shorter distance to set the cello strings in motion. Therefore, it is important to phrase only about two-thirds as many notes under one slur as in a comparable passage for the violin.

15. BOWED TREMOLO

This is extremely effective on the cello, but remember that in double stops a minor seventh is the limit in the lower positions (see Figure 4–10).

16. PIZZICATO

Pizzicato is very resonant and quite common as accompaniment, either single notes or broken chords (if not too fast). The note a^1 is a practical upper limit. Above this the string is too tight and pizzicati become wooden in quality. Pizzicato natural harmonics on the first and second overtone (octave and twelfth above the open string) are quite effective (Figure 4–9).

Figure 4–9

17. THE MUTE

The mute is often used for a veiled tone. A striking example is the beginning of the *Liebestod* (Figure 4–10) with bowed tremoli on the muted strings.

Figure 4–10

Wagner, *Tristan und Isolde*

18. OTHER EFFECTS

The effects described for the violin are also applicable to the cello.

19. THE SOLO CELLO

Although the cello was occasionally used as a solo instrument in the eighteenth century (the Haydn concerto being a case in point), it was used only on rare occasions as a soloist in the orchestra until the nineteenth century (the

viola and double bass were almost never used as soloists). Beethoven's
Creatures of Prometheus is a notable exception. That Beethoven was aware of
the abilities of the solo cello in its upper register is evident since he takes it up
to a high g^2. The example from *Don Quixote* is another exceptional case (Figure
4–11).

Figure 4–11

Beethoven, *Creatures of Prometheus*

R. Strauss, *Don Quixote*

Copyright © 1898 by Jos. Aibl Musikverlag. © assigned 1932 to C. F. Peters.

Henze, *Ode an den Westwind*

Copyright 1955 by Schott & Co., Ltd., London. Used by permission of European American Music
Distributors Corp., Sole U.S. agent for B. Schott's Söhne, Mainz.

20. THE ORCHESTRAL CELLO
SECTION

There are many ways in which the cellos are used in the orchestra. They can take the bass line, usually doubling in octaves with the double basses. Until the nineteenth century, this was their usual task. They also played inner voices, often divided, and frequent melodic passages.

One of the common mistakes of the beginning arranger is to have the cellos and basses play the bass line in octaves all the time. This creates a very heavy bass. There are many ways to break up this monotony:

1. Have the cellos play the bass line alone.
2. Have only half the basses, or one desk, play with the cellos.
3. For a more focused bass line, have the cellos and basses play in unison. This is useful for purposes of emphasis but should not be continued too long.
4. Have the basses play a simplified version of what the cellos are playing (every other note, for instance).
5. Have the cellos play arco while the basses play pizzicato.
6. Have both the cellos and basses divide so that half play pizzicato and half arco (*div. in pizz. e arco*).

It should be noted that many of the above methods can be used in combination. They are not mutually exclusive (for instance, the basses could play a simplified version of what the cellos are playing, both cellos and basses could be divided into arco and pizzicato, and they could be playing at the unison rather than the octave).

Finally, although the cellos and basses are still occasionally written on one staff (the basses sounding an octave lower), this visual association should not discourage the orchestrator from dividing them and using them in independent ways. It is often best to use two separate staves for the cellos and basses at all times.

Figure 4–12

Beethoven, *Symphony No. 8*

Figure 4–12 (cont.)

Mahler, *Symphony No. 4*

Respighi, *Fontane di Roma*

Berg, *Wozzeck*

*get.=geteilt=divided; **am Frosch**=at the frog.

5

The Double Bass

Ital. *contrabasso(i)*   **Ger.** *Kontrabass(bässe)*
Fr. *contrebasse(s)*

1. ORIGIN

The double bass, also called "contrabass," "string bass," or just "bass," is the only surviving orchestral member of the old viol family of string instruments. It retains the sloping shoulders and flat back of that family, specifically those of the old "double-bass viol." The double bass is still sometimes referred to as the "bass viol."

2. DESCRIPTION

The double bass comes in several sizes. The usual orchestral bass is the "3/4 size" bass, about 74 inches (188 cm) long. The bridge is $6\frac{5}{8}$ inches (17 cm) high and the effective vibrating length of the strings is about 43 inches (109 cm). Basses are made with string lengths as great as 46 inches (116 cm).

The smaller "solo bass" has a string length as short as $39\frac{1}{2}$ inches (100 cm).[1]

The double bass rests on a peg, like the cello, and is supported by the player's body and left knee. In the orchestra, the bass player sits on a stool to manage the instrument more easily and avoid fatigue.

3. TUNING

Figure 5–1

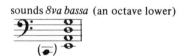

sounds *8va bassa* (an octave lower)

The orchestral bass is tuned to the notes EE, AA, D, and G. These are written an octave higher than they sound, so the instrument's part lies mostly on the bass clef. The double bass is therefore a transposing instrument at the octave below. Although many different tunings were used in the nineteenth century, the only other tuning found today is that of the *solo bass* which, being a smaller instrument, is tuned a whole step higher than the orchestral bass. Because of the greater tension on the bass strings, a system of cogwheels is used instead of tuning pegs.

During the eighteenth century, cello and bass parts were usually written on the same staff. Since the bass transposes at the octave below, the cellos and basses were playing in octaves most of the time. When the bass was unable to play the lowest four semitones of the cello an octave lower (since its lowest string was EE), the bass player would automatically play an octave higher (in unison with the cellos) until he could again return to the lower octave.

Although this procedure was usually satisfactory, occasionally a composer required pitches lower than EE. In this case, scordatura was used, as when Wagner has the double basses tune their lowest string down to EE♭ for the long pedalpoint at the beginning of *Das Rheingold*. Later a fifth string was added, usually tuned to low CC. Such instruments are sometimes still used. (The five-string jazz bass adds a string *above* to extend the upper range of the instrument.)

The most common method of increasing the lower range today is an *extension* on the E string above the nut; there, the four semitones between EE and CC can be obtained by means of keys which are attached to the extension and

---

[1] The solo bass is used in the limited solo repertoire written for the instrument. The smaller size and shorter stretches for the left hand make it easier to play complex passages. Since it has only the three upper strings, the body of the instrument is under less tension and is able to vibrate more freely, producing a better tone. The full-sized bass is too large for most players to manage easily and is seldom seen today.

depressed by the fingers of the left hand. Sometimes an entire bass section will be equipped with these extensions (though none may be found in amateur or school orchestras). If not, those players with the extension will play in the lower octave while the others either stop playing or transpose to the upper octave. Today it is good practice to indicate which method of performance is preferred. Figure 5–2 shows the notation.

Figure 5–2

(basses with extension)

When writing for the lower notes on the extension, one must be careful not to require the player to switch repeatedly from the extension back to the string. Passages such as the one in Figure 5–3 are very awkward and will sound clumsy.

Figure 5–3

4. RANGE

Figure 5–4

harmonics

Sounds *ottava bassa* (an octave lower)

Although it is wise not to write above written e¹ for nonprofessional orchestras, the orchestral bass section normally play up to a¹ or even d². Shostakovich takes his basses up to f² in his Fifth Symphony, though doubled with violas, cellos, and bassoons. The solo bass virtuoso is capable of even higher ranges, especially with his complex artificial harmonic technique. Bass, tenor, and treble clefs are used, all sounding an octave lower, except when harmonics are written in the treble clef at their actual pitch. On most basses, b¹ or c² is the highest stopped note.

5. POSITIONS

On the much-longer strings of the double bass, the normal span from first to fourth finger is only a major second in the lower positions. Above the seventh position, thumb positions are used and the technique and span between fingers becomes more like that of the cello. Obviously, more shifts are needed to play scale passages than on the cello because of the fewer notes available in any one position. Therefore, scales involving open strings (D, G, C, F major) are easiest. For the same reason, chromatic passages (those involving many minor seconds) are easily played and relatively secure.

6. TONE

The tone of the double bass is often described as being rougher than that of the other strings. Although this is true on the lower two strings, the upper strings are capable of surprisingly lyrical expression in the hands of a good player. The dark, forbidding quality of the lower range of the instrument has perhaps been overused for mysterious, threatening, or comic effects. The gradual discovery during the last two centuries of the potential of the instrument in its upper range has liberated it from its former constant enslavement to the bass line.

7. VIBRATO

This is the same as on the cello, though not as intense because of the greater string length.

8. PORTAMENTO, GLISSANDO, TRILLS, FINGERED TREMOLO

All major and minor trills are good but rather "tubby" in the lower range unless doubled with winds. Because of the stretch in the lower positions, fingered tremoli are not practical in the orchestra. Minor thirds become possible above second position. Glissandi are quite effective and, again because of the string length, "sound" well.

9. CHORDS

For the orchestra it is generally best to write the basses divided if they have more than one part to play. Octaves and fifths with one open string are of occasional use (any interval which includes an open string and a note which can be played on an adjacent stopped string are, of course, possible). Thirds, fourths, and fifths are possible on adjacent strings but not of much use in the orchestra since small intervals at low pitches produce such conflicting overtones that they sound dense and muddy.

It is occasionally of use to write broken chords across the strings. This is possible with two to four strings. Only one string should be stopped. See Figure 5–5.

Figure 5–5

10. HARMONICS

Although virtuoso bass soloists have a considerable technique in artificial harmonics in the higher positions, only natural harmonics are worth considering for the orchestral bass section. Because of the long strings, they are easy and of excellent quality. Those on the E string are harder and somewhat unclear. The practical harmonics are shown in Figure 5–6. They are written at their actual concert pitch in the treble clef in the case of harmonics played on the half of the string nearest the bridge. The touched node is indicated for those harmonics nearest the nut. The list given is for the G string. Harmonics on other strings can be found by transposition. Avoid the fifth and sixth harmonics on the E string, which are difficult to produce.

Figure 5–6

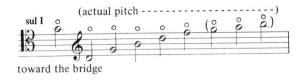

11. THE BOW

The bass bow is about 26 inches (66 cm) long. There are two types, the heavier German bow and the lighter French version. Some players still hold the bow with the palm up in the style of the old bass viol. It takes more pressure than on the other string instruments to set the bass strings in vibration. The bow must move at a relatively rapid pace to produce a satisfactory tone. Therefore, legato slurs for the bass must be very short. They should not include more than a few notes under one bow. Even in quiet passages, the direction of the bow must be changed every few seconds. Of course, long sustained pedal-points are achieved by each player's changing the direction of the bow at will and thereby creating an overall effect of legato (Ital. *cambio d'arco a piacere*). The examples in Figure 5–8 at the end of this chapter show various bowings.

12. ELEVATIONS

Although the bow must cover considerably more distance than on other string instruments, this fact does not affect the technique.

13. AT THE BRIDGE OR FINGER-BOARD, AT THE POINT OR FROG

These techniques are, if anything, even more effective on the bass than on the smaller string instruments.

14. BOWINGS

Although shorter bows must be used, all violin bowings, even off-the-string bowings, are possible, though the greater inertia of the string and weight of the bow make the lighter bowings somewhat less effective.

15. BOWED TREMOLO

Bowed tremoli can be effective but are extremely tiring on the player if prolonged. In the lower range, the tremolo can become muddy and indistinct, producing a rather ineffective sound. Therefore, composers often give the tremolo to the cellos and give the basses a measured tremolo. This has the double advantage of producing a more well-defined rhythmic effect and allowing the bass players to use more bow on each stroke, producing a greater volume of sound. If one wishes a less precise rhythmic effect, the basses can be divided into two sections playing in conflicting rhythm with each other.

16. PIZZICATO

Pizzicato is the bread-and-butter technique of the bass player. Some scores have the basses playing pizzicato more often than arco. The effect is very resonant and the bass line is considerably lightened by its use. Written g^1 should be the upper limit, although Strauss writes a third higher. Pizzicato on the lowest string can be somewhat dull in sound. Rapid pizzicato passages can quickly become tiring to the player.

17. THE MUTE

Although the mute is often indicated, some composers have used unmuted basses with the rest of the strings muted to secure distinctness in the bass line.

18. OTHER EFFECTS

Basically, the techniques are the same as for the other strings, but some additional effects are listed in Chapter 37.

19. THE SOLO DOUBLE BASS

Although solo concerti for the double bass have been written by Bottesini, Dragonetti, Henze, and a few others, the use of the solo double bass in the orchestra is rare even in the twentieth century. The peculiar tragicomic character of the solo that opens the slow movement of Mahler's First Symphony is a case in point. It relies for its effect on the unique "whining" quality of passages played on the upper string of the bass. The contrast of the bass's tone color and the solemn muted timpani accompaniment in combination give a touch of real gallows humor to this funeral march parody of "Frère Jacques."

Figure 5–7

Mahler, *Symphony No. 1*

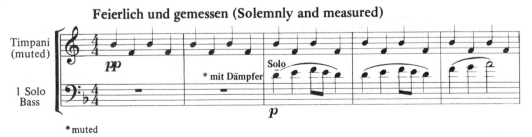

* muted

Figure 5-7 (cont.)

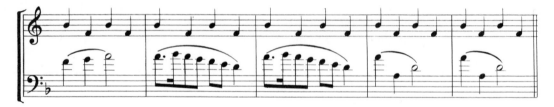

20. THE ORCHESTRAL BASS
SECTION

All the remarks concerning the cellos and basses in the previous chapter (section 20) apply here as well. Additional possibilities include: giving the cellos the bass line and giving the basses an intermittent figure below the real harmonic bass line; dividing the basses in octaves (this is usually a weak effect unless the basses are doubled with some winds; also there should be more basses on the lower part); and using the basses to provide the bass for the winds. Also, difficult passages may be divided between two groups of basses (the symphony orchestra usually includes eight or nine).

Finally, it is most important to avoid one of the common pitfalls of the beginning arranger: don't always keep the basses in the lower part of their range. This can produce an unnecessarily thick, heavy effect.

Figure 5-8

Mozart, *Symphony No. 41*

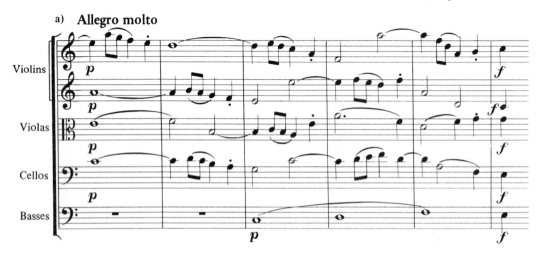

Figure 5–8 (cont.)

b)

Beethoven, *Symphony No. 6*

Verdi, *Otello*

c)

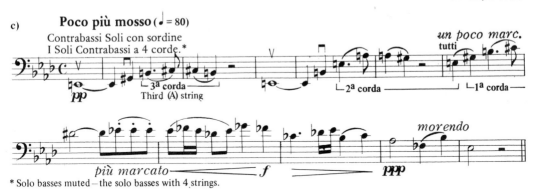

* Solo basses muted — the solo basses with 4 strings.

R. Strauss, *Also Sprach Zarathustra*

d)

Figure 5-8 (cont.)

etc., finally becoming
a four-part fugue

1st desk

2nd desk

Basses

3rd desk

4th desk

Britten, *The Young Person's Guide to the Orchestra*

e)

Basses

Schuller, *Seven Studies on Themes of Paul Klee*

f)

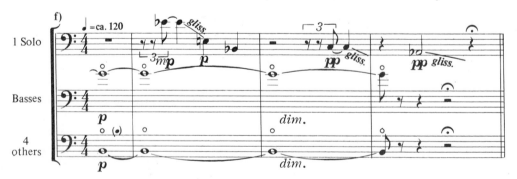

1 Solo

Basses

4 others

6

The Harp

Ital. *arpa(e)*   Ger. *Harfe(n)*   Fr. *harpe(s)*

1. ORIGIN

The most ancient string instrument, the harp existed in Mesopotamia in 3000 B.C. and was a favorite instrument of the ancient Egyptians. It was introduced to Europe by way of Ireland, where it became the national instrument. By the twelfth century it had become popular with the troubadors, trouvères, and minnesingers.

The old harps were tuned to the notes of a single scale, and therefore their use was limited to music written in that key. In 1720 a *single-action* harp was invented with a system of pedals which could quickly tune the strings to various keys by means of a notch which, when the pedal was moved, could change the pitch of a group of strings by one half step. Though a great improvement over previous instruments, the single-action harp still had serious technical drawbacks which were remedied in 1810 when Sébastien Érard introduced the modern (and now universal) *double-action* harp with two notches, so that a string could be either natural, sharp, or flat. In 1897 the Parisian firm of Pleyel introduced a chromatic harp with two sets of strings which were tuned to all twelve notes of the chromatic scale and intersected like the letter X.

This harp had no pedals. It was intended to replace the double-action harp in music of a more chromatic nature. Because of its inferior tone and difficult technique, the instrument never became popular. Although Debussy originally wrote *Danse Sacrée et Danse Profane* (1904) for the chromatic harp, it is invariably played on a double-action harp with minor adjustments in the harp part.

2. DESCRIPTION

Figure 6–1

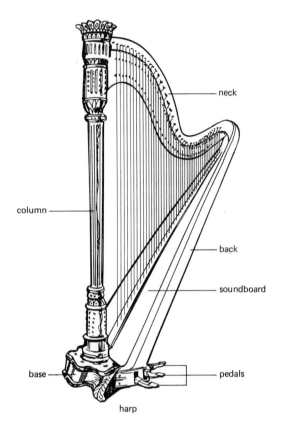

harp

A harp is an instrument with strings attached at a 45° angle to the soundboard. The double-action harp rests on a base (pedestal) in which the pedals are located. From the base rises a *column* (fore-pillar) in front. A curved *neck* to which the strings and their tuning pegs are attached connects to the hollow, tapered *back* of the instrument. The back includes the soundboard, to which the other ends of the strings are attached. The strings themselves are of nylon or gut, the lowest ones wound with metal. The performer distinguishes the strings by a color code (usually all C's red, F's purple, and the rest white). The back of the harp rests against the right shoulder and between the knees of the player.

3. RANGE

Figure 6–2

Figure 6–2 shows the range of the *concert grand* harp, which has 47 strings. Smaller harps with as few as 41 strings are built. The harp part is written on two staves with treble and bass clefs and, like the pianist, the harpist usually performs the part written in the treble clef with the right hand, the bass with the left. Sometimes, when the music lies particularly high or low, treble clefs or bass clefs are used for both staves.

4. TUNING

One feature of symphony concerts with a harp is that, even if one arrives a half hour early, one sees the harpist on stage industriously tuning the instrument. This is because there are 47 separate strings to tune. The harpist accomplishes this with a tuning key which can adjust the tuning pegs in the neck. In each octave there are seven strings, tuned to the notes of the scale of C♭ major.

Figure 6–3

Figure 6–3 shows the seven pedals of the harp in the back of the base from the viewpoint of the player looking down. Each pedal is attached to a mechanism in the column at the front of the harp which operates rotating discs

in the neck under each string below the tuning peg. Each pedal can be depressed and set in either of two notches in the base. When this occurs, a mechanism rotates a disc on the neck attached to all strings of a given letter-name. For instance, if the left foot depresses the pedal on the far left of the harp into the first notch, it will rotate all the discs attached to strings tuned to the note D on the harp. The rotating discs stop all the D strings one half step higher, thereby retuning them from D♭ to D♮. A further depression of the pedal into the second notch sets another set of discs in action and retunes the string yet another half step higher to the note D♯. When any pedal is in its highest position, therefore, the strings it controls will be tuned to the flat pitch; when in the first notch, to natural; and in the second notch, to sharp. Figure 6–3 shows which pedals control which notes. The possibility of retuning each string to two different pitches gives the double action harp its name.

It will be clear from the above that at any moment only one tuning of any particular note is possible. If one C is tuned to C♯, all C's are sharp.

By use of the pedals, the harp can be set in any major or minor (natural or harmonic) key, any mode, or a number of irregular scales. In fact, there are over two thousand possible combinations of pedal tunings on the harp.

The harp can be tuned to the key of g harmonic minor, for example, by leaving the pedals controlling the notes E and B in their flat tuning, depressing the pedals D, C, G, and A to their natural position (first notch), and depressing the F pedal to its sharp position (second notch). Four notations for this tuning are shown in Figure 6–4. The most common notation is a, which shows the tuning of the pedals from left to right; b shows the actual position of the pedals in the notches (first notch is on the line); c shows the pedals for the right foot above those for the left foot; d simply names the scale required. For purely diatonic music, a key signature is sufficient to show the tuning.

Figure 6–4

a) B♭CDE♭F♯GA b) ￩┼┼┼│┼┬┼┼￫ c) [E♭ F♯ G A / B♭ C D] d) g harmonic minor

Clearly, the harp is, by the nature of its mechanism, a diatonic instrument. Changes of pedal can be made at any time, however, and retuning by the pedals is often required as the harpist is playing. Generally the left foot controls the pedals on the left side of the harp, the right foot the pedals on the right, although the left foot can, in an emergency, set the E pedal. Two pedals can be depressed simultaneously if they lie on opposite sides of the instrument. Figure 6–5 shows a case where retuning is necessary during a passage. In this case each pedal change must be indicated under the staff (in the score, Liszt, who was one of the first composers to use the harp in the orchestra, leaves the tuning up to the player).

Figure 6–5

Always use the tuning which gives the harpist the fewest changes of pedal. Figure 6–6a requires ten changes whereas 6–6b (Tchaikovsky's notation) requires four.

Figure 6–6

Tchaikovsky, *Romeo and Juliet*

*B♭♭ played on the A string

There are three other considerations with regard to the pedals:

1. Tunings involving as many flats as possible are most sonorous because the strings are vibrating at their full length (even if the rest of the orchestra is playing in F♯ major, write the harp part in G♭ major).

2. The low CC, and sometimes DD, is not connected to the C pedal and must be tuned by hand at the beginning of the piece. The tuning should be indicated at the beginning of the score and not changed during the piece if the low string is being used.
3. Most important of all, frequent changes of pedal not only are tiring to the harpist, but distract him from his finger technique. Avoid such passages at all cost. The alternative is that the harpist will simply alter such passages to suit the instrument or not play them at all.

5. FINGERING

The strings of the harp are set in vibration by plucking with the fingers. The fingers are numbered 1 to 4 from the thumb to the ring finger. The little finger is not used. In writing for the harp it is important to realize that, so far as the finger technique is concerned, the tuning of the strings makes no difference. The harpist's C string is always in the same position whether it is sharp, natural, or flat.

Fingers 1 and 2 can stretch intervals from a second to a fourth, 1 and 3 stretch a fifth or sixth, and 1 and 4 stretch intervals from a seventh to a tenth (unlike the pianist, the harpist stretches a tenth easily). Parallel thirds, sixths, and even octaves can be played in one hand if not too rapid but such passages are best divided between the hands. In this case, avoid having one hand pluck the string just quitted by the other hand; this will damp the natural vibration of the string and lead to a dull, muffled sound (Figure 6–7).

Figure 6–7

Also avoid writing passages with the hands so far separated that the harpist must play at both ends of the instrument at once (Figure 6–8). It takes little imagination to visualize the awkwardness of such a position.

Figure 6–8   Wagner, *Tannhäuser*

6. TONE COLOR

The plucked strings of the harp have a more resonant sound than the pizzicato strings of the violin family, especially in the lower register. In the upper two octaves the strings are so tight that the effect is of a very sharp staccato accent.

7. CHORDS AND ARPEGGIOS

Chords and arpeggios are typical accompaniment figures for the harp. They can be played in up to four parts in each hand. For maximum resonance, the top note of the lowest chord and the bottom note of the upper chord should be about an octave apart. Normally, the harpist will slightly roll (arpeggiate) a chord to achieve greatest resonance. If this effect is not desired, a bracket or the Italian word *secco* (*non arpeggiando*, not broken, Fr. *sec*) should be added. For a more pronounced arpeggio, a wavy line (sometimes a straight line) is added, often with an arrow to indicate the direction. If the arrow points down, the chord is arpeggiated downward. This effect, though occasionally encountered, is noticeably less resonant than the upward arpeggio (Figure 6–9).

Figure 6–9

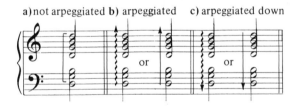

a) not arpeggiated b) arpeggiated c) arpeggiated down

Arpeggios are also possible over a wider range by the player's alternating three or four notes in each hand (Figure 6–10). Naturally, doubling this arpeggio in octaves would not be practical since both hands are already occupied. Also avoid double arpeggios in a rapid tempo.

Figure 6–10

8. GLISSANDO

The harp glissando, which easily walks away with the prize for the most overused of orchestral devices, was introduced by Franz Liszt in the *Mephisto Waltz.* In that score he wrote out each note of the glissando. Today a shorthand notation is used (as Forsyth reminds us, life is simply too short) with usually the first octave being written (to establish the tuning) and a line drawn to the last note of the glissando. Thirty-second or sixty-fourth note beams should connect the first notes of the glissando (Figure 6–11). Sometimes the indication *gliss.* is added below or above the line.

Figure 6–11

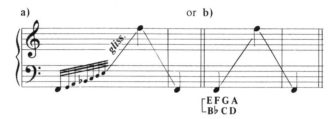

The glissando is performed by simply sweeping the fingers over the strings, up or down. It is most effective over at least two octaves and can be extended by means of *loops* (each hand sweeping quickly over a number of notes in alternation as the forearms bring the hands into a higher or lower range). The notation in Figure 6–12 is recommended:

Figure 6–12

Chords may also be played glissando with up to four notes in each hand descending and three in each hand ascending (where the thumbs cannot be used).

Remember that a glissando cannot be extended for more than a couple of seconds unless loops are employed. A glissando extended too long by this means is likely to sound rather silly. Used with discretion and imagination, however, the harp glissando can still be an effective device.

9. HOMOPHONES

A pitch created by two adjacent strings on the harp tuned enharmonically to the same note is called a *homophone*. Figure 6–13 shows the homophones

Figure 6–13

possible on the harp. It will be noticed that there are homophones possible on every note but D, G, and A. Homophones are useful for the following:

1. To obtain more force by doubling two strings on one pitch (see Figure 6–14).

Figure 6–14

2. To play repeated notes without the dampening effect of successively striking the same string (Figure 6–15).

Figure 6–15

3. To tune the strings of the harp to chords instead of scales (Figure 6–16). By this

Figure 6–16

means, an extremely rapid arpeggio can be played by simply running the hands over the strings as for a glissando. Since all the strings are tuned to notes of a chord, an arpeggio results, as shown in Figure 6–17. It should be noted that all such chords contain three homophones and one single string. All diminished sevenths and many other seventh chords are possible. A triad with added second or sixth is also possible.

Figure 6–17

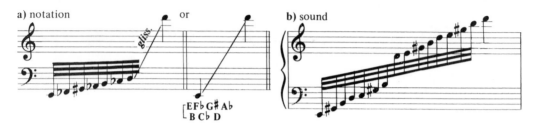

10. HARMONICS

Harmonics are produced on the harp by two means. With the left hand, one to four fingers pluck the strings as the side of the palm touches the node. With the right hand, the thumb plucks the string as the knuckle of the first finger touches the node. Thus up to four harmonics at once are possible with the left hand but only one with the right. Although second and third overtones are possible on the lower strings, only the first harmonic (the octave), found in the middle of the string, is used. The notation is the pitch of the string plucked. The harmonic sounds an octave higher (Figure 6–18). It is wise to add a note to this effect since a few scores write harmonics at pitch.

Figure 6–18

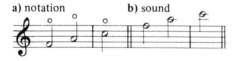

Since harmonics tend to sound flabby on the lower strings and since the higher strings are too tense, the best range is from A to a^2.

Slow melodic fragments can be played in harmonics, and harmonics are often used for accenting the sound of woodwind chords. They have a pure, bell-like tone and blend especially well with the flutes and clarinets. They must be lightly accompanied if they are to be heard in the orchestra.

Figure 6–19

Stravinsky, *Firebird*

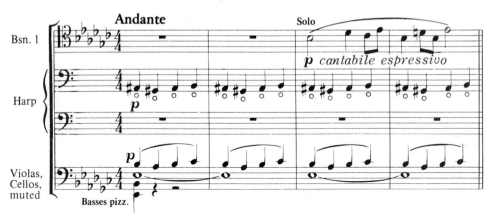

11. TRILLS AND TREMOLO

Trills are generally not too effective on the harp. They are usually played alternately in both hands and are better if they include a homophone. Tremoli are performed by rapidly running the hands over the notes indicated. The notation is the same as that for a string tremolo. Strauss coined the Italian term *bisbigliando* (whispering) to describe this effect.

Figure 6–20

12. SPECIAL EFFECTS

Common effects on the harp include dampening the strings with the palm immediately after plucking. This is indicated by the words *sons étouffés* or the symbol ✛. The return to normal playing is indicated by *laissez vibrer* (l.v.).

The harpist can obtain a guitar-like sound by playing near the soundboard, *près de la table* (p.d.l.t.). Many other effects encountered in contemporary harp literature are discussed in Chapter 37.

13. THE SOLO HARP

The old single-action harp (in E♭, with pedals to raise each set of strings by a half step only) had many disadvantages and could play easily in only a few keys. Nevertheless, Handel wrote a concerto for the instrument and Mozart wrote his concerto K. 299 for flute and harp on commission from a certain Duc de Guines and his daughter, who played the instruments. Mozart was never payed for the work.

Since the invention of the double-action harp, the instrument has appeared as a soloist, primarily in chamber music, in works by composers as diverse as Ravel, Roussel, Schoenberg, Milhaud, Britten, and Henze and by American composers such as Gould, Hovhaness, Luening, and Villa-Lobos.

14. THE HARP IN THE ORCHESTRA

Though the harp was occasionally used in the theater orchestra by such composers as Handel, Gluck, Beethoven (in *Prometheus*), Rossini (*Il Barbiere*), and Meyerbeer, it remained for Berlioz to introduce it to the symphony (the two harps in the waltz from the *Symphonie Fantastique*). Since then, one or two harps have been part of the orchestral arsenal. The use of a harp is almost mandatory in the nineteenth-century ballet orchestra.

Writing for two harps in the orchestra is the norm. It enables the players to divide difficult or chromatic passages between them, gives each player proportionally less to play, and gives added volume when they play together. The *Firebird* used three; Wagner's *Ring*, six; and Berlioz's *La Damnation de Faust*, ten. Usually these parts are boiled down to two for economic reasons.

A few points must be kept in mind in writing for the harp in the orchestra:

1. Chords and arpeggios as accompaniment are the stock-in-trade of orchestral harp parts but must be used with taste and not too often.
2. The use of single notes or chords on the harp to accent the beginning of a phrase in other orchestral sections is often of use.
3. In quiet passages the low octaves on the harp can have a striking effect similar to that of a distant gong.
4. Glissandi, when not overused, are one way of underscoring an orchestral climax.
5. Occasional melodic lines can be given to the harp with good effect.
6. Keep in mind that the harp is not a dynamically powerful instrument. Even the glissando can be lost in a big orchestral tutti.
7. The orchestral harpist is not usually a virtuoso soloist. Do not let the extraordinary difficulty of the solo harp repertory mislead you into writing complex orchestral parts.

8. When arranging piano music, do not fall into the trap of giving the harp an arpeggiated piano accompaniment. The harp is not strong enough to support the entire orchestra.

Figure 6–21

Berlioz, *Symphony Fantastique*

Wagner, *Die Meistersinger*

Figure 6-21 (cont.)

Bartók, *Concerto for Orchestra*

2 Harps

Britten, *The Young Person's Guide to the Orchestra*

Henze, *Elegy for Young Lovers*

7

Writing
For Strings

1. SMALL STRING ENSEMBLES

In spite of the individual tone colors of the various string instruments, they blend well with each other and compete well dynamically (with regard to *balance*). Assuming that the instruments are handled well individually, almost any type of writing will "sound." A word of caution here again about unisons and octave doublings: just as the octave as a double stop on an individual instrument can create problems of intonation, the octave or unison between two or more string instruments is risky in inverse proportion to how many instruments are involved (in a string section, with many instruments on each line, there is an equalizing effect and the problem disappears). Therefore, passages like the one in Figure 7–1 are rare in a small group of strings. Obviously, the octave and unison doubling is occasionally necessitated by the nature of the musical ideas. In this case, if the passage is in a lower position for all the instruments and involves rapidly moving notes, the intonation will be less of a problem. Sustained octaves or unisons in higher, more difficult positions would make differences in intonation more likely to occur and more noticeable.

Since the last half of the eighteenth century, the most important combination of instruments in chamber music (music written for a small group of instruments) has been the string quartet, consisting of two violins, a viola, and a

Figure 7-1

Beethoven, *String Quartet, Op. 95*

*separate bows

cello. The instruments are written on separate staves in descending order of pitch. The four staves are always bracketed together at the beginning of each line. Bar lines can be written separately for each instrument but usually extend through the entire score from first violin to cello. String trios (without the second violin) and quintets (with an extra viola or with double bass) and combinations of piano or winds with strings are also common.

In Figure 7–2, the beginning of the first of Mozart's six string quartets dedicated to Haydn, great richness and variety of texture are obtained. The quartet opens with four measures in four-part harmony (notice the cello is not confined to its lower range). In the next six measures, the viola, second violin, and first violin successively have the main melodic material. In bar 11 the second violin takes up the opening phrase, imitated a bar later by the first violin. The imitation between the two violins continues in measures 12 and 13. In measures 17 and 18, under a sustained b² in the first violin, the lower strings enter one-by-one with an ascending chromatic scale. The first violin immediately inverts this figure in measure 19. In measure 20 the lower strings begin a close rhythmic imitation while the first violin plays a running scale passage, extending the passage until the cadence in measure 24. The second theme begins in the second violin accompanied by the viola and cello. Altogether there have been at least seven major changes of texture within only 28 measures. Notice also the frequent rests in all the parts which serve to lighten the texture and create contrast. As with any other combination of instruments, all the strings playing all the time soon becomes uninteresting.

Figure 7–2

Mozart, *String Quartet in G major,* K. 387

Figure 7–2 (cont.)

Another means of securing variety is giving the melody to the cello (Figure 7–3).

Figure 7–3

Beethoven, *String Quartet, Op. 59, No. 1*

In Figure 7–4 Beethoven suddenly contrasts a section in the lydian mode, which begins with imitation and continues with simple four-part harmony, with a modulation to D major and a section combining double stops, staccato chords, trills, and fleeting scale passages in the Andante.

Figure 7–4

Beethoven, *Quartet No. 15*

The Ravel quartet (Figure 7–5) illustrates the exploitation of the shimmering tone colors of the strings. The Bartók (Figure 7–6), like the Ravel, is a work

Figure 7–5

Ravel, *Quartet in F Major*

written for virtuoso players (though this excerpt is not particularly difficult) and is a study in sonorities of a very different sort.

Figure 7–6

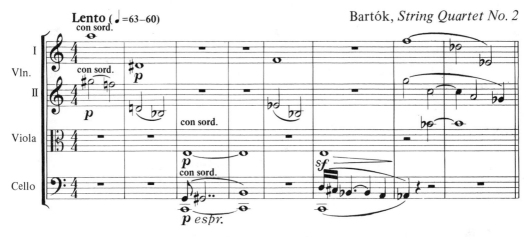

Lento (♩=63–60)   Bartók, *String Quartet No. 2*

Figure 7–7 shows a combination of effects. In the first two measures the violins play *sul tasto* while the viola plays harmonics. The second violin, in measure 3, plays a measured tremolo at the bridge with the point of the bow as the cello plays a broken chord. In the last measure the first violin begins a melodic passage played on the G string which utilizes its particular tone color.

Figure 7–7

Burton, *Quartet Fantasy*

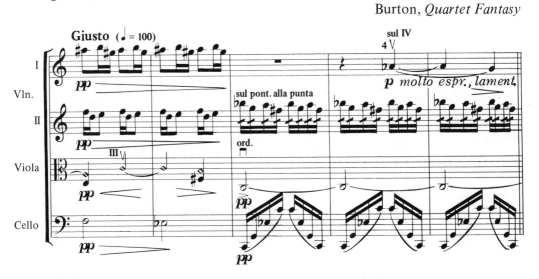

Giusto (♩ = 100)

2. THE STRING ORCHESTRA

MELODIES

Using the first phrase of the Mozart quartet in Figure 7–8, transposed an octave lower, we can illustrate various ways of arranging a melodic line in a group of strings playing together.

Figure 7–8

In actual practice, the choice of what instruments play a melodic line depends on the musical context: what instruments are free to play the melody, what is happening in the accompaniment, what preceded and what will follow the section, and so forth. Putting these considerations aside for the moment, we can say that, all other things being equal, the choice of instruments relies on the following factors:

1. The range of the melody.
2. The tone color desired.
3. The strength (volume) of sound required.

Melodies in the extreme ranges of instruments are usually avoided except for special effects. In addition, a melody in the lower range of an instrument may have quite a different tone color from one in the middle or upper range. Tone color can be the result of using one particular instrument or group of similar instruments (the first violins, for instance) or it can be the result of a combination of different instruments. This aspect will be dealt with more fully in Part II. Finally, the volume of sound depends on many factors. The least effective way of achieving dynamic gradations is by the use of dynamic markings. Some instruments have a rather wide dynamic range, others a quite small one. In any case, the potential strength or softness of the sound should be inherent in the orchestration itself. No amount of triple or quadruple *piano* or *forte* indications can save an intrinsically badly balanced score. Also, it must be understood that dynamics are purely relative. A performer playing in a string quartet interprets a *pp* totally differently from a performer in an orchestra. In addition, that interpretation depends intimately on the context of the music and the other parts that are playing at the same time. These problems of "blend" will be considered in Part II.

The melody in Figure 7–8 clearly lies in the range of the violins. It could also be played by the violas or even the cellos. The double basses in that octave are, of course, out of the question. Other possibilities, for a lighter sound, would be to use part of a section or even a solo instrument.

There are six possible combinations of two sections playing the melody in unison:[1]

1. Vln. I & II
2. Vln. I & Vle.
3. Vln. I & Vcl.
4. Vln. II & Vle.
5. Vln. II & Vcl.
6. Vle. & Vcl.

The effect of combination 1 would be to add strength to the melody. The rich, resonant tone of the violin's G string would dominate most of the melody. Combination 2 might be used if one wished to darken the violin tone by the addition of the violas. Normally, one would expect the seconds also to be playing the melody in this combination, but if they were employed elswhere (in the accompaniment, for instance) or if their added strength was not required, this combination might be used. Combination 3 would impart to the melody the added intensity of the cello's A string, giving the melody an incandescent timbre. Again, the second violins would normally be associated with this doubling. Combinations 4 and 5 have the same effect as 2 and 3. The probable reason for using these combinations would be if the first violins were playing something above the melody (in which case problems of balance might occur) or if they were being saved for a later entrance. Combination 6 might be used for the sound of the lower strings without the intensity of the cello's A string. The violas would effectively darken that timbre.

There are only four combinations of three sections playing in unison:

1. Vln. I, II, & Vle.
2. Vln. I, II, & Vcl.
3. Vln. I, Vle., & Vcl.
4. Vln. II, Vle., & Vcl.

All these combinations are strong and intense. Combination 2 is somewhat brighter than 1. 3 and 4, with one section of violins left out, are darker and weaker.

Finally, all four sections could play the melody in unison for an effect of extraordinary strength. The more striking the effect, as with all things in orchestration, the less often it should be used; extremely noticeable tone colors lose their effectiveness quickly on repetition.

---

[1] The standard abbreviations found in scores are used here. The plural of *viola* is *viole,* properly abbreviated *vle.*

Figure 7–9 shows the first three notes of the melody in its possible octave doublings in the strings. The topmost octave could be played by the first or second violins. Most likely, were a melody to appear in this register, the first violins would take the high octave with the seconds doubling in the octave below. The overtones of the seconds then support the firsts. This is a common procedure between first and second violins in the high register. The second octave is quite comfortable for the violins. Only in rare instances would the violas be asked to play the melody in this octave, such as a unison with first and second violins and other orchestral instruments for an extremely intense melodic doubling. The middle octave, as stated in the previous section, is convenient to all the strings but the double bass. The fourth octave down is fine for the cellos but rather high for the basses, which would be right at home in the lowest octave.

Figure 7–9

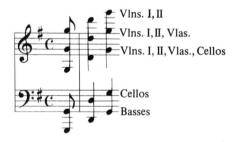

The effect of any combination of strings doubling in one or more octaves should be easy to imagine.

MELODIES WITH HARMONIC
ACCOMPANIMENT

Now let us restore to the melody its original harmonic accompaniment (Figure 7–10) with the parts marked soprano, alto, tenor, and bass so that we can discuss each melodic line independently of its original instrumentation.

Figure 7–10

The simplest and most obvious (and perhaps the best) arrangement of the harmonized melody for string orchestra would be to allot each part to the same instruments as in the string quartet (except here each part would be played by an entire section). The double basses, of course, would then be *tacet* (rest) during the passage.

The basses could also play the bass line an octave below the cellos (remember, the basses play an octave lower than written, even when written on the same staff as the cellos). A much more musical solution, however, would be to drop the basses out in the second measure since the dynamic suddenly changes to *piano* (Figure 7–11). This would enhance the contrast of the first two bars by lightening the texture as well as reducing the number of instruments playing. The difference in effect between this and merely marking the basses *p* is enormous. Good orchestration is made up of such subtle but vital distinctions. Only the continual study of scores and intimate acquaintance with a wide variety of music over a number of years can lead to mastery of this art, which we are just beginning to study in its most elementary aspects.

Figure 7–11

DOUBLING PARTS AT THE OCTAVE

Besides the conventional doubling of the cellos at the octave by the basses, it is possible to double any part at the octave above or below. Following are the possible combinations as well as the criteria for their use:

Doubling the Soprano at the Octave This is a common way to give added strength and brightness to the melody. In our example, this could be done by putting the first violins in the upper octave and leaving the seconds at the octave below. The inner voices would then of necessity be played by divided violas or by violas and the first half of the divided cellos (Figure 7–12). If the violas are divided, the inner parts are greatly weakened. A better balance is obtained by a division of the cellos since the basses still reinforce the bass line an octave below and their overtones lend support to the second half of the cellos.

Figure 7–12

The soprano line could also be doubled in the octave below (assuming that it did not come into too close conflict with the inner voices and thereby obscure the individual lines). In this case either the second violins could take the lower octave and the violas or cellos divide to take the extra part, or the violas could play the soprano line in the lower octave. In this case the second violins could divide on the inner voices (Figure 7–13). This would heavily weight the arrangement in favor of the melody.

Figure 7–13

Doubling the Inner Parts at the Octave   This is not an uncommon practice in orchestration, although it generally occurs in conjunction with the doubling of the soprano line at the octave above. In our example, for instance, doubling the alto in the octave above without doubling the soprano would obscure the melody, which would then become an inner voice (Figure 7–14).

Figure 7–14

In order not to give undue prominence to one inner part, both can be doubled at the octave above and then only when the soprano is doubled as well. In this case, division of the upper three sections of strings to supply the additional three parts is necessary (Figure 7–15).

Figure 7–15

Doubling of inner voices in the octave below is rare, since in the lower registers the confusion of overtones is greater and usually only a muddy mass of sound results (Figure 7–16).

The doubling of the bass in octaves has already been discussed in sections 20 of the chapters on the cello and the double bass. It must be stressed that the doubling of a particular part at the octave is not the same as parallel octaves *between* two separate parts in the harmony. Precisely because the octave, being the first overtone, is the strongest interval (which is why we can transpose a melody at the octave and still hear it as being in the same key), it can strengthen a line doubled at the octave. This is perfectly good when *one* line is being strengthened. For exactly the same reason, this is usually bad between two separate parts (e.g., soprano and alto) since it momentarily gives the parts undue prominence where none is desired. Doubled parts in tonal music must, of course, follow normal voice-leading procedures, resolving dissonances, and so forth.

Figure 7–16

*Here the lower violas had to be altered, as an A would be out of their range.

Filling in the Harmony Additional parts may be added to thicken the sonority. This often occurs in the arrangement of piano music for a group of instruments. An individual added part may double another part at the octave for a few notes and then continue in an independent direction or it may be totally independent. The only criterion is that the usual doublings which are effective in four-part harmony are also effective in orchestration (see the section on *chords* below). Figure 7–17 shows an added part in the violas.

Figure 7–17

It is also common practice to add several additional parts in order to create
an extremely rich sonority. Naturally, the above methods are not mutually exclusive and can be combined. In Figure 7–18, for instance, the filling in of the
harmony is combined with doubling the melody at the octave above.

Figure 7–18

It is also possible to double parts at the unison and divide other sections to
create exceptional stress on one line. This practice is liable to lead to serious
balance problems, however. In Figure 7–19 the violins clearly overbalance the
inner voices.

Figure 7–19

CHORDS

The scoring of chords for the orchestra as a whole will be dealt with in Chapter 28. However, a few words should be said here which apply with equal weight to the other instruments.

The spacing of chords must coincide with the natural spacing of the overtone series (see Appendix B). That is, the lower the part, the wider should be the interval between adjacent parts. Below c, only octaves are likely not to sound muddy because of the confusion of overtones. Fourths and fifths are also rather clear in the low register but usually the lowest part and the next higher part are spaced an octave apart, a fourth or fifth occurring between that part and the next higher. Once thirds pass below c^1 they become progressively less clear, and at c they are useful only for special thick coloristic effects. The extraordinarily ominous effect even of octaves in the extreme low register can be seen in Figure 7–20, which also illustrates the basses divided in arco and pizzicato in two parts.

Figure 7–20

Stravinsky, *The Firebird*

Figure 7–21 shows several chords reduced to two staves for study and comparison of spacing and doubling. Notice that the same practices governing doubling parts of a chord in four-part harmony apply with equal force in many parts. If, for instance, a major triad has the root doubled in four octaves, the fifth will occur in two or three, the third in perhaps only one. Generally, the leading tone, seventh, altered notes, or any other "active" tone will not be doubled. Since Stravinsky, composers have experimented with chords in intentionally unusual spacings with irregular doublings. These and other techniques will be discussed in Part II.

Figure 7-21

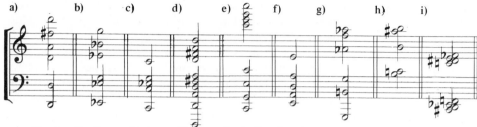

Haydn Beethoven Brahms Strauss Prokofiev Bartók Stravinsky Copland Penderecki

ACCOMPANIMENT FIGURES

Figure 7–22 gives some typical accompaniment patterns for string instruments. Notice that these are not the same as corresponding patterns for the piano. How one can transfer these patterns to orchestral instruments when arranging music written for the piano will be discussed in Chapter 29.

Figure 7-22

Mozart, *Overture to "Die Zauberflöte"*

Schubert, *Symphony No. 8*

*Double basses play an octave higher when the part goes out of their range.

Figure 7–22b (cont.)

Gershwin, *Concerto in F*

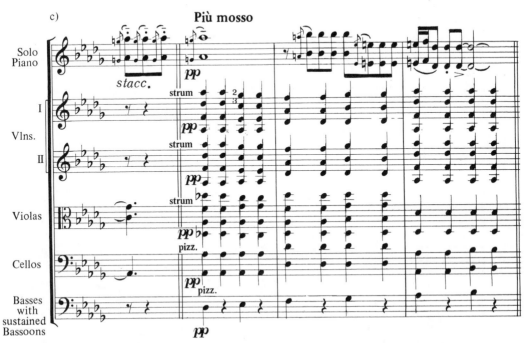

Figure 7-22d (cont.)

Stravinsky, *Rite of Spring*

MUSIC WRITTEN FOR STRING ORCHESTRA

In this chapter we have discussed some of the basics of writing for strings. What has been stated above applies to the strings alone or to the strings as part of an orchestra including other instruments as well. However, there is a substantial literature, especially from the baroque era, for the string orchestra alone. Figure 7–23 gives some examples from various periods.

Figure 7-23

Vivaldi, *Concerto Grosso, Op. 3, No. 8*

Figure 7-23 (cont.)

Mahler, *Symphony No. 5*

(This movement is scored for strings and harp alone.)

Bartók, *Music for Strings, Percussion and Celesta*

Figure 7-23 (cont.)   Barber, *Adagio for Strings*

(Originally the second movement of the **Quartet, Op. 11,** but usually performed by string orchestra)

Martin, *Études pour Orchestre à Cordes*

8

The Flute

Ital. *flauto(i) (flauto grande)* **Ger.** *(grosse) Flöte(n)*
Fr. *(grande) flûte(s)*

1. ORIGIN

Almost all primitive cultures have developed flute-like instruments from the earliest times. The *transverse flute (flauto traverso)* first appeared in Europe about the twelfth century. The lips set the air within the flute in vibration by blowing across a hole near the end of the tube of the instrument, hence the appelation "transverse." Until the eighteenth century these flutes were used primarily for military bands, the end-blown recorder being preferred for artistic purposes. On the transverse flute, then made of wood, one obtained different tube lengths, and therefore different pitches, by simply removing the fingers from various holes bored in the instrument, thereby shortening the length of the tube and raising the pitch. Unfortunately, the instrument was primitive and frequently out of tune. Mozart's aversion to the instrument (in spite of the fact that he contributed two major concertos for it) is well documented. Cherubini, when asked by a conductor if there was anything worse than a flute in the orchestra, replied, "Yes, *two* flutes!"

All this was rectified when, in 1847, after years of experimentation, Theobald Böhm, a famous flutist, perfected the system of keys which is named after him and which has since been almost universally applied to the wood-wind instruments. Böhm added a system of keys to open and close the holes and create an even tone throughout the range. The previous key systems involved so-called *fork-fingerings*, which produced notes of uneven tone color. Previously impossible figures became easy to play, all keys were almost equally simple, and, best of all, the flutes could finally play in tune.

Although the tone of the wooden flute is more mellow, flutes made of metal have now replaced them because of their more brilliant tone and ability to *speak* (be set in vibration) more easily. Wagner refused to allow metal flutes in his orchestra, referring to them as "cannons." Today flutes are generally made of silver, or even platinum or gold. Students use less expensive instruments of stainless steel.

2. DESCRIPTION

The flute is an open cylindrical pipe some $26\frac{1}{2}$ inches (67 cm) long with a bore (inner diameter) of $\frac{3}{4}$ inches (2 cm). Like other woodwinds, the flute consists of several separate sections or "joints" which are fitted together to form the instrument. Flutes with the low b (see section 3) have an additional extension of 2 inches (5 cm).

There is a side hole or *embouchure* (a term also used to denote the mouthpiece of brass instruments and the position of the lips when playing) across which the player blows to set the air in the pipe in vibration. For this reason, the flute is sometimes classified as an air-reed instrument.

3. RANGE

Figure 8–1

The range of the flute is shown in Figure 8–1. Some flutes (most first flutes in professional orchestras) include the extension to the low b. Although it is possible to write *piano* passages for a good player as high as b$^{\flat3}$, the last few notes are possible only in a shrill *ff;* c⁴ is usually cited as the upper limit of the flute, but Strauss and many modern composers have taken the flute as high as d⁴.[1] In his *Sonatina,* Pierre Boulez writes to f⁴.

4. TONE

The tone of the flute is the purest, that is, the least rich in overtones of any instrument in the orchestra. For this reason, the flutes are used more often than any other wind instrument in most orchestration. One does not tire of their tone color easily. The tone of the flute is very even throughout the entire range, but the lowest octave is somewhat thin and breathy, the middle octave sweet and clear, and the upper octave bright and penetrating.

The dynamic range of the flute is not wide, but it is capable of a good *pp* throughout most of its range and in the upper octave can still be heard in an orchestral tutti. The lower octave is quite easily covered unless lightly accompanied and *exposed* (not closely surrounded by other instruments).

5. TECHNIQUE

The flutist plays in the lower octave by successively opening holes in the pipe to produce higher pitches. The second octave is *overblown,* that is, the flutist plays the first overtone by increasing the force of the air against the embouchure. The upper octave is obtained by a combination of overblowing and fingering. It should be noted that the harmonics played on wind instruments as a normal part of their technique (by overblowing) do not have the strikingly different effect of string harmonics although they are sometimes indicated for special effects (see section 8). The player normally imparts a certain amount of vibrato (actually an amplitude, not pitch, variation) to the tone with his breath.

Wide leaps, scales, and arpeggios, rapid repeated notes, and other complex passage work are all possible on the flute, the most agile of wind instruments. Although the player can take a *catch breath* in the middle of a long legato passage when he runs out of air so that almost no break in the line is perceptible (sometimes indicated by a comma above the staff), it is best to phrase wind parts so that each slur indicates those notes taken on one breath. As with the bow on a string instrument, louder passages demand more air (even in quiet passages, ten seconds on one breath would be an outside limit).

---

[1] Mahler obviously had flutes with a low b♭ since he writes this note in his fourth, sixth, and eighth symphonies. Ravel writes the note in *Pictures at an Exhibition.* Milhaud writes up to g♯⁴ in his second symphony, but this must be an oversight.

It is a good idea not to have the flutist play too long without a few measures' rest to give him a chance to relax his lips and breath. This is even more important for the other woodwinds.

If not slurred, each note will be attacked with a separate burst of air from the lips (on the syllable *tu*). This is like the *détaché* bowing of a string instrument. Very rapid passages are *double-tongued* (*tu-ku, tu-ku,* etc.). *Triple tonguing* is used for rapid passages in triple rhythms. These techniques are effective on the flute and the brass instruments, less effective on those instruments played with a reed. If especially sharp tonguing is desired, staccato marks are used. Figure 8–2 shows examples of double and triple tonguing.

Figure 8–2

Tchaikovsky, *Nutcracker Suite No. 1*

a) double-tonguing

Mendelssohn, *Italian Symphony*

b) triple-tonguing

6. NOTATION

Usually, two wind instruments are written on one staff in the score, although the parts from which the players perform are usually copied out separately (see Chapters 26 and 31). In this case, it is necessary to indicate whether both players are playing the same notes or not. Figure 8–3a shows a part played by both players together and marked *a 2* (Ital. *a due*, Ger. *zu 2*, Fr. *a deux*). Two ways of indicating that the first player plays alone are to write I° (*primo*), I, or just 1, or to write stems up and place a rest below for the second player (Figure 8–3b and c). The procedure is reversed if the second player (*secondario*, II, 2) plays alone (Figure 8–3d and e). Finally, if both players have different parts, the two parts are written with one stem connecting the note heads or with stems up for the first player, stems down for the second (Figure 8–3f). The phrasing appears at the end of the stems. If both parts are rhythmically very dissimilar or cross each other so that reading them on the same staff would be difficult, it is best to use two separate staves (Figure 8–3g).

Figure 8–3

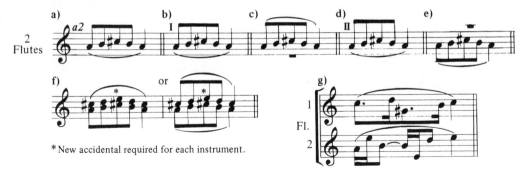

*New accidental required for each instrument.

Note that in Figure 8–3f, the note $c\#^2$ appears twice in the same bar. The accidental must be repeated since the note appears in another instrument. Otherwise the copyist, who copies each part separately, would be likely to leave out the accidental.

7. TRILLS AND TREMOLO

Almost any trill on the flute is good. The exceptions are the trill c^1–d^{b1}, trill $c\#^1$-$d\#^1$, and the tremolo on c^1 to e^{b1} (Figure 8–4). This is because there is only one finger available for the two keys involved. Also, trills above a^3 are impractical.

Figure 8–4

Tremoli are written the same as fingered tremoli in the strings. They are best confined to an interval of a fifth or less in the lower octave, and a major third or less in the upper range, or they may not speak because of the inertia of the air column.

8. SPECIAL EFFECTS

A characteristic effect on the flute is *flutter tonguing* (Ital. *frulando*, Ger. *Flatterzunge*, Fr. *trémolo*). This effect is produced by rapidly rolling the tongue at the front of the palate like a rolled letter R. The result is a "whirring" sound. It was introduced by Strauss in *Don Quixote* and has been used by nearly every twentieth-century composer. Avoid the extreme lower range.

The glissando was first used by Berlioz and is occasionally called for. It is indicated, as on string instruments, by a line connecting the two notes. On all woodwinds, it is performed by rapidly fingering a chromatic scale.

Harmonics (vented overblown notes, which have a typical harmonic sound, unlike unvented notes), can be indicated in the same way as natural string harmonics, by a circle over the note, which is written at its true pitch. They are playable from the first overblown overtone, c^2, to the top of the register.

For other special effects see Chapter 37.

9. THE SOLO FLUTE

Since the baroque period, when the flute began to appear in chamber music (it was then called the *traverso* to distinguish it from the recorder, which was called the *flauto*), many composers have used the flute as a solo instrument, either by itself (in a sonata or concerto) or with other instruments (for instance, a woodwind quintet or a trio sonata). Occasional unaccompanied pieces for flute were written in the baroque era (J.S. Bach) and many have been written in the twentieth century. Some twentieth-century composers who have featured the flute in their works are Debussy, Prokofiev, Hindemith, Honegger, and Varèse.

10. THE FLUTE IN THE ORCHESTRA

Lully seems to be the first composer to have used the transverse flute in the orchestra. It did not become a standard orchestral instrument until the classical period. Even then, Mozart was content to use just one in his symphonies. Beethoven always used two. Haydn even used three in the opening of Part III of *The Creation*. In the nineteenth century three or even four flutes were common. Often one of these (second or third) would *double on* piccolo (see section 13) when required. In the case of three flutes, at least two staves are, of course, needed. On occasion, more flutes are called for; Mahler writes for four flutes and two piccolos in his Eighth Symphony, Schoenberg for four flutes and four piccolos in the *Gurrelieder*. Naturally, these are very large orchestras.

Following are some considerations for writing for the flute in the orchestra:

1. It is common for flutes to play in unison for added strength.
2. When the flutes are in octaves with each other, the lower flute will strengthen the overtones of the upper flute. This applies to all instrumental octave doublings. Doublings with other instruments will be considered in Part II.
3. Flutes in thirds are often found.
4. Flutes playing separate parts are not uncommon.
5. Flutes in harmony with other instruments (the flute sometimes taking the lower or middle parts in which case one must be careful about balance) is also common.

6. The flutes brighten the orchestral color by reinforcing the upper partials of the orchestra.
7. Flutes kept always in their upper range tend to lend the orchestration a shrill sound. Utilize the entire range of the instrument.

Figure 8–5

Mozart, *Cosi Fan Tutte*

Rossini, *Overture to "William Tell"*

Bizet, *Carmen*

Debussy, *Prelude to the Afternoon of a Faun*

Figure 8–5 (cont.)

Berg, *Wozzeck*

Varèse, *Density 21.5*

Burton, *Stravinskiana*

frullando = flutter-tonguing

11. THE PICCOLO

It. *flauto(i) piccolo(i), ottavino(i)*   **Ger.** *kleine Flöte(n)*
Fr. *petite flûte(s)*

The piccolo is half the length of the regular flute and therefore is pitched an octave higher. It is written an octave below the true pitch and is therefore a transposing instrument. Note that its range begins at d^2 (Figure 8–6). The fingering is like that of the flute. Although many scores call for the second or third flute to double on piccolo, in most symphony orchestras there are specialists on these *auxiliary* instruments (instruments such as the English horn, bass clarinet, and contrabassoon). Therefore, in a score calling for two flutes, the second of which doubles on piccolo, three players will actually be employed.

Figure 8–6

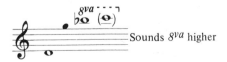

Sounds *8va* higher

The top notes b[4] and c[5] are difficult and extremely shrill. Trills are good up to a[4]. The upper octave is shrill and useful only for an exceedingly bright strengthening of the upper orchestral octave or for solo passagework (which, if overdone, can easily begin to sound like a Sousa march). The lower octave is thin and flabby. It is best to have the flutes play anything written in that register; their tone is much better. It should be noted that notes as high as c#[5] and as low as c[2] are found in some scores, notably those of Mahler. Perhaps he was writing for a different type of piccolo. In any case, these notes are not in the range of the instrument as we know it today.

In writing for the piccolo:

1. Avoid long, sustained notes. They sound extremely thin unless doubled with violins or flutes.
2. For the same reason, beware of the use of the piccolo as a part of a woodwind chord. It is likely to stand out.
3. The piccolo works well in octaves with the flutes for extra brightness on top.
4. The piccolo unison with the flutes is often valuable for a strong top line without quite the shrillness of the piccolo alone an octave above.
5. Two piccolos can be useful for an occasional striking effect. They are diabolically shrill (Figure 8–7c and d).
6. Sometimes the flutes and piccolo can divide a passage, especially one which begins in the flute range and rises into the range where only the piccolo can play.
7. Flutter tonguing is not as effective on the piccolo as on the flute but is used in the middle and lower register.
8. Above all, avoid overuse of the piccolo. Its sound quickly becomes tiring, even unpleasant, as when it is continuously doubling the upper orchestral octave.

Figure 8–7

Beethoven, *Symphony No. 5*

Figure 8–7 (cont.)

Rimsky-Korsakov, *Scheherezade*

Stravinsky, *Rite of Spring*

Copyright 1921 by Edition Russe de Musique. Copyright assigned 1947 to Boosey & Hawkes, Inc. Reprinted by permission.

Schuller, *Seven Studies on Themes of Paul Klee*

Copyright © 1962 by Universal Edition, Ltd., London. Used by permission of European American Music Distributors Corp., sole U.S. agent for Universal Edition, Ltd., London.

12. THE ALTO FLUTE

Ital. *flauto(i) contralto(i)*   **Ger.** *Altflöte(n)*
Fr. *flûte(s) alto(s), flûte(s) en sol*

The alto flute, or flute in G (mistakenly called bass flute), is a larger (34 inches or 87 cm) version of the flute and transposes a perfect fourth lower than written. It is the first instrument discussed in this book which transposes at an interval other than the octave. The part is written a perfect fourth higher than the sounds which result; thus, the written key signature has one more flat or one fewer sharp than the key of the actual music. As a result, a flutist can play an alto flute part with exactly the same fingerings he would use on the flute (everything is the same as on the flute, but since the instrument is larger and has a lower fundamental pitch, everything comes out that much lower). Were the part written at its actual *concert* pitch, the alto flute player would have to learn an entirely new method of fingering. Many modern scores are written at concert pitch for the benefit of the conductor, but the parts are transposed by the copyist.[2]

Figure 8–8

Sounding down a perfect fourth (in G basso)

The alto flute is not just a lower-pitched version of the flute, but has its own unique tone color, more mellow and vibrant than that of the flute. It is used in the orchestra specifically because of this quality. Although it is stronger in the lower register than the flute, it must still be lightly accompanied to be heard. Its upper range is weak and it is much better to use the flutes in that register. Slow, lyric melodies in the lowest twelfth of its range are characteristic of the instrument. The alto flute is also useful as the bass for a harmony in the flutes.

Figure 8–9   Ravel, *Daphnis et Chloé*

Copyright 1910 Durand et Cie. Used by permission of the publisher.
Theordore Presser Company Sole Representative U.S.A.

Stravinsky, *Rite of Spring*

Copyright 1921 by Edition Russe de Musique. Copyright assigned 1947 to Boosey & Hawkes, Inc. Reprinted by permission.

Henze, *Symphony No. 5*

Copyright © 1963 by B. Schott's Söhne, Mainz. Used by permission of European American Music Distributors Corp., sole U. S. agent for B. Schott's Söhne, Mainz.

[2] It is easy to forget which way transposing instruments transpose (a fourth up or a fourth down, for example). The easiest way to orient oneself is to imagine the instrument is reading a c in its part. That c would then sound (at concert pitch) a G on an alto flute, a B♭ on a clarinet in B♭, an F on a horn in F, and so forth. See also the Transposition Chart in this volume.

13. DOUBLING

When a player doubles on (that is, switches to) another instrument (for example, second flute to piccolo), the change is indicated after the final notes of the first instrument: "Change to (take) piccolo."

Ital. *muta in (prende) l'ottavino*
Ger. *Fl. 2 nimmt kl. Fl., kl. Flöte nehmen*
Fr. *prendre (change en) la P^{te} Fl.*

At least a few bars' rest should be given the player to make the change. It is best to have the player begin playing the new instrument in some subsidiary part rather than in an exposed solo because a *cold* instrument (one which has not been played in some time) is likely to be somewhat flat.

9

The Oboe

Ital. *oboe(i)*   **Ger.** *Oboe(n), Hoboe(n)*   **Fr.** *hautbois*

1. ORIGIN

Oboe-like instruments existed as long ago as 2800 B.C. in Sumer and double-reed folk instruments are still common throughout Asia and Africa. They were probably brought to Europe in the twelfth century from the Near East, where they were known as *shawms* (or *pommern*, or *bombarde*). The oboe which developed in the mid-seventeenth century from the shawm had a broader reed and a considerably more nasal tone quality than the modern oboe. Improvements made during the course of the nineteenth century included the addition of the Böhm key system and the use of narrower reeds. Various refinements of manufacture and technique carried out in France brought the oboe to its present stage of development.

2. DESCRIPTION

The oboe is a double-reed open-tube instrument of slightly conical bore. The reed is made of a piece of cane bent double, shaved to the correct shape, and tied with nylon twine around a *staple* (tube) which, in turn, is inserted into the upper end of the instrument. The player places the reed, which must be kept carefully moistened, between his lips and blows through the thin opening between the two ends of the reed (hence "double-reed"). Slight differences of moisture or temperature, or imperfections in the reed, can have a serious if not disastrous effect on the tone of the instrument.

The oboe itself, with reed, is about $25\frac{1}{2}$ inches (65 cm) long. It is now made of a hard wood such as granadilla. The bore varies from three sixteenth inches ($\frac{1}{2}$ cm) at the upper end to five eighth inches (1.5 cm) at the *bell* (slight flaring at the bottom end of the instrument).

3. RANGE

Figure 9–1

Although the basic pipe of the oboe is, like the flute, in D, it is written for as a nontransposing instrument in C. The range is shown in Figure 9–1. Additional lower notes are obtained by additional holes at the bottom end of the instrument. The low b♭ is of bad quality and is seldom used in exposed passages. Although the oboe has a high a³, it is so difficult and of such unsatisfactory tone color that it is almost never written. The high g♯³ is found on rare occasions in twentieth-century scores. Except when an extraordinary effect is wanted, or when the oboe is doubled by several other instruments, the notes above f³ are seldom used.

4. TONE

The notes below d¹ on the oboe are quite "honky" in tone and incapable of being played quietly. Those above a² become increasingly thin and strident. The middle register, from d¹ to a², is the range used for most melodic passages on the oboe. It has the characteristic reedy sound of the instrument combined with a certain vibrant sweetness which makes the tone of the oboe so suitable for expressive melodies. The upper register is useful for certain effects such as satirical passages or brightening of the orchestral tutti. Vibrato is used on the oboe as well.

The dynamic range of the oboe varies from *p* to *ff*, though it is not capable of the extreme *pp* of the flutes or clarinets, especially in the lower register. Because of the oboe's extremely rich overtones, its tone quickly becomes tiring to the ear and it should not be used prominently for a sustained period.

5. TECHNIQUE

Like the flute, the oboe overblows at the octave. Its key system is also similar to the flute's.

Although the oboe's usual function is to play legato melodies in its middle range or take part in orchestral harmony, it is capable of the most precise, biting staccato of any instrument in the orchestra. This is accomplished by single tonguing and can be performed rather rapidly. Double tonguing is not so easy or effective on the double reeds.

Runs and arpeggios are quite playable on the instrument but tend to be quite prominent in the orchestra because of the oboe's tone. They do not blend as well as similar passages on the flute or clarinet.

Because of the small opening in the reed, the oboist faces a unique problem. Whereas all the other wind instruments take a good deal of air to set the air column in vibration, and therefore the players must breathe fairly often to refill their lungs, the oboe uses very little air. This affects the oboist in two ways:

1. Sustained passages are effective because the oboist can play for several measures before taking a breath.
2. The oboist runs out of oxygen in his system before he runs out of air. Therefore, unless he is given rests fairly often between sustained passages, he faces the necessity of gasping for breath in every available pause. Anyone who has noticed the oboist at the end of a long solo passage at a concert will recall the uncomfortable feeling that the oboist was about to pass out as his face turned a deeper shade of red at each succeeding phrase.

Because of this problem and because of the striking tone color of the oboe, oboe parts often contain only about half as many measures to play as the other woodwinds. The instrument should certainly be used sparingly.

6. TRILLS AND TREMOLO

Trills, especially on more than one oboe, are quite penetrating and should be used only if that effect is intended. They are best in tone between d^1 and a^2. Avoid the trill on $b^\flat$ to $c^{\flat 1}$. This is difficult to perform rapidly because one finger must play both notes.

Tremoli of intervals up to the fourth are possible, but again have a penetrating sound. They sound quite awkward above the staff except when covered in a tutti.

7. SPECIAL EFFECTS

Flutter tonguing is not very effective on the oboe and is usually found in combination with other instruments.

Normally, an oboist uses the second overtone from the d¹ and e♭¹ to produce the notes a² and b♭² in certain pianissimo passages. These are never indicated in scores. No other harmonics are dependable.[1]

Glissandi are occasionally found in scores from the time of Berlioz.

Berlioz also introduced the offstage oboe in his *Symphonie Fantastique* (where it imitates a distant shepherd playing his pipes). Prokofiev also uses this device in *Alexander Nevsky*.

Mahler calls for the oboes to raise their bells in the air to direct their sound out more strongly to the audience in especially loud passages.

Eng.	**Ital.**
bells up	*campane in alto*
Ger.	**Fr.**
Schalltrichter auf	*les pavillons en l'air*

This technique is more often employed in the orchestra with the French horns, since their bells normally point down and back. It has been a common technique for obtaining more sound in dance bands since the 1920's, especially with the clarinets.

Muted oboes are required by Stravinsky in the *Petrouchka Suite*. The oboist simply inserts a piece of cloth into the bell. This affects only the lowest notes on the instrument. (See also Chapter 37.)

8. THE SOLO OBOE

Handel, K.P.E. Bach, Mozart, Bellini, Schumann, Hindemith, Poulenc, Britten, and many others have written for the solo oboe, both with orchestra and in chamber groups. An oboe is almost invariably included in chamber music involving woodwinds. Complex passagework and considerable virtuosity, seldom found in orchestral writing, are common in music for solo oboe.

9. THE OBOE IN THE ORCHESTRA

The orchestra generally includes two oboes or two oboes and an English horn. Rarely are three oboes called for (Bruckner, Symphony No. 9). Unusually large orchestrations include *Götterdämmerung*, which calls for three oboes and English horn; Mahler's Symphony No. 8 and Stravinsky's *Sacre*, calling for four oboes and English horn; and Schoenberg's *Gurrelieder*, which calls for three oboes and two English horns.

---

[1] Naturally, the oboist uses the first overtone in the overblown octave. This overtone, however, does not have the pure tone color we associate with harmonics on a string instrument and therefore is not a special effect unless it is played unvented, in which case the harmonic sound results.

The types of passages appropriate to the oboe and the difficulties involving its unique and striking tone quality and breathing problems have all been discussed above. It remains to analyze the oboe section.

Because of the instrument's penetrating tone quality, oboes generally do not double in the unison on one part of a chord as the flutes often do. Usually the oboes are spaced in close position on chords in their middle or upper register, where they lend solidity and brightness to wind chords. They are also useful for reinforcing the upper partials of the other sections of the orchestra. The English horn acts as a better bass to the oboe section than does a third oboe.

Figure 9–2

Beethoven, *Missa Solemnis*

Rossini, *Barber of Seville*

Tchaikovsky, *Symphony No. 4*

Debussy, *Prelude to the Afternoon of a Faun*

Figure 9–2 (cont.)

Ives, *Three Places in New England*

e) **Animato** (about 120 = ♩)

Oboe I

10. THE ENGLISH HORN

Ital. *corno inglese*   **Ger.** *englisches Horn*   **Fr.** *cor anglais*

The English horn, which is neither English nor a horn, replaced the old *oboe da caccia* (oboe of the hunt) used by Bach, an instrument that was curved like an animal's horn—thus the name. "English" may be a mistranslation of the French *angle* (angle) since the *oboe da caccia* was curved (in French, *anglais*, meaning English, and *angle* sound similar).

Haydn and Mozart occasionally wrote for the instrument in chamber works, but it did not begin to appear regularly in the orchestra until Rossini used it in *William Tell*.

The English horn is really an alto oboe, $31\frac{1}{2}$ inches (80 cm) long, with a pear-shaped bell. It is pitched a perfect fifth below the oboe and is written as a transposing instrument in the key of F. That is, everything playable on the oboe is playable on the English horn with essentially the same fingering except that it sounds a fifth lower (it is written with one fewer flat or one more sharp than the key of the music).

Figure 9–3

Sounding down a perfect fifth (in F basso)

*rare

The range can be seen in Figure 9–3. Instruments with an extension for the low written b♭ are extremely rare. The English horn's upper range is seldom used since the oboe's tone is better in that register. The top f³ and f♯³ have been called for by Milhaud, Britten, Copland, and others. As with all transposing instruments, if the music is in an extreme sharp key, it is best to write the

English horn in a flat key with fewer accidentals (for example, if the music is in F♯, write the English horn in D♭, not C♯).

The tone of the English horn is even more *reedy* than that of the oboe. It has a quality of richness which makes it particularly well suited for sustained, lyric melodies of a somber or melancholy character. Even more than with the oboe, one must be careful not to write too many such solos because of the striking tone of the instrument. Another common use of the instrument is to add to the sonority of woodwind harmony.

Trills are good up to d³. In any case there seems little reason to write this high in the orchestra.

Figure 9-4

Berlioz, *Symphonie Fantastique*

Franck, *Symphony in D minor*

R. Strauss, *Ein Heldenleben*

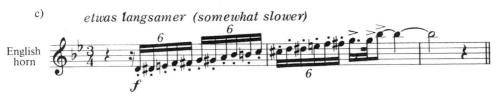

Bartók, *Concerto for Orchestra*

10

The Clarinet

Ital. *clarinetto(i)*   Ger. *Klarinette(n)*   Fr. *clarinette(s)*

1. ORIGIN

Although single reeds were historically much rarer than double reeds, a single-reed instrument existed in ancient Egypt. The medieval ancestor of the clarinet was the *chalumeau*, a small, single-reed shawm. Around the turn of the eighteenth century, Johann Christoph Denner and his son added keys to create the forerunner of the modern clarinet. The name comes from the sound of these early instruments, which was something like that of a distant trumpet (*clarino, clarion*). During the early part of the eighteenth century the clarinet was occasionally called upon to play trumpet-like parts in the opera by composers such as Rameau, Gluck, and Stamitz. Mozart's friendship with a clarinetist by the name of Stadler led to his use of the clarinet as a virtuoso solo instrument in his later works. From Beethoven's time, it became a standard member of the orchestra. Other refinements during the course of the nineteenth century, including the addition of the Böhm key system (preferred in America) and the Ehler system (preferred in Europe), led to the modern clarinet.

2. DESCRIPTION

The clarinet is a single-reed cylindrical pipe which the player overblows at the twelfth (see Appendix B) by opening a *register (speaker)* key at the node which produces the third harmonic, encouraging the air to vibrate in thirds within the pipe. The best clarinets are made of granadilla wood. A single reed is connected to a mouthpiece by means of a screw clip known as a *ligature*. The B♭ clarinet is about 26 inches (66 cm) long. The lower end flares into a bell.

3. RANGE

Figure 10–1

B♭ Clarinet sounding down a major second
A Clarinet sounding down a minor third

*rare

The range is shown in Figure 10–1. Although the clarinet is built to give a fundamental pitch G, additional holes extend the range down to e. Rarely, one finds a clarinet with the low e♭. The clarinet in B♭ is the most common, and the one for which band music is universally written. Orchestra players also use the clarinet in A when particular passages are more easily or satisfactorily played on that instrument. The composer indicates which instrument is wanted, but the individual player will choose the instrument he prefers. The difference in the resultant sound is negligible. Simply write for the clarinet pitched in the most convenient key for professional orchestras. It is wise to stick to the B♭ clarinet in all other cases.

The clarinet in B♭ will play in two more sharps or two fewer flats than the key of the written music; the clarinet in A will play in three more flats or three fewer sharps than the key of the written music. On the B♭ clarinet, written C sounds as B♭. On the A clarinet, written C sounds as A.

Most professional clarinetists have a smooth, even control over their instruments, dynamically and in terms of intonation, from the low e to the high b♭³, though music for students had best avoid the upper octave. The last two half steps on the instrument are shrill and available only in the *forte*. The clarinettist has no difficulty with the low notes of the instrument as does the oboist.

There must have been a clarinet which played down to low C in the late eighteenth century, since Mozart often writes this low in works such as *Clemenza di Tito.* Stravinsky, in *Chant du Rossignol,* writes down to low (written) d. This may have been an oversight, or Stravinsky may have had clarinets with that note, or he may have intended a bell extension to be used.

4. TONE

Figure 10–2

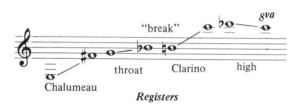

Registers

The tone color of the clarinet in its upper and lower ranges is like that of two different instruments, and the instrument is treated quite differently in each register. The lowest octave is known as the *chalumeau (chalumeaux)* register and has a rich, full tone. The last few notes before the first overblown note, b¹ are in what is known as the throat register. These notes are slightly weaker than the other notes on the instrument. This need not concern the arranger unless a passage is made up primarily of those notes, in which case the clarinet will not sound quite so full. Above the *break* (between the lowest twelfth and the first overblown note) the clarinet in its *clarino* register has a pure, brilliant tone. The upper octave (the high register) is liable to be even more brilliant and penetrating.

The clarinet has great powers of crescendo and decrescendo and has a wide dynamic range from the quietest *pp* to a solid *ff* throughout almost its entire range. Below the break, the clarinet is less capable of playing *forte* and is easily covered. The tone of the clarinet is partly due to the fact that, in a closed pipe, only the odd-numbered harmonics are strongly emphasized.

5. TECHNIQUE

The clarinet, like the flute, is extremely agile. Runs, arpeggios, wide leaps, trills, and an expressive legato are all good on the clarinet. Double tonguing is used only when the passage is too rapid to be played by single tonguing, but single-tongued passages can be written up to a moderately rapid tempo. Though not as biting as the oboe staccato, the clarinet staccato (Figure 10–3a) is quite pointed. Slurred staccato (Figure 10–3b) and an expressive semi-detached effect not unlike the *louré* bowing on a string instrument (Figure 10–3c) are also possible.

Figure 10–3

The clarinet has the widest range of attacks possible of any woodwind, from a soft *pp* to a sharp, accented *sforzando*. Figure 10–4 at the end of section 9 illustrates typical passages for the clarinet.

6. TRILLS AND TREMOLO

All trills are possible on the clarinet. They have an "oily" quality which makes them particularly suitable for blending with other instruments. Tremolos of an octave are possible, but they are safest if restricted to a major sixth in the chalumeau register, a perfect fourth above the break, and a major third above the staff.

7. SPECIAL EFFECTS

Berlioz introduced several special effects on the clarinet, among them muting the instrument by tying a leather bag around the bell (in *Lélio*). He also introduced the *echo tone,* or *subtone* (Ital. *come un eco,* Ger. *Echoton,* Fr. *écho*). This muted effect is produced by the tongue's lightly touching the reed as the instrument is played.

Flutter tonguing is not very effective on the clarinet and generally appears in combination with other instruments. Bells up are called for by Mahler and Schoenberg (*Pierrot Lunaire*), and *vibrato* and *non vibrato* (Copland's *Appalachian Spring*) are also indicated, although the clarinet does not normally use vibrato in the orchestra. Harmonics are not written in parts for the clarinet.

The glissando is characteristic of the jazz style and has been used by composers such as Gershwin, Grofé, and Copland. See also Chapter 37.

8. THE SOLO CLARINET

Because of the clarinet's wide range of technique, dynamics, and expression, it has been a favorite solo instrument since Mozart wrote his famous concerto K. 622. Since then, Weber, Debussy, Hindemith, Berg, Bartók, and others have contributed important solo works for the instrument and it is often used in chamber music.

9. THE CLARINET IN THE ORCHESTRA

In the classical orchestra two clarinets were the norm. In nineteenth- and twentieth-century scores two clarinets and bass clarinet with sometimes a third clarinet doubling on E♭ clarinet are common. In exceptional cases, more are called for; Strauss, in *Elektra*, calls for eight members of the clarinet family: four clarinets, one bass clarinet, one E♭ clarinet, and two basset horns (see Appendix A).

Because of their tone, clarinets blend well with almost any instruments. Although the clarinets are written below the oboes in an orchestral score, they are often most effective when placed above the oboes in a high orchestral harmony. When the harmony is lower in pitch, the clarinets, because of their lower range, often are placed beneath the oboes. The general rule is to keep each instrument in the strongest and most effective part of its range. The clarinet is the only instrument other than the piccolo capable of emphasizing the upper range of the orchestra in a big tutti section if the passage is too high for the oboes and the flutes are not sufficiently strong.

Figure 10–4

Mozart, *Clarinet Concerto*

Wagner, *Overture to "Tannhäuser"*

Brahms, *Symphony No. 1*

Figure 10–4 (cont.)

Tchaikovsky, *Symphony No. 4*

Schönberg, *Pierrot Lunaire*

Used by permission of Belmont Music Publishers, Los Angeles, California

Gershwin, *Rhapsody in Blue*

10. THE BASS CLARINET

Ital. *clarinetto(i) basso(i), clarone(i)*   **Ger.** *Bassklarinette(n)*
Fr. *clarinette(s) basse(s)*

Figure 10–5

Sounding down a major ninth

The bass clarinet, in B♭, is pitched an octave below the ordinary clarinet and written a major ninth above (older scores sometimes use the notation a major second above the concert pitch in the bass clef). The range is shown in Figure 10–5. It was introduced to the orchestra by Meyerbeer, and by the time of Wagner it had become a regular member of the orchestra. The parts for the now-obsolete bass clarinet in A are now played on the B♭ instruments. In Russia there are bass clarinets which have the low written B♭. Janáček takes the instrument (in his *Sinfonietta*) as low as G (sounding FF). Most instruments in the West, however, have the same written range as the clarinet, with the addition of a (written) e♭ at the bottom of the range to enable the instrument to perform parts originally written for the bass clarinet in A. Some have low (written) c.

The technique of the bass clarinet is almost as facile as that of the clarinet and everything which has been said of the clarinet holds true of the bass clarinet, transposed an octave lower. It is often used in the orchestra as a more satisfactory bass for the woodwinds than the bassoon, partly because of its tone color, which blends well with all instruments, and partly because of its greater dynamic range in passages where a softer bass is required. The rich (odd-numbered) harmonics of the bass clarinet reinforce the upper winds or strings much better than the bassoons. In these combinations, the bassoons are often given inner parts. The upper range is not much used since the clarinets in B♭ sound much better in that range. Wagner was the first to discover the somewhat somber beauty of an occasional bass clarinet solo.

Figure 10–6

Wagner, *Die Walküre*

*written originally for bass clarinet in A, a minor third above concert pitch (old notation)

Strauss, *Sinfonia Domestica*

*originally in old notation.

Copyright 1964 by Boosey & Hawkes Music Publishers Ltd. Reprinted by permission.

Figure 10–6 (cont.)

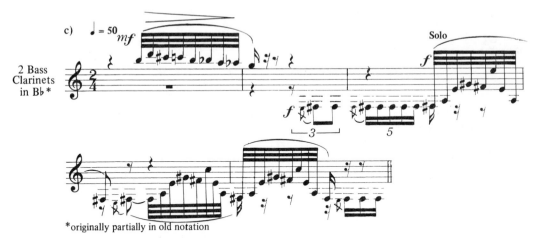

*originally partially in old notation

11. THE CLARINET IN E♭

Ital. *clarinetto(i) in Mi♭*   **Ger.** *Klarinette(n) in Es*
Fr. *clarinette(s) en Mi♭*

Figure 10–7

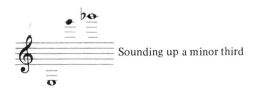

Sounding up a minor third

The *soprano* clarinet in E♭ (not to be confused with the *alto* clarinet in E♭—see Chapter 32) is a smaller version of the B♭ clarinet. It transposes a minor third above the written notes. Therefore, its part has three flats fewer or three sharps more than the key of the music. Figure 10–7 shows the range.

It is primarily used for strengthening the upper partials of a large orchestral tutti (two are used in Mahler's Symphony No. 8 and in Schoenberg's *Gurrelieder*), but is also used for satirical purposes because of its high, squeaky tone. Berlioz portrays the nightmare of the Witches' Round Dance and Strauss the pranks of *Til Eulenspiegel* with the instrument (Figure 10–8). The lower register is usually avoided because of its weakness (B♭ clarinets are better) and the upper range because of its intense, stabbing tone (the Strauss excerpt is exceptional). It is almost useless to write for the instrument in *piano*.

Figure 10–8

Berlioz, *Symphonie Fantastique*

R. Strauss, *Til Eulenspiegel*

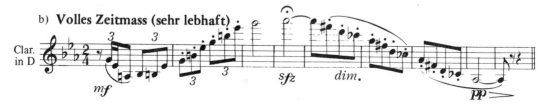

11

The Bassoon

Ital. *fagotto(i)*   **Ger.** *Fagott(e)*   **Fr.** *Basson(s)*

1. ORIGIN

The bassoon developed from the medieval bombard, the low-pitched ancestor of the oboe family. Later the instrument was shortened and came to be called the *curtal*. This developed into the *Dulzian*, an instrument which resembled our modern bassoon. Its pipe was bent double, hence its Italian name, *fagotto* (a bundle of sticks).

2. DESCRIPTION

The bassoon is a double-reed, conical-bore woodwind made of maple, plastic, or hard rubber. The pipe, bent double, is 9 feet, 2 inches (2.88 meters) long. The reed, $\frac{1}{2}$ inch (14 mm) wide, is attached to the instrument by a curved tube called the *bocal* or *crook*.

3. RANGE

Figure 11–1

*rare   *

Although built in G, the bassoon, like the oboe, is written as a nontransposing instrument. Both bass clef and, for high passages, tenor clef are used. See range in Figure 11–1. BB♭ is the lowest note available on most bassoons, though instruments are made with the low AA. Wagner, Mahler and Prokofiev write this low for the instrument (this note may also be obtained by a bell extension). Shostakovich in his Third Symphony writes down to the low AA♭, and Stravinsky exploits in the solo at the beginning of *The Rite of Spring (Sacre)*.

It is not uncommon in twentieth-century scores to see the instrument play as high as d^2, although the notes above $b♭^1$ tend to be more and more difficult. Stravinsky and Ravel take the instrument as high as e^2, and Berg calls for f^2 in *Lulu*.

4. TONE

The tone of the bassoon, with its weak fundamental, is less nasal and not as penetrating as that of the oboe. The lower fifth, which is somewhat thick and reedy, can be played quietly only with difficulty (helped by mute, special reeds, and fingerings). The top octave has a somewhat pinched quality which Stravinsky exploits in the solo at the beginning of *The Rite of Spring*.

Although the bassoon has a considerable dynamic range throughout most of its register, its tone is easily absorbed by other instruments. This makes it ideal for background accompaniment and unobtrusive doublings. Vibrato is used on the bassoon.

5. TECHNIQUE

Scales, arpeggios, repeated notes, wide leaps of up to two octaves (easier ascending than descending, as is true of other wind instruments), legato, rapid single tonguing, and (at a pinch) double tonguing, can be performed with considerable agility on the bassoon. Because of the larger reed, a considerable air flow is needed to keep the reed vibrating. Therefore, as with most winds, slurs of more than six or eight beats in a moderate tempo are generally impractical (this, of course, depends on the dynamic and type of passage).

6. TRILLS AND TREMOLO

Since the Böhm system has not been applied to the bassoon with complete success, and since there are both French and German types, it is not possible to list those trills which are difficult on all instruments. However, it is good to avoid trills on the notes indicated in Figure 11–2 and trills below the note F.

Figure 11–2

Tremoli should be no wider than a fourth. It is best to avoid the upper and lower octaves.

7. SPECIAL EFFECTS

Flutter tonguing is rather ineffective on the bassoon although it is occasionally used in combination with other instruments. The bassoon glissando is found in Mahler's Third Symphony, Ives' *Three Places in New England*, and Schoenberg's *Fünf Orchesterstücke*. Liadov, in *The Enchanted Lake*, writes for muted bassoons. This effect is achieved by stuffing a cloth in the bell. See Chapter 37 for other effects.

8. THE SOLO BASSOON

As a solo instrument, the bassoon is allowed to show off its varied technique much more than it usually is in the orchestra. It is also allowed to play throughout its very wide range. Concerti have been written for the instrument by Vivaldi, Mozart, and Weber. The chamber literature includes a sonata by Hindemith.

9. THE BASSOON IN THE ORCHESTRA

The bassoon first appeared in the orchestra in the early seventeenth century. Two bassoons or two bassoons and contrabassoon are the rule today. Sometimes three bassoons and contrabassoon are required (*La Mer, Daphnis et Chloé, Alpine Symphony*), or even three bassoons and two contrabassoons (*Gurrelieder, Sacre*).

The common classical procedure was to use the bassoons to reinforce the bass line. They were gradually freed from this drudgery during the nineteenth century. They are often used for inner harmonic parts; to play accompaniment figures; to double the other woodwinds, usually at the octave; or to double the strings (with which they blend particularly well) in unison or at the octave. They are also often used in combination with the French horns. In most orchestral doublings the bassoons add solidity to the line without asserting their own tone color. This sort of doubling will be discussed in detail in Part II.

Although Beethoven occasionally gave the bassoon short solos in his symphonies, it was the Russian composers, especially Tchaikovsky, who fully realized the instrument's great potential for melodic expression. In writing solo passages, one must keep in mind that the bassoon is easily covered by other instruments. It is also important to remember not to keep the instrument always in the bottom, and least effective, part of its range.

Figure 11–3

Mozart, *Bassoon Concerto*

Moussorgsky, *Pictures at an Exhibition*, arranged by Ravel

Stravinsky, *Rite of Spring*

Figure 11–3 (cont.)

Bartók, *Concerto for Orchestra*

d) **Allegretto scherzando**

p staccato

N. B. see also Chapter 3, Ex. 6-b

10. THE CONTRABASSOON

It. *contrafagotto(i)*   **Ger.** *Kontrafagott(e)*

Fr. *contrebasson(s)*

Figure 11–4

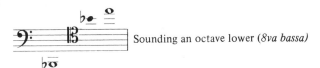

Sounding an octave lower (*8va bassa*)

The contrabassoon is twice the size of the ordinary bassoon, 18 feet (5.7 meters) long. The instrument is bent back on itself three times and rests on the floor. It is written an octave above its concert pitch (see Figure 11–4 for range), and therefore is to the bassoons what the double basses are to the cellos.

Stravinsky writes down to the low written AA (sounding AAA, the lowest note on the piano), which is available with a bell extension. Beethoven, in his Ninth Symphony, takes it up to written a[1], and Ravel, in *Ma Mère L'Oye*, to b♭[1].

The tone of the instrument is like that of a darker bassoon. The lower fifth has a decided buzzing sound and, while it is not possible to play extremely quietly, the lower range is somewhat softer than the bassoon's. The upper register is thin and the bassoons have a much better tone in that register. When the contrabassoon is taken into its higher range, it is usually doubled with other instruments. Rapid passages tend to sound somewhat thick and heavy on the contrabassoon. It is wise to give the instrument plenty of rests, both because of its heavy tone and because the player tires easily.

Handel wrote for a forerunner of our modern contrabassoon (which was developed by Heckel about 1880), as did Haydn and Mozart. Beethoven was the first to employ it in a symphony (his Fifth, in which he also introduced the piccolo and the trombones). Beethoven wrote one of the most effective solos for the instrument in his opera *Fidelio,* where it invokes the depths of a dungeon (Figure 11–5a). Such solo passages, used with great discretion, when made up of a few notes and not appearing too frequently, can be highly effective in conjuring up the somber or the grotesque. As with the bassoons, don't keep the instrument always in the basement; the effect of great depth is obtained even in the middle register of the instrument. Gunther Schuller has written a concerto for the instrument.

Figure 11–5

Beethoven, *Fidelio*

Dukas, *The Sorcerer's Apprentice*

Burton, *Dithyramb*

12

The Horn

Ital. *corno(i)*   **Ger.** *Horn (Hörner)*   **Fr.** *cor(s)*

1. ORIGIN

From the earliest times wind instruments were constructed with a cup-shaped *mouthpiece* (against which the lips are placed in playing) inserted into the end of a hollowed animal horn. It was soon discovered that an instrument made of metal not only was more durable but produced a better sound. Early horns were coiled so they could be carried over the shoulder; they were used solely for the purpose of signaling by huntsmen, postmen on stage coaches (*Posthorn*) (see Appendix A, No. 42), foresters, watchmen, and the like. These are also called *French* horns in English because they receive their present wide circular form in seventeenth-century France.

These early, *natural* horns (Ital. *corno naturale*, Ger. *Waldhorn*, Fr. *cor d'harmonie*) were able to produce (by overblowing) only the notes of the overtone series generated by the fundamental pitch of the instrument, which in turn was determined by the length of the air column. An instrument with a fundamental pitch of C, for instance, would produce the overtone series in Figure 12–1. By means of increased tension in the lips, the first fifteen overtones could be sounded. The fundamental itself was not practical on some instruments (see

Figure 12-1

Overtones: 1 2 3 4 5 6 7 8 9 10 11 12 13 14 15

Fundamental

section 2). The overtones marked with a + in the figure are, as on all natural wind instruments, slightly out of tune with our tempered scale (see Appendix B). No notes other than these fifteen were available on the natural horn; furthermore, the last three are very difficult because of the tension of the lips. Therefore, music written for the horn was necessarily of the "fanfare" type since the instrument could play stepwise melodies only in its upper register. Figure 12–2 shows a typical example of music written for the natural horn.

Figure 12-2

Handel, *Giga*

It was not until the early eighteenth century that the horn was improved by the addition of *crooks*, additional lengths of tubing that could be inserted into the instrument, thereby lowering the fundamental pitch and creating an entirely new series of overtones. The crooks could be changed in just a few measures of music, but at any one time only one overtone series was available. This system had been applied to the trumpets nearly a century earlier. Following is a list of horn crooks in use in the eighteenth and early nineteenth centuries:

E♭ alto   sounding up a minor third (rare—see Mozart Symphony No. 19, K. 132)

C alto   sounding at the written pitch (rare—used by Bach and Haydn)

B alto   sounding down a minor second (also rare—used by Haydn)

B♭ alto   sounding down a major second

A   sounding down a minor third

A♭	sounding down a major third (uncommon)
G	sounding down a perfect fourth
F♯	sounding down a diminished fifth (rare—see Haydn Symphony No. 45, "Farewell")
F	sounding down a perfect fifth
E	sounding down a minor sixth
E♭	sounding down a major sixth
D	sounding down a minor seventh
D♭	sounding down a major seventh (rare—see Berlioz *Roméo et Juliette*, Bizet *Carmen*)
C	sounding down an octave
B basso	sounding down a minor ninth (rare—see Brahms Symphony No. 1)
B♭ basso	sounding down a major ninth
A basso	sounding down a minor tenth (rare—occasionally seen in Italian opera scores)

As can be seen, except for the horns in C alto, all the natural horns were transposing instruments. Although this can cause inconvenience to someone studying eighteenth- and nineteenth-century scores—and this is why it is necessary to discuss the natural horn in such detail—it was a perfectly logical procedure from the standpoint of the horn player. The switch from one crook to another changed the fundamental pitch of the instrument, but not the player's technique with regard to the lips, which were the natural horn player's only means of controlling the pitch in the first half of the eighteenth century. He still read the fifteen overtones available to him in the key of C. No other notes were written in his part. The resultant sound, however, would be in the key of the crook. It should be noted that crooks for all keys were not necessary since by means of a *tuning slide* the player could lower the pitch of the horn a semitone. Therefore a horn "in D" (with the D crook) could be converted to a horn in D♭ merely by pulling out the slide. It is also worth noting that all horns except the rare E♭ alto transposed *down* from the written pitches. Horns "in C" meant horns sounding an octave lower unless written "in C alto."

About 1750 it was discovered that if the right hand was inserted into the bell of the instrument and half closed the opening, the fundamental, and therefore any overtone being played, could be lowered a semitone in pitch. By inserting the hand all the way, the player could lower the note a whole tone. Thus was the *hand horn* (Ital. *corno a mano*) born. Now players had a whole new series of notes available and were able to adjust the pitch of the natural overtones that were out of line with the tempered scale. Unfortunately, the tone of these altered notes was dull and muted in quality and not at all like the rich, open tones of the horn. Figure 12–3 shows all the notes written for the horn in F by Beethoven in his Sonata Op. 17. All notes marked + had to be *stopped* (played with the hand in the bell). Mozart's Horn Concerto No. 3, K. 447, requires a

Figure 12–3

complete chromatic range of the natural horn from e¹ to a²! These works were both written for virtuoso soloists, however. Mozart and Haydn hardly ever employ stopped notes in their symphonies. Beethoven was the first composer to require them extensively, and then only in solo passages.

It was also common practice after Beethoven to require two sets of horns in different keys in order to make available more notes on the horns at any one

Figure 12–4

Beethoven, *Symphony No. 9*

time (Figure 12–4). As music became more chromatic during the early nineteenth century, composers were sometimes forced to go to extraordinary lengths to make their music playable on the natural horn. To write the melody in Figure 12–5, Berlioz had to divide the part among four horns, each in a different key.

Given a few bars' rest, the player could switch crooks and play in a new key. This was indicated by writing the pitch of the new crook, "in D," "in B♭ basso," etc. In Figure 12–6, Schumann gives the horns plenty of time to warm up on the new crook.

In about 1815, *valves* were applied to the horn, creating basically the instrument we know today. By means of rotary or piston valves, extra lengths of tubing could be instantaneously added to the instrument, thereby altering the pitch of the fundamental and the entire overtone series. On the modern horn, the first (index) finger of the left hand operates a valve which lowers the pitch of the instrument a whole step, the second valve lowers the pitch a semitone, and the third valve lowers it a minor third. By various combinations of these valves, the player can produce the overtones of any fundamental from a semitone lower to a diminished fifth lower (all three valves depressed, a whole step + a

Figure 12–5

Berlioz, *Treatise on Instrumentation*

Horn
in E

Horn
in E♭

Horn
in G

Horn
in F

Sounding

Figure 12–6

Schumann, *Piano Concerto in A minor*

2
Horns
in C

2
Horns
in A

*Change to A (crooks)

Figure 12–6 (cont.)

semitone + a minor third = a diminished fifth). Eventually, a technique was developed whereby, through fingering of various combinations of valves, a chromatic scale was possible throughout almost its entire range. Halévy, in his opera *La Juive* (1835), is usually credited as the first composer to introduce the valve horn (Ital. *corno ventile, corno chromatico*, Ger. *Ventilhorn*, Fr. *cor-à-pistons*) and trumpet to the orchestra. Schumann and Wagner pioneered the use of the instrument in Germany (but see footnote 5), Wagner often writing for a quartet consisting of a pair of natural horns and a pair of valve horns.

In this regard, the time is long overdue to correct an error which has been passed down for almost a century from Prout in 1897 to Kennan in 1970 in nearly every book on orchestration. This is the matter of Wagner's notation of his horn parts, especially in the score of *Lohengrin*, where examples such as Figure 12–7 are to be found. The assumption is that Wagner is asking the

Figure 12–7

Wagner, *Lohengrin*

player to read a confusing notation. Prout "utterly fail(s) to conceive why Wagner . . . adopted this impractical notation."[1] Forsyth,[2] Piston,[3] and Kennan (who says, "It is difficult to follow the logic of this strange system,"[4]) all perpetuate the idea that Wagner simply didn't know what he was doing when it came to writing horn parts. In fact, nothing could be further from the truth.

Wagner wrote *Lohengrin* when he was *Hofkapellmeister* at Dresden. The first horn at the Opera was one Joseph-Rudolf Lewy, one of the first virtuoso

---

[1] Ebenezer Prout, *The Orchestra* (London: Augener, 1897), p. 196.

[2] Cecil Forsyth, *Orchestration* (New York: Macmillan, 1914), p. 98.

[3] Walter Piston, *Orchestration* (New York: Norton, 1955), pp. 231–32.

[4] Kent Kennan, *The Technique of Orchestration*, 2nd ed. (Englewood Cliffs, N.J.: Prentice-Hall, Inc., 1970).

soloists on the valve horn; Figure 12–8 shows an excerpt from Lewy's *Douze Etudes* for the valve horn.[5] Obviously, Wagner's notation has nothing to do

Figure 12–8

Lewy, *Study No. XI*

with changing crooks. When one remembers that the valve horn was in its infancy and that the first players of the instrument had all been trained in the old hand horn technique, the explanation appears quite simple. The early valve horn players looked on the valves as merely a quick way of changing crooks, thereby creating a new overtone series. Although a rudimentary chromatic technique had begun to develop (see the last four notes on the F horn in Figure 12–8), most valve combinations were used to quickly put the instrument in a new key. Far from not understanding the instrument, it seems clear that Wagner consulted with Lewy and was writing in accord with the latest developments in horn technique.[6]

Much has been written about the better tone of the natural horn compared with that of the valve horn, despite the enormous technical superiority of the newer instrument. This may have been true of the early models of the valve horn; however, the modern valve horn is so vastly superior in intonation and evenness of tone that we should not for a moment mourn the disappearance of the older instrument. Yet it took nearly a century for the valve horn to replace the natural horn, partly because players of the older instrument were justifiably afraid of being replaced by valve horn players. Hand horns were still to be heard in Berlin and Paris at the beginning of the twentieth century.

2. DESCRIPTION

The modern valve horn is a brass instrument coiled into a spiral, ending with a flaring bell. It is 12 feet (3.66 meters) long, 17 feet (5.19 meters) counting

---

[5] Lewy played the horn obbligato to Schubert's *Auf dem Strom* (1828). There is internal evidence that this part may have been written for a valve horn. Lewy also, according to tradition, played fourth horn in the first performance of Beethoven's Symphony No. 9, which would explain the difficulty of the solo passages. R. Morley-Pegge, *The French Horn* (London: Benn-Norton, 1960).

[6] Morley-Pegge, *The French Horn*, pp. 107–8.

the rotary valve extensions. Because of the mostly conical bore, the horn is a *half-tube* instrument which cannot sound the fundamental tone (see Appendix B), but only the overtones. The most common horn today is the *double horn*, which is a three-valve horn in F with a thumb valve which puts the horn in B♭ alto. This additional valve facilitates the performance of certain passages, especially in the high register where, for instance, c^2 can be taken as the ninth harmonic of BB♭ rather than the twelfth of FF, in which case the harmonics would be closer together and more difficult to pick out. The part is written in F throughout, the player deciding when to utilize the B♭ key. The wider-bore German instrument is more popular than its lighter French cousin.

3. RANGE

Figure 12–9

Sounding down a perfect fifth

The range of the horn is shown in Figure 12–9. Low harmonics are possible by means of a very loose lip, but they are only possible in *piano* and have an unpleasant, grunting quality which makes them of little practical use in either solo or orchestral writing. The low F is occasionally written, and Mahler and Shostakovich have written down to E.

Because of the extreme lip tension, notes above g^2 tend to sound extremely high. b^2 and c^3 are difficult and the horn is liable to "crack" on the notes, though $c\sharp^3$ is found in works of Ives and Schoenberg, and Strauss writes as high as e^3 (*Sinfonia Domestica*).

The bass clef is used only if the part lies in a low range for several measures. Although today most composers write a fifth above the concert pitch in both clefs, until fairly recently it was common to write a fourth *below* the actual pitch in the bass clef. It is wise to add a footnote in the score explaining which transposition is being used.

4. TONE

Partly because of the conical bore, the horn has a mellower tone than the trumpet or trombone. Much has been written about the "noble" or "heroic" tone of the horn. One has only to open the score of nearly any nineteenth-century work to see that the horn was one of the favorite instruments of the Romantic era. It retains nearly as important a place in many twentieth-century works as well.

The tone is fairly even throughout the range of the instrument, though below g the notes tend to become weak dynamically and unfocused in tone. The extreme high is possible only in *forte*. The best part of the range is g to g², where the tone is bright and clear and where the horn has a good dynamic range from the softest *pp* to a *ff* exceeded only by the trumpets and trombones.

5. TECHNIQUE

The horn is primarily a lyrical instrument. Rapid, mechanical technique, such as scale passages, arpeggios, repeated notes, and so forth are not as effective on nor as characteristic of the horn as, say, the trumpets or the woodwinds. Nevertheless, these techniques may be quite effective in virtuoso solo writing or for an occasional solo in the orchestra. Slurs, in brass writing as in writing for woodwinds, indicate breathing.

It should be remembered that passages which lie in a high register for more than a bar or two are extremely taxing. Double and triple tonguing are used on the horn, though they are not as sharply defined as on the trumpet. The parts should indicate plenty of rests, especially after the player has been playing for an extended period of time.

6. TRILLS AND TREMOLO

Trills are not often written for the horns because of their rather ponderous and striking sound. There are two types of trills, those performed with the valves, and *lip trills*, performed by rapidly alternating the lip pressure to pick out two adjacent overtones. They are best from g¹ to f². Tremoli are rarely encountered.

7. SPECIAL EFFECTS

Stopped notes are still used on the horn to create two quite different effects. One is a muted *pp* created by inserting the hand into the bell (Ital. *chiuso*, Ger. *gestopft*, Fr. *bouché*). The other effect combines the stopped horn with a *brassy* (It. *squillato*, Ger. *schmetternd*, Fr. *cuivré*) sound obtained by increased air pressure, creating a sharp, pungent accent. The *pp* stopped notes are effective down to about g. A mute of metal, wood, or cardboard is also used. Since the right hand is at the bell, a mute can be inserted or withdrawn as the player is playing. This works with hand-stopped notes as well. Rarely an *echo* (Ital. *lontano*) effect is required. Without more specific directions, players perform this either with mutes, stopped, or simply by playing very quietly. Gluck even directs two horns to play with their bells placed up against each other to obtain

a distant effect ("*Caron t'appelle*" from *Alceste*). The sign for a stopped note is
+. Sometimes ° is used to indicate an open note (Ital. *aperto*, Ger. *offen*, Fr.
ouvert). A stopped horn and an open horn can be combined in unison on the
same note.

Figure 12–10

Stravinsky, *Rite of Spring*

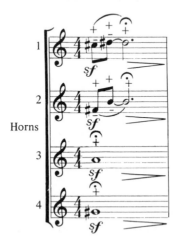

The glissando is a particularly striking effect on the horn and should be used
with discretion. It is performed by increasing the lip pressure (sometimes with
the aid of the valves) to run rapidly up the overtone series from one note to
another. It can only be effective ascending (Figure 12–11).

Figure 12–11

Stravinsky, *Rite of Spring*

The horns are sometimes asked to play with their bells up. With four or more good players, this can be a particularly hair-raising effect. See also Chapter 37.

8. THE SOLO HORN

Composers who have written works for solo horn and orchestra include Mozart, Haydn, Schumann, Strauss, and Hindemith. Important chamber works including horn (which is also found in every "woodwind" quintet) have been written by Beethoven, Brahms, Britten, and Henze. Because there are some notes which were unattainable on the hand horn and because the first performance was played by Wagner's friend Lewy, the horn obbligato in Schubert's *Auf dem Strom* may be the first example of a work by a major composer for the valve horn (see footnote 5).

9. THE HORN IN THE ORCHESTRA

From the first appearance of the horn in the orchestra, around the turn of the eighteenth century, two horns were the rule. Mozart was one of the first composers to write for four horns (*Idomeneo*). Since the early nineteenth century, four horns have been the rule. Six or eight horns are used in large orchestras (Wagner's *Ring*, Mahler's Symphony No. 8, Stravinsky's *Sacre*). *Tannhäuser* calls for four horns in the pit and twelve offstage, but Strauss holds the record with eight in the orchestra and twelve offstage, a total of twenty (*Alpensinfonie*)! Such large numbers of horns are often prohibitively expensive today and usually the parts are divided among fewer performers.

The horns blend well with almost everything. Their traditional use is for sustaining notes or chords in the middle of the orchestral range, acting as a sort of sonic glue to hold everything together. Almost any score of the last two centuries provides copious examples of this use of the horns. The horns also lend a more homogeneous sound to the woodwinds and they are often used as members of the woodwind choir. In very loud passages where the trumpets and/or trombones are playing *f* and the horns are expected to balance these instruments, it is a good idea to double each horn part. This is one reason why four horns are the norm.

Horn parts are written on two staves, the first and second horns above, the third and fourth below. The parts are interlocked, with the first horn taking the highest part, the third the next highest, the second the next, and the fourth horn the lowest part. This is because horn players specialize in playing either high or low notes, since a different embouchure (lip musculature) is required for each register. Occasionally the second and fourth horns will be asked to play high notes, as when the horns are in unison. In this case, try to avoid the extreme high (above a²). More rarely, the first and third horns play in the lower range (avoid writing below a). If the first and third horns are playing in unison for an extended period or the second and fourth are in unison, it is possible to write horns I and III on the upper staff and parts II and IV on the lower staff, though this should be brought to the attention of the parts copyist.

Figure 12–12

a) Horn solos

Wagner, *Siegfried*

Brahms, *Symphony No. 3*

R. Strauss, *Til Eulenspigel*

Berio, *Tempi Concertati*

*flutter tonguing

b) Horns in unison

R. Strauss, *Don Juan*

Figure 12–12 (cont.)

Bartók, *Concerto for Orchestra*

4 Horns
in F
(unison
with
trumpets
and
trombones)

c) Horns in harmony

Beethoven, *Symphony No. 3*

Horns
in E♭

Rossini, *Semiramide*

Horns
in D

Wagner, *Tristan und Isolde*

Sehr ruhig und nicht schleppend (very quiet and not dragging)

Horns

in E

Figure 12–12 (cont.)

d) Horns in octaves

Hindemith, *Symphonic Metamorphosis*

e) Pedal tones

Beethoven, *Symphony No. 7*

f) Horns divided on a difficult passage

R. Strauss, *Don Quixote*

13

The Trumpet

Ital. *tromba(e)*   Ger. *Trompete(n)*   Fr. *trompette(s)*

1. ORIGIN

Primitive trumpets were in use in Egypt at least by the second millennium B.C. They were used for both ceremonial and military purposes. The Hebrew *shofar*, a ram's horn with a mouthpiece, is still blown in synagogues during *Rosh Hashanah*, the Jewish New Year.

The ancestor of the modern trumpet was the medieval *buisine*, descended from the Roman *tuba* (no relation to the modern tuba), a bronze instrument some 4 feet (122 cm) in length. The smallest buisine was called the *trombetta*. About the fifteenth century, trumpets began to be folded back in an elongated loop to make them shorter. At this time the trumpet was an aristocratic instrument and often was played only by official court trumpeters. During the early seventeenth century, crooks appeared and the trumpets made their first appearance in the orchestra (Monteverdi's *Orfeo*, 1607). It was not until later in the century, however, with the development of *clarino* playing, that the trumpet began to be used consistently for art music. Like clarino horn players, clarino trumpet players specialized in playing in the extreme upper range of the trumpet where the overtones were close enough together to play stepwise melodic passages (Figure 13–1).

161

Figure 13–1

J. S. Bach, *Cantata: Der Himmel Lacht*

Like the natural horn, the natural trumpet (Ger. *Naturtrompete*) was written in C and transposed up or down by an interval determined by the crook which was being used at the time. Also like the natural horn, the natural trumpet was able to lower the pitch of any crook a semitone or even a whole step by means of a tuning slide. With the dawn of the classical era, the art of clarino playing disappeared, probably because it did not fit with the new homophonic style of composition. Mozart was one of the last composers to write for clarino in eight curious pieces for two flutes, five trumpets and four timpani. *Valve trumpets* (Ital. *tromba ventile*, Ger. *Ventiltrompete*, Fr. *trompette-à-pistons*) appeared about 1815 and gradually replaced natural trumpets as well as trumpets with side holes and keys (the old keyed bugle of the nineteenth century) and with slides (the slide trumpet, Ger. *Zugtrompete*, Fr. *trompette à coulisse*). This was perhaps Bach's *tromba da tirarsi* and Mozart's soprano trombone in the unfinished *Mass in C Minor*.

Following is a list of trumpets found in older scores (since 1700) alongside the modern trumpets.

Modern Trumpets	Transposition	Older Trumpets
B♭ piccolo	sounds m7* up	
(also in A by means of tuning slide)	sounds m6 up	A♭ (very rare according to Berlioz)
G	sounds P5 up	G (rare—used by Auber)
	sounds d5 up	G♭ (rare—alteration of G trumpet produced by tuning slide)
F	sounds P4 up	F (The valve trumpet was usually crooked in this key in the nineteenth century.)
	sounds M3 up	E
E♭	sounds m3 up	E♭
D (original "Bach" trumpet)	sounds M2 up	D
	sounds m2 up	D♭ (rare—produced by tuning slide—used by Schumann)
Standard Orchestral Trumpets { C	sounds as written	C
	sounds m2 down	B (rare—produced by tuning slide—used by Wagner in *Tannhäuser*)
B♭	sounds M2 down	B♭

Modern Trumpets	Transposition	Older Trumpets
A (A few B♭ trumpets are equipped with a tuning slide to convert into A trumpets, which are now obsolete.)	sounds m3 down	A (rare—produced by slide—used by Schubert in "Great" C Major Symphony)
	sounds M3 down	A♭ (very rare—produced by double lengthening slide—poor in intonation)
	sounds m6 down	E ⎫ bass trumpets (Conceived by
	sounds M6 down	E♭ ⎬ Wagner for the *Ring*. The E,
	sounds m7 down	D ⎬ E♭, D, and B♭ instruments are
C bass trumpet (Used to play Wagner's bass trumpet parts; supplied with trombone mouthpiece and played by trombonist; really a valve trombone; though available to most major orchestras, not what could be called a common instrument.)	sounds octave lower (sometimes written in bass clef at pitch)	now obsolete, although the bass trumpets in E♭ and B♭ persisted in bands until the twentieth century. Stravinsky
	sounds M9 down	B♭ ⎭ writes for E♭ bass trumpet in *Sacre* [1913].)

The primary difference between the older and modern trumpets (besides the addition of valves) is that the older instruments are twice as long as the modern ones. The old C trumpet had a tube length of 8 feet (244 cm) compared with 4 feet (122 cm) for the modern trumpet. Therefore the fundamental pitch and overtone series were an octave below those of the modern trumpet (Figure 13–2).

Because trumpets are narrow-bore, half-tube instruments (see Appendix B), the fundamental cannot be obtained with ease. Therefore the older natural trumpets were limited to the series of notes from the first overtone up. Most

Figure 13–2

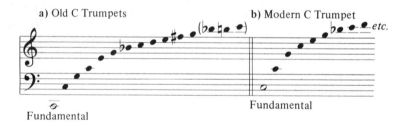

a) Old C Trumpets   b) Modern C Trumpet

Fundamental

Fundamental

players developed an embouchure (lip musculature) to play from the first over-tone to about the eleventh. The clarino players developed an embouchure to play in the octave above that where stepwise melodic lines were possible. The crook, of course, determined which overtone series was available. After the disappearance of clarino playing, notes above the eleventh overtone were seldom written.

When valves were added to the older instrument, the trumpet became chromatic throughout its range, though, like the hand horn, the natural trumpet survived into the twentieth century. By the turn of the twentieth century, according to Strauss, the preferred orchestral trumpets were the modern, shorter trumpets in A, B♭, or C for the first trumpet players (who had to play the higher part), and the older, longer trumpets in F, E♭, or D for the second trumpet players. When playing high passages, the first trumpets were playing on shorter-tube instruments and therefore in a correspondingly lower part of their overtone series than were the older instruments playing the same passage. This somewhat facilitated execution of high passages. It must be remembered, however, that the pitch is produced on a brass instrument by the lips against the mouthpiece acting as a sort of living reed. There is a limit to the muscular development possible to the human lip and therefore to the playable range on any instrument, no matter what its basic tube length. In fact, the modern B♭ trumpet is able to encompass almost the entire range of all the older trumpets except parts written for specialized clarino players. These parts are today played on the much smaller "Bach" trumpets (in D) which began to appear in 1890 to play the high clarino parts in the music of Bach. The B♭ piccolo trumpet, built an octave above the standard trumpet, has a tube length of only 2 feet, 3 inches (69 cm).

Theoretically, of course, it should be possible to play in an extremely high range on the modern, standard trumpet in B♭ if one develops an extremely tight embouchure as in the clarino style. Modern jazz trumpet players have, in fact, done this and are able to play up to f[3] and above. These notes are available only in *forte*, however, and in order to develop this lip musculature, these players have sacrificed the ability to play with a satisfactory tone and secure intonation in the middle register of the instrument, where the orchestral trumpet player is most at home. It should be added that a jazz trumpet player usually uses a narrower, shallower mouthpiece in order to facilitate playing in the extreme high register.

Much has been written about the sound of the older, longer instruments and the superiority of their tone over that of the modern trumpet. It is true that the now-obsolete valve trumpet in F has a richer, fuller tone, especially in soft passages in the lower or middle range of the instrument. Its tone is unique, but might be compared to a hybrid between the trumpet and the trombone. Nevertheless, its relative lack of brilliance, lower range, and less secure intonation doomed it to extinction.

The modern "Bach" trumpets (simply called D trumpets today) are occasionally used by twentieth-century composers and have found their way into some bands.

2. DESCRIPTION

The modern trumpet is a brass instrument of mostly cylindrical bore except for the last foot and a half toward the bell, where it becomes conical. Its tube length is 4 feet (122 cm). There are three piston valves, which lower the basic pitch of the instrument by a whole step, a semitone, and a minor third. Professional trumpet players play instruments with two tuning slides operated by the thumb and little finger of the left hand, which help with minor adjustments in intonation. A cup-shaped mouthpiece is used.

3. RANGE

The range of the B♭ trumpet is shown in Figure 13–3. This is the most common instrument, although C trumpets are more common in European or-

Figure 13–3

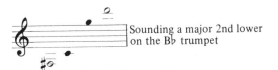

Sounding a major 2nd lower on the B♭ trumpet

chestras. Classical composers seemed content with an upward range of written g² for their trumpets, though during the nineteenth century, scores commonly call for c³. Since the turn of the twentieth century, composers have written higher and higher for the trumpets, perhaps aware that modern trumpet players play a part on whichever size trumpet is best no matter which trumpet the piece is written for. The piccolo B♭ trumpet in the author's *Dithyramb* ascends to f³ (see Figure 13–4). In the several times this work has been performed by major orchestras, no player has missed the note. Nevertheless, it is far from easy. The author is not aware of any higher parts written for the instrument.

Figure 13-4

Burton, *Dithyramb*

By pulling out the valve and tuning slides, one can obtain pitches lower than f♯, though these notes are used very rarely. Figure 13–5 shows some extreme low notes written for the old crooked trumpets; these notes were obtainable as fundamentals (with an extremely loose lip on the higher crooked instruments), as first overtones, or as second overtones (the lowest possible notes in the series obtainable on the lower-pitched instruments).

Figure 13-5

Occasionally, the trumpets, like the horns, were written in the bass clef, in which case they sounded above the written pitch. In modern scores they are always written in the treble clef. Wagner used this notation for an unusually low passage for valve trumpets in E in the overture to *Tannhäuser* (Figure 13–6). Prokofiev writes the low c in his little-known work *Chout.*

Figure 13-6

4. TONE

The modern trumpet possesses a brilliant, penetrating tone throughout nearly its entire compass. Great dynamic range is possible from *pp* to *fff*. In fact, the trumpet is one of the few instruments able to dominate the orchestral tutti in a solo. Even in *pp*, the trumpet tone is penetrating. Below c¹ the tone becomes weaker and unfocused and above g² it becomes harder to play at a dynamic less than *forte*.

5. TECHNIQUE

The trumpet is the most agile of the common orchestral brass instruments. Double and triple tonguing, repeated notes, diatonic and chromatic runs, even wide leaps and arpeggios are part of the solo technique of the instrument, although because of the striking tone of the instrument, these techniques are best used with discretion in the orchestra.

6. TRILLS AND TREMOLO

Although a few lip trills are possible in the higher register, most trumpet trills are done with the valves. All are possible although some call for awkward fingering (all valves off to all valves on, for instance). In any case, they are used sparingly in the orchestra because of their extremely strident sound (Figure 13–7).

Figure 13–7   Verdi, *Falstaff*

Tremoli are occasionally found in a massive tutti. They are best confined from c^1 to f^2 and limited to a major third.

7. SPECIAL EFFECTS

Flutter tonguing is used, as on other brass instruments, either for an extremely vulgar "Bronx cheer" effect in the *forte* or for suggestive effects such as the bleating of sheep in Strauss's *Don Quixote* (Figure 13–8).

Figure 13–8   Strauss, *Don Quixote*

(with horns and trombones)

The glissando, bells up, and the direction to play with a "brassy" sound by increased air pressure are found in trumpet parts. Offstage trumpets have been used since before Beethoven's famous fanfare to announce the arrival of the minister Don Fernando in *Fidelio*, which occurs both in the opera proper and in the famous *Leonore Overture No. 3* (Figure 13–9). Respighi (*The Pines of Rome*) and Mahler (Symphonies No. 2 and 8) have used offstage trumpets for dramatic effects. Verdi uses four in his *Messa da Requiem* to announce the Day of Judgment, and Wagner uses eight onstage in *Lohengrin*.

Figure 13–9   Beethoven, *Leonore Overture No. 3*

The standard mute used in the orchestra is the *straight* mute. Mozart (*Zauberflöte*) was one of the first composers to employ the mute. It is usually used to soften the tone of the trumpet and make it sound as if it were being played at a distance. Wagner discovered that the mutes used *forte* or with an accent have a harsh, acid tone. This effect was much used in music of the early twentieth century and is still a standard, if sometimes overused, orchestral effect. Figure 13–10 shows both uses.

Figure 13–10   Stravinsky, *Firebird*   Stravinsky, *Rite of Spring*

The many other types of mutes as well as other effects developed for jazz are described in Chapter 34.

8. THE SOLO TRUMPET

Concertos by Haydn and Hummel, as well as sonatas and other works by composers such as Purcell, Vivaldi, Bach, Enesco, and Hindemith are included in the wide solo repertory of the instrument.

9. THE TRUMPET IN THE ORCHESTRA

Besides what has been said in section 4 about the trumpet, it should be added that trumpets in unison are occasionally used for an extraordinarily powerful and sharply defined melodic line. Trumpet octaves are also powerful. The trumpet does not blend well with most instruments in unison but is occasionally used with woodwinds, particularly in quieter passages in the lower middle register of the instrument, and especially when muted.

During the classical period the orchestra generally employed two trumpets, or sometimes none at all. Three or even four were found in the theater, however, and became standard in the nineteenth-century symphony orchestra. Stravinsky uses five in *Sacre,* Schoenberg six in *Gurrelieder.*

Figure 13–11

Verdi, *Otello*

Bartók, *Concerto for Orchestra*

*today played on one of the higher-pitched trumpets (such as a D-trumpet).

14

The Trombone

Ital. *trombone(i)*   **Ger.** *Posaune(n)*   **Fr.** *trombone(s)*

1. ORIGIN

Sometime in the fifteenth century a slide mechanism was applied to a large
trumpet (*trombone* = large *tromba*) and the trombone was born. Until the
seventeenth century this instrument was generally known as the *sackbut* (probably from the French *sacqueboute*, or "pull-push"). In Germany the trombone
is still called *die Posaune*, from the medieval *buisine*, the ancestor of the
trumpet. At first glance, this older instrument is indistinguishable from the
modern trombone, which makes it the earliest orchestral instrument to develop
its present, modern form.

By means of extending the slide of the trombone, the tube of the instrument
could be lengthened to produce entirely new overtone series. Therefore, the
trombone was capable of playing chromatically throughout almost its entire
range over three hundred years before the other brass instruments. There is an
extensive sixteenth- and seventeenth-century repertoire for the instrument by
composers such as Gabrieli, Biber, Schütz, and others. Often antiphonal music
was written for groups of trombone "choirs" to be played in church. Courts and

municipalities often retained trombone bands for ceremonial occasions. The tone of these instruments was somewhat softer and less brilliant than that of the modern trombone, and they were therefore able to blend better with voices, which they often accompanied, and with strings and Renaissance wind instruments.

There were four sizes of trombone which survived into the eighteenth century: the soprano trombone, or slide trumpet (see Chapter 13), built (in pitch) an octave above the tenor trombone and with the range of the trumpet; the alto trombone, built a perfect fourth above the tenor trombone; the tenor trombone, our standard instrument today; the bass trombone, usually built a perfect fourth below the tenor trombone. (See also Appendix A.) The trombone family was almost inevitably used together as a trombone quartet, a survival from the Renaissance when groups of different-sized instruments of the same family were often used "in consort" (playing together). The soprano trombone seems to have survived as late as Mozart's time (see Chapter 13, section 1).

Throughout the late eighteenth and most of the nineteenth centuries, three trombones—one alto (pitched a fourth above the tenor), one tenor, and one bass—were used in the orchestra. Three notations were common:

1. Three staves: alto, tenor, and bass clefs.
2. Two staves: alto and tenor trombones written on one staff with alto or tenor clef, bass trombone written on one staff with bass clef.
3. One staff: all three trombones on bass clef.

The alto trombone, which had a more brilliant tone but was less powerful than the tenor trombone, was gradually replaced by a first tenor trombone. The standard trombone section today consists of two tenors (the first of which plays any alto trombone parts) and a tenor-bass trombone (see section 10). Russian scores still show alto and tenor trombones on one staff with alto clef.

Valves were applied to the trombone in the nineteenth century, but because of the inferior tone of that instrument, it has not survived in the orchestra. It is used in some bands, however.

2. DESCRIPTION

The trombone is a brass instrument with a large, mostly cylindrical bore which becomes conical in the last third of the tube toward the bell (the instrument used in dance bands has a smaller bore). It is folded back on itself twice, with the *bell joint* being held over the left shoulder. The right hand manipulates the slide mechanism (see section 3). The tube of the trombone is 9 feet (2.75 meters) long, 12 feet $7\frac{1}{2}$ inches (3.85 meters) with the slide extended. It is played with a cup mouthpiece larger than that of the trumpet.

3. RANGE

The range of the tenor trombone (Ital. *trombone tenore*, Ger. *Tenoreposaune*, Fr. *trombone tenor*) (Figure 14–1) is determined by how high or low in the overtone series the trombonist can play and the position of the slide. When the

Figure 14–1

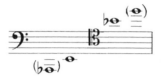

slide is pulled in all the way and the tube is at its shortest, the fundamental is BB♭. This is the basic key of the instrument although the trombone is written as a nontransposing instrument at concert pitch. The slide is now in *first position*. When the slide is pushed out a bit more than 3 inches (7.5 cm), the tube is lengthened and the fundamental becomes AA. This is called *second position*. In all, a total of seven positions can be obtained. In the seventh position, the arm is extended all the way. Each position lowers the fundamental, and therefore the entire overtone series, by a semitone. The fundamental, or pedal tone (Ital. *tono di pedale*, Ger. *Pedalton*, Fr. *ton de pédale*), is playable in the first three positions with a very loose lip. The term "pedal tone" probably comes from the low notes of the organ played on the pedal board. Figure 14–2 shows the notes playable in the overtone series of each position on the trombone.

Figure 14–2

Positions: 1 2 3 4 5 6 7

Since the overtones are closer together in the higher range of the instrument, they are available in more than one position. In the lower range, however, some pitches are available in only one position. Therefore, passages with alternating notes which are available only in distant positions, such as first and seventh, can involve a movement of the right arm of two feet or more (see Figure 14–3). In a rapid tempo, such passages were extremely awkward, both musically and visually, until a valve was added; operated by the left thumb, it adds an extra length of tubing to put the trombone in FF, a fourth lower. Most trombones in the professional orchestra come equipped with this valve, and some have a second valve which can lower the pitch of the instrument a

Figure 14–3

semitone. Obviously, this not only facilitates many passages such as the one in Figure 14–3 by making available a greater number of positions on which any one note can be played, but also fills in the gap between EE and the first pedal tone BB♭ (Figure 14–4).

Figure 14–4

Berlioz was the first composer to write for the pedal tones of the trombone (Figure 14–5). He remarks that "although at the first rehearsal of this work five or six of the eight trombone players exclaimed with indignation that this was impossible," the passage nevertheless came out "quite full and pure—played by artists who did not believe in the existence of these notes" on their instruments.[1] Some time (a beat or two) should be allowed to prepare the loose embouchure before playing the pedal tones. They are possible only as slow, sustained notes and it is not possible to play them softly. They are of better quality on the bass trombone (section 10).

The first trombone is often asked to play as high as d^2 in twentieth-century scores such as *Sacre* and, of course, to f^2 in parts originally written for the alto trombone.

Figure 14–5   Berlioz, *Requiem*

4. TONE

The tone of the trombone is more dignified and solemn, though less brilliant, than that of the trumpet. This is due partly to the larger mouthpiece. In the lower range, the tone is dark and rich. The tone is remarkably smooth throughout the entire range of the instrument.

---

[1] Berlioz-Strauss, *Treatise on Instrumentation*, rev. ed. (New York: Belwin-Mills, 1904), p. 300.

The trombone has the greatest dynamic range in the orchestra, from the loudest *fff*, in which a solo trombone can dominate the orchestral tutti, to the vibrant trombone *pp*.

A good *fff* is possible throughout almost the entire range, although the lowest few notes tend to be weaker. It becomes harder to play *p* above f¹, but a good player can play surprisingly softly in the upper register.

5. TECHNIQUE

A true legato is not possible on the trombone because of the fact that the slide moving between two notes will produce every pitch in between, and therefore trombonists generally make a slight break between each note to avoid the continual portamento that would otherwise result. This can be done so smoothly that one is usually not aware of it, as when a violinist changes bows (Figure 14–6). The effect is of a true legato.

Figure 14–6   Mozart, *Requiem*

A sort of legato is obtainable between two adjacent notes of the same over-tone series by means of a *lip slur*. This simply means that the player plays up or down the series by tightening or loosening his embouchure (Figure 14–7).

Figure 14–7

Being a large-bore instrument, the trombone takes proportionally more air than the trumpet or horn and therefore should have shorter phrases, especially when playing *forte*, when more air is expended. For the same reason, frequent rests in the part save the player from fatigue. Extremely rapid passages are awkward. Figure 14–8 shows the fastest passage work one can demand of the

Figure 14–8   Wagner, *Götterdämmerung*

trombone without its sounding imprecise and sluggish. Long passages of this nature are extremely tiring.

Double or occasionally triple tonguing is possible, though wide leaps are out of character for the instrument. As with all wide-bore, lower-pitched instruments, the notes take more time to "speak" and are therefore not as crisp as on the higher brass such as the trumpet.

6. TRILLS AND TREMOLO

Trills and tremoli are not possible with the slide since a portamento would result between the notes (although one might make use of this effect). Lip trills, though rare, are possible from b♭ up. They are possible only on adjacent overtones and are therefore limited to major second trills and minor and major third tremoli. They occur in scores by Ravel, Stravinsky, Sibelius, and others.

7. SPECIAL EFFECTS

The glissando, first used by Schoenberg in *Pelleas und Melisande*, is the most characteristic effect on the trombone. It can be performed by means of the slide from any note in one position to the corresponding overtone in any other slide position. Therefore, the maximum range of a trombone glissando is an augmented fourth, the maximum interval for one overtone between first and seventh positions. Wider intervals are possible by means of a "fake" in technique. The glissando begins from the first note and the player changes slide position in the middle of the glissando to obtain the final note. This produces a break which is usually noticeable between the end of the glissando and the final note. The glissando can also be combined with flutter tonguing to produce the *flutter gliss*. These techniques create an extremely raucous sound and must be used with care to overcome the connotations of the circus or burlesque which they almost inevitably evoke.

Muted trombones can be quite effective in *piano*. In *forte*, they are not so

Figure 14–9

Bartók, *Concerto for Orchestra*

Burton, *Dithyramb*

piercing as the muted trumpets, but here the mutes sometimes tend to make the whole trombone vibrate and create a rattling sound.

Strauss (*Tod und Verklärung*) and Mahler (Symphony No. 9) write for the trombones with bells up. Both composers (*Alpensinfonie*, Symphony No. 8) write for offstage trombones or, in the Mahler, trombones in another part of the hall from the orchestra.

8. THE SOLO TROMBONE

The eighteenth and nineteenth centuries almost totally ignored the trombone as a solo instrument, but the twentieth century has contributed solo repertory by such composers as Stravinsky, Hindemith, Poulenc, Henry Cowell, and Alan Hovhaness.

9. THE TROMBONE IN THE ORCHESTRA

Bach and Handel occasionally used the trombone to double the chorus. Gluck seems to have been the first composer to use trombones in the theater to supply chordal accompaniment. Mozart used the trombones effectively in *Don Giovanni* and *Die Zauberflöte* and introduced the solo trombone into the *Tuba mirum* of his *Requiem*. Beethoven was the first composer to use the trombones in symphonic music, in his fifth symphony.

Usually, two tenor and one bass trombone (see section 10) are used in the orchestra, often with a tuba. Some orchestras for lighter musical theater make do with one trombone. Beethoven uses two in *Fidelio* (but three in the *Leonore No. 3 Overture*). Some French and Italian scores in the nineteenth century were written for three tenor trombones. *Otello* calls for three tenor trombones, one bass trombone, and no tuba; the *Alpensinfonie* for four trombones and two tubas; and *Gurrelieder* for six trombones, one contrabass trombone, and *Wagner tubas* (see Appendix A).

The trombones are often used, both in the *piano* and *forte,* for chordal thickening in the orchestra. The trombone unison on a melodic line is the most powerful in the orchestra and should be reserved for big climaxes. It should be remembered that the trombones are primarily harmony instruments and are least effective in doubling the orchestral bass line, where they tend to assert their particular tone quality and lend undue weight. They can also easily overpower and smother voices, especially solo voices, unless playing *pp*.

10. THE BASS TROMBONE

This is the instrument used to play the parts written for the old bass trombone, which is now nearly extinct. The bass trombone was simply an instrument pitched a perfect fourth below the tenor trombone and manufactured with a wider bore to produce greater facility in playing the lower notes and produce a bigger tone. The instrument was pitched in FF, although, like the tenor trombone, it was written as a nontransposing instrument. Some bass trombones were made in GG and EE♭. The parts for the tenor-bass trombone are usually still indicated as simply *bass trombone* (Ital. *trombono basso*, Ger. *Bassposaune*, Fr. *trombone basse*).

The modern tenor-bass trombone has the same mechanism as the tenor trombone but is made with a wider bore and therefore has a deeper, richer tone. Only six positions are possible with the added tube length in F because each position, being lower in pitch, requires a correspondingly greater movement of the slide between positions. With the E valve, which lowers the pitch a semitone, the low BB is obtainable, thus filling in the gap down to the first pedal tone of the B♭ trombone. Because of the wider bore, pedal tones are of comparatively good quality on the bass trombone. Composers such as Strauss, Janáček, and Berg have written down to the low GG or even GG♭, and Varèse (*Hyperprism*) writes down to FF, the first pedal tone of the trombone in F.

The bass trombone (or tenor-bass trombone) is written at pitch (not an octave higher like the double bass or double bassoon) and uses the bass clef almost always. Figure 14–10 shows the range. It requires even more air than the tenor trombone and should therefore be given shorter phrases and more rests. It is difficult to play *piano* above the note d¹.

Figure 14–10

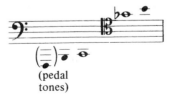

(pedal tones)

Today the two tenor trombones share a staff in bass or, if the part lies high, tenor clef. The bass trombone may have a staff of its own in the bass clef or share the staff with the tuba. The degree of independence of the parts should be the criterion as to whether separate staves are used.

Figure 14–11   Bach, *Cantata : O Jesu Christ, mein's Leben's Licht*

Figure 14–11 (cont.)

Feierlich (Solemnly)   Schumann, *Symphony No. 3*

b)

alto*
tenor

trbs.

bass

*played today on the tenor trombone.

Maestoso   Wagner, *Das Rheingold*

c)

bass trb.
double
bass trb.

Allegro energico e passionato   Brahms, *Symphony No. 4*

d)

3
trbs.

e) **Andante**   Tchaikovsky, *Symphony No. 6*

3
trbs.
and
tuba

Sehr getragen (Very drawn-out)   Mahler, *Symphony No. 3*

f)

trb.

Figure 14–11 (cont.)

g) **Ruhig bewegt (Restfully moving)** Hindemith, *Symphony: Mathis der Maler*

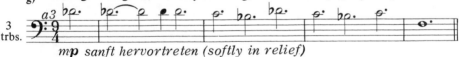

*m**p** sanft hervortreten (softly in relief)*

Sostenuto (♩=56)   Burton,*Symphony No. 1*

15

The Tuba

Ital. *tuba(e), tuba(e) bassa(e)*   **Ger.** *Tuba(en), Basstuba(en)*
Fr. *tuba(s), tuba(s) basse(s)*

1. ORIGIN

The tubas are a family of brass instruments which were developed during the nineteenth century to supply the low bass to the brass choir in the band and orchestra. Parts written for the *ophicleide* (ŏf′ ə klĭd′), a low–pitched keyed brass bass of the nineteenth century (Mendelssohn's *Overture to a Midsummer Night's Dream*), are now played on one of the standard orchestral tubas. Wagner developed a set of low-pitched horns for use in the *Ring*. They are known as *Wagner tubas* and have been utilized by Bruckner and Strauss (see Appendix A).

2. DESCRIPTION

The orchestral tubas are oblong, wide conical-bore, low-pitched, valved brass instruments with three to five, or even six, valves, played with a deep-cup mouthpiece to facilitate the production of low tones. They come in three sizes:

1. The *euphonium*, sometimes called the tenor tuba (Ital. *eufonio, flicorno basso*, Ger. *Tenortuba, Baryton*, Fr. *basse à pistons*) a 9-foot (2.74-meter) instrument pitched in B♭ but written, as are all orchestral tubas, at concert pitch. Stravinsky writes for the euphonium in *Petrushka*. Some instruments are equipped with a sixth valve with the aid of which the euphonium can reach the low notes possible on the bass tuba. Some French tubas have been built in 8-foot (2.44-meter) C.

2. The *bass tuba* (Ital. *tuba, tuba basso*, Ger. *Tuba, Basstuba*, Fr. *contrebasse à pistons, tuba contrebasse, tuba basse*) (formerly the *bombardon*), a 12-foot (3.66-meter) instrument with five valves, pitched in F but written at concert pitch (this is the orchestral version of the band bass tuba pitched in E♭). It is used for higher tuba parts such as are found in French scores and parts originally written for the ophicleide.

3. The *contrabass* or *double C* tuba (Ital. *tuba contrabasso*, Ger. *Kontrabasstuba*, Fr. *contrebasse à pistons*[1]), a 16-foot (4.88-meter) instrument pitched in CC and written at pitch (originally developed as Wagner's *Kontrabasstuba*; see Appendix A). This instrument is preferred by many players for most tuba parts, especially those that lie in a low range and demand a heavy tone. (The band version of this instrument is the double B♭ bass tuba pitched in BB♭; see Chapter 32.)

3. RANGE

The euphonium is commonly taken as high as b♭¹. The contrabass tuba is often written as low as DD. The ranges are shown in Figure 15–1. Prokofiev and Respighi write as low as DD♭, and Berg, in his violin concerto, takes the tuba down to CC. Notes above d¹ on the contrabass tuba are insecure and are better played on the bass tuba or euphonium.

Figure 15–1

4. TONE

Because of the conical bore, the tuba, like the horn, has a rounder tone than the trombones. It is velvety and "oily" in *piano* and full and hearty in *forte*. Except for the lowest third of the register, which tends to be somewhat unfocused and speaks with difficulty, the tuba has a smooth and even range throughout its compass.

[1] The nomenclature of the various tubas is not precise and is often treated in a cavalier fashion by composers.

5. TECHNIQUE

Slow, sustained passages are characteristic of tuba writing. The tuba demands a great deal of breath, especially when playing in its lower range, and short phrases and plenty of rests are more essential than for any other instrument. Often, tuba players must breathe after every note in even a moderately fast passage.

Even with these restrictions, the tuba has a surprisingly agile technique. Wide leaps are possible on the tuba, as well as rapid passage work, unhampered by the limitations imposed on the trombone by its slide mechanism.

6. TRILLS AND TREMOLO

Trills are quite smooth and even on the tuba. They are performed with the valves and therefore some are more awkward in terms of fingering than others, as on the trumpet, though all are possible. They are best in the middle and upper range of the instrument. They tend to speak with difficulty in the lowest third of the instrument.

Tremoli, though possible up to a fourth, are almost never written for the tuba. They might be useful for some effect, especially doubled with other instruments in a tutti.

7. SPECIAL EFFECTS

Composers such as Milhaud and Honegger have written flutter tonguing for the tuba, though this effect is better on higher-pitched instruments. It is somewhat muddy on the tuba and almost always used in combination with other instruments. Mahler and Strauss have written glissandi for the tuba. Strauss (*Don Quixote*) introduced the muted tuba, and an offstage (later onstage) tuba is found in Henze's opera *Der Junge Lord*.

There is no point in directing the tuba to play with a brassy tone since it is hardly possible to create this effect on an instrument of such length and with such a wide bore. Also, since the bell of the instrument already points up, "bell up" would have no meaning for a tuba player.

8. THE SOLO TUBA

While the tuba is capable of playing music of considerable technical difficulty, the repertoire for the solo tuba is limited to a few minor twentieth-century works.

9. THE TUBA IN THE ORCHESTRA

Although most scores merely specify "tuba" and leave it up to the player to decide which instrument to use, it is good practice to write for a specific instrument. Otherwise, tuba parts can range from high-pitched melodies effective on the bass tuba or euphonium to low-pitched basses more appropriate to the contrabass tuba. Often the result is that players will change instruments in the middle of a piece.

Most scores call for just one tuba, though Berlioz's *Symphonie Fantastique* requires two (originally ophicleides). *Sacre* and the *Alpensinfonie* are other rare examples of works requiring two tubas.

The typical use of the tuba is to double the orchestral bass line in passages requiring additional sonority. It is often used in unison with the double basses or as the bass to a harmony of trombones, horns, or woodwinds. The bass trombone can often supply a more well-defined bass to the winds than can the tuba, but the tuba blends better with harmonies of strings and the general orchestral tutti. It is also useful for adding breadth to expansive melodic material in a middle or low orchestral register when combined with other instruments at the unison or octave.

Though the tuba has often been used for occasional short solos of a satirical or grotesque nature (Strauss's *Don Quixote*, where it parodies Sancho Panza, and Wagner's *Siegfried*, where it depicts the dragon Fafner), it is capable of broad melodic statements of considerable nobility, especially in its middle and upper range, where it has considerable powers of *pp*, (Figure 15–2).

Figure 15–2

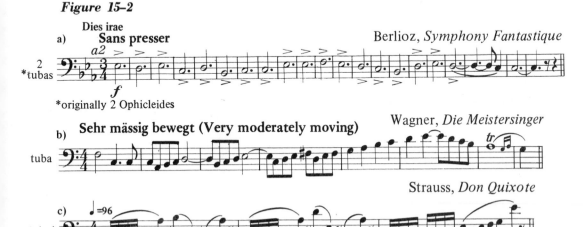

*originally 2 Ophicleides

*originally written for tenor tuba in B♭, a transposing instrument.

Copyright © 1898 by Jos. Aibl Musikverlag. © assigned 1932 to C. F. Peters

Figure 15–2 (cont.)

Sempre moderato pesante   Mussorgsky, *Pictures at an Exhibition,* arr. Ravel

e) **Molto allegro** ♩=166   Stravinsky, *Rite of Spring*

16

Writing
For Winds

1. SMALL WIND ENSEMBLES

There are some important differences between writing for winds and writing for strings. Besides allowing for the techniques and capabilities of the individual instruments, one must consider the differing tone colors and dynamic strengths of the winds among themselves. Unisons of just two wind instruments are common and do not present such noticeable difficulties in intonation (unless they are playing in their upper register) as two string instruments in unison. These doublings are usually found in louder passages, often supported by other instruments, such as strings. In quieter, more exposed passages, solo winds are the rule except when one wants the effect of thick sonority.

Many different combinations of wind instruments have been used in chamber music. Figure 16–1 illustrates three textures. In the first two bars the melody is taken by the first oboe. The clarinets and basset horns (a type of alto clarinet; see Appendix A) play broken chords in their lower register, typical of clarinet writing, and the horns and bassoons sustain the harmony.

In bars 3 and 4 the clarinets play repeated chords off the beat and the bass is shared between the bassoons in sustained notes and the contrabassoon in shorter note values. The second oboe has a simple countermelody.

In the last two bars the oboes play in thirds, later joined by the basset horns while the bassoons and horns play the bass.

Figure 16–1   Mozart, *Serenade for Winds No. 6*

Figure 16–2 begins with the oboe alone on the melody, joined in the second bar by the flute in thirds. In the third bar the lines diverge and join again in thirds in the last measure. A rhythmic accompaniment is shared by the clarinet and bassoon while the horn sustains a pedal tone.

In Figure 16–3 the main melodic line is the clarinet (H̄, Ger. *Hauptstimme*, main voice) while the horn has a countermelody (N̄, Ger. *Nebenstimme*, secondary voice). The other instruments are treated contrapuntally.

Figure 16–2   Hindemith, *Kleine Kammermusik für fünf Bläser*

* In German, **B** is B♭, **H** is B♮.

Figure 16–3   Schoenberg, *Wind Quintet, Op. 26, No. 3*

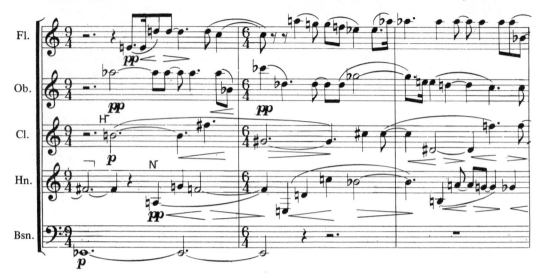

2. WIND ENSEMBLES

MELODIES

To illustrate various ways of arranging melodic lines for winds, we will use the well-known theme from Mussorgsky's *Pictures at an Exhibition* (Figure 16–4).

Figure 16–4

As with the strings, there are many considerations in the decision of which instrument(s) plays the melody, three important ones being range, tone color, and strength (volume). The extreme upper ranges of the flute, clarinet, and oboe are shrill and difficult, the lower range of the flute weak and breathy; the lower ranges of the oboe and bassoon are not possible for very quiet passages and are inferior in tone quality. The extreme upper ranges of the brass are possible only in *f*, and the extreme lower ranges are generally weak. Tone color can vary widely in different ranges of an instrument such as the clarinet. As with the strings, dynamic markings alone cannot make a badly balanced passage sound good. Remember too that the various wind instruments have much more widely varying dynamic ranges than the strings.

One of the more popular combinations of winds has been the wind quintet, consisting of flute, oboe, clarinet, horn, and bassoon. We can use this combination to illustrate many considerations of writing for winds which are encountered on a larger scale in the orchestra.

A unison doubling of the melody in Figure 16–4 could be made by flute, oboe, and clarinet in any combination. The leap to the f² is in the range of the horn, but it would be difficult and could be done only *f*. Unison doublings an octave higher could be played by the flute, clarinet, or oboe. The clarinet, horn, and bassoon could double the melody in the lower octave. Only the bassoon could comfortably play the melody in the next lower octave, since the horn is weak in that range.

Although any combination of tone colors could be used, the oboe, with its rich overtones, blends less well with other instruments. The flute and clarinet, with fewer strong overtones, blend well with other instruments. Though the horn and bassoon blend well in larger combinations of instruments, their tone tends to assert itself more strongly in smaller combinations. The flute or clarinet playing in unison with the oboe tends to soften its tone. By the same token, the oboe lends a certain bite to the tone of the flute or clarinet, though a true blend of oboe and clarinet is difficult to achieve (see Figure 7–22b). Flute and clarinet together create a smooth but bright color. The horn adds a strong, mellow tone to the woodwinds.

OCTAVE DOUBLING OF MELODIES

Figure 16–5 shows possible octave doublings within the woodwind quintet. Any combination of octaves could be used with any combination of the instruments indicated. With woodwind quintet, one practical solution in all four octaves would be obtained with the flute on the upper octave, oboe and clarinet on the next, and horn and bassoon on the two next lower octaves.

Figure 16–5

MELODIES WITH HARMONIC ACCOMPANIMENT

Figure 16–6 shows the melody with its original harmonic accompaniment. With woodwind quintet, the only practical solution would be to allot each voice to each instrument in order: flute, oboe, clarinet, horn, and bassoon. The

Figure 16–6

oboe and flute could switch parts in order to emphasize the melody, since the flute in its lower range is weak in relation to the other instruments.

Figure 16–7 shows various ways of arranging the beginning of our example for woodwinds in pairs. Section a simply utilizes two instruments per part in the upper voices; b gives a brighter sound with the melody doubled at the octave above; c doubles all three parts at the octave above for a thicker texture; d shows another disposition of the flutes and oboes for a slightly more homogeneous texture.

Figure 16–7

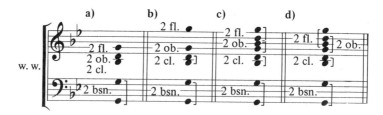

Figure 16–8 shows possible arrangements for brass. Section a sounds bright and powerful; octave doubling would be impractical because of the range later in the example. Section b would be mellower because of the tone of the horns; c doubles two horns on each part, since in loud passages a horn is about half as powerful as a trumpet or trombone; d shows Ravel's solution in his arrangement of *Pictures at an Exhibition,* with horns doubling the trumpets and trombone to mellow the tone of the brighter instruments.

When woodwinds and brass play together, the woodwinds are usually kept

Figure 16–8

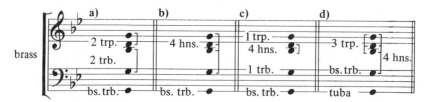

above the brass, where they are more easily heard, in order to reinforce the upper overtones of the brass (Figure 16–9a), although they can double the brass in the unison to mellow the brass tone (Figure 16–9b).

Figure 16–10 shows the usual order of winds in a score. Here two trombones double the melody an octave lower. (as in Figure 16–9a) The dashes which ap-

Figure 16–9

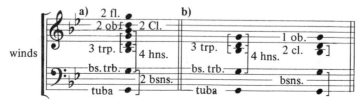

Figure 16–10

pear over or under note heads on the opposite side from the stems indicate detached notes like the string *détaché.* If the parts are not too independant rhythmically, two winds are usually written on one staff. They must be the same type of instrument, such as two flutes or two trumpets. Occasionally three winds are written on one part but usually only when they are playing mostly in parallel unisons, octaves, thirds, sixths, or chords and all in the same rhythm. *Auxiliary instruments* (piccolo, English horn, bass clarinet, contrabassoon) appear on the staves below the primary instruments.

The notation 1., I° (*primo*), or upward stems with rests below for the second instrument (when the parts diverge for only a few bars) is used to indicate that only the first chair is to play (Figure 16–11a). Similar indications are used if only the second chair is to play (Figure 16–11b). If both instruments are to play in unison, *a 2* (*a due*) or double stems are used (Figure 16–11c). The notation *a 3* is used for three instruments playing together. *Divisi* is used only in the strings. See also Chapter 8, section 6.

Figure 16–11

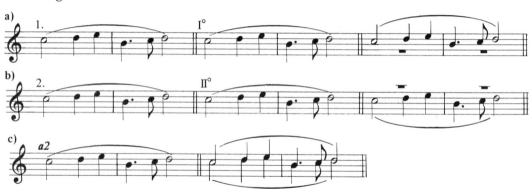

Remember that the horn parts are always dovetailed in the score, the first and third horns playing the higher parts, the second and fourth playing the lower parts.

The first two trombones are written on one staff, the third (bass) trombone and tuba on another. Families of instruments are bracketed together (woodwinds, brass) and additional brackets connect instruments of the same type written on more than one staff (horns, trombones). Bar lines are usually drawn through entire sections (woodwinds, brass, etc.)

The remarks in Chapter 7 on the scoring of chords apply with equal force here. Figure 16–12 shows some examples of wind chords, reduced to two staves for study and comparison.

Figure 16–13 shows various wind phrasings.

An example of music written for the symphonic wind section is Stravinsky's *Symphonies of Wind Instruments* (Figure 16–14), in itself a study of writing for winds.

Accompaniment figures and further considerations in scoring for winds will be discussed in Part II. Examples of music for band are to be found in Chapter 33.

Figure 16–12

a) Mozart, *Overture to The Magic Flute* d) Brahms, *Symphony No. 1*
b) Schubert, *Symphony No. 4* e) Bartók, *Concerto for Orchestra*
c) Berlioz, *Symphonie Fantastique* f) Stravinsky, *Symphony in Three Movements*

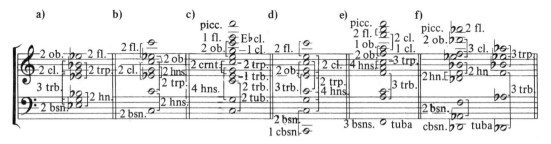

Figure 16–13

Figure 16–14(a)   Stravinsky, *Symphonies of Wind Instruments*

Figure 16–14(b)

194

Figure 16–14(c)

17

The Timpani

Ital. *timpani*   **Ger.** *Pauken*   **Fr.** *timbales*

1. ORIGIN

The timpani (or kettledrums) originated in Asia. In India, huge silver timpani were suspended on each side of an elephant and played on ceremonial occasions. They were introduced to Europe through Hungary primarily as cavalry instruments, suspended on each side of a horse and used on the march. From Hungary they found their way to France in the fifteenth century and were taken to England in the sixteenth century by Henry viii, who was "mightily impressed" by them.[1] Sachs quotes an early European impression of the timpani: "They are enormous rumbling barrels. They trouble old people, the ill, . . . the devotees in monasteries who study, read and pray, and I think and believe that the devil has invented and made them." [2] Like the trumpets and trombones, the timpani were instruments of the aristocracy.

They may have made their first appearance in the theater in Monteverdi's *Orfeo* in 1607, but it was not until the last quarter of the seventeenth century that their use in the orchestra became common. During the eighteenth century

---

[1] Cecil Forsyth, *Orchestration* (New York: Macmillan, 1914), p. 41.

[2] Curt Sachs, *The History of Musical Instruments*, New York, 1940.

two timpani tuned to the tonic and dominant notes were the rule. The timpani were required to retune only between movements. The tuning would appear in the score at the beginning of the part (e.g., "Timp. in D and A") and then the notes C and G would be written, representing the tonic and dominant. Thus the timpani were written as transposing instruments (Figure 17–1).

Figure 17–1

Later, composers began to write the correct pitches, but without accidentals (Figure 17–2). Finally, when Beethoven began writing timpani tuned to notes other than the tonic and dominant, the timpani were written at actual pitch with accidentals, though key signatures were seldom used (Figure 17–3).

Figure 17–2

Figure 17–3   Beethoven

By the early nineteenth century Weber was writing for three timpani and composers began to demand retuning during movements. In order to facilitate retuning, various mechanical drums were developed which the player could almost instantaneously retune by moving one master screw which was connected to all the other screws around the outside of the drumhead or by rotating the entire top of the drum, screwing it up or down on the shell to lower or raise the pitch. Berlioz experimented with multiple sets of drums and numerous players and also replaced the wooden-, rubber-, or ivory-tipped sticks used in the eighteenth century with leather- and sponge-headed sticks.

By the twentieth century the pedal timpani had been invented. These drums connect a foot-pedal mechanism to the screws around the drumhead. By a movement of the foot, the drum can be changed to a new pitch.

2. DESCRIPTION

The body of the drum is a hemispheric or parabolic shell of copper, alloy, or fiberglass. A calfskin or plastic head is stretched over a metal hoop and placed over the opening of the drum. Various screws around the *rim* (circumference) tune the head by stretching or loosening the skin. On mechanical drums these are connected to a master screw; on the pedal timpani, to the pedal mechanism within the drum.

Today four timpani are standard in the orchestra. These may all be pedal timpani, though many players prefer the outside drums to be mechanical. One reason for this preference is that if all pedal timpani are used, only two drums may be retuned at one time, one with each foot, whereas with drums retuned by a master screw on the outside, all four drums can, in an emergency, be retuned at once with both feet and both hands. Obviously, a score which requires much of this sort of retuning is not very well-written for the instrument.

3. RANGE

Figure 17–4

Before the twentieth century, composers seldom wrote outside the limits of F to f, the normal range of the two medium-size drums referred to in Figure 17–4. Today professional orchestras have larger and smaller sizes available. The choice of sizes for any particular piece depends on the range required for any particular drum. For instance, three large drums would be used for the tuning in Figure 17–5a, three small drums for the tuning in Figure 17–5b. The reason is that any drum sounds dull and murky if extended below its normal range of a fifth, and dry and wooden if extended above. To accomodate extremely low or high parts, timpani are built in larger and smaller sizes than those shown here. Mahler writes down to C♯, Stokowski, in his Bach transcriptions, to C. To properly resonate, this music would require a drum of almost 36-inch (91.5-cm) diameter. Such drums are rare.

Figure 17–5

The upper range of the timpani has been extended since Schubert, who wrote as high as f♯, and Rossini, who wrote (in his *Stabat Mater*) to g. With the development of the small *timpano* (Ital. *timpano piccolo*, Ger. *kleine Pauke*, Fr. *petite timbale*) in the late nineteenth century, composers have written as high as b (*Sacre*), d¹ (Ravel's *L'Enfant et les Sortilèges*), e¹ (Delibes' *Lakmé*, 1883), and f♯¹ (Milhaud's *La Création du Monde*). These smaller drums are not universally available. A timpanist in Munich once substituted a bongo for a high timpano with no great loss in effect.

4. TONE

The timpani are generally played about a third of the way from the rim to the center, where the resonance seems to be best and the pitch clearest. Composers occasionally indicate that the drums should be played in the center or on the edge of the head (see Chapter 37). The timpani have an enormous dynamic range from the quietest *pp* to the loudest *ff*.

5. TECHNIQUE

Because of the wide dynamic range, it is extremely important to be quite specific in marking dynamics for the timpani. A crescendo or decrescendo must be preceded and followed by the precise dynamics desired. There is, for instance, an enormous difference in effect between Figure 17–6a and b.

Figure 17–6

Since the tone of the timpani sustains for a second, staccato notes are normally dampened with the hand or stick immediately after they are struck. Sometimes the word "dry" (Ital. *secco*, Ger. *trocken*, Fr. *sec*) is added. In Figure 17–7a the timpani should be written staccato, like the rest of the orchestra, or they will ring through the rests. The correct notation is shown at b. At 17–7c, the timpani would be dampened unnecessarily while the rest of the orchestra sustains. The better notation is shown at d.

Figure 17–7

The timpani *roll* is the equivalent of a sustained note on a string or wind instrument. It is written either as a trill or with three or more beams through the stem, like the bowed tremolo on a string instrument. The trill, of course, takes place on the same note, not the note above as with most other instruments. The trill superseded the earlier "tremolo" notation, although most composers have returned to the earlier notation (Figure 17–8b) as being more descriptive of the sound produced (Figure 17–8).

Figure 17–8

If there is no slur between the note heads, a new attack will be made and an accent produced for each note (Figure 17–9a). With a slur (solid or dotted), the roll is continuous and there is no new attack (b). It is also good to show exactly where the roll should end (c), especially if a new attack is desired to accent the end of the roll on the following beat (d). When there is an accent at the beginning of the roll, it is better to notate the accented note as having specific value so that the note can resound a fraction of a second before the roll is taken up (Figure 17–10). This will produce a much more effective accent than if the resonance of the initial stroke is immediately muffled by beating of the head.

Figure 17–9

Figure 17–10

The timpani are played with two sticks, the ends of which are covered with felt of varying degrees of hardness. The timpanist will choose whichever hardness is appropriate for the passage he is playing, harder sticks generally giving a sharper attack with less resonance and producing more nonharmonic overtones than the softer sticks. Composers sometimes indicate which stick the timpanist should use:

1. Soft sticks (Ital. *bacchette molle*, Ger. *weicher Schlegel*, Fr. *baguettes molles*).
2. Hard sticks (Ital. *bacchette dure*, Ger. *harte Schlegel*, Fr. *baguettes dures*).
3. Wooden sticks (Ital. *bacchette di legno*, Ger. *Holzschlegel*, Fr. *baguettes de bois*). These are used for extremely sharp, percussive sounds with little resonance and less sense of definite pitch.

Sticks of materials other than felt or wood are used as well (see Chapter 37). Although most orchestration texts (Kennan, 1952; Piston, 1955) still recommend indicating Berlioz's sponge-headed sticks (Ital. *bacchette di spugna*, Ger. *Schwammschlegel*, Fr. *baguettes d'eponge*), few living timpanists have seen them and it is time the expression be retired to the annals of music history.

Although the pedals can be changed rapidly from one notch to the next and the master screw turned quickly, there is no guarantee that the drumhead will be exactly in tune, especially if the more pliant calfskin heads are used. Therefore, although the timpanist *can* retune in a fraction of a second, and on the pedal timpani even while playing, he prefers to have ten seconds or so to check the pitch of the new note and make whatever fine adjustments are necessary by hand. One of the arts of the timpanist is to be able to listen to the pitch of the drums by lightly tapping them and unerringly retune them even while the whole orchestra is playing *ff* in a different key or even no key at all. Just as one should indicate the tuning of the drums at the beginning of the score, one should also mark each change of tuning as far before it is required as possible, in the following manner:

change G to G♯ (Ital. *muta G in G♯*. Ger. *G in Gis umstimmen*, Fr. *changez Sol en Sol♯*)

6. SPECIAL EFFECTS

Figure 17–11 illustrates the following special effects:

a. The *glissando* on the pedal timpani, performed by playing a roll with the sticks while moving the pedals up or down. This can also be performed with a single drum stroke with the pedal being immediately changed while the note is still sounding. It is better ascending than descending since a slackening drumhead dampens the vibrations.

b. *Muted* (muffled, dampened) timpani (Ital. *coperti, sordi*, Ger. *gedämpft*, Fr. *sons voilés, sourdine*). A cloth is placed on the drumhead, deadening the vibrations. Mozart was the first to use this effect in the first act finale of *Die Zauberflöte*.

c. *Both sticks* (Ital. *ambedue bacchette*, Ger. *mit beide Schlegel*, Fr. *tous les deux baguettes*) on one note for great resonance and volume.

d. Two drums tuned to the same note for double the volume.

e. Two drums played at the same time with different pitches.

f. A *tremolo* on two drums. This is not as effective as the roll on one drum since only one stick is available for each drum.

g. Two players on the same part.

h. Played in the center of the head (Ital. *al centro*, Ger. *in der Mitte*, Fr. *au centre*), giving a dull thud.

i. Played near the rim (Ital. *al margine*, Ger. *am Rand*, Fr. *au bord*) giving a dry sound like a bongo drum.

Figure 17-11

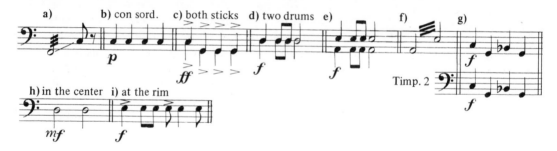

7. THE TIMPANI IN
THE ORCHESTRA

The timpanist holds a special position in the orchestral percussion section. While scores rarely call for other percussion instruments until the nineteenth century and seldom employ them extensively until the twentieth, it is difficult to think of an orchestral work in the standard repertory which does not call for timpani. While other percussion players may be required to double on any number of different instruments, the timpanist plays only the timpani.

The standard orchestral work now usually requires four drums played by one timpanist. Occasionally, more are required. Stravinsky writes for two players on five drums in *Sacre,* Berlioz for four on four (hand-tuned) drums in the *Sinfonie Fantastique,* and ten players on sixteen drums in his *Requiem!* The author uses two players, each with a set of four drums on opposite sides of the stage, in his *Dithyramb.*

The timpani are commonly used to add force to orchestral tuttis, but they are also useful for outlining a rhythm in the orchestra. Persistent pedal rhythms, often combined with crescendo and decrescendo, accenting a single note or chord in the orchestra either *p* or *f,* rolling in combination with the tremolo of the low strings, or occasionally having a short solo, preferably one requiring little or no retuning, are all common uses of the timpani.

Sometimes composers such as Rossini have written passages in which the timpani play pitches not part of the orchestral harmony at the moment because there was no chance to retune but the composer wanted the sound of the drums anyway. This compromise works to the extent that the timpani's playing a wrong note does not conflict with the sound of the orchestra so much as a trombone's playing a wrong note. Nevertheless, there is a definite feeling of an independence to the timpani part in such cases which can sound confusing.

Finally, like any instrument of strongly individual tone and great dynamic power, it is best to use the timpani judiciously and not always in the *forte.* Many of the most effective uses of the timpani are *pp.* The beginning of the Beethoven *Violin Concerto* is a case in point. Other examples are shown in Figure 17–12.

Figure 17–12

Figure 17–12 (cont.)

Langsam Hindemith, *Concerto for Violin and Orchestra*

d)

Timp.

*these figures are quintuplets, though not notated as such.

Copyright © 1925 by B. Schott's Söhne, Mainz. Copyright renewed. Used by permission of European American Music Distributors Corp., Sole U. S. agent for B. Schott's Söhne, Mainz.

Fugue: Allegro William Schuman, *Symphony No. 3*

e)

Timp.

Copyright © 1942 G. Schirmer, Inc. Used by permission.

Allegro Henze, *Elegy for Young Lovers*

f)

Timp.

Copyright © 1961 by B. Schott's Söhne, Mainz. Used by permission of European American Music Distributors Corp., Sole U. S. agent for B. Schott's Söhne, Mainz.

18

Other Common
Orchestral Drums

Ital. *tamburo(i), cassa(e)*   **Ger.** *Trommel(n)*
Fr. *Tambour(s), Caisse(s)*

1. SNARE DRUM

Ital. *tamburo militare*   **Ger.** *Militärtrommel*
Fr. *tambour militaire*

Of military origin, the snare drum first appeared in the orchestra in a 1706 opera by Marais and later in Rossini's *La Gazza Ladra*, though it did not become a regular member of the orchestra until the twentieth century.

The snare drum is a two-headed, cylindrical drum with *snares* of wire or gut stretched across its lower head, giving it its characteristic pungent sound, rich in overtones. The drum is set horizontally on a stand and the upper head played with two wooden sticks about 16 inches (40 cm) long with small olive-shaped tips. Snare drums come in all sizes from 3 inches (8 cm) to 10 inches (25 cm) deep. The diameter is about 14 inches (35 cm). The common orchestral snare drum is between 5 inches (13 cm) and 8 inches (20 cm) deep. Smaller snare drums are often indicated. "Jazz" or "bop" snare drums are usually between 3 and 4 inches (8 and 10 cm) deep. The French *caisse claire* is also a small snare drum. The Italian and German terms *piccolo tamburo* and *kleine Trommel* can be used to indicate the smaller instrument, but since there is yet no standardization of terminology, the approximate size of the drum desired should be indicated where there is any question.

The basic technique of the snare drum includes isolated single notes, rhythmic figures of any degree of complexity, rolls, and the following standard embellishments:

1. The *flam,* a rapid two-stick figure which can be accented either on the second note (a *closed* flam, see Figure 18–1a) or, less commonly, on the first note (an *open* flam, see Figure 18–1b).
2. The *drag* or *ruff,* consisting of two or more grace notes before an accented beat (Figure 18–1c).

Notation is either on a single line or one line of a five-line staff.

Figure 18–1

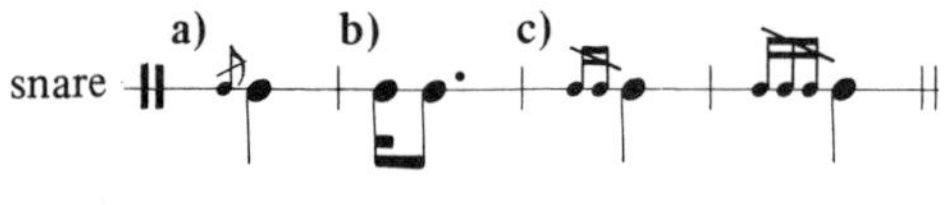

The left and right hands seldom alternate on repeated notes as they do on the timpani. Rather, the natural resiliance of the head allows two quickly rebounding strokes from each stick. Therefore, a more even rhythm can be obtained by alternating two beats in each hand. In Figure 18–2 the strong beat falls on alternate sticks each time. This type of beating is known onomatopoetically as the *paradiddle.*

Figure 18–2

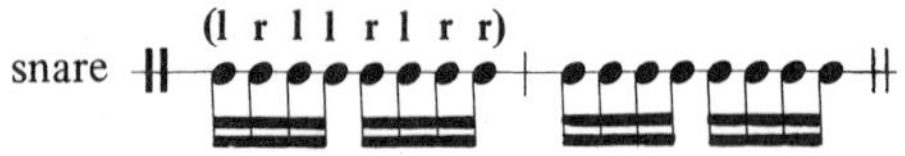

The snare drum roll is a common and sometimes overused effect (in the later Shostakovich symphonies, for example). Often composers seem unaware that the crescendo and the decrescendo on the snare, while possible from the quietest *pianissimo* to the loudest *fortissimo,* can take place only over a few measures, though, to indicate an overall "feeling" of crescendo, Ravel writes a snare crescendo through the entire *Bolero.* All the techniques are illustrated in Figure 18–3.

The snares can be loosened by a lever so that they are not in contact with the

Figure 18–3   Mahler, *Symphony No. 3*

head and thereby produce a less strident sound. This effect is indicated by "without snares" (Ital. *senza corde*, Ger. *ohne Schnarrseite*, Fr. *sans cordes, relâchées*). The return to normal playing is indicated by "snares on" (Ital. *con corde*, Ger. *mit Schnarrseiten*, Fr. *avec cordes*).

Snare drums can also be muffled by means of a small piece of felt placed on the head. In this case, the notation should be clear as to whether the snares are off or the drum is muted (Ital. *coperto*). A piece of cloth and even paper have been used to cover the head for different effects. Some models have a lever which clamps a piece of felt to the underside of the head internally. This is called a "tone control" (Ital. *sordino interno*, Ger. *Obertonkontrolle*).

As with all drums, a deeper sound is created when the head is struck in the center and a sharper sound, richer in overtones, when the drum is struck at the outer 2 inches (5 cm), near the rim, where an extraordinarily quiet, distant sound can be obtained (for terminology see Chapter 17). A roll can begin at the center and work toward the rim or vice versa.

The tension of the head can also be adjusted for a more muffled sound (loose) or a sharper sound (tight). Vaughan Williams calls for a snare tuned high in his Symphony No. 6.

The *rim shot* (Ger. *Randschlag*) is produced by holding one stick with the knob in contact with the head and the side of the rim and then hitting it sharply with the other stick. This produces a sound like a pistol shot. The abbreviation *r.s.* (rim shot) is understood in most countries. This abbreviation also refers to the *hoop crack*, less sure of execution but louder, used in "popular" music but seldom in the orchestra. It is performed by striking the head and rim simultaneously with one stick.

Wire brushes (Ital. *spazzole (metallica) di jazz*, Ger. *Jazzbesen, Drahtbürste*, Fr. *ballais métalliques*) have been used in the orchestra by such composers as Walton, Gould, and Bernstein. In jazz style, one brush makes a circular pattern on the head, producing a tremolo effect, while the other plays a rhythm. Any number of other sticks has been called for (see Chapter 37).

Other effects include playing with the fingers, turning the drum over and playing, picking or scratching the snares lengthwise, and playing on the rim (or shell) of the drum (Ital. *sulla cassa*, Ger. *auf dem Holzrand*, Fr. *sur le cadre, contre le pupitre*). Stravinsky uses offstage snare (and tambourine) in *Petrushka*.

2. FIELD (PARADE) DRUM AND TENOR DRUM

Ital. *tamburo rullante*   **Ger.** *Rühr- (Wirbel-)trommel*
Fr. *caisse (tambour) roulante*

Side drums (a generic term for all drums suspended at the side to be played while marching) are larger than the snare drum, from 10 to 20 inches (26 to 50 cm) deep in the case of the field drum and to 17 inches (43 cm) in the case of the tenor drum. Some continental models (such as the German *Landsknechttrommel*) are as much as 20 inches (50 cm) deep. Both are similar in construction and technique to the snare drum except that the tenor drum, in the orchestra at least, is always played without snares and usually with hard felt mallets. Gluck was the first composer to introduce them into the orchestra and Wagner calls for them in *Die Walküre*.

3. TOM-TOM

Ital. *timpano di jazz, tamburo muto*   **Ger.** *Jazzpauke*
Fr. *caisse sourde*

The name "tom-tom" is common to most languages but they are also referred to by the terms above. Double-headed toms (as they are also called) are cylindrical drums which usually come in sets of two and vary from 12 to 18 inches (30 to 45 cm) in diameter and 8 to 20 inches (20 to 50 cm) in depth, although instruments from 6 inches (15 cm) to 20 inches (50 cm) in diameter are available. Although used in jazz for years, having been adapted from Oriental instruments, they found their way into the orchestra only after the Second World War. They have no snares and are usually played with yarn, cord, or timpani mallets, or snare sticks.

Typical techniques are beating rapidly from one drum to another (composers often write for more than two tom-toms, five or six being not unusual in contemporary music), hitting two drums at once, and, of course, all the usual drum techniques mentioned above. As many staff lines as needed are written, or the five-line staff can be used, higher lines denoting higher-pitched drums. The *neutral* clef is used (two parallel vertical lines).

Figure 18–4

Although usually treated as instruments of indefinite pitch, tom-toms can be tuned to specific pitches. Their actual range varies from E to b♭ although they are often written an octave higher because of the strength of the upper partials. Stravinsky writes for toms tuned to g♭ and b♭ in *Agon*, and Henze writes for six tom-toms tuned diatonically from d¹ to b¹ (*Heliogabalus Imperator*) and from c² to b♭² (Symphony No. 6).

The *single-headed toms* (Ital. *tom-tom a una pelle*, Ger. *Einfell-Tom-Toms*, Fr. *tom-toms à une peau*), also called "concert toms" and "mambo set," have been used in orchestral music since the 1950's. They are from 6 to 12 inches (15 to 30 cm) deep and have a more open sound than the double-headed toms. They sound about an octave higher than the timpani. In *Gruppen*, Stockhausen writes for twelve toms tuned from C to g^1!

4. BASS DRUM

Ital. *gran cassa, cassa grande, cassa*   **Ger.** *grosse Trommel*
Fr. *grosse caisse*

The bass drum found its way into the orchestra as part of the Janizary (Ger. *Janitscharren*) music, which included a large battery of percussion and accompanied the Turkish sultan in his royal progressions. This music became quite the vogue in Vienna in the late eighteenth century, and Mozart (*Abduction from the Seraglio*) and Beethoven (Symphony No. 9) used the bass drum, often with cymbals attached, and the triangle to invoke this music. Mozart sometimes indicated that the bass drum was to be hit with switches (Ital. *verghe*, Ger. *Ruthe*, Fr. *verges*), a large bundle of sticks. Mahler revived this practice in his symphonies.

The usual orchestral bass drum is a two-headed cylindrical instrument about 16 inches (40 cm) deep and from 32 to 36 inches (80 to 90 cm) in diameter. Bass drums are made up to 24 inches (60 cm) deep. The bass drum used in jazz is usually 20 to 24 inches (50 to 60 cm) in diameter and is played with a foot beater. The bass drum used in marching bands, the "Scotch" drum, is about 10 inches (25 cm) deep and 28 inches (70 cm) in diameter and is played on both heads with two sticks.

The bass drum is usually played with a large lamb's wool beater, sometimes double-headed (Fr. *mailloche*), but yarn or felt sticks are often used for rolls, and in contemporary scores almost any beater can be required. The drum is usually placed vertically on a stand but may also be turned horizontally to facilitate certain methods of beating.

The standard technique of the bass drum includes isolated single strokes, rhythmic figures which are not too rapid (since the heads ring for some time after being hit), and rolls. The bass drum can be effective from the quietest *pianissimo* to the loudest *fortissimo* (indeed, the bass drum has often been used to simulate cannon shots). One should avoid using the bass drum simply to accent beats in loud passages unless one wishes to invoke a marching band.

When it is played in the center of the head, the sound is hard and dry, and near the edge it becomes more vibrant and reverberant. Sometimes the drum is muted with a cloth or other object placed on the head. For a particularly crisp rhythm, Britten directs the drummer to play with snare sticks. Occasionally more than one bass drum or more than one player on one drum are required.

Verdi (who usually indicates *gran cassa* when he wants the bass drum and attached cymbals to be played simultaneously, and just *cassa* when the drum is to be played alone) indicates the heads of the drum are to be loosened (Ital.

scordata) to create a dull, booming sound (*Requiem*). Gunther Schuller, in a possibly unique example, has directed that the bass drum be tuned to a definite pitch (C). A stick pressed to the center of the head and rubbed with a rosined cloth has been used to turn the bass drum into a large friction drum (see *Cuica*, Chapter 36, section 9). The drum can be played on both heads at once, sometimes with different beaters (Ital. *dalle due parti*, Ger. *auf beiden Fellen*, Fr. *sur tous les deux côtés*).

The *gong drum* is a bass drum head suspended on a shallow shell attached to a stand and is sometimes used in English orchestras instead of the bass drum. This instrument is based on the theory that the drum shell is there simply to hold the head taut and has little effect on the sound. Since the gong drum is a single-headed drum, it tends to take on more of a definite pitch in sympathy with whatever notes are being played in the bass of the orchestra (bass drum players will usually tune one head on the regular drum slightly tauter than the other in order to avoid this effect and keep the pitch indefinite). Two examples from Britten's *War Requiem* show contrasting uses of the bass drum (Figure 18–5).

Figure 18–5   Britten, *War Requiem*

b)   (S. D. sticks)

5. TAMBOURINE

Ital. *tamburo basco, tamburino*   **Ger.** *Schellentrommel*
Fr. *tambour de basque*

The tambourine was introduced to the orchestra in 1820 by von Weber (*Preciosa*). Berlioz called for as many as three. It was traditionally used to imply exotic locales (Wagner, *Tannhäuser;* Tchaikovsky, *Capriccio Italien,* Arabian dance from *Nutcracker;* Rimsky-Korsakov, *Capriccio espanol*) but today is used as any other percussion instrument, for its individual sound disassociated from extra-musical implications.

The tambourine is a shallow, one-headed drum with jingles (small metal discs) attached around the shell. It is played in the following ways:

1. The head is struck with the knuckles, fingers, fist, back of the hand, or against the knee (for an especially loud effect).
2. The hoop is shaken (notate as a tremolo with slashes through the stem (Ital. *agitare,* Ger. *schütteln,* Fr. *agité*).
3. The thumb is moistened and rubbed around the outer edge of the head to produce the *thumb roll* (Ital. *col pollice,* Ger. *mit dem Daumen,* Fr. *avec le pouce*). This is usually indicated by a trill sign with the direction "thumb roll."
4. The tambourine is placed on a table and played with mallets or fingertips (for a quiet sound). For an extremely quiet sound, the tambourine can be held steady and the jingles alone brushed.

Figure 18–6 illustrates the tremolo and thumb roll.

Figure 18–6   Stravinsky, *Petrushka*

tambourine

Stravinsky (*Petrushka*) has the tambourine dropped on the floor. Elie Siegmeister has it placed on the snare drum and has the drummer play on the tambourine with sticks. Manuel de Falla asks for a tambourine without jingles.

The *jingle ring* (Ger. *Schellenrief*) is a hoop with jingles but no head. It is sometimes used instead of the tambourine when only the jingle effect is desired, often in rock music.

19

Common
Percussion Instruments
of Definite Pitch

---

1. BELLS

Ital. *campane* **Ger.** *Glocken* **Fr.** *cloches*

Bells are hollow bodies, usually of metal, which are struck inside with a clapper or from the outside with a mallet. It is believed they were first made in their now familiar form about 400 A.D. in the Italian district of *Campania* (hence the Italian name). Bells have been made in all sizes from tiny hand bells to the 19-foot (5.8-meter) high, 180-ton (164,000-kilogram) "Tsar Koloko" in the Kremlin. Sets of 23 to 72 or more bells in church steeples played with a mechanism are called a *carillon*. Outdoor music, such as Tchaikovsky's *1812 Overture*, sometimes employs them. Handbells are made in sets of 61 (C to c⁴).

In 1791 Nicolas Dalayrac introduced the bell to the orchestra, and nineteenth-century composers were fond of writing for the sounds of very deep bells (Figure 19–1). Unfortunately, these low pitches were unattainable on bells

Figure 19–1 Berlioz, *Symphonie Fantastique*   Wagner, *Parsifal*

weighing less than several tons. This problem was solved in several ways. The Paris Opera had bells specially cast for Meyerbeer's *Les Huguenots* (1836) but they sound an octave higher than the c and f written in the score. The Bayreuth opera house used a combination of tuba, gongs, several pianos, and metal bars for the Parsifal chimes to imitate the characteristic tone color of church bells. The metal bars, tuba, and piano gave the "strike tone" or "tap tone" (the clear definite pitch heard when the bell is struck) and the gongs and the reverberation of the bars and pianos gave the "hum note," a tone about a major sixth below which creates the rich and dissonant upper partials characteristic of bell timbre (see Appendix B). Large opera houses, such as La Scala and Covent Garden, possess mushroom-shaped bells and large bronze plates (as does the Concertgebouw Orchestra) and the Bolshoi theater has a collection of 38 bells of various sizes. *Clock chimes* attached to a resonating box have also been used to imitate bell sounds (some sets sound BB♭, E♭, F, and G). The recorded sound of actual bells has also been used. The instrument that is almost universally used to produce bell sounds in the orchestra today is the chimes, or tubular bells (see also Bell Plate in Chapter 20).

2. CHIMES (TUBULAR BELLS)

Ital. *campane tubolari*   **Ger.** *Röhrenglocken*

Fr. *cloches, tubes*

Introduced in 1885, the chimes are a set of metal tubes, 40 to 66 inches (100 to 165 cm) long, closed at the top, and hung in two rows in the order of the keys of the piano. They are played with a rawhide hammer at the top of the tube. Sometimes, if only one or two bells are called for, they will be taken out of the frame and hung separately. There is a pedal mechanism which can dampen the tubes, which have a very long reverberation.

The range of the chimes is seen in Figure 19–2; few models have the g². Chimes are notated on one staff in the treble clef. Because of the hum tone, the chimes sometimes seem to sound an octave lower than their actual pitch. This makes them an effective substitute for church bells, though the deep sound of large bells cannot be obtained.

Figure 19–2

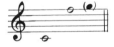

Chimes can also be played with two hammers (or, more commonly, with two players), or with other types of mallets. Three and four notes simultaneously are possible if one or both mallets are turned on their side against several tubes (two, three- and four-note clash).

The following special effects are possible:

1. One hand dampening a single chime after it has been struck.
2. Chimes muted by being covered with a cloth.
3. Glissando with rubber or cord mallets.
4. One-note tremolo with two vibraphone sticks.
5. Two-note tremolo with wood stick between two adjacent tubes.
6. Glissando with wire brush.
7. Several tubes struck simultaneously with a metal bar.
8. Offstage chimes (Mahler, Symphony No. 3; Tchaikovsky, *Manfred*).

Figure 19–3   Mahler, *Symphony No. 3*

3. ORCHESTRA BELLS

Ital. *campanelli, campanetti*   **Ger.** *Glockenspiel*
Fr. *carillon, jeu de timbres*

In *Saul* (1738), Handel wrote for an instrument consisting of small bells struck by a keyboard mechanism. The range of that part is from c^1 to g^3, sounding presumably an octave higher. Mozart's *strumento d'acciaio* (instrument of steel) in *The Magic Flute* was probably a similar instrument. In that opera it was used to create the sound of the magic bells played by the bird-man Papageno. It is irresistible to repeat the story of Mozart's going backstage during a performance and playing the bells at the wrong time in order to play a joke on Emanuel Schikaneder, who, in the role of Papageno, was on stage with a set of fake bells which he was to shake when the offstage bells were played.

A *keyed glockenspiel* (Ital. *campanelli a tastiera*, Ger. *Tastenglockenspiel*, Fr. *jeu de timbres*) with plates of metal instead of bells has been used by composers such as Dukas and Ravel. Its range is from c to c^3 or occasionally d^3 and it sounds two octaves higher. The instrument is rare, especially in the United States. The *tubaphone*, in which metal tubes are substituted for bells, has been used by Khatchaturian and others. Its range is c^1 to c^3.

The modern orchestra bells are a refinement of the *bell lyre* or *lyra glockenspiel* used in bands, in which metal bars on a frame are struck with a mallet (range a to a^2, sounding two octaves higher). Orchestra bells consist of a set of steel bars mounted in a carrying case in the same configuration as the piano keyboard (natural notes in a row on the bottom, accidentals arranged in twos and threes above). They are played with brass mallets, although rubber, plastic, cord, yarn, or wooden mallets can be used as well for special effects. The notation is on one staff in the treble clef, sounding two octaves higher. The range is shown in Figure 19–4. Instruments are also manufactured with larger (to c) or smaller ranges but the range shown here is standard in the orchestra. A set known as *song bells* sound an octave lower but are not generally available.

Figure 19–4

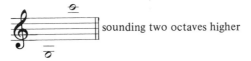

sounding two octaves higher

The orchestra bells, like the chimes, have a wide dynamic range, but even when played quietly they have a tone which, because of the rich overtones, easily slices through the thickest orchestral texture. For this reason, as with all instruments of striking tone color, the most effective parts for the orchestra bells usually consist of just a few notes, either accenting and lending brilliance to a line in the orchestra (often only highlighting certain notes of a melody) or occasionally playing a line of their own. Two-part writing is possible, of course, although special effects, such as the glissando or dampening with a cloth, are rare. Carl Orff has written for three sets of bells at once.

It should be noted that Wagner and others wrote their bell parts an octave rather than two octaves below actual pitch.

Figure 19–5   Tchaikovsky, *Capriccio Italien*

Campanelli
(Glockenspiel)

4. CELESTA

Ital. *celesta*   **Ger.** *Celesta*   **Fr.** *célesta*

Though strictly speaking a keyboard instrument (and usually played by a pianist), the celesta is used only in association with the percussion and is therefore considered here. The celesta was invented in 1886 and found its way into the orchestra almost immediately. It was only five years old when Tchaikovsky wrote for it in *The Nutcracker*. It consists of steel plates with wooden resonators played with a keyboard mechanism. The technique is the same as that of the piano. There is always a brief reverberation. Although there is a damper pedal which allows the bars to vibrate longer by removing the felt dampers on each bar, the tone quickly dies away. In fact, the dynamic level of the celesta is extremely narrow and it is futile to write dynamic variations in a celesta part. The sound, unlike that of the orchestra bells, is extraordinarily delicate and can be easily absorbed by any but the lightest *pianissimo* orchestration. The notation is on two staves in treble and bass clefs (two treble clefs for high passages), sounding an octave higher. The range is shown in Figure 19–6.

Figure 19–6

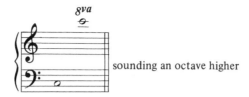

sounding an octave higher

Typical uses of the celesta in the orchestra are highlighting quiet melodic passages, giving delicate background embroidery, and occasionally playing short melodies. Mozart's glockenspiel part in *The Magic Flute* (see section 3) is usually played on the celesta today.

Figure 19–7   Mozart, *The Magic Flute*

Figure 19-7 (cont.)

Tchaikovsky, *The Nutcracker*

b) **Andante non troppo**

c)

Bartók, *Music for Strings, Percussion and Celesta*

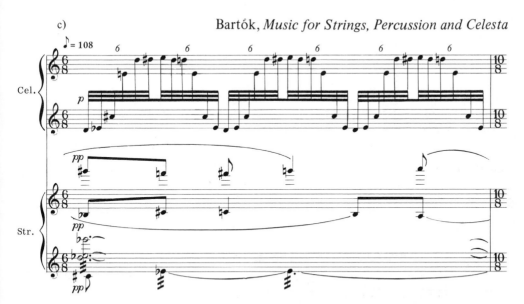

5. CROTALES, ANTIQUE CYMBALS

Ital. *crotali*   **Ger.** *antike Zimbeln*
Fr. *crotales, cymbales antiques*

Crotales are modeled after ancient Greek finger cymbals used by dancing girls. One pair, dating from 500 B.C., is inscribed OATAS EIMI (I am Oata's) and still sounds a clear f#4. Berlioz introduced them to the orchestra (*Romeo and Juliet*, 1839).

Modern crotales are made of brass or copper and are from $\frac{1}{3}$ to $1\frac{1}{4}$ inches (1 to 3 cm) thick and from 2 to 5 inches (5 to 13 cm) in diameter. They are available either in individual pairs or in chromatic sets of single cymbals mounted on a board. They can be played by striking two cymbals together or by striking one crotale with a triangle beater or a mallet. They are written on one staff in the treble clef, sounding an octave higher. Since some scores notate the crotales at pitch or two octaves lower, a footnote regarding octave transposition should be added in the score.

Sets of thirteen crotales, covering the range shown in Figure 19–8, are not uncommon. Some sets made in Europe extend the range an octave higher by the addition of twelve smaller crotales.

Figure 19–8

sounding an octave higher

Like the celesta, crotales are delicate in tone and are commonly used in very transparently orchestrated passages to play either a few notes highlighting a melody or a line of their own. See Figure 19–9.

Figure 19–9   Debussy, *Prelude to the Afternoon of a Faun*

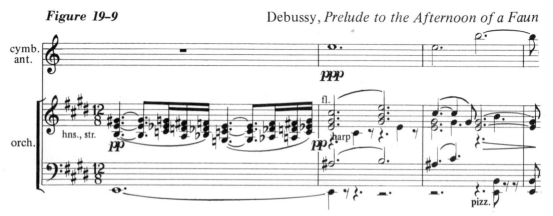

Used through the courtesy of Belwin-Mills Publishing Corp.

218

Finger cymbals or *metal castanets* are thinner then crotales and have no definite pitch. They are popular in Arabic and Spanish music. Bowl-shaped crotales known as *bell crotales* are also available.

6. XYLOPHONE

Ital. *Silofono, Xilofone, Zilafone*   **Ger.** *Xylophon*
Fr. *Xylophon*

The xylophone was imported to Europe from the East in the fifteenth century. It was a popular instrument of the street musician until the Russian Gusikow, whom Mendelssohn accompanied, elevated it to the level of a solo instrument. Saint-Saëns first used it in the orchestra in *Danse Macabre* (1874).

The name *xylophone* comes from the Greek *xulon phone* (wood-voice). Originally, the xylophone consisted of four rows of wooden bars set on straw on a table. This was superseded by the modern instrument consisting of two rows of wooden bars arranged chromatically and mounted on a stand with or without tubular resonators set beneath each bar. Mallets of rubber (also cord, plastic, or even wood) are used. At one time there was a xylophone played with a keyboard mechanism, but this has long since become extinct.

The range of the xylophone is shown in Figure 19–10. European models can extend down to c. One staff is used in the treble clef, sounding an octave higher, the *8va* sign being used for high passages, as on the other percussion of definite pitch.

Figure 19–10

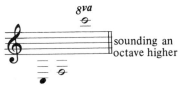

sounding an octave higher

The xylophone has a sharp, staccato tone with little resonance and can easily penetrate rather thick orchestral textures, especially in its upper range. The lower range is less rich in upper partials and tends to be mellower, like the marimba. Typical orchestral use is to give a pointed accent to single notes or melodies and to play occasional short solo lines.

Cross-hammerings, passages where mallets have to cross over each other, should be avoided. The easiest passages are those which alternate high and low pitches and can be played by alternating mallets in each hand. Rapid alteration of the mallets produce a tremolo effect, though this technique is more characteristic of the marimba or vibraphone.

Chords can be played with two or three mallets in each hand. They must be spaced fairly equally for both hands so that the player has to make as little adjustment as possible between mallets in each hand. In other words, in four-part chords with two mallets in each hand, do not suddenly write a chord with three notes together separated from the fourth note by an octave or more. Also, a combination of accidentals and naturals on one hand is more difficult than all accidentals or all naturals, since one pair would have to play on both rows of keys at once. The above remarks apply with equal force to the other *mallet percussion* (marimba, vibraphone, etc.).

Special effects on the xylophone include:

1. Glissando over the natural row of bars or the accidentals (less effective on the accidentals), either up or down. Simultaneous glissando in opposite directions are also possible.
2. Using a cloth to dampen the tone.
3. A glissando on the resonator tubes.
4. Using a cello bow to play the edge of a bar.

Figure 19–11   Barber, *Medea's Meditation and Dance of Vengeance*

Messiaen, *Oiseaux Exotiques*

The *xylorimba* is a large xylophone-marimba combination with resonators and a range of C (or even F) to c⁴. It is more common in Europe than America.

7. MARIMBA, MARIMBAPHONE

Ital. *marimbafono*   **Ger.** *Marimba(-phon)*
Fr. *marimba(-phone)*

The marimba is a Mexican version of an African instrument which found its way to the United States about 1915 and soon was used in jazz. Berg, Stravinsky, and Milhaud were some of the first European composers to write for the instrument. It has been standard in the orchestra since the 1950's.

The marimba, which always has resonators, is mellower and more resonant in tone than the xylophone, with a much less brittle sound and a tone much more easily absorbed by thick or loud scoring. One or two staves with treble or bass clefs are used, sounding at pitch. The range is shown in Figure 19–12. American models often have the low a; European models sometimes have the high f⁴.

Figure 19–12

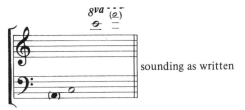

sounding as written

Much of what has been said about xylophone technique applies to the marimba except that chords with four mallets, derived from jazz, are more characteristic of marimba technique. In fact, if a simple chord is written for the marimba, the notes may be rolled if not otherwise indicated. It is good to indicate specifically which method of performance is desired. The roll can be indicated in the same manner as a bowed tremolo in string writing (Figure 19–13). Crescendo and decrescendo are effective with rolled chords. The tone blends especially well with woodwind harmonies. Rubber, yarn, or cord (even wood or timpani) mallets can be used.

Figure 19–13

In addition to the special effects possible on the xylophone, the following have been employed on the marimba:

1. Playing with the fingers for extremely soft passages.
2. Two players on the same instrument for more complex textures.

8. VIBRAPHONE, VIBES, VIBRAHARP

Ital. *vibrafono*   **Ger.** *Vibraphon*   **Fr.** *vibraphone*

The vibraphone was invented in 1923 by Joe Green, a jazz musician, though the English claim a similar instrument invented in 1916. Berg used the vibraphone in *Lulu* in 1934 and it is common in late twentieth century scores.

The vibraphone consists of a double row of chromatic steel bars with resonators. At the top of each resonator is a metal disc which spins when an electric motor is turned on. The spinning disc alternately opens and closes each resonator, producing a variation in intensity of sound (an *intensity* vibrato as opposed to the *pitch* vibrato characteristic of string instruments). This produces a tremulous sound, rich in overtones; however, it is easily covered by heavy orchestration. The vibraphone can also be played without vibrato (*fan off*).

The range shown in Figure 19–14 is standard in the orchestra, though models are manufactured with ranges of c to c⁴, c¹ to f³, and f¹ to f⁴ (the "soprano" vibraphone). The vibraphone is notated on one or two staves in the treble clef at pitch.

Figure 19–14

sounding as written

Cord, yarn, rubber (characteristic of jazz), or felt mallets are used. Techniques characteristic of the marimba are used, plus rapidly arpeggiated chords, particularly effective because notes on the vibraphone sustain for several seconds. For this reason, there is a damper pedal which allows the notes to vibrate when depressed. Its use is usually left up to the player, although pedal indications can be written in as for the piano (*ped.* and a long line under the passage, or the symbol * to indicate when the pedal is to be released). Notes are also dampened with the fingers. This too is usually left to the discretion of the player, though it can be indicated by the symbol +. It is important to notate the exact duration of notes on the vibraphone so that the player knows when to dampen. Newer models have a mechanism by which the rate of vibrato can be varied from three to eight pulses per second. The indications are slow, medium, and fast vibrato.

Special effects include:

1. Dampening only certain notes of a chord.
2. Gradually turning the fan off or on while playing.
3. Rolling a chord while performing a glissando (also possible, but less effective on the marimba).
4. Glissando with wire brushes.
5. Playing with jazz *slap mallets,* which "give" and dampen the sound, producing a dull attack.

Figure 19–15   Henze, *Symphony No. 3*

20

Common
Percussion Instruments
of Indefinite Pitch

1. CYMBALS

Ital. *piatti, cinelli*   **Ger.** *Becken, Schallbecken*   **Fr.** *cimbales*

The name derives from the Greek *kymbē* (hollow of a vessel). Cymbals arrived in Europe along with the bass drum and triangle in the Turkish Janizary music and were first used in the orchestra by Gluck in 1764. Originally, one cymbal was attached to the shell of the bass drum and another was crashed against it. This arrangement continued well into the nineteenth century (see *Bass Drum* in Chapter 18).

Cymbals indicated alone means *crash cymbals*, two cymbals with leather thongs through the center by which they are held and brushed together. In 1869 Wagner invented the *suspended cymbal* (Ital. *piatto sospeso*), which is merely one cymbal attached horizontally to a stand through its center hole so that it can be played with mallets, especially for rolls. Berlioz used as many as ten pairs of crash cymbals and recent composers such as Nono and Berio have called for as many as eight suspended cymbals of different sizes.

The exact ratio of metals used to make cymbals are usually closely guarded secrets of the families who make them. The best cymbals still come from Turkey. Cymbals are thick or thin metal discs from 8 to 26 inches (20 to 66 cm) in diameter (in *Antigonae*, Orff writes for *kleine Zimbeln* 6 inches [15 cm] in diameter). The normal orchestral crash cymbals are between 17 and 22 inches (44 to 57 cm). Composers often write for suspended cymbals in three sizes, small, medium, and large. Small cymbals generally vary from 10 to 14 inches (25 to 35 cm) in diameter, medium from 15 to 18 inches (38 to 45 cm) and large from 19 to 24 inches (48 to 61 cm). The circumference is called the *edge* or *rim*. There is a hemispherical bulge in the center of the cymbal known as the *bell* or *dome*. The area between the bell and the edge is called the *bow*.

When struck, cymbals produce a confusion of overtones which fall between 100 and 9,000 cycles per second. The nearer the edge the cymbal is hit, the richer in overtones and brighter the sound will be. Hit on or near the bell, the cymbal produces a dull, gong-like tone with fewer overtones.

1. At the edge (Ital. *al margine*, Ger. *am Rande*, Fr. *au bord, blousez*)
2. In the middle (Ital. *alla metà*, Ger. *in der Mitte*, Fr. *au milieu*)
3. On the bell (dome) (Ital. *alla campana, sulla cupola, al centro*, Ger. *auf die Kuppe*, Fr. *sur la protubérance*)

Yarn, marimba, or vibraphone mallets, snare sticks, triangle beaters (Mahler asks for a steel rod in his Symphony No. 3), fingernails or the blade of a knife (Bartók), and even coins and sawblades have been prescribed for suspended cymbals. Besides the roll on the suspended cymbal, which is possible over a wide dynamic range (the crescendo being a common effect), individual notes or rhythmic patterns are common, often over three or more cymbals of different size. Since the cymbal can ring for some time after being struck, exact note values should be indicated. The cymbal can be dampened by grasping with the hand; this maneuver is called the *choke*.

Figure 20–1 shows three ways of notating three suspended cymbals of different sizes: high (or small), medium, and low (or large).

Figure 20–1

Crash cymbals can be sounded over a wide dynamic range. The cymbals are not simply brought straight together, which would produce a dull, dampened sound, but are brushed by each other so that both cymbals can ring freely. A common nineteenth-century effect was the *two-plate roll* (Fr. *frottées*) invented by Berlioz: both cymbals are continuously brushed together. It is notated like a drum roll, with slashes through the stem. This effect is more smoothly performed as a roll with mallets on a suspended cymbal. Another effect is to hold the crash cymbals together and lightly brush them apart. This creates a quiet, swishing sound (Ital. *strisciato*).

Special effects on the cymbals include:

1. The cymbal struck and a wire brush immediately placed against it, giving a "sizzling" effect from the vibration of the brush against the cymbal.
2. A cymbal placed on a timpani head and played with glockenspiel beaters (Sir Arthur Bliss).
3. The cymbal struck with a triangle (Sir William Walton).
4. The cymbal bowed with a cello bow (Schoenberg, *Five Pieces for Orchestra*).
5. The cymbal dampened, after being struck, progressively from the bell to the edge or vice versa, thereby producing respectively more or fewer upper partials as the tone diminishes.

2. TAM-TAM

Ital. *tam-tam*   **Ger.** *Tam-tam*   **Fr.** *tam-tam*

The tam-tam is a large gong of indefinite pitch. Although it is habitually called the *gong*, precise terminology reserves the term "gong" for instruments of definite pitch. The tam-tam originated in the Far East, and the best instruments still come from there. It first appeared in the opera orchestra in 1791 in a work by a composer named Gossec. In the early nineteenth century it became standard fare in the opera house and later in the symphony orchestra.

The tam-tam is a large hammered metal plate turned over at the edge and suspended from a frame. Tam-tams exist with diameters of from 16 inches to 5 feet (40 to 150 cm) but in the orchestra the instrument generally ranges from 20 to 36 inches (50 to 91 cm).

Single, isolated notes from *pianissimo* to an orchestra-dominating *fortissimo* are characteristic of the tam-tam. Rhythmic figures must be rather slow to be clear because of the enormous reverberation of the tam-tam which lasts at least several seconds. A soft, chamois-headed stick is used, but timpani sticks can be used for rolls, and mallets of all kinds as well as wire brushes and even fingers have been used. Strauss and Stravinsky use the triangle beater to create a glissando effect by having it drawn in an arc on the surface or along the edge of the tam-tam.

Although the tam-tam is normally dampened with the arms, large felt mutes are sometimes found in Germany. Stravinsky writes for two different sizes and contemporary scores sometimes call for as many as four (in one case six) sizes. De Falla has the tam-tam laid horizontally to sound without resonance, and Charles Griffes asks for it to be kept in vibration by friction on the edge (*The*

Pleasure Dome of Kubla Khan). He does not specify what mallet (or bow) is to be used.

Other effects on the tam-tam include:

1. Roll with triangle beaters.
2. Striking with snare stick (Stravinsky).
3. Bowed gong (Penderecki) sounding a harmonic at a low dynamic level.

As with all instruments of indefinite pitch, one line of the five-line staff or a single line can be used. A passage for the tam-tam is shown in Figure 20–2.

Figure 20–2   Tchaikovsky, *Symphony No. 6*

*The key signature notation is now obsolete

3. TRIANGLE

Ital. *triangolo*   **Ger.** *Triangel*   **Fr.** *triangle*

Part of the Turkish Janizary music, the triangle was first used in the orchestra at the Hamburg Opera in 1710. In 1800 Boieldieu called for two sizes in one of his operas. Haydn was the first to use the triangle in the symphony orchestra ("Military" Symphony).

A bar of metal bent twice into a triangular shape and played with a short cylindrical bar of metal, the triangle is from 6 to 10 inches (15 to 25 cm) on a side. Larger triangles, which tend to have definite pitch, are used as dinner gongs in the country, and a giant one 2 feet, 3 inches (68 cm) on a side exists (American Cemetery at Epinal).

The triangle has a wide dynamic range. Single notes (often pointing up important accents), rolls (performed on the inside angle of the triangle), rhythmic patterns, and flams and drags (see Chapter 18, section 1) are typical triangle techniques. The tone is between 700 to about 15,500 cycles per second and rich in nonharmonic overtones. In the *forte* it has a penetrating tone which can be heard over the entire orchestra.

Two beaters can be used for complex rhythms or wooden sticks for softer effects. The triangle can be muted by the player's holding a cloth around one side or simply grasping a side in the hand. Sometimes several different sizes are called for. Mahler uses offstage triangle in his Symphony No. 2.

Figure 20–3   Liszt, *Piano Concerto No. 1*

4. COWBELLS

Ital. *campanaccio*   **Ger.** *Kuhglocke*
Fr. *cloche de vache, bloc de métal*

The cowbell is a clapperless bell made of thin metal. It may be single (the *cencerro* of Latin music) or a pair in two sizes (the *au-go-go* or *agogo*, usually tuned a third apart). Cowbells are usually played with a snare stick and can be muted with a cloth placed in the bell. Rolls can be performed within the bell or between two bells.

Mahler wrote for offstage cowbells in his Symphonies No. 6 and 7, and Strauss used them in his *Alpine Symphony.*

Tuned sets of cowbells, more common in Europe than in America, are mounted in two rows and have chromatic ranges of an octave or more (available from c to a³). Though they are of definite pitch, they are sometimes written as instruments of indefinite pitch (high, medium, low, etc.). These tuned bells are known in Germany as *Almglocken, Viehschellen,* and *Herdenglocken.*

5. SLEIGHBELLS

Ital. *sonagli*   **Ger.** *Schellen*   **Fr.** *grelots*

Sleighbells are small circular metal spheres, with metal pellets inside, strung on a belt or stick. They are shaken in simple rhythmic patterns or continuously in a roll.

Although sets of tuned bells are manufactured today, sleighbells are commonly written as instruments of indefinite pitch. They appear in scores of Cherubini, Massenet, Mahler, Respighi, Elgar, Copland, Stockhausen, and many others. A unique example of the use of sleighbells is in the Mozart German Dances K. 605, where they are tuned to definite pitches (c^2, e^2, f^2, g^2, a^2).

Figure 20–4   Mahler, *Symphony No. 4*

6. ANVIL

Ital. *incudine*   **Ger.** *Amboss*   **Fr.** *enclume*

The anvil, first used in the opera by Auber in 1825, is a thick steel bar played with a hammer. Single strokes or rhythmic patterns are characteristic. Wagner wrote for eighteen anvils in three different sizes in *Rheingold.* Tuned sets are now available but are expensive and not found in most orchestras.

Figure 20–5   Wagner, *Das Rheingold*

7. THUNDER MACHINE, THUNDER SHEET

Ital. *lastra (del tuono)*   **Ger.** *Donnerblech*
Fr. *tôle, plaque de tonnerre*

A large sheet of aluminum or other metal which is beaten with a large tam-tam stick or shaken to imitate thunder, the thunder machine was first used in the theater by Gounod. The thunder sheet at the Vienna Opera is 12 feet (3.6 m) high and suspended from an enormous ladder.

The *bronteron* or thunder drum was a huge drum filled with heavy balls which made a rumbling sound when the drum was rotated. Strauss used it in his *Alpine Symphony* but it is now extinct. Today electronic recordings are sometimes used to imitate thunder.

8. BELL PLATE

Ital. *campane a lastra d'acciaio*   **Ger.** *Plattenglocken*
Fr. *plaque d'acier*

The bell plate is a rectangular steel plate a few inches on a side used to give a bell-like sound of indefinite pitch. Henze writes for tuned bell plates (f$\sharp^1$, g$\sharp^1$) but this is possibly a unique case.

9. WOOD BLOCK, CHINESE WOOD BLOCK, TONE BLOCK

Ital. *blocco (cassa) di legno (cinese)*
Ger. *(chinesische) Holzblock, Holztrommel*
Fr. *bloc de bois (chinois)*
(Also called clog or tap box in England)

A hollow wooden box $1\frac{1}{2}$ to $2\frac{1}{4}$ inches (4 to 6 cm) high, 3 inches (8 cm) wide, and $6\frac{1}{2}$ to 8 inches (16 to 20 cm) long, the wood block was introduced to the orchestra by composers such as Barber, Copland, Walton, and Prokofiev. It is played with wooden, rubber, or plastic sticks. Single notes or rhythmic figures are common, and a glissando across several blocks has been written.

It has a high, penetrating tone from c^2 up but is used as an instrument of indefinite pitch. Often three sizes are used (high, medium, low). They can be muffled with a cloth.

The *cylindrical wood block* or *wood cymbal* (Ital. *nacchera cilindrica*, Ger. *Röhrenholztrommel*, Fr. *bloc de bois cylindrique*) is a modernization of the slit drum of the central American Indians. At either end of a connecting piece of wood, it has two hollow cylinders of different size, generally producing tones a major third or perfect fourth apart. The cylindrical wood block is from 4 to 6 inches (10 to 15 cm) long and is played like the rectangular wood block.

10. (CHINESE) TEMPLE BLOCKS OR DRAGON'S MOUTHS

Ital. *blocchi di legno coreani*   **Ger.** *Tempelblocks*
Fr. *temple blocks*

These are large, clam-shaped wooden slit drums (originating in Korea, not China) mounted on a stand and painted red with elaborate designs. Walton introduced them to the orchestra in 1923 (*Façade*). Previously they had been used to imitate hoofbeats, replacing coconut half shells on leather (Ferde Grofé, *Grand Canyon Suite*). They have since lost this connotation. Their modern technique often involves quite complex rhythmic figures played with felt or rubber sticks, across sets of blocks of different sizes mounted together. Sets of five are common although they may come in sets of from three to seven. The *mokubio* is a very large block which forms a part of some sets.

Quite a penetrating tone can be obtained from the temple blocks. Although they have definite pitches (from about g^1 to f^3), these are not commonly in tune with our Western scale and therefore the instrument is written as one of indefinite pitch. Usually the five lines of the staff represent the five sizes of blocks. In an unusual case, Sir Michael Tippett has written for tuned temple blocks (d¹, e¹, f¹, g¹, c♯²).

11. CASTANETS

Ital. *nacchere, castagnette*   **Ger.** *Kastagnetten*
Fr. *castagnettes*

Originally instruments of the Spanish peasants, tied together in sets and played with the fingers while dancing, these were originally made of chestnut wood (Sp. *castaña,* hence the name). They consist of a pair of saucer-shaped pieces of ebony or rosewood. Orchestral sets consist of single or double sets mounted on a handle for easier playing; "machine" castanets are mounted on a block with springs so that they can be played simply by tapping with the fingers.

Although they used to be associated with exotic locales (Wagner, *Tannhäuser*; Bizet, *Carmen*), today they do not necessarily carry such implications. Saint-Saëns and Milhaud both wrote for metal castanets, sometimes classified as a type of finger cymbal.

12. WHIP, SLAPSTICK

Ital. *frusta*   **Ger.** *Peitsche, Holzklapper*   **Fr.** *fouet*

Known since ancient Assyria, the whip is simply a long slat with a handle, total size about 2½ by 18 inches (6 by 46 cm), to which another slat is attached with a hinge. A flick of the wrist makes the two slats come together with a loud slap. Mascagni was the first composer to use the instrument to imitate the sound of a whip, although today it is often used purely for a sharp accent. Obviously, occasional single notes are the limit of the instrument's technique.

Figure 20–6   Copland, *Rodeo*

13. RATTLE, RATCHET, COG-RATTLE

Ital. *raganella*   **Ger.** *Ratsche, Knarre*   **Fr.** *crécelle*

Derived from the instrument used to signal the arrival of the watchman, the rattle is a wooden cogwheel which, when turned by a handle, sets a wooden slat in vibration. It was first used by Beethoven to imitate rifle fire in *Wellington's Victory* (or the *Battle Symphony*), which was illustriously premiered with Beethoven conducting, Spohr in the violin section, Meyerbeer and Hummel on bass drums, Moscheles playing cymbals, and Salieri directing the cannonade of percussion. Strauss revived the ratchet to imitate the watchman's rattle in *Til Eulenspiegel* and it has been used by many composers since.

14. WIND MACHINE

Ital. *eolifono*   **Ger.** *Windmaschine*   **Fr.** *éoliphone*

A large barrel with thin wooden slats. When turned by a handle, it rubs against silk or canvas, giving a sound of anything from a light breeze to a stiff gale. Strauss introduced it in *Don Quixote* (the *Ride Through the Air*), where he wisely directs that it be kept in the wings out of sight of the audience. The notation is as for a drum roll.

21

Latin
Percussion Instruments

Although derived from instruments used in Latin dance music, these instruments have become established in the orchestra since 1950. At one time they were used only for 'Latin' works, such as Louis Moreau Gottschalk's Symphony No. 1, *A Night in the Tropics*, written in the 1850's, and George Gershwin's *Cuban Overture* (1932). Today they are used for their individual tone colors without reference to Latin popular music.

The Latin names are used in all languages.

1. BONGO

The bongo (not *bongos*) is a set of single-headed Cuban drums with depressed rims (the heads are stretched over the rims) about 5 inches (13 cm) deep and 6 to 8 inches (15 to 20 cm) in diameter. It is usually played with the fingers and hands (though mallets are often used in the orchestra). Different sounds can be produced by the player's hitting different parts of the head with fingers and hands:

1. Flat index finger on rim.
2. Tip of finger one-third of the way to center.
3. Thumb in center of head.
4. Four fingers together.
5. Tremolo with index fingers (or index and middle finger) on rim.

Though one could notate these effects, they are better left up to the player in most cases. The usual notation is on two lines, one for the high (small) drum, one for the low (large) drum. Occasionally, "high" and "low" sounds have been indicated on different parts of each drum by using two lines per drum. The notation in Figure 21–1 shows high and low sounds for each drum.

Figure 21–1

The drums are tuned anywhere from a perfect fourth to a minor sixth apart, though they are written as instruments of indefinite pitch. With sticks, the technique is like that of the tom-toms except, of course, with no rim shots.

2. TIMBALES

Fr. also *timbales creoles* (to distinguish them
from *timbales,* the French for kettledrums)

A pair of single-headed Cuban drums 8 to 10 inches (20 to 26 cm) deep. The smaller drum has a diameter of from 7 to 9 inches (18 to 23 cm), the larger 9 to 14 inches (22 to 35 cm). They are played with wooden sticks smaller than snare sticks. The notation is on two lines, one for each drum.

In Cuban music the right hand plays the cowbell or wood block on the beat, the left hand playing the timbales off the beat. In the orchestra they can be played with timpani or marimba mallets or with the hands and fingers. The technique is like that of the tom-toms.

Special effects include muffling the drum with one hand while the other hand strikes the drum with a stick, and playing with one stick on the head and one on the shell.

3. CONGA, TUMBA, TUMBADORA

This is a deep, tapered, single-headed drum with depressed rim, 15 to 19 inches (37 to 48 cm) deep and 10 to 12 inches (26 to 30 cm) in diameter. It is played like and sounds like a large bongo. It is often used in sets of two: a small, high drum (*conga*), and a large, low drum (*tumba*). In this case two lines are used in the notation.

4. MARACAS, SONAJAS

Ger. also *Rumbakugeln*   **Fr.** also *noix de coco*

A pair of gourds about 4 inches (10 cm) in diameter and 7 to 12 inches (18 to 30 cm) long, including handles. The gourds contain seeds or pebbles. The usual method of playing is to hold one in each hand and shake the maracas alternately to produce a rhythmic pattern. It is also possible to make a continuous sound by moving the maracas in circles (Ital. *girare*), and a sharp staccato by tapping the maraca with the finger. The *shaker* is a large maraca.

5. TUBO, TUBOLO, TUBO SONORA, CHOCALHO, BEAN CAN SHAKER

This is a cylindrical shaker, usually of metal, filled with seeds, shot, or similar material.

6. CLAVES

Ital. also *legni per rumba*   **Ger.** also *Schlagstäbe*

A pair of sticks which, when struck together, make a sharp sound of higher pitch than the wood block. Their typical rhythm in Latin music is shown in Figure 21–2. They have been used in the orchestra by Varèse, Orff, Roldán, Russell, Boulez, and others.

Figure 21–2

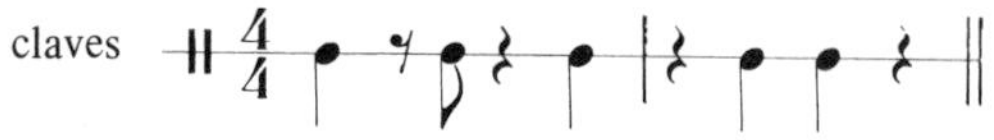

7. GÜIRO, GOURD, RASPER

Fr. also *râpe guero*

This is a large gourd about 13 inches (33 cm) long with parallel serrations cut in one side. When a stiff wire or wooden stick is rubbed across the notches, a rasping sound results. The gourd was first used in the orchestra by Stravinsky (*Sacre*). Villa-Lobos writes for it both rasped and beaten.

Other gourds are the *kameso*, a hollow wooden tube filled with buckshot, the *guáchara*, made of wood or bamboo and smaller than the güiro with a correspondingly higher, sharper sound, and the *raspador*, made of metal.

8. CABAZA, CABACA, AFUCHÉ

A large gourd (some are made of metal) about 8 inches (20 cm) in diameter, with a handle, seeds inside and a net on which beads are strung covering the outside. The handle is held in the right hand and the cabaza shaken or slapped against the palm of the left hand. In Latin dance music it is used only in sambas.

9. JAWBONE, QUIJADA

Originally the jawbone of an ass with the teeth loosely attached with string or springs, it is now often made of plastic. Sometimes jingles are attached as well. When it is struck with the fist, the teeth rattle. It is used in dances such as the conga and by orchestral composers such as Amadeo Roldán and William Russell.

10. CENCERRO AND AU-GO-GO, AGOGO

See *Cowbells* in Chapter 20.

For additional percussion which has appeared in the orchestra since the Second World War, see Chapter 36.

22

Writing
For Percussion

---

1. SMALL PERCUSSION ENSEMBLES

With the increase in the variety of percussion instruments, especially those of definite pitch, in the twentieth century, works began to be written for one or more percussionists either alone or with other instruments. The possible combinations of percussion instruments and techniques are, of course, myriad.

One important consideration in writing for percussion is that although some percussion instruments, such as the tam-tam and vibraphone, ring for some time after they are struck, the only percussive sound which approximates the sustained notes of the winds and strings is the roll. Also, the percussion have an immense dynamic range, and exploitation of their subtler and quieter tone colors is much more aesthetically rewarding than making a lot of noise.

Percussion ensembles are of two types; those requiring a large number of players for a small number of instruments (Figure 22–3) and those requiring a small number of players for a large number of instruments (Figures 22–1, 22–7). Today percussionists are accustomed to switching frequently from one instrument to another.

One of the earliest examples of percussion used extensively in chamber music is Stravinsky's *L'Histoire du Soldat* (1918) for seven instrumentalists, one of them a percussionist who plays two snare drums (one without snares), two

238

tom-toms, bass drum, tambourine, triangle, and cymbal. Stravinsky writes the tambourine and snare drums on different lines of one staff, the bass drum on a separate staff or line (Figure 22–1).

Figure 22–1   Stravinsky, *Histoire du Soldat*

Bartók's *Sonata for Two Pianos and Percussion* (1937) requires the use of two percussionists who utilize a variety of techniques (Figure 22–2). Varèse's *Ionisation* requires the services of a dozen percussionists plus piano (Figure 22–3).

Figure 22-2   Bartók, *Sonata for Two Pianos and Percussion*

* ♩ = in the centre.   ♩ = on the extreme edge of the skin.

©Copyright 1942 by Hawkes & Son (London) Ltd. Renewed 1973. Reprinted by permission of Boosey & Hawkes, Inc.

2. THE ORCHESTRAL PERCUSSION SECTION

The unusual introduction of Janizary music into the symphony by Haydn in his *"Military" Symphony* has already been noted. In Figure 22–4, stems down on the lower staff indicate the bass drum, stems up, the attached cymbals.

More complex rhythms are characteristic of *The Rite of Spring* (Figure 22–5). The *Háry János Suite* uses a large percussion section with bells and winds in canon (Figure 22–6). Henze's *Antifone* uses four percussionists, each playing a variety of instruments, deployed in a half-circle at the back of the orchestra for *antiphonal* (spacial) effects (Figure 22–7).

Other notable works with large percussion groupings have been written by Orff, Stravinsky (*Les Noces*), Milhaud (*Les Choëphores, Christopher Columbo*), Chávez (*Toccata for Percussion*), Boulez (*Pli selon pli*), and Stockhausen (*Zyklus*). Berlioz's ideal orchestra (*Treatise on Instrumentation*) would have included 53 percussionists! Luigi Nono's *Diario Polacco* and Havergal Brian's rarely performed Second Symphony call for 16 percussionists each. Elliott Carter's *Double Concerto* utilizes 45 different percussion instruments.

Figure 22–4   Haydn, *Symphony No. 100*

Figure 22–5   Stravinsky, *Rite of Spring*

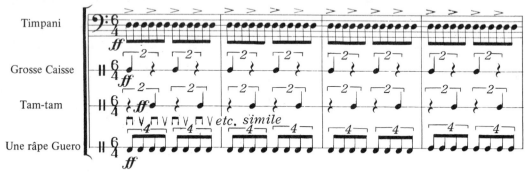

Figure 22–6   Kodály, *Háry János Suite*

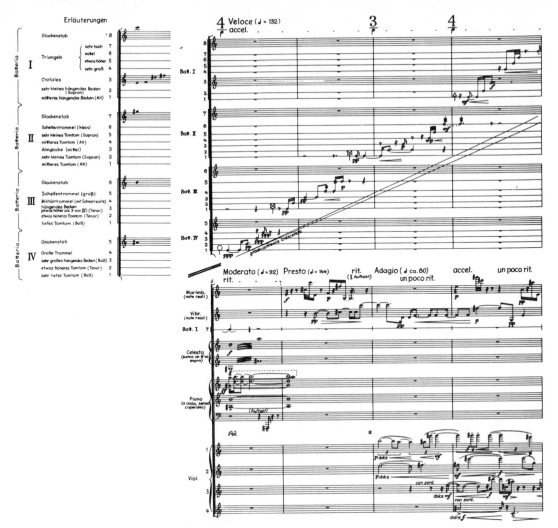

Following are some of the ways percussion have been used in the orchestra:

1. Melody. Solo or doubling other instruments for attack or tone color. Also *Klangfarbenmelodie,* a melody that is passed from one instrument to another.
2. *Harmony.* Chords on marimba, vibraphone, or other instruments of definite pitch either alone or doubling other instruments.
3. Tone color. Separate timbres of wood, metal, or membrane instruments contrasted or combined.
4. Dynamic reinforcement of the orchestra.
5. Ostinati (repeated rhythmic figures).
6. Naturalistic, exotic, ethnic, or abstract sound effects.

Further information on percussion notation can be found in Chapter 26. New percussion techniques and their notation are discussed in Chapter 37.

23

The Piano

Ital. *pianoforte*   **Ger.** *Klavier*   **Fr.** *piano*

1. ORIGIN

The piano was created when Bartolomeo Cristofori added a hammer mechanism to the harpsichord around 1709, allowing the performer to produce gradations of loudness. His original instrument was called the *gravicembalo col piano e forte*, from which was derived the name *pianoforte*, shortened in English to *piano*. Around 1772 the *English action* was invented; this required a heavier touch but allowed greater volume and dynamic range. In 1825 Alpheus Babcock invented the one-piece cast-iron frame to hold the thicker strings required for increased loudness and brilliance. By 1855 the grand piano had reached essentially its present-day form.

2. DESCRIPTION

Modern *grand pianos*, with strings set on a horizontal frame over a sound-board, vary from the *concert grand* with a length of 9 feet (2.75 meters) to the *baby grand* with a length of about 5 feet, 2 inches (1.57 meters), though shorter and longer grands (to 11 feet [3.36 meters]) are built.

244

Pianos with vertical frames and soundboards include the *upright* or *studio upright,* about 46 inches (1.17 meters) high, the *console,* about 40 inches (1 meter) high, and the *spinet,* about 36 inches (91 cm) high.

When a key on the piano is depressed, the *damper* which stops the string from vibrating is raised and a felt hammer strikes the string. The force with which this hammer strikes is regulated by the force with which the key is depressed. As long as the key is depressed, the damper remains raised and the string is allowed to continue to vibrate. In the high range, there are three strings for each note; in the middle-lower range, two; and in the lowest range, one.

All pianos are equipped with a *damper pedal* operated by the right foot. When depressed, it raises all the dampers, allowing all the strings of the piano to vibrate. If a note is struck with the damper pedal depressed, sympathetic vibrations will be created in those strings tuned to the harmonics of the note struck, thereby creating greater resonance.

The soft pedal (It. *una corda,* Ger. *mit Verschiebung*), operated by the left foot, shifts the mechanism so that only two of the three strings in the high are set in vibration and only one of the two in the middle-lower range, so that a muted effect is created. Beethoven was one of the first composers to utilize this effect.

Grand pianos, especially those made in America, usually have a third pedal in the center, operated by either foot, called the *sostenuto.* When keys are depressed and the sostenuto immediately engaged, the dampers over those notes will remain raised until the pedal is released. While those notes are sustained, other notes may be played in the normal manner. As soon as the key is released, the dampers stop the vibration.

Indications for the pedals are shown in Figure 23–1.

Figure 23–1

a) Damper pedal: Ped. ______⌋ / Ped. ❋ / Ped. ⊕

b) una corda *una corda* ______⌋ (❋ or ⊕)

c) sostenuto: *sost.* ______⌋ (❋ or ⊕)

3. RANGE

The piano is notated on two staves connected by a bracket. Range is seen in Figure 23–2. The right hand plays the upper staff and is usually written in the treble clef unless the part descends into the lower range, in which case the bass clef is used. The left hand plays the lower staff and is written in the bass clef unless the part ascends into the treble clef range. Dynamic markings are usually written between the staves unless there are different dynamics for each hand. Usual markings for legato, staccato, accents, and other effects are used. Tempo markings appear above the upper staff, pedal markings below the lower staff.

Figure 23–2

8va bassa⌐
*found rarely on pianos
such as the Bösendorfer.

4. TONE

The piano combines attributes of the strings and percussion because of the method in which the strings are set in vibration. The tone of the piano always has a slight accent, even in *piano*, but it quickly drops in dynamic volume, though the vibrating string may be audible at a low level for several seconds. Therefore the piano has no sustained tone comparable to that of the strings or winds. For this reason its orchestral use is generally like that of the percussion instruments.

5. TECHNIQUE

Considerable control over the tone of the piano is possible through various finger techniques. Extremely rapid and complex figures are possible due mainly to the highly developed technique of the professional pianist. The average stretch between the thumb and little finger of each hand is an octave, though tenths are possible for some pianists if there are not too many other notes between and they do not occur rapidly in succession. Four- and five-note chords are possible in each hand. The hands can cross on occasion, though this is usually reserved for solo work. Octaves in one or both hands are possible at moderately rapid tempi although rapid passages in thirds are more difficult and generally demand considerable practice. Counterpoint in up to four or five parts is possible if the voices are carefully arranged. Rapid scales and arpeggios and even parallel triads or sixth chords in one or both hands are also common. Everything from sharp staccato or *sforzando* to a smooth legato over a wide dynamic range is standard procedure.

Orchestral piano parts should not be extremely difficult, largely because of the limited time available to practice such parts. Solo music, of course, can be much more difficult although performance chances increase in inverse propor-

tion to the difficulty of a composition. Soloists generally have limited practice
time as well.

6. TRILLS AND TREMOLI

Trills are possible over the entire range of the piano. Tremoli are somewhat
less effective unless combined with other instruments, though they are quite
easy up to the interval of an octave in each hand. The notation is the same as
for the bowed string tremolo or the wind tremolo (Figure 23–3).

Figure 23–3

7. SPECIAL EFFECTS

The glissando is usually on the white keys (Figure 23–4a) since the gaps between the black keys make the glissando uneven and probably painful.
Glissandi in two directions are also possible (Figure 23–4b). This was first used
in the orchestra by composers such as Ives and Bartók.

Figure 23–4

Tone clusters are sometimes used for a percussive effect. Figure 23–5a
shows the notation for a cluster on white keys alone, 23–5b on black keys
alone, and 23–5c on both black and white keys. The cluster can be played with
the fist (range of a third of fourth), the palm (range of an octave), or the
forearm (range of about three octaves). Boards have also been used for more
specific or larger ranges.

Many other effects are to be found in Chapter 37.

Figure 23–5

8. SOLO PIANO

The extensive solo literature for the piano makes it unnecessary and impractical to discuss this subject in detail in this text. The use of the piano as a solo instrument with the orchestra in such forms as the concerto is discussed in Chapter 30.

9. THE PIANO IN THE ORCHESTRA

The first composers to treat the piano as an orchestral instrument were Méhul, Donizetti, and Berlioz, who wrote for two pianos in *Lélio*. Piano four hands was first used by Saint-Saëns and later by Debussy and Bartók. In the later twentieth century the piano has become a standard orchestral instrument.

The most common uses of the piano in the orchestra are for high, bright, percussive figures either alone or doubling other instruments, and for low, darkly colored octaves, usually in combination with other instruments. Percussive chords (the opening of Stravinsky's *Symphony of Psalms*) or clusters in high or low registers, both loud and soft, and rapid figures in octaves between hands either alone or with other instruments are common.

It is usual to use a grand piano with the orchestra since smaller pianos have thinner tone and less dynamic power. In the chamber orchestra the piano often does much to compensate for the absence of a larger number of instruments (see Copland's original version of *Appalachian Spring*, Chapter 29).

Figure 23–6   Stravinsky, *Petrushka*

Copyright by Edition Russe de Musique. Copyright assigned to Boosey & Hawkes, Inc. Revised version copyright 1947 by Boosey & Hawkes, Inc. Reprinted by permission.

Figure 23–6 (cont.)

Menotti, *Sebastian Suite*

b)

24

The Voice

1. VOCAL PRODUCTION

"Vocal" sounds, other than whispering and whistling, are produced by the vibration of the membranes known as *vocal cords*, which form a slit-like opening over the larynx. When kept tense, they act like a reed to produce pitch when air is expelled from the lungs under pressure by the action of the diaphragm. The overtones are modified by the air cavities of the mouth, nose, sinuses, throat, and even the lungs themselves. The human voice is particularly rich in overtones as high as the 35th partial. To *vocalize* is to produce melody on a neutral vowel sound. Vocalizing is used for singing excercises, and occasionally in music written for performance (for example, Villa-Lobos's *Bachianas Brasileiras No. 5). Humming* is vocalizing with the mouth shut. All other vocal singing consists of a combination of melody and enunciation.

Any sustained singing is done on vowels, sounds in which the passage of air from the throat is relatively unimpeded. Consonants are produced by the action of the tongue against or near the teeth or roof of the mouth and are momentary. They are either *voiced* (using the vocal cords) or *unvoiced.* They are further classified as explosive if followed by a rush of air. Explosive consonants can be either dental stops (*d, t*) or guttural (*g, k*). In addition, there are *semivowels* or *sonorants,* with relatively little obstruction (such as *l* and *m*), and *fricatives,* with relatively great obstruction (such as *s* and *f*). The intelligibility of the words largely depends on the enunciation of the consonants. *Closed* vowel sounds, such as pure *ee*, are harder to sing on high notes than are *open* sounds, such as pure *ah*. However, this depends on vocal technique, which is somewhat individual. Many male singers find closed vowels better on high notes. Nevertheless, this should not greatly trouble the composer, since singers coming across an awkward vowel in the extreme ranges commonly mix or substitute vowel sounds which are easier to sing (and sound better). This may lead to a slight difficulty in understanding the word, but since this is a problem only in extreme ranges, it is not of great concern.

There are two types of singing voice: the *chest voice*, consisting of the lower tones which resonate in the chest, and the *head voice*, consisting of the higher tones which resonate in the smaller air cavities in the head, something like the overblowing of a wind instrument. Singing technique requires the control and mixture of these two sounds to produce an even tone throughout the range. A proper mixture results in a sound with can *carry*, or be heard in a large hall and cut through other voices or instruments, without being forced. This technique, which began in the sixteenth century and continues to the present day, is known as *bel canto* (Italian for "beautiful voice"). Other aspects of *bel canto* style include the ability to perform rapid and difficult figurations, trills, passage work, and the like with technical security and ease (Ital. *agilità, passaggio, fioritura*).

The overtones of the head voice in men is called *falsetto* and can be used unmixed for comic or other effects. It is indicated by the word *falsetto* or by the usual circle above the note denoting a harmonic. The words *sotto voce* are often used to indicate a passage which is to be sung *half voice*, in an undertone. A *piena voce* means *full voice*. *Mezzo voce* is in between.

2. VOCAL TYPES AND RANGES

The simplest division of voices is simply soprano and alto for female voices, tenor and bass for male voices. This is the usual chorus division, though many "altos" are sopranos without the high range and, since tenors are also rare, many may be baritones with a good high range. Figure 24–1 shows practical ranges for chorus voices that are untrained and not of solo quality. Extreme ranges are shown in parentheses. The tenor, of course, sounds an octave lower. Older scores use soprano, alto, tenor, and bass clefs. Though a few singers in a chorus will be able to sing in the extreme range with good quality, most will sound shrill and unpleasant. The repeated a^2's in Beethoven's Symphony No. 9 are an oft-cited example of choral miscalculation, though pitch was lower then,

Figure 24–1

so perhaps Beethoven was right after all. In any case, unless one wishes a rough and wild effect, it is best to avoid these extreme ranges. In the lowest range, the voice loses its power and sings at a low dynamic level. Russian *octavists* (Ital. *contrabassi*, Fr. *contrebasses*) sing as low as BB♭ and soloists to FF, but only in *piano*. Most bass parts don't descend below F. Mozart's *Osmin* reaches D and Handel's *Polifemo* C♯.

Music for women's chorus is usually in three parts: first soprano, second soprano, and alto. It is wise to avoid the extreme high indicated in Figure 24–1 and to keep the second sopranos below g^2. Men's choruses are usually divided into first tenors (with a range of e to a^1), second tenors (c to f^1), baritones or first basses (A to e^1), and second basses (E or F to c^1). This distribution more closely fits the types of voices found in most choruses. Berlioz suggests the combination of these divisions to form a seven-part *mixed chorus* (three-part women and four-part men). Often sopranos are divided (largely because there are usually more of them available) to make a five-part chorus (such as Bach's *Mass in B Minor*). Other divisions are found as well. A *choir* is a chorus used in church.

Solo voices are usually categorized as soprano, mezzo-soprano, contralto, tenor, baritone, and bass, with the general ranges shown in Figure 24–2. The solid notes in the middle of the range show where the *break* usually occurs between the chest and head voice. In a well-trained voice this should not be audible, but it is best not to write repeatedly in this range.

Figure 24–2

As can be seen, extreme ranges vary widely in these categories. More important, some voices are more powerful than others, some lighter, some darker, and so on. Therefore, further divisions (Ger. *Fächer*) are used:

1. Coloratura soprano (Ital. *soprano leggiero*). A high, light, extremely agile voice. Mozart's Queen of the Night sings up to f^3, and he writes to $f♯^3$ in a concert aria. Lucrezia Agujari (1743–1783) was reputed to have sung as high as c^4.
2. Lyric soprano. A light, flexible, *cantabile* (song-like) voice seldom singing above c^3.
3. *Soubrette*. A lighter lyric soprano, often used for *comprimario* or supporting roles (see page 253) such as the young lover or the lady's maid.
4. *Spinto*. A heavier lyric, halfway between lyric and dramatic.
5. Dramatic soprano. A powerful, cutting voice, singing to c^3 but often somewhat shrill in the high.

6. Mezzo-soprano. A darker soprano voice with generally lower *tessitura* (average range of a part) but often singing to b♭² or c³.
7. Contralto (often, though incorrectly, shortened to *alto*, especially in choruses). A deep, rich, dark, almost masculine female voice with a range of f or g to f² or g². True contraltos are rare.
8. Male alto. A yet rarer voice, with the quality of a female contralto and a range to c² and above.
9. Countertenor (Fr. *haute-contre*). An extremely high, light tenor with a pure, almost colorless tone, singing as high as f².
10. *Tenore leggiero*. A high tenor singing as high as the countertenor but with a more masculine tone and great agility (the "Rossini" tenor). In Bellini's *I Puritani*, the tenor sings to f².
11. Lyric tenor. Like the lyric soprano, an agile, cantabile voice singing to b♭¹ or c².
12. *Tenorino (altino)*. A lighter lyric tenor; to the lyric tenor as the soubrette is to the lyric soprano.
13. *Heldentenor (tenore drammatico* or *robusto)*. A voice singing to b♭¹ and, like the dramatic soprano, very powerful and cutting. Often somewhat strident in the high. Used in the works of Wagner, Mahler, Strauss, among others. Often singing only to f¹ in German scores (e.g., *Siegfried*).
14. Lyric baritone. A light, cantabile voice, darker than the tenor, singing to f♯¹ or even a¹.
15. Baritone. A rich, masculine voice singing to f¹ or f♯¹.
16. Bass-baritone. A voice with the range of the baritone but the low notes and power of the bass.
17. *Basso cantante* (Fr. *basse chantante*). A lyric bass voice with a good high to at least f¹.
18. *Basso buffo*. An agile comic voice with the range of the basso cantante, specializing in characterization. May be rough in quality.
19. *Basso profundo*. A deep, dark, powerful male voice singing down to C or D.
20. *Contrabasso*. The "Russian" bass, singing as low as FF.

Various voices fall in between these categories and are characterized accordingly: dramatic-coloratura, lyric-mezzo, mezzo-contralto, and so forth. They are known as *mezzo-carattere*. This term also includes extremely versatile voices which are equally at home in two or more categories. Voices can also change over the years and singers may retrain for a totally different category. The extreme high disappears with age and the voice tends to grow in power, so a singer may change from a lyric tenor to Heldentenor, for instance, though many singers have lost their voices trying to force them unnaturally. Some voices are *incomplete* in the sense that though they may be beautifully trained, they lack the high or are unusually weak in the low. Sometimes such singers are cast in *comprimario* or supporting roles.

Though specific vocal types may not be specified in the score (it may say "tenor" instead of "lyric tenor," for instance), it is usually obvious to the person casting the work which type of voice is required. A considerable body of music still exists for another type of voice that existed up until the end of the eighteenth century (though some survived until the late nineteenth century). This was the *castrato*. In Italy since the sixteenth century, young boys, usually orphans, were castrated in order that the male hormones released at puberty would not change their voices. They trained to become, in effect, male sopranos. They were rare even in Berlioz's time. He wrote that their complete disappearance was not to be regretted. One of the last, Alessandro Moreschi, recorded some examples of his art in 1904. Considering the state of the art of recording in those days and his advanced age, it is difficult to form an impression of how the *castrato* actually sounded. Today these roles are sung by a female soprano, mezzo, or contralto, or by a male countertenor, male alto, or even a tenor. The practice of taking the part down an octave usually does violence to the musical conception.

Another class of voice is the boy soprano (Ital. *voce biancho*), with a range of c^1 to f^2 or g^2 (with trained voices b^{b2}) for the first sopranos, c^1 to e^{b2} or f^2 for the second sopranos, and b to d^2 or e^2 for the altos. Young girls' voices, usually quite shrill, have ranges of from a or c^1 to f^2 or a^2.

Trained voices are usually antithetical to folk music, popular musical theater, and commercial music. These singers are generally untrained or minimally trained and rely on stylization rather than extraordinary technique for their musical effects.

3. WRITING FOR SOLO VOICE

The most important consideration in writing for the voice, whether solo or in chorus, is that of *tessitura*. The average range of the part, or where the part *lies*, is much more important than whether or not it has a few high notes. If the voice is kept in the upper or, to a lesser extent, lower part of its range for some time, the vocal cords begin to tire and the voice begins to weaken. Even prominent composers have written parts of extraordinary vocal difficulty without realizing it simply because they did not understand the instrument. One finds this error consistently in the works of younger composers, possibly because most orchestration books usually pass over the voice briefly if they mention it at all, and unless the composer has had the advantage of working with singers, he has no way of knowing how far astray he has gone.

Also, there is an enormous amount of difference between, say, the high c^3 of the soprano voice and $c\#^3$. Just a half step can make the note twice as difficult to sing in extreme ranges. Usually beginning composers write in the extreme high in order to make an effect. Everything in the soprano voice from f^2 up *sounds* high, however, and a climax can be made on a g^2 or an a^2 just as well as the high c^3. Also, these very high notes should not occur more than once or twice in a piece or they lose their effect. A few singers are capable of a beautiful *pianissimo* in the high, but don't expect it of nonprofessionals.

It should also be borne in mind that the singer, unlike the instrumentalist, sings a pitch by ear alone, with no keys or places on the fingerboard to guide him. Therefore, the singer's note should be clearly audible in the orchestra before he sings or at least a chord or interval given from which he can find his pitch. For the same reason a singer should not be forced to sing a half step away from another singer or instrument unless the part is approached or left in such a manner that he can easily find his way. All this holds especially true if the singer must be thinking about acting at the same time. Some singers have perfect pitch or at least an uncanny sureness of pitch, but the more difficult the music one writes, the fewer singers will take the time to learn and perform it.

Though rapid, syllabic settings (Ital. *parlato*) are sometimes very effective, the voice is by nature a lyrical instrument and the singer needs some notes of longer duration in order to shape the tone. As with any wind instrument, frequent rests are necessary. Breathing, if not obvious in the musical texture, should be indicated either by a comma above the staff if there is no rest, or by slurs. Even the most powerful voice tires after singing for some time and should be given adequate rest.

Traditionally, beams are not used for vocal music, except to indicate several notes sung on one syllable, in which case a slur is also necessary (Figure 24–3). Some twentieth-century composers have abandoned this practice and beam notes whenever feasible as with other instruments. Words are generally divided before the consonant of the following syllable or between double consonants, though this depends on subtleties of language. The syllables are separated by a hyphen. For a tied note, the syllable on which it is sung is followed by a dash which is as long as the duration of that note. Older scores seldom indicate dynamics for the voice, though it is common to do so in contemporary music. The dynamics should be written above the staff; the words, of course, are always below.

Figure 24–3   Mozart, *Cosi fan tutte*

One of the difficulties of setting words to music is the tendency to follow slavishly the rhythm of the text. This results in a syllabic, recitative-like patter that soon becomes tiring. The composer must learn to make music out of the words, not just "set" them. Also, it takes several times as long to sing words, if they are set with musical interest, than to speak them. The beginning composer tends to choose texts that are far too long. It is much better to choose a shorter text and repeat an important line here or there than to draw out the musical structure longer than it can sustain interest. Also, poetry with more complex rhythms and meter tends to be most difficult to set since there is a strong tendency to set the verse meters in the musical rhythm in order to retain the rhythm of the original poetry. Simple meter allows much more musical freedom in the setting. Remember, the musical setting will have a relatively complex rhythmic structure of its own superimposed on the poetry in any case.

Vibrato is a natural part of vocal technique, as it is of string technique. Some singers use wider or more rapid vibrato than others. This is largely a matter of style, taste, and different styles of music. When age, oversinging, or incorrect singing have taken their toll on the vocal cords, however, an extremely wide, slow vibrato known as a *wobble* results. This can be corrected only with extensive retraining, if at all.

Writing for vocal ensembles generally contrasts changing textures of harmony, imitation, and more independent counterpoint between voices. The most important melodic material is usually alternated between voices. When singing in harmony, voices are generally a third, sixth, or tenth apart. Octaves are occasionally used for extreme emphasis (the duet in the last act of *Tosca*). Duets are usually between similar voices, such as two females voices, two male voices, soprano and tenor, or contralto and bass, though any combination can be used. In larger ensembles, there is generally great rhythmic distinction between the voices; there are many rests in the parts and many pauses and reentries for each voice to maintain clarity and textural variety. For instance, one voice may have the main melodic material, another a countermelody, and the others an intermittent harmony.

Many composers, such as Mozart and most of the Italian opera composers, have written for specific singers with extraordinary capabilities. Subsequent productions must find voices of similar type. While good lyric sopranos, mezzos, baritones, and basses are rather common, a good coloratura, dramatic soprano, tenor of any kind, or basso profundo is rare (these are called "money" voices in opera). Some young singers try to force themselves into these more unusual vocal categories, often with disastrous and sometimes permanent results (the vocal cords cannot be replaced as an instrument can). The lighter voices tend to develop young, the heavier later.

When one is casting singers, many considerations must be taken into account: the range of the voice, the size of the voice, the stamina required by the part, the tessitura of the part, the color of the voice, the control of the high, the strength of the low, the vocal technique and musicianship of the singer, and, for a stage work, the looks, age, and acting ability of the singer. Finally, it must be decided if the singer fits vocally and dramatically with others in the cast. Some roles are naturally easier to cast than others and not a few singers have made highly successful careers on one or two roles in which they specialized.

Figure 24–4 shows writing for coloratura soprano (a), Heldentenor (b), an ensemble of high voices (c), lyric soprano (d), and an ensemble of women's voices (e).

Figure 24-4

a)

Mozart, *The Abduction from the Seraglio*

Figure 24–4 (cont.)

b)

Wagner, *Die Walküre*

c)

Verdi, *Requiem*

Figure 24–4 (cont.)

d)   Berg, *Wozzeck*

Figure 24–4 (cont.)

e)

Burton, *The Duchess of Malfi* (I, ii).

4. WRITING FOR CHORUS

The size of choruses varies from over a hundred voices for large-scale choral works with large orchestra to the *chamber chorus* of eight or ten singers (two on a part) which usually specializes in *a cappella* (unaccompanied) singing, early music, and more difficult twentieth-century repertoire.

Most important to remember is that in writing for chorus, especially large chorus, one is dealing with mostly untrained voices and cannot expect of them anything like what one can expect of a professional singer.

By division of the sections of the chorus, more than four parts are possible (see section 2 above). One should remember, however, that division also lessens the power of each section. Combinations of the four basic sections are as follows:

SATB	SA
SAT	ST
SAB	SB
STB	AT
ATB	AB
	TB

Of course, each of the four sections can also sing alone. It is good to think of alternating the above combinations to obtain textural variety rather than having all four sections singing all the time. This also allows the singers to rest. This practice is evident in choral writing of all periods.

For emphasis, the combination SA in unison or TB in unison can strengthen a melodic line. AT is less common. Octaves between SA and TB are also common, less common between AT. Divided parts (such as SI, SII) are seldom in octaves since the reason for dividing a section is not for greater emphasis of a line but for more complex or thicker texture. An exception to this is the divided bass line. For extreme emphasis, SA and TB can be in unison an octave apart. Double octaves with SA in unison, T an octave below, and B an octave below that, or S with AT in unison an octave below and B in the lower octave, are also possible. Naturally, doublings at the third, sixth, or combinations of these with the octave are also common. Another possibility is to emphasize a line by having two sections in unison (SA) and the other sections divided to provide the accompaniment. Emphasis can also be obtained on a line by contrasting it rhythmically with the rest of the chorus or by having a particular section sing high. Once the tenors sing above e^1, for instance, they will be heard as an important melodic element. Parts can also cross to emphasize a particular line.

In female or male choruses, or when using SA or TB alone in a section of a larger work, close harmony naturally prevails because of ranges. Also, when women are singing alone, the bass line is generally left to the instrumental accompaniment, the women singing the three upper parts.

The chorus director or choirmaster will obtain balance among parts, especially when they are divided, through the assigning of voices in each section. He may, for instance, assign some altos to the tenor part if the tenors are weak. Individual taste determines whether a director prefers a brilliant high or rich low or middle parts. Therefore the distribution of voices and weight in choruses varies widely.

With choruses one must be even more careful than with soloists to write clearly and simply, helping the singers whenever pitch is a difficulty, especially in wide leaps and those involving dissonant intervals. On the other hand, phrasing is possible over long sections since the chorus can employ staggered breathing, parts of each section breathing at different times to obtain an overall legato. It is even more difficult for the chorus than for the soloist to sing quietly in the extreme high. A good upper limit for sopranos is f^2 for a real *pianissimo*. Rapid vocalization is also best produced in the middle register.

It is possible to divide a line between sections, especially if it is of extraordinary range. As with instruments, it is best to have one section double the next for a note or two as the line moves from one section to the next. Finally, a vocal *Klangfarbenmelodie* is common in some twentieth-century choral writing: each note of a line is sung by a different section of the chorus. Naturally, this divides the words as well. Antiphonal double choruses, a typical Renaissance and baroque device (Bach's *St. Matthew Passion*), have not been used much in the twentieth century, but have unexplored possibilities.

In the theater, especially the lighter musical theater, the chorus is usually treated as simply as possible, often singing in unison or octaves or simply in two parts, one for women, one for men. Imitative effects are common. Foremost to remember is that the theater chorus has to act as well as sing and must have their part memorized. Also, because of the staging, it is not always possible for them to see the conductor clearly or to hear the orchestra. Under these conditions, it is often a wonder they get the notes out at all.

Figure 24–5 gives some examples of choral writing from various periods. See also Figures 25–2, 26–1, 29–13, 30–2, 30–3, and 37–89.

Figure 24–5

Figure 24–5 (cont.)

Britten, *War Requiem*

Figure 24–5 (cont.)

c)   Dorati, *Missa Brevis*

Some of the lower strings of the orchestra (from front): violas, cellos, basses. Photo: Bert Bial, courtesy of the New York Philharmonic Orchestra.

A large orchestral wind section.
   last row: horn, trumpets
   third row: horns, two tenor trombones, bass tuba
   second row: clarinets, bassoons, contrabassoon
   first row: piccolos, flutes, oboes, English horn
Photo: Christian Steiner, courtesy of the New York Philharmonic Orchestra.

The percussion (from left): grand piano, xylophone with resonators, triangles on music stands, tambourine on xylophone, tam tam in back, snare drums, five timpani, cymbals (suspended and crash) on table, bass drum. Photo courtesy of the Detroit Symphony Orchestra.

PART II

WRITING

FOR

ORCHESTRA

25

Introduction
to Orchestration

---

1. THE ART OF ORCHESTRATION

Rimsky-Korsakov wrote, "To orchestrate is to create, and this cannot be taught."[1] If by *orchestrate* one means to create original music for orchestra, this is quite true. Indeed, orchestration is, or should be, part of the original creative thought, inseparable from the structure of the music itself. Music originally written for the piano or other instruments has been successfully *arranged* for orchestra; many of Ravel's works, for instance, were originally written for piano. Although seldom heard today, *transcriptions* (arrangements, usually of keyboard works) for orchestra such as Stokowski's transcriptions of Bach's organ works formed an important addition to the symphonic repertoire during the first half of this century. It must be emphasized, however, that these arrangements were produced by basically reconceiving the work in orchestral terms, not by merely assigning various notes of the original version to instruments of the orchestra. Arranging is discussed in Chapter 29.

Almost anything in orchestration can be effective in the proper musical context, and although there are no formulas, no secrets to instant success as an arranger, orchestration is nevertheless a practical craft as well as an art and there are general considerations and examples which will be of help to the neophyte orchestrator.

---

[1] Nikolai Rimsky-Korsakov, *Principles of Orchestration*, ed. Maximilian Steinberg, trans. Edward Agate (New York: Dover, 1905), p. 1.

In addition to these guides, an intimate knowledge of each instrument, its possibilities and its limitations, is indispensable. The score must be practical to play, should avoid awkward technical difficulties as much as possible, and should achieve its effect with the simplest means. Only in this way will the performer be able to devote himself to playing the music beautifully rather than just playing the notes.

The continual study and analysis of scores of all periods and styles are necessary to develop the musical literacy requisite to a practitioner of this craft. In limiting one's familiarity with any type of music, one merely limits one's creative horizons. No composer has achieved distinction who had not first mastered the technique and styles from which his own period and his personal style developed. Originality is achieved only through the most dedicated and continuous study and mastery of compositional technique.

To this end, it is especially important that a composer/arranger play at least one instrument well, preferably the piano or some other keyboard instrument which can play more than one part at a time, both so that he can learn to think in several parts, and also play from orchestral scores at the piano, an invaluable means of study.

In addition, the beginning composer must develop his aural imagination (his "ear") not only to identify and mentally reproduce melodic and harmonic combinations, but also in order to hear various instrumental timbres, both singly and in combination. This may seem like an extraordinarily difficult process. He will usually discover, however, that continual practice in trying to imagine orchestral sounds over a few years will lead to a highly developed aural imagination capable of synthesizing the most complex orchestral textures in his mind.

It is also desirable, though by no means necessary, that the orchestrator take up an orchestral instrument and attain some experience in performing in an orchestral ensemble. In that way he can learn to appreciate the difficulties faced by the performer who has to *play* what the arranger or composer has written.

Regular attendance at professional concerts is also a necessity for the would-be orchestrator. Nothing can replace the experience of hearing the orchestral ensemble live, preferably with study score in hand. Recordings and broadcasts are also invaluable aids to the study of the orchestra but, because of the distorted impression even the highest fidelity reproduction gives to the sound of a live performance (such as artificial balance and reverberation added by electronic means), they are valuable only as an adjunct to live performance. Attending rehearsals can also be an enormously educational experience whereby the neophyte composer can learn what is practical and especially what is not practical in the orchestra.

In addition to playing from scores at the piano, writing reductions of orchestral scores either for piano or simply on three or four staves is an important way to gain an intimate knowledge of the processes of orchestration. It forces one to reason *why* a particular score is orchestrated as it is. This method was practiced by Bach and Mozart in studying the scores of other composers and, though laborious, it is equally effective today. It develops the link between the visual and aural conception of a score.

Finally, by striving to express one's orchestral ideas in the clearest and most effective way, by hearing one's orchestrations rehearsed and performed (or, better still, by conducting them oneself), one will gradually achieve mastery of the difficult but fascinating craft of orchestration.

2. THE DEVELOPMENT OF THE ORCHESTRA

During the Middle Ages and Renaissance, instruments were used primarily to accompany voices, to substitute for voices in music originally written for voice, and to perform dance music. Until the end of the sixteenth century no specific instruments were prescribed. Whatever instruments were available simply played the part which was within their range. Groups of instruments were used together in the Renaissance, the choice of instruments being determined by whether the music was being performed indoors or out. For outdoors there was the *high consort* (group) of any loud instruments, and for indoors the *low consort* of any soft instruments.

Probably the first music to indicate specific instruments on a part were the *Sacrae Symphoniae* of Giovanni Gabrieli (1597). In these works all instruments, strings and winds, are treated in the same manner, as is typical of the imitative polyphonic style of the time, with apparently no consideration being given to differing orchestral timbres or dynamic strengths (Figure 25–1).

Figure 25–1   G. Gabrieli, *Sacrae Symphoniae*

In Monteverdi's *Orfeo* (1607) an orchestra of 38 instruments of 14 different types is prescribed, but only general indications of which instruments are to play at any particular time are given. The choice of which part is to be played by which instrument is left open.

The orchestra with a group of strings playing in chorus (several to a part) did not become established until about 1700. By that time the *basso continuo* (consisting of whatever bass instruments were available on the bass line and a keyboard instrument such as the harpsichord filling in chords according to the "figured bass" numbers beneath the bass line) was *de rigeur*. The wind, string, and voice parts, however, were still treated contrapuntally and seldom given parts characteristic of their tone color or technique. Only rarely were dynamics or phrasing indicated. See Figure 25–3.

Many different clefs were used in older scores. Although many modern editions have transferred parts written in the less common clefs to more familiar ones, a knowledge of how to read the older clefs is necessary for studying many editions of Bach or other early composers. In fact, the older clefs were still in use in much vocal music up to the first half of the twentieth century. Following is a list of the standard clefs in baroque music. These are illustrated in Figure 25–2. The whole note shows the position of middle C.

Figure 25-2

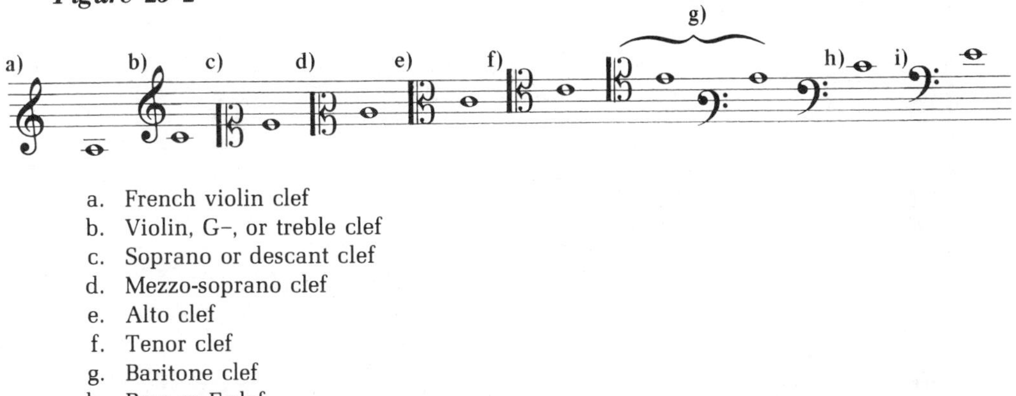

a. French violin clef
b. Violin, G–, or treble clef
c. Soprano or descant clef
d. Mezzo-soprano clef
e. Alto clef
f. Tenor clef
g. Baritone clef
h. Bass or F-clef
i. Sub-bass clef

A knowledge of clefs is also useful in reading transpositions. For instance, if one can read the tenor clef, one can mentally substitute it for the treble clef and read music written for a B♭ instrument as if it were at concert pitch, though an octave higher. Music written for in instrument in F could be read at concert pitch by mentally substituting the mezzo-soprano clef, and so on.

During the baroque period the orchestra was usually led by the continuo player, who would set the tempo; by motions of his head, or his hands if they were free, he would lead the orchestra. At the beginning of the eighteenth century Lully was one of the first such conductors. He led the orchestra by beating

Figure 25–3   J. S. Bach, *Cantata:Meine Seele erhebt den Herrn*

time on the floor with a large staff, a particularly hazardous occupation, it seems, for he died of complications from having hit his foot with the staff. Later, the *concertmaster,* or first chair violinist, would lead the orchestra. Beethoven's conducting consisted of indicating dynamics and expression without regard to beating time. Berlioz was the first conductor in the modern sense, both beating time and indicating expression as well. Composers usually conducted their own music until the late nineteenth century, when conducting became a specialty in its own right.

Publication of orchestral *parts* was common in the late eighteenth century, but it was not until the early nineteenth century that orchestral *scores* began to be published, undoubtedly because the presence of a conductor was not considered a necessity until that time. The first scores usually had the winds and percussion in reverse order (timpani on top, flutes on the bottom) and vocal parts and trombones between the violas and cellos. After a few years, however, an order closer to that presently accepted was adopted, though exceptions are found well into the twentieth century.

With the emergence of homophonic instrumental music in the mid-eighteenth century, the continuo disappeared and scores were written which began to exploit the individual techniques and tone colors of the instruments. It can be said that the art of orchestration really began with the classical period, though indications of expression were rare; the only dynamic markings used were *p* and *f* and only with Beethoven did the *crescendo* and *diminuendo* begin to be commonly used as orchestral effects (with the exception of the Mannheim orchestra, which was famous for its *crescendo* before Beethoven's time).

The constitution of the orchestra also became more or less standardized in the classical period, with pairs of flutes, oboes, bassoons, horns, and often trumpets and timpani in addition to the usual strings. Later clarinets were added. Haydn introduced the Janizary instruments, triangle, bass drum, and cymbals, and Beethoven added to the symphony orchestra the trombones (commonly used only in the opera house previously), piccolo, and double bassoon. In the nineteenth century other wind instruments were added, the design of wind instruments improved, and a few additional percussion appeared sporadically in the orchestra. The primary development in the nineteenth century was the growth of the *size* of the orchestra, winds in threes and even fours by the end of the century and a corresponding increase in the number of strings.

Bach's orchestra in Leipzig consisted of 12 strings and 9 winds. Haydn's orchestra at the Esterházy court had 17 strings and 8 winds. Nevertheless, classical composers often used larger orchestras when they could get them. Mozart wrote to his father describing the wonderful sound of a large section of strings. The Mannheim orchestra consisted of 33 strings and 14 winds. Beethoven conducted a concert in 1814 with 79 strings, a larger number than in our orchestras today! The number of winds is not recorded. Even by 1754 the Paris Opera orchestra included 34 strings, and a Handel commemorative concert in 1784 in London used an orchestra of 230. Other large festivals collected orchestra and chorus combinations of as many as 680 (Cologne, 1835). But the record seems to be the orchestra of 2,000 and chorus of 20,000 conducted by Johann Strauss the younger at the World Peace Jubilee in Boston in 1872.

The standard professional symphony orchestra today consists of approximately the following instrumentation, any of which may be deleted for smaller works:

3	flutes
1	piccolo
3	oboes
1	English horn
3	clarinets
1	bass clarinet
3	bassoons
1	double bassoon
4–6	horns
3–4	trumpets
3–4	trombones
1	tuba
1	timpani
3+	percussion
1	piano
1–2	harps
18	first violins
16	second violins
12	violas
10	cellos
8	double basses

These forces often include *assistant first chair* players, that is, players who share the duties with the first chair (or *principal*) players, or *associate firsts,* that is, players who are on an equal footing with and equally divide the responsibilities of first chair. This assistance is necessary with the demanding rehearsal, performance, touring, and recording schedules of major orchestras today. In addition, some orchestras may have a few more strings in each section or hire additional players for exceptionally large works.

Symphony orchestras as established ensembles which rehearse and play public concerts together on a regular basis are rather recent phenomena. Until the end of the eighteenth century most orchestras were attached to a court and only a few were established organizations performing publicly. Some notable examples are the Gewandhaus in Leipzig (1781) and the Paris Conservatory Orchestra (1792). The New York Philharmonic was established in 1842, the same year as the Vienna Philharmonic, but most of the great orchestras of Europe and America were established at the end of the nineteenth century. Before that time, public concerts were usually arranged by the composer, and musicians hired especially for that event, usually from the local opera house orchestra.

In the following chapters, musical examples will be taken from a variety of periods and styles. The classical approach to orchestration may be said to begin with Haydn and Mozart and continue to the end of the nineteenth century with such composers as Mendelssohn, culminating in the works of Brahms. The Romantic tradition, with its greater concern with orchestral colors and sometimes massive effects, begins with the influence of Beethoven and continues through Berlioz, Liszt, Wagner, and others, culminating in the works of Strauss, Bruckner, and Mahler.

In the twentieth century, though many works are still written for symphony orchestra, much emphasis has also been placed on smaller groups and unusual combinations of instruments as well as experimentation with new techniques and with a wide variety of percussion instruments (see Part IV).

Finally, although at any time in the history of music there have been several styles of composition and orchestration existing side by side, it is difficult to comprehend today the violent factionalism of the adherents of particular styles in the past, resulting, for instance, in the battles of the supporters of Wagner and Brahms or Wagner and Verdi. In our own day more *avant-garde* or more conservative composers are extolled or reviled with equal vigor. It may be that in the next century people will find it as difficult to understand what was so different in what we now see as contradictory stylistic trends. It is good to remember that George Gershwin was a great supporter of the music of his friend Arnold Schoenberg, which was considered too cerebral, and that Schoenberg defended Gershwin's music against the charge of being "too popular." Understanding, if not appreciation, of the widest possible variety of music should be the goal of the musician today.

26

Notation
of the
Orchestral Score

1. TYPES OF SCORES

There are four types of orchestral score:

1. *Conductor's score.* The large, easily readable, *full* score used by the conductor; expensive and often, in the case of works still protected by copyright, available from the publisher only on a rental basis.
2. *Study, miniature, or pocket score.* Usually a photographic reduction of the conductor's score; small, inexpensive, and used for study purposes.
3. *Manuscript score.* The composer's finished product which can be sent on to the publisher for engraving or hand copying but is usually written on special paper which is copied by a black-line blueprint process (Chapter 31 deals in more detail with this subject as well as with the extraction of orchestra parts).
4. *Short score.* The composer's shorthand score on two, three, four, or more staves from which the manuscript score is derived. Also, a score reduced to a few staves from the full score.

2. TITLE PAGE

Often scores begin with the first page of music printed on the first odd-numbered (right-hand) page. Figure 26–1 shows the first page of Britten's *War Requiem.* In this case, the title of the piece appears at the top center of the

Figure 26–1

I. REQUIEM AETERNAM

Britten, *War Requiem*
Op. 66

page, the composer's name (and opus or catalog number, if any) below the title to the right of the page. If there are vocal parts, the name of the poet appears below the title to the left. The dedication appears below the title, the copyright notice at the bottom of the page.

Not uncommonly, however, there is a separate title page, the first odd-numbered page, with the composer's name above the title. The second (first left-hand) page may have a list of instruments used in the composition, including all percussion instruments. This is often the case with contemporary works which employ an unusual combination of instruments. Additional pages may have special performance instructions, special seating charts in the case of works which utilize antiphonal spacial arrangements, and other such information.

3. FIRST PAGE OF SCORE

The names of each instrument are written to the left of the first bar (see Figure 26–1). Each section is bracketed together (woodwinds, brass, percussion, chorus, strings). Timpani, harp, piano, soloists (except for solos within a regular orchestral section) are usually not bracketed within a section.

Secondary brackets connect instruments of the same family or type within a section (flutes and piccolo, clarinet and bass clarinet, horns, trombones and tuba, first and second violins, and so on). Auxiliary woodwinds are placed *below* the primary instruments (piccolo below flutes, English horn below oboes, and so forth). One or two winds are written on each staff. Voices and instrumental solos appear above the strings, vocal soloists above the chorus.

4. GENERAL CONSIDERATIONS

On succeeding pages of the score either the instruments are bracketed on the left of each page just as they are on the first page, in which case names of instruments can be deleted, or only the number of instruments needed for any particular page are indicated by the number of staves, in which case the names of the instruments must appear on the left. In other words, staves can be deleted for instruments which are *tacet* (resting) for a page. In printed scores, often two or more separate systems (groups of staves with instruments playing together) can appear on the same page if there are enough lines. In manuscript, it is good to leave as many empty staves as possible between the separate systems and to separate them with a parallel pair of diagonal solid lines at both the left- and right-hand side of the page to avoid confusion.

Some scores are *concert* scores, written at absolute pitch. This is a convenience for the conductor (and composer), but of course the individual parts must be transposed so that the player can read them in the normal manner. In this case, different clefs may be used in the score than in the parts (bass clef instead of treble for low horns, for example). The instruments which transpose at one or two octaves (piccolo, double bassoon, celesta, bells, xylophone, double bass, and others) still transpose in the usual way because, obviously, an awkward number of leger lines would be necessary which would make the score harder, rather than easier, to read. A footnote should be added at the beginning of the score indicating that it is in C except for the instruments which usually transpose at the octave.

The language used in tempo markings and other musical indications should be the same throughout the score. If one is writing only for American (or British) distribution, English is acceptable. Italian, however, remains the *lingua franca* of music; there are special musical connotations to such terms as *andante* (which literally means "in a walking tempo" but means much more to a musician because of its previous musical associations). Italian is understood all over the world by musicians whereas other languages are not.

The notation *8va* (*ottava:* an octave higher) and *8vab* (*ottava bassa:* an octave lower) followed by a dotted or sometimes solid line for the duration of the passage indicates that something is to be played an octave higher or lower and it is used to avoid leger lines; however, it should be used only where more than a few leger lines would otherwise be required and when the passage stays high or low for more than a few notes. It should never be used for instruments such as the clarinet, where a different fingering is used in the upper octave. It would be more confusing than helpful to the player. The notation *15ma* (*quindicima,* 15th) means two octaves higher.

Bar lines are best written continuously through each section (woodwinds, brass, percussion, strings, and so on) although many scores have bar lines continuous from top to bottom.

Rehearsal letters or numbers must be supplied in the score both at the top and over the strings. The conventional ways of doing this are as follows:

1. Every ten bars (the first complete measure counting as bar one) are numbered.
2. The first bar of every page is numbered.
3. Each bar is numbered.
4. Letters are placed at the beginning of sections where a conductor would be likely to stop in rehearsal. In longer works, after Z is reached, double letters start (AA, etc.).

The fourth method seems to be the one most generally accepted and preferred by conductors. The first method makes checking numbers of bars in the parts somewhat easier.

In works of more than one movement or act, each movement or act is numbered separately, beginning again at 1 (or A).

When an extremely high, low, or difficult section is written, it is often wise to add an alternate version of less difficulty. This is written in smaller notes above (or below) the original version, or even on a separate staff; the word *ossia* is added and a dotted line connects the bars at the beginning and end of the *ossia* (Figure 26–2). The performer will perform the original version unless it is too risky, in which case he will take the alternate version.

Figure 26–2

5. TEMPO MARKINGS

The initial tempo marking, changes of tempo, ritards, accelerandos, and other tempo markings appear both at the top of the score and above the first violins. In manuscript, at least one extra staff should be left above the violins so that these indications can be clearly written.

Some composers prefer to indicate tempo with words (*allegro con brio*), some with words and metronome markings (*allegro con brio*, ♩ = 152), some with metronome markings alone (MM ♩ = 152, or just ♩ = 152). It is difficult to predict the exact tempo for a piece of orchestral music. For one thing, the resonance of the orchestra and the reverberation (or lack of it) in a particular hall, as well as slight differences of momentum in each individual performance, may affect the "best" tempo for one piece. Wagner gave up metronome markings altogether, stating that if the conductor didn't understand the music, metronome markings would be of no help, and if he did, he didn't need them. Often, however, it is possible to determine the tempo within certain limits or indicate an approximate marking to serve as a guide to the conductor. This can be indicated in any of the following ways:

1. ♩ = ca. 152, ♩ = app. 152 (meaning circa or approximately 152)
2. ♩ = 152–168 (152 to 168)
3. ♩ = ± 152 (more or less 152)

6. METER

Meter should appear at the beginning of the score on each staff after the clef and key signature and on each staff every time the meter changes (see Figure 26–1). If the meter changes on the first bar of a page, it must appear on the previous page after the last bar line. Most modern scores show meter only at the top and above the first violins or over each section. It must appear in each of the orchestra parts, however. Contemporary German scores often use the note itself to show that it is the unit of beat; ♩ instead of 4/4.

7. CLEFS

Clefs must appear at the beginning of each line on every page for each instrument. If there is a change of clef at a bar line, the new clef should be written *before* rather than after the bar line. Always remember to change back to the original clef after a passage in a new clef. Clefs should be changed only if a passage lies in a new range for several notes or if the part suddenly goes extremely high or low. Never change clefs just to avoid two or three leger lines. Remember to use only the clefs appropriate for the particular instrument which is playing the part.

8. KEY SIGNATURES

Key signatures, if used, must appear after the clef in each part at the beginning of the score, at the beginning of each page, and whenever there is a change of key. Cancelled accidentals from the previous signature are usually shown as well. For instance, in changing from a key signature of D major to G major, an F sharp and a C natural would appear in the new signature. Changes of signature taking place on the first bar of a page must, like tempo indications, also appear after the last bar line of the previous page.

9. DYNAMICS AND PHRASING

Dynamic indications must appear *beneath* (never above) each staff except in the case of instruments such as the piano and harp which are written on two staves, in which case they usually appear *between* the staves. This is also true of crescendo and decrescendo markings. A dynamic indication should be written each time an instrument reenters after resting for more than a bar.

Phrase indications of all types generally appear on the opposite side of the note head from the stems unless there is a problem of space with the next staff or unless there are two separate parts written on one staff, in which case they are written on the stem side of both parts (see Figure 26–1).

Sim. (*simile*) is used to indicate the continuation of a certain type of phrasing or dynamic (see Figure 26–1).

10. NOTATION OF WIND PARTS

Two wind parts should be written on one staff only if they are the same type of instrument (two flutes, two bassoons, two horns) and if the parts are clearly distinguishable. Parts that have radically different rhythms or parts that often cross are best written on two staves. In any case, separate orchestral parts should be written for each wind instrument even if they appear on the same staff in the score.

What has been said in regard to notation of individual wind parts in Chapters 8 (section 6), 12 (section 9), and 16 should be reviewed. In addition, it is important to emphasize that phrase markings *must* be included in wind parts where a legato is desired; otherwise each note will be separately tongued, resulting in a totally different effect. Sufficient rests *must* be included (especially in the brass) to enable the players to rest their embouchures. A comma is sometimes used in wind parts to indicate the point at which a catch breath is to be taken. Since a comma can also mean a slight pause in tempo (Ger. *Luftpause*) the interpretation can be ambiguous (Figure 26–3).

Figure 26–3

11. ORDER OF PERCUSSION IN THE SCORE

In the average symphony orchestra there are always a timpanist and at least three percussionists available. While all percussionists are able to play all percussion instruments, they also specialize in particular groups of instruments. The timpanist, for instance, is almost never asked to play anything but the timpani. Should he be asked to play an additional percussion instrument, an additional player might be hired, thus increasing the cost of rehearsal and performance. Also avoid adding an additional percussionist for just a few notes, since the additional expense might well result in cancellation of the performance altogether. Of course, in most cases the timpanist plus one or two percussionists will be sufficient.

Only rarely will a score call for the entire standard orchestral percussion; however, since there is no way of knowing what combination of instruments may be required for a particular score, the order of instruments in a hypothetical score requiring them all will be discussed here. To decide how to order any combination of these instruments, simply delete the instruments not required.

There are many considerations in ordering the percussion and dividing the instruments among the players. Such factors as the distance between the instruments and their relative positions, the direction in respect to the conductor, the specialties of each player, the order of instruments from left to right all come into play. Since each group of percussionists has its own way of arranging its section and since the available space on any stage or in any pit varies, it is not always possible for the composer to predict the best arrangement for any score involving many percussion instruments. For this reason, a *percussion score* containing all the percussion parts is usually copied out rather than a separate part for each percussionist, and several extra copies are made so that the percussionists are free to determine the most convenient setup for themselves and exchange assignment of parts at their convenience. The only exceptions are when the composer indicates a particular spacial arrangement of instruments for antiphonal effects or always assigns the same instruments to the same player. In general, try to keep the number of players to a minimum in assigning parts in the score, but if they must make frequent changes of instruments in a short time, it is best to add another player. Otherwise, in a fairly complicated score the percussion section can begin to look like a tag-team wrestling match.

Sometimes the same group of instruments are always assigned to the same player, in which case one player should play all the mallet instruments (xylophone, marimba, vibraphone), another all the drums if possible. Usually, though, there is no standardization of the order of percussion instruments in a score; however, the following arrangement seems to be the most common and logical:

(winds)
timpani
instruments of indefinite pitch
    drums
      metal instruments (triangle, cymbals, gong)
      wood instruments (temple blocks, etc.)
      other instruments
bells
chimes
xylophone
marimba
vibraphone
celesta/piano
(harp)
(any soloists, voices)
(strings)

Within each section, instruments should be ordered by pitch from high to low:

drums	*metal*
bongo	triangle
snare	cymbals
tenor	tam-tam
bass	

12. NOTATION OF INDIVIDUAL PERCUSSION

All that was said in Chapters 17 to 22 applies here. In Figure 26–4, three different drums are assigned separate lines. They would be played by one percussionist. At Figure 26–4b, three sizes of cymbals are indicated, while at section c, a set of five temple blocks are assigned a line each. The highest instruments are always on top. The various sizes can be indicated as follows:

Eng.	Ital.	Ger.	Fr.
small	piccolo	klein	petit
medium	medio	mitte	moyen
large	grande	gross	grand

Figure 26–4

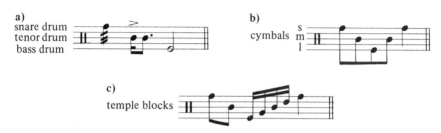

The *neutral clef* (two parallel vertical lines between the second and fourth lines of the staff) indicates that the lines do not refer to definite pitches. It should always be used, especially after the player has switched from an instrument of definite pitch.

Another means of notating instruments of indefinite pitch utilizes from one to four lines depending on how many are needed at the time. With one line, three instruments or three different sizes of the same instrument can be indicated. With two lines, five separate levels are possible, and so on (Figure 26–5).

Figure 26–5

Both systems can also be used to indicate different ways of playing on the same instrument (fingers, palm, stick, for example). If there is any advantage to the five-line system it is that manuscript paper comes with five-line staves already printed (though some is available with sets of two or three single lines for the percussion).

13. CHANGING INSTRUMENTS

Notation for the entry of each percussion instrument either after a rest of several measures or when a player has switched from one instrument to another (in which case at least several measures' rest should be allowed) must include the name of the instrument (often abbreviated), the size of the instrument if more than one size is being used, the method of playing (if unusual), and a dynamic marking *below* the staff.

When a change is made from one instrument to another, the last notes on the previous instrument should be followed by "change to" or "take" and the name of the new instrument (Ital. *prende* or *muta*, Ger. *nehmen*, Fr. *changez*). The same applies to an instrument which is to be retuned for the following passage. If a timpano tuned to the note *a* is to be retuned to g, for instance, the last note of the previous passage can be followed by: "tune (Ital. *muta*, Ger. *stimmen*, Fr. *accordez*) a–g," although this can also be left to the player.

14. INDICATING DURATION

Each percussion instrument has a different *decay rate*, that is, the amount of time it takes for the instrument to stop vibrating after it has been struck. It is of utmost importance that in those instruments which vibrate for several seconds (such as tam-tam or cymbals) the precise duration of the sound be indicated by the note values (tying into notes in the next bar if necessary). The player will dampen the sound with his hand at the end of the indicated duration if the instrument is still vibrating.

With instruments of rapid decay, the method of notation which is easiest to read is preferred. For instance, though the xylophone never sustains for more than a split second, it is much better to write as shown in Figure 26–6a rather than 26–6b. The sound will be the same, but the first version is much easier to read.

Figure 26–6

If the sound is to last as long as the instrument keeps vibrating, the indication "let ring" (Ital. *lasciare vibrare*, Ger. *klingen lassen*, Fr. *laisser vibrer*, abbreviated *l.v.*) is used, or a half tie follows the note (whole rests are always used for empty bars no matter what the meter). See Figure 26–7.

If the note is to be immediately dampened, a staccato mark will suffice (Figure 26–8), although to make doubly sure, the indication "damp" or "choke" (Ital. *secco*, Ger. *dämpfen*, Fr. *sec* or *étouffés*) can be added.

Figure 26–7

tam-tam

Figure 26–8

cymbals

If rests are written in the part of an instrument which would otherwise "ring" through, the player will dampen the sound. Therefore Figure 26–9a will result in a different sound than Figure 26–9b.

Figure 26–9

B.D.

15. ROLLS, TRILLS, AND TREMOLI

Notation for rolls on drums and other instruments written as in Figure 26–10a and b would indicate an accent over the bar line, sections c and d indicate a continuous roll with no accent, and e and f are ambiguous and therefore to be avoided. Sometimes a dotted line is used for the tie (Figure 26–10g). Measured repeated notes had best begin with at least a beat written out so that they are not confused with the roll (Figure 26–10h).

The end of a roll should be indicated with a note, either without accent on the beat (Figure 26–11a), with accent (b), or ending just before the next beat (c). The notation at Figure 26–11d is ambiguous and should not be used.

The notation for the roll between mallets on mallet instruments should be written like the bowed tremolo on string instruments (Figure 26–12a), not like

Figure 26–10

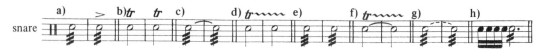

snare

Figure 26–11

B.D.

Figure 26–12

the fingered tremolo (Figure 26–12b), which is more difficult to read. It should not be confused with the trill on a note and its upper neighbor (Figure 26–12c). If rolled and single notes and chords are both written in a part, it is wise, especially for the marimba and vibraphone, to indicate "not rolled" or to write a footnote at the beginning of the part saying that only those notes and chords indicated as rolls are to be rolled, since a sustained chord is normally rolled on these instruments whether indicated or not.

The final note of a glissando (such as on the timpani) must be shown. Figure 26–13a would indicate a glissando lasting three beats. At 26–13b, the glissando occurs quickly at the end of the roll.

Figure 26–13

16. UNUSUAL METHODS OF PLAYING

Normally, no special indications are necessary, as the players will choose the mallets or sticks which give the best effect for a particular passage. However, if the composer has a specific effect in mind, he can indicate the use of a special mallet (the return to normal mallets must, of course, be indicated).

There are soft, medium, and hard sticks with ends of rubber, cord, or yarn. There are also mallets of brass (which will damage instruments of wood such as the xylophone), plastic, and wood, as well as jazz brushes, maraca sticks (with handles filled with beads), double-headed bass drum sticks, and others. These can be specified if the composer is sure of an exact effect (better worked out in advance with a percussionist).

Soft mallets, especially those of a large contact area with the instrument, tend to smother vibrations of high frequency, thereby eliminating the upper partials of the sound and producing a mellower, more muted tone. Hard mallets, especially those of small contact area, allow the upper partials to come through, producing a bright, clear tone.

By the same token, playing at the edge of an instrument such as the cymbal or drum allows the upper partials to predominate; playing at the center has the opposite effect (see Chapter 20, section 1).

17. NOTATION FOR STRINGS

As with two wind parts playing on the same staff, each part of a divided string section must have all accidentals. The return to undivided playing is indicated by *unis. (unisono)*.

Figure 26–14

Remember that bowings are seldom indicated by name in the score (such as *spiccato, martellato*), but rather by the phrasing, accent, staccato markings, and the like (see Chapter 2). Even though string players will undoubtedly alter the arranger's bowings on numerous occasions to facilitate performance, it is best to mark them anyway so as to give the string players an idea of what was intended. With experience the arranger will find that less and less of his bowing must be altered in performance.

18. MANUSCRIPT SCORES

It is most important that a manuscript score be done in ink and be perfectly clear, neat, and correct. Notes must be aligned vertically from top to bottom of the score, bar lines must be ruled at right angles to the staves.

In scores that are to be sent to copyists or engravers and therefore are not in their final form, certain shortcuts are allowed:

1. Full-measure rests may be omitted.
2. If the instruments of one section are playing exactly the same notes as those of another, with the same phrasing and other indications for a number of measures, the symbol *col* or *colla* (with) may be used followed by a wavy line to avoid the necessity of writing out the same notes for more than one part. Naturally, transposing instruments (other than the octave) and instruments playing in different clefs cannot be so indicated. Instruments playing an octave higher or lower can be indicated by *col*, the name of the instrument, and *8va* (an octave higher) or *8vab* (an octave lower).
3. A diagonal line through a bar along with dots on either side of it indicates that the preceding bar is to be repeated (this is a shorthand symbol used in orchestra parts). Several repeated bars should be numbered. A similar line through two bars indicates that the previous two bars are to be repeated.

Figure 26–15 shows a second violin part from a manuscript score in which all these methods have been used. The parts themselves must not, of course, use *col 8vab* but must have all the notes copied out.

Figure 26–15

Excerpts from Orchestral Scores

The following excerpts should be analyzed in the following manner. First, their component parts, primary and secondary melodic lines, bass line, inner parts, and other elements should be determined. Next these elements should be compared. Finally the distribution of each element between different instruments should be determined and each part independently studied.

The full scores of these and other examples should be studied with recordings if possible. The balance and blend of the component elements and their tone color both individually and together should be considered.

These excerpts are referred to in subsequent chapters by score and bar number (6:8–10 means excerpt number 6, bar numbers 8 to 10).

The choice of excerpts for study will certainly be questioned. The great difficulty was deciding what to omit. Such a brief collection cannot hope to be completely representative, but an attempt was made to represent different periods and styles in the belief that an entire section of a score is more valuable than brief excerpts of a bar or two and that the comparison of these excerpts will be of great value.

Beethoven, *Symphony No. 3*

Score No. 1 (cont.)

Score No. 1 (cont.)

Score No. 1 (cont.)

Score No. 1 (cont.)

Score No. 1 (cont.)

Score No. 1 (cont.)

Score No. 1 (cont.)

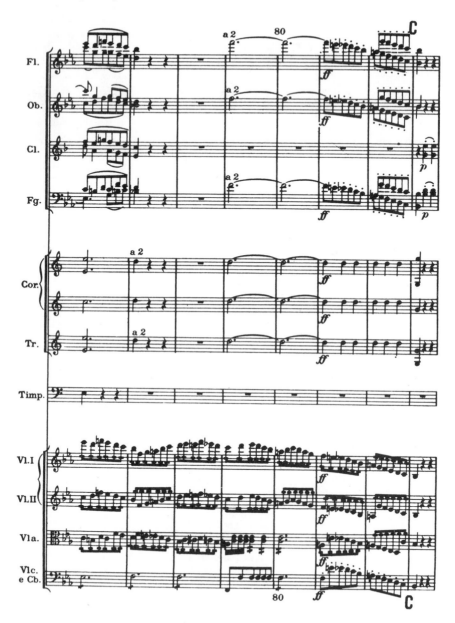

Score No. 1 (cont.)

Used through the courtesy of Belwin-Mills Publishing Corp.

$\frac{6}{8}$

Langsam und schmachtend   Wagner, *Tristan und Isolde, Prelude*
Lento e languente

Score No. 2 (cont.)

10

Score No. 2 (cont.)

Score No. 2 (cont.)

20

30

Score No. 2 (cont.)

Used through the courtesy of Belwin-Mills Publishing Corp.

Mahler, *Symphony No. 5*

5. Rondo-Finale.

Score No. 3 (cont.)

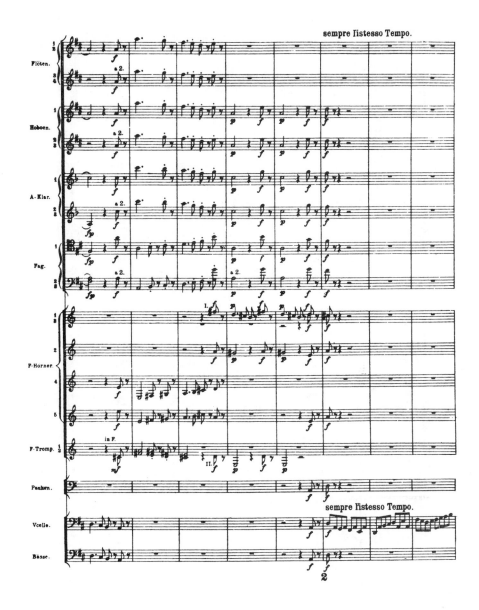

Score No. 3 (cont.)

90

Score No. 3 (cont.)

Used through the courtesy of Belwin-Mills Publishing Corp.

314

Debussy, *Prelude to the Afternoon of a Faun*

Score No. 4 (cont.)

Score No. 4 (cont.)

Score No. 4 (cont.)

Score No. 4 (cont.)

Used through the courtesy of Belwin-Mills Publishing Corp.

*leading   H main voice

†accompanying   N secondary voice

10

*) event. zur Verstärkung der Violinen (if needed to strengthen the violins)

**) ♩ = 30 bis ♩ = 42 - 48

Score No. 5 (cont.)

*let the violins through, horns continue   †if possible with the upper octave

Score No. 5 (cont.)

*divisi   †quickly mute

SCORE NO. 6

Bartók, *Concerto for Orchestra*

I
(INTRODUZIONE)

Score No. 6 (cont.)

Score No. 6 (cont.)

Score No. 6 (cont.)

Score No. 6 (cont.)

SCORE NO. 7

Stravinsky, *Symphony in Three Movements*

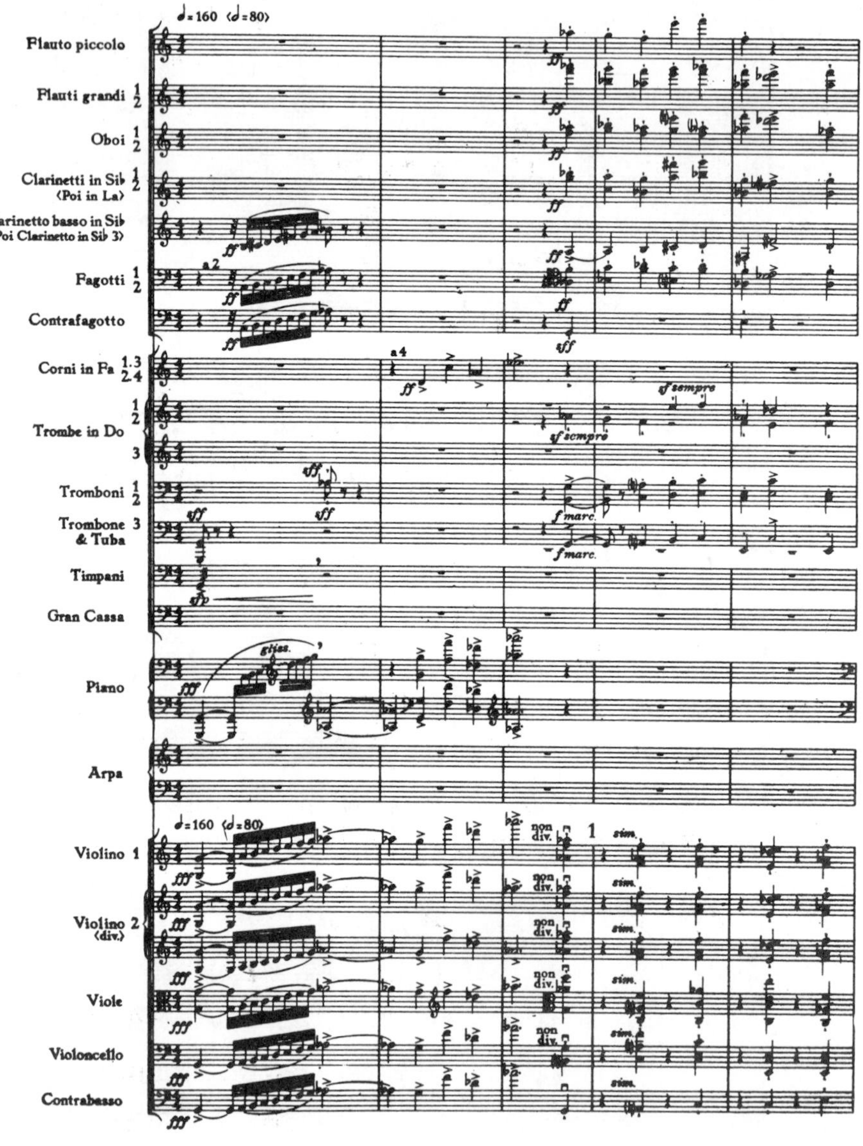

10

Score No. 7 (cont.)

SCORE NO. 8

Henze, *Symphony No. 5*

$\frac{3}{4}$

Moto perpetuo $\;\text{♩.} = 72$

Score No. 8 (cont.)

Score No. 8 (cont.)

27

Scoring Individual
Melodic Lines

Any orchestral score consists of individual parts, called *voices* or *lines*, which are made up of melodic intervals occurring in a certain sequence, along with simultaneous combinations of harmonic intervals producing chordal structures. Though the treatment of these two basic elements of music varies greatly from the classical period to the present day, certain considerations remain basic to "effective" orchestration, that is, orchestration in which the various parts have the tone color the orchestrator imagined and in which they *balance,* or are in correct dynamic proportion to each other so that the important musical ideas stand out and the less important support without overwhelming them. These basic considerations of color and balance will be dealt with in the following chapters from the standpoint of individual instrumental combinations; these considerations are always relative to the particular musical situation and no general rules can be applied.

In various periods and styles certain combinations which have seemed "ugly" or not aesthetically pleasing can, at another time, seem beautiful and correct. Therefore the score excerpts have been taken from a wide variety of styles and periods to illustrate the widest possible range of application of various orchestral combinations.

A melodic line can be the main° or primary melody, secondary or countermelody, or simply a relatively unimportant part within the accompaniment. In all cases, the same basic considerations apply, though naturally the goal is to keep the main melody in the foreground and arrange the less important parts so as not to *cover* it.

1. ORCHESTRATION OF MELODIC LINES IN SINGLE INSTRUMENTS

The choice of a particular instrument to play a *solo* line depends on the particular tone color of the instrument, its range, its technical capabilities, and its ability to be heard in proper relation to the other instruments playing at the same time. Some instruments sound pinched in their extreme upper range and some lack volume and adequate tone in their extreme lower ranges. These considerations have been dealt with in Part I of this book. It remains to discuss the dynamic power of various instruments in the orchestra. Naturally this depends upon whether the instrument is playing in its strongest range, upon the rhythmic independence of the line in relation to others occurring at the same time, upon the contrast in tone color to the other instruments, and upon dynamic markings. It must again be stressed, however, that dynamic markings are only partially useful in securing good balance. A weak instrument playing *fff* can still be covered if the passage is not intrinsically well balanced.

Following is a list of the relative strengths of instruments. Of course, in a very lightly scored passage *any* instrument can be heard in a solo. Only when the orchestration begins to thicken does the problem of balance arise. The following list can be open to question because so much depends on range, tone color, and other considerations, but generally speaking it should be a useful categorization of instrumental strengths. The only percussion instruments considered here are those of definite pitch.

Easily Covered
celesta
crotales (antique cymbals)
Moderately Easily Covered
flute
bass clarinet
double bassoon
harp
double basses
Relatively Strong
oboe
English horn
clarinet
bassoon

Relatively Strong
horn
tuba
violas
cellos
Very Strong
piccolo
trumpet
trombone
timpani
chimes
orchestra bells
xylophone
violins

Some of the above instruments fall into strong (piccolo) or weak (double bass) categories because of their range or because of the presence or lack of strong overtones (flute).

Naturally, the melody in an upper part will stand out better than that in an inner or bass part. Any instruments playing above an important melodic line tend to absorb the upper partials of the instrument and therefore reduce its volume.

Examples of instrumental solos are to be found in Part I.

2. DOUBLING MELODIC LINES

Melodic lines may be doubled at the unison or in one or more octaves with instruments of the same type or different instruments. Naturally, each string section is an example of the continual unison doubling of a melodic line. Doubling is generally done for one of the following reasons:

1. To add strength.
2. To combine tone colors.
3. To alter (mellow or make brighter) the tone color of the instrument which dominates the combination.

Following is a list of wind and string instruments whose ranges lie comfortably in each octave:

$c^4 - b^4$
    piccolo (also violin in extreme high register)
$c^3 - b^3$
    piccolo, flute, violin
$c^2 - b^2$
    flute, oboe, clarinet, trumpet, violin, viola
$c^1 - b^1$
    flute, oboe, English horn, clarinet, bass clarinet, bassoon, trumpet, horn, trombone, violin, viola, cello
$c - b$
    bass clarinet, bassoon, horn, trombone, tuba, viola, cello
$C - B$
    bass clarinet, bassoon, double bassoon, trombone, tuba, cello, double bass
$CC - BB$
    double bassoon, double bass (also tuba in extreme low register)

It should be noted that most instrumental ranges lie within the range of the human voice (about F to c^3). Instruments in the extreme ranges of the orchestra are often used to double the highest part in the orchestra at the octave above for increased brilliance (emphasizing upper partials) or to double the bass line at the octave below for added weight and depth.

Generally speaking, the less doubling, the more transparent and clear the orchestration, and the more doubling, the more resonant and thick. Effective orchestration often makes use of continual contrast between sections of a piece which are transparent and sections which are thick, as a means of adding variety and contrasting textures.

3. DOUBLING OF MELODIC LINES IN THE STRINGS

It is important to keep in mind that a section of ten strings playing together is not ten times as loud as a solo string instrument. There is an acoustical phenomenon which absorbs much of the added volume of each string instrument into the overall sound. What does result from a group of strings playing together is a different tone color, one that is mellower, less bright than that of a solo instrument due to (one hopes) imperceptible differences in pitch and rates of vibrato. These differences cause the characteristic "shimmering" quality of a section of strings.

Following are common *unison* doublings between string sections:

1. Vln I + II — for greater strength and sonority (Score No. 6: bars 76–85; 7:1–11).
2. Vln (I or II or both) + Vla — darker color (3:90–93; 7:1–3, 8–11; 8:8–9)
3. Vla + Vcl — stronger and darker than cellos alone (1:57–58, 81–82; 3:88–89, 94)
4. Vln + Vcl — strong and very intense
5. Vln + Vla + Vcl — very strong and rich sonority

Because of their range, basses rarely take part in a string unison (but see 6:51–75—basses in unison with cellos).

Single octave doublings:

1. Vln I + II — increased brillance (1:55–60, 63–64, 76–82; 3:88–89; 4:2–13 soli; 5:9–15; 6:58–63 [3 octaves])
2. Divisi Vln section in octaves — same, but weaker (6:51–58)
3. Vln + Vla (1:10–15, 82; 2:7–9 viola *above* violin, 10–13, 18–23, 25–26, 28–32; 7:1–3, 8–11)
4. Vln + Vcl (1:23, 27, 81–82; 2:20–27; 4:3–5 soli)
5. Vla + Vcl (1:37–40, 59–62; 6:22–34, 37–75; 7:1–2, 8–11)
6. Vcl + basses — usually for heavier bass line (basses alone on the bass line are weak), frequent examples in all excerpts. The combination of violas and basses at the octave is rare without the cellos.

Double octave doublings:

1. Vln I + II + Vla
2. Vln I + II + Vcl
3. Vla + Vcl + basses (6:22–34)

All the above combinations strongly emphasize the melodic line. Violins, cellos, and basses in octaves without the violas is rare. In addition, octave doublings and unison doublings are often combined:

1. Vln and II + Vla + Vcl
2. Vln I + Vln II and Vla and Vcl + bass (1:81–82)

Triple octave doublings:

1. Vln I + Vln II and Vla + Vcl + basses — well balanced (1:55–57)
2. Vln I and II + Vla + Vcl + basses — somewhat top-heavy

Quadruple octave doublings are usually supported by winds (as, of course, any of the above combinations may be) to avoid the thinness of sections each playing an octave apart. *Divisi* strings occur in 4:1–13.

For more on writing for strings, see Chapter 7.

4. DOUBLINGS OF MELODIC LINES IN THE WINDS

The flute, with its relatively weak overtones, and the clarinet, with only odd-numbered harmonics, tend to blend best with other instruments. Their tone is also more easily absorbed and dominated by the sound of other instruments. The oboe and English horn, rich in overtones, do not blend so well; they tend to assert their particular nasal quality, especially in combination with each other. This is true to a lesser extent of the bassoon; in its middle register it blends well with horns or clarinets (although in the latter combination the bassoon tone will often predominate).

The horns are often used in combination with woodwinds, usually as a tenor part. In fact, the horns blend well with nearly any combination of instruments and are often used as the connecting links between woodwinds, brass, and strings.

The trumpet has an incisive tone which will stand out in most combinations unless playing quietly in its middle-low range. Likewise, the trombones tend to assert their tone in most combinations.

The piccolo, double bassoon, and tuba, while capable of occasional effective solos, are usually used to double upper and lower orchestral octaves for extreme brightness and reinforcement of upper partials or for adding weight and sonority to the bass line.

Combinations of woodwinds alone at unison or octave are:

1. Picc + Fl — added brightness (8:4–8, 10–18 with violins)
2. Fl + Ob — oboe tone predominates (2:6–7; 4:3–6, 9 partial doubling, 12)

3. Fl + Cl — clarinet softened by flute (1:13–14, 15–17 with horn)
4. Fl + Bsn (usually at one or two octaves) — "hollow" but effective sound, favorite of Mozart (1:21–23 with clarinet)
5. Ob + Cl — oboe predominates, penetrating sonority (3:90–94)
6. Ob + Bsn — thick, reedy, penetrating sonority (1:89–91 with violins)
7. Cl + Bsn — rich, mellow tone, bassoon predominates (3:31–35)

Combinations of three or four types of woodwind at the octave (sometimes doubled two or more on a part) are not uncommon, especially doubled with strings. Either these doublings can be with a different instrument in each octave (highest octave, two flutes in unison, next octave, two oboes, and so on) or a blend of tone colors can be achieved by combining different colors in each octave (highest octave, first flute, second octave second flute, first oboe, third octave second oboe, first clarinet, and so on). In cases of multiple octave doublings with winds alone, it is generally best to distribute the weight in the middle. Putting more or stronger instruments on the outer parts tends to give the octaves a hollow sound.

The order of instruments in a score need not be observed in octave doublings, the clarinets sometimes being found above the oboes, for instance. Balance problems can occur, however. For instance placing the flutes under the oboes would put the strongest instrument on top and considerably overpower the flutes.

The combinations of the subsidiary instruments—English horn (with oboe, 2:10–11, 31–32; 8:3–9), bass clarinet, double bassoon—with other woodwinds have similar effects to their primary instruments (for example, in the list of woodwind combinations above, read "English horn" for oboe in the various combinations). Nevertheless, the subtleties of various combinations of tone color can be understood only by much score study and experience.

Combinations of trumpets in unison or octaves, horns in unison or octaves, and trombones and tuba in unison or octaves are all powerful. Other possibilities are:

1. Trp + Hn — less bright and mellower than trumpets alone (5:14–15)
2. Trp + Trb — powerful and extremely strong (6:47–50)
3. Hn + Trb — mellower than trombones alone, rich timbre

The tuba adds great weight to any combination of brass. Usually two horns double in the unison against one trumpet or one trombone, especially in loud passages where two horns are needed to balance with each of the other brass instruments (3:94–99).

In combinations of brass and woodwinds, the woodwinds are generally placed *above* the brass, where they can strengthen the upper partials and where they have a better chance of being heard (1:1–2, 23–35; 7:3–7, 11–19). Woodwinds placed among the brass, especially in loud passages, tend to lessen the brilliance of the brass without lending any strength or color of their own.

Generally speaking, two or more woodwinds are needed to compete in loud passages with one horn, four or more to be heard at all with the trumpets and trombones. The woodwinds tend to soften the brass tone.

Combinations of woodwinds and brass:

1. Trp + Fl (and Picc) — added brilliance
2. Trp + Ob (or Eng Hn) — added bite and nasality
3. Trp + Cl — rounder tone
4. Hn + Cl — less brassy (2:10–11, 12–13, 29–30)
5. Hn + Bsn — mellow (2:28–31; 3:39–46, 51–53)
6. Hn + Ob — lack of blend, each instrument stands out
7. Trb + Cl — mellow, especially with muted trombones
8. Trb + Bsn — bassoons tend to deaden the trombone tone
9. Tuba + Bsn (and Dbl Bsn) — strong, heavy bass for brass

It should be noted that the bass trombone is an excellent bass for the brass, fully capable of balancing in loud passages, when the added weight of the tuba is not desired.

For extraordinary power or thick sonority, doublings of most or all of the woodwinds and/or brass can be used (1:79–80; 2:14–21, 24–28, 30–53, 39–41 woodwinds, 54–56 woodwinds and trumpet, 88–89, 95–98 woodwinds; 5:1–9, 16–18 woodwinds; 6:58–62 woodwinds and horns).

For more on writing for winds, see Chapter 16.

5. DOUBLINGS OF MELODIC LINES IN WINDS AND STRINGS

Combinations of winds and strings generally occur to create a new timbre, to give more resonance to the strings, or to soften the winds. These combinations add cohesiveness to the string tone. The addition of one woodwind to a string section in unison adds cohesion and definition but allows the string tone to predominate. In a loud passage two winds can perform the same function. Four or more woodwinds added to the strings begin to predominate in tone color, especially the double reeds. When winds and strings are in octaves, both octaves are often doubled in both instruments for better blend (highest octave, Vln I + Fls; lower octave, Vln II + Obs; [6:51–57]. Except for the horns, which blend well with the violas and cellos, combinations of brass and strings tend not to blend well. Combinations of all three sections create a rich and heavy sonority which is effective in *piano* as well as *forte* (1:37–40; 7:11–19 bass line, 14–19 woodwinds, trumpet, piano).

Combinations of winds and strings:

1. Vln + Fl (and Picc) — added brilliance and intensity (1:63–64; 3:79–89; 5:4–8, 10–18 with piccolo)
2. Vln + Ob — oboe tone will penetrate somewhat, rich tone (8:9–18)

3. Vln + Cl — mellow tone (3:79–83; 4:2 with violins)
4. Vln + Bsn — rare, possible only in lower range of violin in unison
5. Vln + Trp — blends best in tutti (5:9–12, 16–18 with viola)
6. Vln + Hn — rich sonority, moderately good blend
7. Vla + Cl, Bsn, or Hn (4:9) — rich sonority, good blend (8:3–18 with alto flute)
8. Vla + Trb — do not blend as well
9. Vcl + Bsn (and bass Cl) — good blend (frequent examples, 4:3–4 clarinet with solo cello and violins)
10. Vcl + upper winds in octaves — rare, blend often not good (4:7–8 solo cello and flute)
11. Vcl + Hn — very rich, sonorous blend (6:51–56 with basses, partial doubling)
12. Vcl + Trb (and tuba) — less common, blends less well
13. Basses + Hn (3:38–46) — blend well
14. Basses + Dbl Bsn — heavy bass, good blend
15. Basses + Trb — good blend, good bass reinforcement
16. Basses + tuba — good for heavy bass in thick texture, less appropriate in more transparent textures where the lack of blend of the sonority of the double basses and tuba is more evident

Other doublings of several winds and strings together occur in the following excerpts: 1:44, Fl, Cl, Bsn, Vln II, Vla; 1:55–57, tutti octaves; 1:57–58, Bsn and Vla with Vcl in doubling in thirds; 1:81–83, tutti octaves; 2:13–31, low winds with low strings; 6:65–69 woodwinds and low strings; 7:1, 8, 10–11, 14, low winds and strings with piano; 7:2, 9, strings with Hn and piano.

The percussion instruments have not been considered above because of their highly individual melodic uses, which were discussed in Part I.

6. OTHER CONSIDERATIONS IN DOUBLING MELODIC LINES

Entrances of new melodic lines are usually preceded by rests in the participating instruments to make more effective the entry of the new tone color. Melodies which reappear are usually orchestrated with a different combination of instruments each time for variety. Melodies can also be doubled in thirds or sixths (often in combination with octave doublings as well). In this case, the same timbre should be used for each part if blend is desired.

Also, a melody can be doubled by a simplified version of itself in another instrument or group of instruments (every other note, only strong beats, or another pattern; see "partial doublings" in the examples cited in this chapter, as well as 1:35–36, 75–76 woodwinds and strings). This type of doubling gives more rhythmic strength to the melody and defines it better. Often this happens in the bass line, with the bassoons and/or cellos playing legato and the basses pizzicato on the strong beats. If it happens in an upper part, the two versions of the melody are usually in instruments of contrasting timbre and often at the octave. One part will often play legato and the other staccato.

Melodic lines (and their doublings) can be divided among instruments, either to give instruments a rest in long passages, in which case the division will occur from one instrument of the same type to another, or when a melodic line goes out of the range of an instrument and is taken over by another. In these cases, the first instrument should always end in unison on the first note played by the succeeding instrument in order to obtain continuity in the line. When one instrument stops playing before the next instrument enters, there is always a perceptible break. Composers of all periods have consistently joined melodic lines passing from one instrument to another in this manner (7:11–19 trombone and tuba, 21–22 horns; 8:10–18 cellos and basses). When melodic lines are divided each instrument can take a melodic figure of the phrase in turn or close imitation can occur between two different instruments which seem to echo each other (1:46–55, 83–98 woodwinds and strings; 2:1–7 woodwinds and strings; 3:1–23; 6:55–57 woodwinds and strings; 8:4–18 brass, 4–18 timpani).

In passages where the woodwinds or strings are playing a rapidly ascending scale with a glissando in the harp leading up to a strong beat, if the effect of a rapid flourish is desired, there is no need to have all the instruments play the same notes at the same time. In fact, their doing so would be ineffective. While the winds are covering one octave in a scale, the harp can cover two or more. For the greatest effect, each instrument should play over the widest possible range in the time available. It matters not at all that they may all be playing different notes of the scale at a different time (8:18 with violin and flutes).

In addition to the primary melody, more often than not there is also a countermelody of secondary importance. This may be in imitation with the primary melody, or a different melody contrasting in rhythm and range. It should be orchestrated less strongly then the primary melody but stronger than the accompaniment and in a contrasting timbre (2:10–27 primary melody in doubled woodwinds, countermelody in strings; 2:28–32 primary melody in imitation in strings, countermelody in imitation in winds; 3:24–51 imitative melody and countermelody in horns, winds, then winds and strings, from 62, fugal texture; 4:1–6 melody in flutes, countermelody in solo violins; 5:1–9 melody in brass, countermelody in woodwinds; 5:10–15 melody in strings, countermelody in horns; 5:16–18 melody in woodwinds, countermelody in cellos and bassoon; 6:51–63 melody in violins and woodwinds, countermelody in lower strings and horns; 8:1–18 main material in imitation in brass, countermelody in woodwinds and upper strings, bass in timpani and low strings).

Many twentieth-century scores use the concept of the *Klangfarbenmelodie* (tone-color melody; see Chapter 37), a melody which alternates between instruments of different color, each instrument playing only a few notes of the melody. Naturally, the scoring has to be very transparent for the necessary and difficult balance to be achieved in order to bring out a line which is continually passing from one instrument to another. German scores often indicate the primary melodic material at any particular moment with the indication H for *Hauptstimme* (primary voice) followed by a line over the passage until the instrument no longer has the primary melodic material. Countermelodies are designated by N̄ for *Nebenstimme* (secondary voice). (See also Chapter 16, p. 185.)

With more than two melodic lines, the problems of balance between different parts and emphasis of important parts become more complex, though no new rules are needed to deal with these contrapuntal textures. Score excerpts Nos. 1, 4, 6, and 7 are basically homophonic in texture. Score No. 5, with one or more countermelodies, becomes somewhat contrapuntal, and score Nos. 2, 3, and 8 are increasingly complex contrapuntally but completely transparent and clear because of the instrumentation and the fact that the motives are rhythmically differentiated, are preceded by rests before each entrance, are in different registers, and are distinguished by different tone colors.

28

Scoring Chords, Accompaniment, and Other Textures

---

1. SPACING AND DOUBLING OF CHORDS

The most sonorous spacing of chords follows the distribution of overtones in the natural overtone series. The upper partials of the lower notes are thereby reinforced by the upper instruments. In other words, below middle c, parts of chords are usually separated by intervals of the octave, fourth, or fifth (*open position*), and above middle c there are usually no chordal tones left out (*close position*), especially in loud passages. Open position chords in quiet passages are better because the overtones are more clearly audible and fill in the harmony.

Chords in close position in lower registers produce conflicting overtones with many dissonances which make the chord sound thick and muddy. Occasionally this can be useful for special effects (8:1–18 trombones). Figure 28–1 compares the overtones generated by chords in a low register in open and close position. The close position chord generates closer overtone clashes in a lower range.

Doubling different degrees of a chord also follows the distribution of notes in the overtone series. In the first sixteen harmonics are found five roots, three fifths, and two thirds. Therefore, it is preferable to double the root more often than the fifth, the third even less. Sevenths, ninths, and other dissonances are

Figure 28-1

also seldom doubled and usually appear in the upper parts. In other words, the rules of doubling taken from four-part vocal harmonization are merely expanded to apply to chords in the orchestra, which usually contain more than four parts and which are spread over a wider range. In the twentieth century composers began writing chords with unusual spacings and doublings to create unusual sonorities (see Chords in Chapters 7 and 16).

2. BALANCE AND BLEND

Balance means that all parts of a chord are distributed among the various instruments in proper dynamic relation. *Blend* has to do with the way in which the tone colors of the different instruments complement each other. Certain instruments blend less well than others because of their overtones (see Chapter 27). Generally, all other things being equal, those instruments which have greater dynamic power or a more penetrating tone color are given the root and fifth of the chord, those which are weaker or blend better the third, seventh, and so on.

Much, of course, depends on whether the passage is loud or soft. What is proper balance in *piano* might be destroyed were the instruments playing *forte*, since some instruments are capable of playing much louder than others. For this reason, during a crescendo or diminuendo, instruments and doublings are often added or deleted to obtain proper balance (6:63–75).

The balance of a particular chord depends on the strength of the individual instruments in the register in which they are playing (another reason why an intimate knowledge of each instrument is mandatory for good orchestration), on the number of instruments playing, and on the dynamic markings. It must again be emphasized that of these, the dynamic markings are the least effective way to balance a chord. For one thing, dynamics are purely relative, each player making individual decisions as to exactly how to interpret those dynamics, depending on the context of the music. A great deal is done by listening to each other and balancing by ear. Also, few players make a noticeable distinction between more than four or five levels of dynamics, depending largely on which instrument they play and what its dynamic range is. Most of the time *pp*, *p*, *f*, and *ff* should suffice. Experiments with finer shadings of dynamics in some twentieth-century scores have not met with noticeable success in performance. Indeed, the difference between *p* and *mp* or *f* and *mf* is vague and dependent entirely on the musical situation of the moment. Dynamic markings such as *ppppp* or *fffff* found in many late romantic scores are there purely as a precaution to the player and found only in rare instances where the softest or loudest possible tone is required. It is doubtful if anything beyond *ppp* or *fff* has any meaning to an orchestral player. Verdi, in order to ensure that the solo cello in *Otello* would play as quietly as possible, marked one passage *pppp*. At a rehearsal, Verdi said to Toscanini, who was playing first cello at the premiere, "I can't hear you." Toscanini replied, "But Maestro, you marked the passage *pppp*." "Ah," said Verdi, "that's for other cellists, not for you!"

So-called *terrace dynamics,* marking each part with a different dynamic to achieve balance, are useful to only a limited extent and cannot compensate for an intrinsically badly balanced chord. In addition, the weight of the chord should be in the middle, where most instruments should be playing. Avoid chords which are top- or bottom-heavy except for special effects.

3. WOODWIND CHORDS

In scoring chords for woodwinds, one may be dealing with chords of from three to six or more parts (with octave doublings) and may have woodwinds in pairs or threes with or without subsidiary instruments. The number of instruments playing will, of course, depend upon the sonority and dynamics of the particular chord in relation to the rest of the orchestra. Combinations of different colors and strengths are many. Figure 28–2 shows various ways of combining woodwinds in pairs on chords.

Figure 28–2

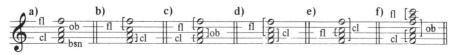

a. *Separate instruments on each chord degree.* No blend, somewhat better in open position.
b. *Superposition.* Good, but less blend than in section d, often used in open position when necessitated by the ranges of the instruments. Clarinets (or oboes) above flutes would overbalance the top.
c. *Overlapping.* Common in classical scores; first flute will balance because it is the highest part, but undoubled second clarinet is relatively weak.
d. *Dovetailing, interlocking, or crossing.* Usually achieves the best blend, though second flute is weak, and if oboes were playing instead of clarinets the balance would be worse. If clarinets doubled the flutes and oboes played the root and fifth, greater sonority and a better balance would be achieved (more desirable in louder or more sonorous passages).
e. *Enclosure.* Good for emphasizing the octave with the same tone color. With flutes on the outside and oboes in the middle, the balance would be bad.

f. *Combinations of the above.* In actual practice, scoring chords for woodwinds will usually entail a combination of methods. In this chord, the flute,
being on the upper parts, will balance with the oboes and clarinets, which
will blend well, being dovetailed.

4. BRASS CHORDS

Brass chords are usually arranged in close position for the trumpets and
horns, both for greater sonority and because of the ranges of the instruments.
Trombones are often in open position. Trombones, especially in quieter
passages, are effective in close position if they are not playing too low.
Remember that in loud passages with all the brass, the horns are almost always
doubled two to a part because they are about half as powerful as one trumpet
or trombone (remember too that the first and third horns have the higher parts,
the second and fourth the lower, that is, they are always written dovetailed).

Avoid using just one trombone in brass chords since it tends not to blend as
well except as a bass for two or three trumpets. Chords with trumpets playing
above or overlapped with the trombones are bright and powerful. With horns,
they are more mellow. The tuba adds weight. The trumpets or trombones can
also be used with the horns, either overlapped, dovetailed, or enclosed, in
which case the horns take the edge off the tone of the other brass. Two horns
playing in unison are a good bass to the trumpets, and the bass trombone is a
good bass for the trombones or entire brass if the weight of the tuba is not
desired.

5. CHORDS IN THE WOODWIND AND BRASS TOGETHER

The horns are often used separately from the other brass, blending well,
especially with the bassoons, in woodwind chords. In chords involving all or
most of the brass and woodwind, the woodwinds are generally in close position, often with three or more winds on a part in loud passages, above the brass
where they reinforce the upper partials of the brass. In unison with the brass
they take away brilliance and mellow the tone. The woodwinds and brass can
also be overlapped, and, in quieter passages, dovetailed or enclosed, though
special attention must be given to balance in these cases. Double basses added
to wind chord basses give added cohesion.

6. STRING CHORDS

Chords in the strings can be in four or five parts or, if sections are divided or
multiple stops used, in more (4:1–13). A group of solo strings in harmony is a
useful effect, as is dividing one section, often the cellos, to play in harmony. In

dividing sections, one must take care to achieve a good balance. For instance, *divisi* first and second violins with violas on an inner part and cellos and double basses on the bass line would create an overbalance on the bass which could be rectified by having only half the cellos play. Although the winds are usually in close position, widely spaced string chords are more common and can be quite resonant, especially when combined with winds in close position (1:1–2).

7. CHORDS IN WINDS AND STRINGS TOGETHER

Doubling parts of the chord in the winds and strings in unison can be effective, but usually the winds and strings have separate and independent chords complete in each section, for although the overall orchestral sonority is heard, each section tends to retain its separate color; therefore, parts of chords cannot be assigned indiscriminately to any instruments. Often the violins will carry the upper part, the upper woodwinds and violas share the harmony, and the bassoons and lower strings the bass. Woodwinds enclosed in strings are seldom well-balanced, though winds overlapped above the strings or dovetailed on upper and inner parts can blend. The combination of strings and brass, though sometimes very effective, does not blend as well except for horns on inner parts (2:10–32).

A typical well-balanced and blended chord for woodwinds, brass, and strings might have the brass, with horns doubled, in the middle in close position, except for the trombones; the upper woodwinds grouped above the brass in close position; the strings spread more widely from top to bottom, with the bass in the bassoons, lowest trombone, and tuba; cellos and double basses on the bass in octaves. A good procedure is to arrange the brass parts first, grouping the woodwinds above in close position, then arranging the strings in open but complete chords. The winds give the required fullness to the chords so that the strings can be spread out without causing a sense of thinness. Although in quieter passages terrace dynamics can be of help in achieving balance in unusual combinations of instruments, their effect in loud passages is minimal, since the players will tend to play at the dynamic level they hear from the other players anyway. Examine the chords in score Nos. 1:1–2, 25–35, 65–75, 83–99; 2:1–9; 4:1–17; 5:1–9, 16–18; 6:6–10; 7:3–7; 8:1–18 brass.

8. ORCHESTRAL TEXTURE

No matter in what style a score is written, it will be made up of melodic intervals and harmonic intervals, that is, pitches occurring in succession or simultaneously. Therefore, in even the most complex and dissonant orchestral texture, the considerations of blend (or contrast) and balance will be considered both in individual lines, though they may no longer be termed "melodic," and in harmonic aggregates, whether tonal harmonies, polychords, or tone clusters. Following are the six basic types of orchestral texture:

1. *Chordal.* Based exclusively on a progression of harmonic structures; in this case blend is usually to be desired.
2. *Unaccompanied melody.* Either in unison or octaves, in a solo instrument or combinations up to the entire orchestra. Again, blend is usually desired.
3. *Melody with accompaniment.* Coloristic contrast between melody and accompaniment with usually a strong melodic line so that it can be heard against the accompaniment.
4. *Melody with one or more countermelodies and accompaniment.* Again, contrast between the elements, melody strongest, countermelody less strong, accompaniment in the background.
5. *Contrapuntal texture.* Two or more independent melodies without accompaniment. Contrast desirable.
6. *Complex textures.* Combinations of many elements of varying degrees of importance, used for a massive sonic effect, a *collage* of notes and rhythmic figures, including tone clusters (Figure 28–3, see page 354).

9. ASPECTS OF ORCHESTRATION

There are various things which must be considered in the analysis or orchestration of any score. They will be discussed in this section.

MELODIC LINES

Independent melodic lines must be sufficiently strong and/or differentiated in tone color to stand out against the accompaniment.

COUNTERMELODIES

Countermelodies must be subsidiary to the primary melodic line. Most often a countermelody of some sort is present even if it is of relatively minor importance.

BASS LINES

The bass line must be next in strength to the melody or countermelody to support the accompaniment. These lines can be sustained or intermittent or a combination of both.

INNER PARTS

The accompanying parts must be orchestrated so as not to overpower the

Figure 28–3   Ives, *Three Places in New England*

melody but must be thick and sonorous enough to support it. This balance, of course, depends on how many and what type of instruments are playing the melody, the dynamic markings, and so on. Doublings and harmonic fillers (Chapter 29) can thicken and add volume to the accompaniment.

SUSTAINING ELEMENTS

In all periods and styles of orchestration the use of a sustaining element is probably the most universal method of adding cohesion to the orchestra. A sustaining element can be simply a sustained note in one or more instruments, usually in an inner part, but often in the bass or upper part as well. It can also be an interval or chord. The sustaining element acts like a glue which can hold together the most rhythmically hectic passages. In fact, the rhythmic excitement is increased rather than diminished by the added contrast of a sustaining element.

This sustaining element might be compared to the effect of the sostenuto pedal on the piano. These elements can either be part of the harmony or a pedal tone. If they exist over many measures in the winds, they are usually alternated between winds, one instrument being tied over to the first beat of the measure in which the second wind enters, giving the effect of a continuously sustained tone while giving the wind players a chance to breathe and rest their embouchures. In the strings, the note is simply tied for its entire duration, the players changing bows where necessary; since each player changes bows at a different time, the effect is that of a continuous tone. A sustaining element can also be an ostinato figure or a roll on an instrument of definite or indefinite pitch (1:47–53, 57–63 horn; 2:20–21 horn, 28–31 low woodwinds and strings; 3:4–11, 16–18 horn, 30–38 bassoon and horn, 39–41 woodwinds; 4:9 horn and violas, 14–15 basses; 5:9–17 low woodwinds; 6:58–62 woodwinds and horns, 63–75 horns, 7:20–23 bassoon).

RHYTHMIC ELEMENTS

Usually the melody and accompaniment form at least two separate rhythmic elements. Often each of these elements can be further broken down into the overall rhythm and one or more simplified versions of it. For instance, the melody may be accented by being partially doubled, perhaps on strong beats, by another instrument or group of instruments of different color playing staccato. The accompaniment may be continuous in one instrument, another may play only on the strong beats, another on the offbeats, adding both rhythmic accent and variety of color to the various elements (1:65–69 intermittent chords; 5:16–18 intermittent chords; 6:76–85 intermittent chords; 7:1 trombone accents melody, 4–7, 13 intermittent chords).

TEXTURE

Most orchestration makes use of continual contrast between thick and thin textures to emphasize structural sections of the music. Continuation of the same texture for more than a few pages becomes monotonous. Furthermore, most passages, including all the excerpts quoted in this text, contain changes of texture every few beats.

BALANCE

At all times the most important elements should be orchestrated more powerfully than the background elements. Choice of instruments should depend on their range, technique, the strong and weak parts of their range, the number of instruments playing, and the dynamic of the passage. A crescendo or decrescendo will usually upset the balance and therefore instruments will be added or deleted in the course of the dynamic change. This addition and deletion of instruments also result in increased or decreased sonority which helps support and make more effective the dynamic change. Also, a better crescendo will be attained by the addition of instruments over the course of the crescendo. By the same token, a *fp* or any note or chord with a strong accent can be enhanced by giving the brass, percussion, and strings a sharp staccato accent on the beat and letting just woodwinds (or woodwinds with tremolo strings, etc.) sustain. In quieter passages, *any* instrument can accent a beat for any other (for example, a pizzicato in the strings, a note on the harp, the crotales). Likewise, sections in which the outer parts diverge or converge in pitch must add or delete instruments to maintain a consistent texture and balance.

TONE COLOR

The choice of tone color for a passage will depend on whether one wishes to contrast elements or blend them. Usually moving and stationary parts are arranged in contrasting colors. Groups or sections can also be juxtaposed on notes of a melody or chords to create an imitative effect, or a chord can be passed from one section or group of instruments to another, sometimes while one section makes a diminuendo and the other a crescendo to gradually transfer the sonority.

In a typical score, some combination of winds and strings are playing together about three-quarters of the time, the strings alone about one-fifth of the time, and the winds alone rarely (1:83–99). Even though the strings can play more or less continuously, various sections and the entire group of strings should be allowed to rest. Short rests within parts tend to lighten the overall sonority. Nothing sounds thicker than continuously sustained notes in all parts. It is a good idea to look through scores of all periods and notice how many rests there are even in sections where the instrument is "playing" all the time.

Flutes, clarinets, bassoons, and horns are the winds used most often within a score, the oboes somewhat less often, then the trumpets, trombones, and tuba. Notice that the more powerful instruments are usually saved for less frequent powerful effects. As with all extreme effects of color, dynamics, or anything else, the effect varies in inverse proportion to how often it is used. Therefore avoid using strong brass too much, avoid using the percussion just to create noise, and avoid scoring which depends on nothing more than a succession of sound effects.

STRUCTURE

Much of the effectiveness of an orchestration depends on the contrast of various sections in terms of the structure of the whole piece, not just in terms of individual sections. Instrumental use should be balanced over an entire score. Thickness and lightness, highly colored and homogeneous sections, homophony and counterpoint, should appear in proportions which create continual interest as the orchestral treatment unravels. An instrument entering on an important part should have rested for several measures before playing so that the new entrance will be as fresh and effective as possible. In fact, if an instrument is allowed to rest, any number of entries of the same instrument can be made within the same work, each sounding fresh and new. Also, instruments should enter and contrasts of different combinations of instruments should be made at important structural joints, not in the middle of a phrase, unless a dramatic effect is desired.

The return of a musical section should be varied in some way. Often only the instrumentation will be changed. If there are more extensive changes in the musical structure of the section—variation, a different octave or transposition to another key, change of dynamic or other alteration—certain changes in orchestration will usually be necessary, such as different instruments, addition or deletion of instruments, new combination of instruments, additional or deleted doubling, or filling.

Figure 28–4 shows two highly contrasting appearances of the same theme in *Scheherezade* (a-1 and 2) and the gradual orchestral buildup of a simple repeated phrase through a long crescendo by canonic imitation and the addition of instruments (Figure 28–4b).

SPACIAL EFFECTS

Many Renaissance scores, a few eighteenth- and nineteenth-century scores, and many twentieth-century scores make use of specific spacial arrangement of instruments and/or the use of spacially separated instrumental groups for imitative or antiphonal effects. In this case another dimension is added to the considerations of balance, contrast and blend.

As a final example, compare Britten's scoring of the same music for each section of the orchestra and, finally, the full orchestra (Figure 28–5).

Figure 28–4

Rimsky-Korsakov, Scheherezade

Figure 28–4 (cont.) a-2)

359

Figure 28–4 (cont.)   Bernstein, *Overture to Candide*

b)

Figure 28–4 (cont.)

Figure 28-4 (cont.)

362

Figure 28-4 (cont.)

a) woodwinds alone

b) brass alone

Figure 28-5 (cont.)

c) strings alone

d) percussion alone

Figure 28–5 (cont.)

e) full orchestra

Figure 28–5 (cont.)

29

Arranging
For Orchestra

1. TYPES OF ARRANGING

When one is writing original music, the orchestration is, or should be, part of the original creative conception. The composer's first sketches should include copious indications of instrumentation. He should not think up a line and then decide which instrument should play it, but be thinking of a particular instrument or group of instruments as he is conceiving the music for the first time. This is true *orchestration*.

Arranging, however, is done from a preexisting musical work and has several possible levels of complexity:

1. Transcription. In its simplest form, this is simply recreating preexisting orchestration from, say, memory or a record (as occasionally required by ballet companies when scores are not available).
2. Additional instrumentation (as in Mozart's arrangement of Handel's *Messiah*; Figure 29–13) or substitution of other instrumentation (such as reduction for small orchestra).
3. Transcription for orchestra of a work originally written for another instrument or instruments, such as piano, organ, or a chamber group.
4. The orchestration of a melody to which one has added original accompaniment, harmonization, countermelodies, and so on.
5. The orchestration of a melody or melodies to which one has added accompaniment and also written transitional passages.

6. The use of a preexisting melody in a larger work where the melody forms only the thematic material and where much of the development is original. This approaches original composition and is the sort of work done by Broadway arrangers in dance sequences and transitional sections.

Arranging of preexisting music is a good way to gain practical experience with the problems of orchestration. It is also a practical skill which can be put to use to create new repertoire for various groups.

Arrangement for full orchestra of pieces written for chamber ensembles or string orchestra (see Figure 29–17) is a useful exercise. Next best is arranging organ music or music written for two pianos or piano, four hands. The greatest problems and the greatest challenges arise in arranging for orchestra music originally written for solo piano. This is because the piano, being a mechanical instrument, often breaks chords that would be sustained in at least some of the instruments of the orchestra. The sostenuto pedal on the piano allows the strings to vibrate sympathetically with the overtones of the notes being played on the piano and therefore creates sustained notes and chords which are possible in the orchestra only by held notes. Also, piano technique does not allow for more than an octave in each hand, and therefore the piano work lacks much filling in of the middle parts and doubling of parts which would take place in the orchestra. A work arranged from a piano score simply by assigning different notes to different instruments without any doubling of parts or harmonic filler would sound thin and empty. To reproduce the sonority of the piano, many more notes are usually needed in the orchestra.

Another useful method of analyzing orchestration is to make reductions for piano of orchestral works. This is also a necessity for the composer in cases of works involving voices or instrumental soloists for rehearsal purposes (the *vocal score* or *piano reduction*). Reducing orchestral scores to three or four staves for study purposes is also valuable.

Another useful learning technique is to take a piano reduction, reorchestrate it for full orchestra, and then compare one's orchestration with the original.

2. PROCEDURES IN ARRANGING

The instruments chosen for an orchestral arrangement should fit with the period and both general and personal style of the piece. Throughout the nineteenth and twentieth centuries instrumental color has become an increasingly important aspect of orchestral music, so that while a classical symphony arranged for piano still makes musical sense, many contemporary works would make no sense whatsoever stripped of their orchestral colors.

The score paper should be prepared beforehand with all bar lines drawn so that the instrumentation of various sections can be sketched out and planned in advance for maximum effect. Then the arranger must break the music down into its constituent elements: melody, countermelody, bass line, inner parts, counterpoint, and so on and choose which instruments or combinations of instruments he wants for each element, with proper regard to balance, contrast, and blend.

3. ARRANGEMENT OF PIANISTIC MELODIC LINES FOR ORCHESTRAL INSTRUMENTS

It is important to remember that each line on the piano is single, but that there are always several instruments available in the orchestra to play the same line, solo, doubled at the unison or octave(s), or in two separate versions, one simplified to add rhythmic emphasis (Figure 29–1).

Figure 29–1

Melodic lines with wide leaps, though often perfectly playable by instruments such as the flute, clarinet, or violin, are often divided among instruments of similar tone color for ease of playing or for rhythmic emphasis. If they are not of primary melodic importance, they may be more effective orchestrally in a simplified version (Figure 29–2).

Figure 29–2

Often melodic lines on the piano are written in broken octaves, thirds, sixths, or combinations of both. In this case the strongest sonority on string or wind instruments is obtained by repeated notes on each part; this also gives a stronger rhythmic pulse (Figure 29–3a). Also, one part may be simplified for greater rhythmic emphasis and clearer outlining of the melodic line (b and c). Never should an instrument or group of instruments be asked to play only off the beat in a rapid passage. The effect will be rhythmically weak, treacherous in performance, and not half so good as the first three arrangements in Figure 29–3 (compare 29–3d). Of course, in a moderate tempo, syncopated chords in winds or strings are quite practical (e).

Figure 29–3   Chopin, *Étude, Op. 25, No. 11*

Often melodic lines and inner voices are combined in the right hand on the piano in broken chords. In this case, the melody must be sustained by an orchestral instrument, preferably of differing tone color from the instruments of the accompaniment. The inner parts can alternate in winds or strings (Figure 29–4a) or, often in winds, be reduced to repeated notes (b).

Figure 29–4

Naturally, any appropriate unison or octave doublings can be combined with any of the above.

4. ARRANGEMENT OF PIANISTIC CHORDAL ACCOMPANIMENTS FOR ORCHESTRAL INSTRUMENTS

A sustained chord (or note or interval) on the piano can be arranged in the orchestra for (Figure 29–5a) instruments sustaining the chord, (b) a tremolo on the strings, (c) trills or tremoli in the winds, (d) repeated notes in the winds, or (e) a roll on percussion such as the timpani in combination with any of the above.

Figure 29–5

Repeated chords can be arranged by (Figure 29–6a) alternating notes in winds or strings, (b) repeated notes, (c) tremolo on the strings, (d) alternating repeated chords between different groups of instruments, or any combination of these techniques.

Figure 29–6

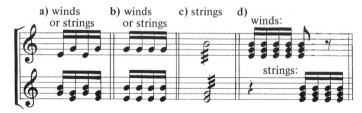

Broken chord accompaniments consist generally of a bass line and two or more inner parts, all of which should be treated as separate lines in the orchestra, either with sustaining or intermittent bass lines and with or without sustaining instruments on the inner voices, doublings, and fillers (see Figure 29–7). Although it is possible and sometimes desirable for instruments such as the clarinet or harp to play broken-chord accompaniments, the effect is useful only in very light textures and is not at all the same effect as the arpeggiated accompaniment in the piano with the sustaining (sostenuto) pedal.

Figure 29–7

Wider arpeggios are often simplified by utilizing relatively smaller ranges in each instrument (Figure 29–8).

Figure 29–8

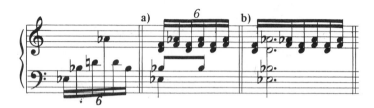

Syncopated chordal accompaniments, if not too fast, can either be arranged by combining the syncopation with notes on the beat to give the instruments greater rhythmic security and force (if syncopation continues for a few measures without notes on the beat, it becomes the beat in itself to the listener)

or by combining syncopation in one group of instruments with repeated notes in others (Figure 29–9).

Figure 29–9

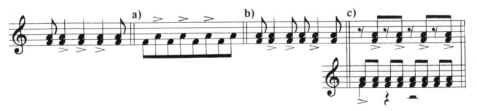

Arpeggios can also be divided between instruments or filled in for greater sonority (Figure 29–10).

Figure 29–10

Finally, arpeggios which take place over a wide range on the piano can either be divided among different instruments or rearranged in smaller limits, or a combination of these methods may be used (Figure 29–11).

Figure 29–11   Chopin, *Étude, Op. 25, No. 12*

5. GENERAL CONSIDERATIONS

Following is a list of some general things to keep in mind when arranging piano music for orchestra.

1. Melodic lines, either as primary melody, as countermelody, or in counterpoint, must be clearly distinguished from and well balanced with the other lines or accompaniment. A new entry on an important melodic line should be preceded by a few measures' rest in that instrument if possible.

2. Don't divide melodic lines between instruments or groups of instruments of different color unless a contrast in tone is desired. If a melody leaves the range of an instrument, try to continue it with an instrument of similar color.

3. Doublings and harmonic fillers (added inner parts), and sustaining notes, intervals, or chords are usually necessary in arranging piano music for orchestra. Often the melody will be doubled at the octave above, or occasionally at the octave below. When it is doubled at the octave above, the inner parts may also be doubled at the octave above. In certain cases it might be useful to switch the alto and tenor lines for better spacing or balance. The bass is often doubled at the octave below for greater resonance. A better blend is achieved with instruments of similar tone color on doubled parts. Generally, the harmony is filled in above middle c.

4. If a separate inner part is added, it must fit with the harmony and other parts. Separate countermelodies can be added but must be treated with discretion since they add a new creative element to the work. Each line in each instrument must function as an independent part, just as in vocal harmonization.

5. Many scores mix or alternate homophonic and contrapuntal sections. Contrast and blend are important considerations for obtaining clarity in the orchestration.

6. Loud sections are generally doubled and filled more than quiet sections, which can be more transparent.

7. The same texture should be kept for each section unless imitative or dramatic contrasts are desired. The most striking changes of texture usually occur at important structural divisions. Echoing of one section or group of instruments by another is common, often with contrasts of loud and soft between sections.

8. Sometimes the original music is transposed to another key to make it simpler for orchestral instruments or for reasons of range or sonority.

9. It is, of course, impossible to obtain the sound of the piano in the orchestra or vice versa. Arranging consists of being as faithful to the original spirit of the music as possible while creating an effective version in the new medium. It is not possible, for instance, to imitate on the piano the string sounds shown in Figure 29–12.

Figure 29–12   Mozart, *Symphony No. 40 in G Minor*

6. EXAMPLES OF DIFFERENT TYPES OF ARRANGEMENTS

1. In the examples from Mozart's additional instrumentation to Handel's *Messiah* (Figure 29–13), several degrees of alteration mentioned above are illustrated. Handel's original instrumentation (generally only strings) is double-bracketed on the lower staves and Mozart's added without brackets on the upper staves. It should be mentioned that many musical purists insist that the *Messiah* should be performed as originally written, without additional instrumentation. It is known, however, that Handel himself performed the *Messiah* with as many oboes, bassoons, flutes, trumpets, horns, and timpani as were available. At one performance five horn players were paid for performing. Trombones seem not to have been available to Handel. In any case, Mozart uses them only in the overture. Whatever one's feelings about the "original" *Messiah,* if there is such a thing, Mozart's accompaniments are a fascinating study in instrumentation.

A. Overture (Figure 29–13a). Harmony is filled in.
B. No. 5 (29–13b). Imitation is added in the flute.
C. No. 8 (29–13c). Unison doublings and additional inner parts (fillers) are added.
D. No. 22 (29–13d). Sustaining chords are added in the woodwinds.
E. No. 24 (29–13e). Countermelody in octaves is added in the winds.
F. No. 38 (29–13f). Sustained chords are added in the winds against repeated notes in the strings; there is a new rhythmic element in the trumpets and timpani.
G. No. 48 (29–13g). A beautiful two-part counterpoint in the violas sometimes parallels vocal lines and sometimes is independent.

Figure 29–13   Händel, *The Messiah*

a)

Figure 29–13 (cont.)

b)

c)

Figure 29–13 (cont.)

d)

8287

e)

8287

Figure 29-13 (cont.)

f)

g)

2. Beethoven's arrangement of the Funeral March from his piano sonata Op. 26 for his incidental music to *Leonore Prohaska* illustrates the following (see Figure 29–14):

A. The music has been transposed from a^b minor to b minor, perhaps because it is an easier key for the orchestral instruments to play in, perhaps because of the ranges of the instruments, perhaps so that the timpani could be tuned to play the dominant *below* the tonic rather than above (since the timpani range in Beethoven's day was F to f), but most likely because of the keys in which the horns were crooked.

B. Notice the brighter oboes and trumpets have been left out of the instrumentation and the violins and violas enter only to add their color and sonority to the cadence chords at the ends of the phrases.

C. The flutes and clarinets double the soprano, alto, and tenor lines an octave higher.

D. The horns in D double the fifth of the chord at the octave, enclosing the bassoons.

E. The first horn in E doubles the first bassoon on the important melodic line, which happens to be in the alto.

F. The second horn in E doubles the bass in the first bar and then drops to the third of the chord in the second measure. It then rests until the fifth bar.

G. The timpani plays a somewhat independent rhythm to the bass, partly because of the two notes available to it, partly for rhythmic emphasis.

Figure 29–14

a)

Andante maestoso

Beethoven, *Sonata, Op. 26*

Piano

Figure 29–14 (cont.)

Beethoven, *Leonore Prohaska*

In the arrangement of the beginning of the trio of the same movement (Figure 29–14b), note the following:

H. The tremolo in the piano has been arranged with a timpani roll combined with a string tremolo and a sustained octave in the horns.

I. Note the division of the music between strings and winds.

Figure 29–14 (cont.)   Beethoven, *Leonore Prohaska*

Figure 29-15

Weber, *Invitation a la Valse*

382

3. In Berlioz's transcription of Weber's *Invitation to the Dance,* transposed from D♭ to the easier orchestral key of D (Figure 29–15), notice:

A. The bass line is divided between sustained cellos and double basses on the beat only for rhythmic emphasis.
B. The inner parts are doubled in second violins, violas, and horns.
C. The melody is alternated between first violins and woodwinds in octaves for a particularly colorful sonority.

4. In Ravel's orchestration of Mussorgsky's *Pictures at an Exhibition* (Figure 29–16):

A. Flutes doubled by oboes, later by clarinets and bassoons, accented by pizzicato strings and xylophone, have the chords that are in the right hand of the piano version.
B. The bass line is divided between muted tuba and muted trumpet (to maintain a legato line and allow the tuba to breathe). Timpani, double bassoon, and pizzicato lower strings accent the beginning of each phrase.
C. The octaves in bar 9 are divided between low woodwinds, horns, and low strings.

In the repeat (bars 11 to 20), Ravel has changed not only the tone color but the dynamics of the original as well, making it a quiet echo.

D. Now the chords are in the celesta, accented by pizzicato strings and harp harmonics.
E. The bass line, divided between bass clarinet and horn (stopped at the end) is accented by pizzicato lower strings.
F. A new sustaining element, a glissando, has been added in the strings playing from an open string up to a natural harmonic, bowing at the fingerboard.
G. The harp has the final octave alone.

Figure 29–16   Mussorgsky, *Pictures at an Exhibition*

a)

Figure 29-16 (cont.)   Mussorgsky-Ravel, *Pictures at an Exhibition*

b)

Figure 29–16 (cont.)

385

Figure 29-16 (cont.)

  5. Copland's *Appalachian Spring* was originally written for thirteen instruments and later orchestrated by the composer for full orchestra:

  A. Greater variety of color is obtained with more woodwinds available; triangle is used to add color and rhythmic emphasis (Figure 29–17a).
  B. The two-part hymn tune originally in the strings is now in the brass; the scale fragments are in the strings rather than the piano (29–17b).
  C. Doublings create richer sonority and a climax with an effect quite different from that of the original suite (29–17c).

Doublings in the orchestra version create richer sonority and a climax with an effect quite different from that of the original suite.

Figure 29–17   Copland, *Appalachian Spring*

Figure 29–17 (cont.)

b-1)

Figure 29–17 (cont.)

b-2)

30

Scoring for
Other Ensembles

1. CHAMBER MUSIC

Chamber music simply means music written for a small group of instruments, to be played in a room rather than in the concert hall. Some common categories are:

1. *Sonata*. A work for solo instrument or for a solo instrument with piano accompaniment. Sonatas have been written for nearly every conceivable instrument.
2. *Duo*. A work for two instruments of the same or different types (except if one is a piano, in which case it is a sonata). Duos for the same type of instrument are often used as teaching pieces, the teacher playing one part and the pupil the other.
3. *Trio*. A work for three instruments, often three strings or two strings (usually violin and cello) with piano. Occasionally winds, strings, and piano are combined, as in Mozart's and Schumann's trios for clarinet, viola, and piano, and Beethoven's and Brahms's trios for clarinet, cello, and piano.
4. *Quartet*. A work for four instruments. The string quartet for two violins, viola, and cello is the most popular form of chamber composition, with works by Mozart, Haydn, Beethoven, Bartók, Carter, and others (see Chapter 7).
5. *Quintet*. A work for five instruments. Woodwind quintets, consisting of flute, oboe, clarinet, horn, and bassoon, have been a popular form in the twentieth

century. Mozart wrote quintets, adding a second viola to the usual string quartet. Schubert added a double bass; he also used four strings with piano ("*Trout*" *Quintet*).

6. *Sextet.* A work for six instruments, such as Beethoven's for two clarinets, two bassoons, and two horns.
7. *Septet.* A work for seven instruments, such as Beethoven's *Septet* combining strings and winds.
8. *Octet.* A work for eight instruments, such as Mendelssohn's *Octet* for eight strings. Mozart's *divertimenti* for winds were usually for two oboes, two bassoons, and two horns with often two clarinets or two English horns added. Schubert's *Octet* combines strings and winds.

Music for chamber ensembles usually presents greater technical demands than that for orchestral instruments. The individual parts are generally more independent and interesting even in homophonic textures. Melody with simple accompaniment is found less often. The individual parts also tend to be treated more equally in the overall musical structure. Parts commonly cross more often than in the orchestra. As in the orchestra, the composer should avoid only two solo string instruments playing in unison; slight differences of intonation and rates of vibrato, producing "beats," will be clearly audible. Strings in octaves are also better with more than just two. This is true to a lesser degree with winds, especially if they are the same type of instrument and are not playing in their extreme high range.

Winds often juxtapose their contrasting colors, but use of instruments such as the trumpet and trombone in chamber music requires careful calculation of balance and sonority as well as players sensitive to these considerations. The horn must also be carefully handled. A sustained high note on the horn, even in *piano*, can drown the rest of the winds in a small ensemble. The penetrating tone of the oboe must also be remembered. It is interesting to note that Mozart made three versions of his G minor Symphony No. 40, one with no clarinets, which he later added in the second version. In the third version he replaced oboes with clarinets whenever the winds were playing alone.

Music for strings, winds and percussion alone has already been considered in Chapters 7, 16, and 22.

A *chamber orchestra* is one with a small number of strings and winds singly or in pairs.

2. SOLO INSTRUMENTS WITH ORCHESTRA

Solo instruments used with orchestra in works such as concertos must be treated in such a way that they will be heard against the orchestra. Therefore accompaniments are usually light when the soloist is playing. Fewer and less powerful instruments, lighter textures with more rests and short note values, and quiet dynamics are the rule. Of course, more powerful solo instruments are better able to compete with the orchestra. For big climaxes requiring an orchestral tutti with the soloist, the soloist is usually given the melodic material along with the orchestra in unison or octaves or some figuration in a different rhythm.

The most popular solo instruments are the piano and violin, largely because of their technical capabilities. The cello, woodwinds, brass, other strings, and percussion follow in that order. Following are the ways in which soloist and orchestra can be combined:

1. Passages in which either the soloist or orchestra play alone.
2. A melody in the solo instrument with orchestral accompaniment. (In the Mendelssohn excerpt (Figure 30–1a) the solo violin easily balances against the orchestra because of the contrasting timbre of the solo instrument, its position above the other instruments, the fact that the winds rest every other bar, and the fact that the strings are playing spiccato and pizzicato with frequent rests at *pp*.)
3. A melody in the orchestra with arpeggios or other figuration in the solo instrument (such as the opening of the second Rachmaninoff concerto).
4. A dialogue between soloist and orchestra (as in the second movement of the fourth Beethoven concerto).
5. More complex texture, with the soloist and orchestra taking equal parts.

Most works with soloist continually alternate these combinations to create contrast of texture. Works with solo winds carefully treat combinations of the soloist with the orchestral winds so that he will not be covered. Often, use of the same type of wind in the orchestra is restricted to orchestral tuttis or the instrument is omitted from the orchestra altogether. The organ (see Appendix A) is used with the orchestra either as a solo instrument (Saint-Saëns' Symphony No. 3) or as reinforcement of orchestral sonority, playing chords in tutti passages, for example, or sustaining pedal tones with the instruments, (as in many large choral works such as the Mahler Symphonies Nos. 2 and 8). Figure 30–1 shows two contrasting styles of writing for solo violin and orchestra.

3. SOLO VOICE WITH ORCHESTRA

Accompaniment to the voice must be particularly carefully dealt with. It is not just a matter of not covering the voice, but of not forcing the singer to sing loudly in order to be heard over the orchestra. Thus the singer is free to interpret the music and the words can be clearly heard. Loud orchestral tutti should be used only when the singer is silent, though loud staccato chords in the orchestra can be interpolated while the singer is singing. Sustained notes in winds or strings, especially in high registers, are likely to cover the voice. The shorter

Figure 30–1

a)

Figure 30–1 (cont.)   Berg, *Violin Concerto*

the note values and the more rests in the parts, the more likely that the singer will be easily heard. Strings are least likely to cover the voice, woodwinds somewhat more likely, and brass quite likely. Mozart used trumpets, trombones, and timpani in only four numbers in *Don Giovanni*. Again, just marking parts *ppp* is often not enough. These considerations are especially important when the singer is in a low register. The voice is heard best when it is the highest part in the orchestra or, since this is not always possible, especially with male voices, when there is some space between the voice and the instruments. The eighteenth-century *recitativo secco,* in which words were sung in a *parlato* (spoken) style with the accompaniment only of harpsichord, was revived by Stravinsky in *The Rake's Progress. Recitativo accompagnato,* in which strings or winds supply the accompaniment, is still used, though styles of harmony may have changed. Both these styles are used to allow the words to come through clearly with a minimum of musical complexity.

A countermelody, or *obbligato,* is often added in an instrument, usually a woodwind. Doubling of the vocal line is usually done only for climaxes, when the voice is singing full voice in the high, or for special coloristic effects. Doubling in quiet passages is rare. The instrumental doubling can also represent a simplified version of the vocal melody (repeated syllables on the same note are seldom given separate attacks in the orchestra); a few notes may be doubled for accent or doubling may occur for isolated phrases. Female voices are often doubled at the unison with instruments such as violin or viola, oboe or clarinet; men's voices are often doubled with viola or cello, bassoon or horn. Doublings at the octave above can add color to the part but must be carefully handled so as not to cover the voice.

The excerpt from *Il Trovatore* in Figure 30–2a is unusual in its combination of orchestral tutti and voice for coloristic reasons. The *pp* marking helps, but the real reason the passage balances is that the notes are of brief duration and each instrument is playing in a range where it is able to produce a controlled, quiet tone. Notice in Figure 30–2b how Mahler thins the orchestration when the voice enters (see pages 396–99).

Accompaniments for ensembles of two or more voices tend to be somewhat more heavily orchestrated and more doubling is used. Three or four voices can produce quite a good deal of sound.

4. CHORUS WITH ORCHESTRA

The chorus, having greater dynamic power than solo voices, is generally much more strongly supported by the orchestra and parts are often doubled, especially in contrapuntal textures. Lighter orchestration must be used with male chorus, still lighter with female voices. Much, of course, depends on the size of the chorus, which can vary from a few voices to over a hundred, depending on the work and the orchestral forces involved.

Figure 30–2   Verdi, *Il Trovatore*

Figure 30–2 (cont.)

Figure 30–2 (cont.)

Mahler, *Das Lied von der Erde*

Figure 30–2 (cont.)

Passages for solo voice with chorus and orchestra need quiet choral writing, preferably in a different register than the soloist's, and an orchestration as light as for solo voice alone. Offstage voices must be accompanied with the very lightest orchestration if they are to be heard. Note the different orchestral accompaniments for solo quartet and chorus in the Beethoven excerpt in Figure 30–3a.

It is important in general to write choral parts as simply as possible, and especially to avoid close dissonances. Choral singers are not generally trained as professional soloists (see Chapter 24). Also, singers rely entirely on their ears to sing pitches and therefore music must be much clearer and simpler than for instruments, unless, of course, one is writing for a specially trained chorus that specializes in difficult music. Note how Stravinsky has the chorus singing the mere outlines of the harmony, with the orchestra doing the doubling and harmonic filling (Figure 30–3b). This is much more effective than dividing sections of the chorus, which is a useful and practical effect only in *a capella* (unaccompanied) passages. Much greater distinction and clarity are obtained by giving the chorus simple lines and intervals and letting the orchestra do the busy work. In the Schoenberg excerpt (Figure 30–3c) clarity is obtained by using few instruments at any one time with the chorus and wide spacing between the chorus line and the instruments. The doubling of the chorus in the trombone helps with the difficult intervals.

5. PIT ORCHESTRAS

Opera orchestras range from the chamber orchestras of Britten to the mammoth symphonic ensembles of Wagner and Strauss. It must be realized, however, that of the several hundred opera houses in the world, only the largest have pits that can accomodate orchestras of this size; it is largely for this reason that these works are performed only by major companies. Triple winds, especially if there is a large complement of percussion, will tend to limit performance opportunities. Forty instruments can be contained in most pits but over sixty becomes problematical.

Most ballets (with the exception of works like *The Rite of Spring,* which are almost invariably performed in the concert hall anyway) employ orchestras of double winds, four horns, two trumpets, three trombones, tuba, timpani, one or two percussionists, and strings. Since ballet companies often perform on tour and use *pick-up* orchestras hired on the spot with little rehearsal, ballet music should be easy to play, be functional, and use frequent doublings to reinforce what may possibly be an uneven string section.

Figure 30-3

a)

Beethoven, *Missa Solemnis*

Figure 30–3 (cont.)

Figure 30–3 (cont.)

Figure 30–3 (cont.)

Figure 30–3 (cont.)   Stravinsky, *Symphony of Psalms*

Figure 30-3 (cont.)

Figure 30–3 (cont.)   Schoenberg, *A Survivor from Warsaw*

31

Bringing
The Score
To Performance

1. REPRODUCTION OF THE
ORCHESTRAL SCORE

Printed scores are produced by a process of engraving. This process is so expensive, however, that it is seldom used with new scores unless they enjoy an unusual popularity. Most final scores are copied by the composer on transparent paper from which copies are made by a black-line blueprint process. Black opaque ink must be used such as Pelikan drawing ink, Higgins Engrossing ink, China ink, or other similar ink. Although various brands of music writing pens are on the market, they tend to become clogged after several uses even if carefully washed after each use. The most convenient pen is a simple music writing point, medium italic, or artist's sketch point that fits in a handle. The point should draw a thick horizontal line for note heads and beams, and it should draw a thin vertical line for the writing of stems.

Various sizes of paper with various numbers and sizes of staves are available. Paper is available already bracketed with the names of the instruments for various standard ensembles—orchestral, band, and jazz—as well as for piano or piano-vocal scores. This paper is also available with bar lines, usually four to a page. This can save an enormous amount of time when one is scoring larger works and it is, of course, visually clearer than manuscript. The copies of the score are then ring bound.

The following firms sell reproduction paper and make copies. They all do business by mail. Since prices and quality of work differ, it might be wise to shop around. It should be mentioned that any blueprint company can do black-line music reproduction but they are unlikely to have paper sensitive on both sides or the proper binding.

Alpheus Music Corporation
1433 North Cole Place
Hollywood, Cal. 90028

Huey Company
19 South Wabash Avenue
Chicago, Ill. 60603

Associated Music
  Copy Service Corporation
231 West 54th Street
New York, N.Y. 10019

Independent Music
  Publishers, Inc.
215 East 42nd Street
New York, N.Y. 10017

Henry Bonar
22 West 48th Street
New York, N.Y. 10036

Music Graphics
117 Washington Street
San Diego, Cal. 92103

Circle Blueprint
225 West 57th Street
New York, N.Y. 10019

Valle Music Reproduction
12441 Riverside Drive
North Hollywood, Cal. 91607

2. ORCHESTRA PARTS

If a work contains instrumental soloists or voices, it is necessary for rehearsal purposes to have a piano reduction (or *vocal score*) which includes solo or vocal parts and the orchestral music arranged for solo piano. With complex scores, one can try to include all the orchestral material in the piano part, making it virtually unplayable, or include the important material, especially that from which the singers or soloist will take their pitch or cue. Some scores include additional, unplayable material on separate staves in smaller notes.

Individual parts must also be copied out for each instrument in the orchestra. Orchestra parts, as well as piano reductions, are copied on transparent paper. The best size paper to use is ten-stave, 11 by 14 inches (28 by 35 cm) though $9\frac{1}{2}$ by 13 inches (24 by 33 cm) is also used as are other, less convenient sizes. If the score is a concert score, the copyist must naturally transpose the parts for the transposing instruments such as the clarinets and horns. Separate parts should also be made for each wind instrument, even if they appear two to a staff in the score. The parts must be planned so that each odd-numbered page ends at a place where there are rests in the part so that the player can turn the page without having to stop playing, even if half a page has to be left blank in order to do so. When this is not possible, accordion binding can be used: here the pages are bound together in a continuous strip that can be opened out three pages at a time. Of course, winds normally need rests to breathe anyway, so it would be a rare circumstance or a badly written score that did not have places for page turns. The strings, on the other hand, often play for prolonged periods without rest. In this case, since they play two players to a desk, one of the players can turn the page while the other keeps playing, although this is to be avoided if possible.

Following are rules for notation of orchestral parts:

1. The top of the first page of each part should contain the title of the work with the composer's name to the right. At the top left-hand corner should appear the name of the instrument and its position in its section (Fl. 1, Bsn. 2, Vln. I) as well as its transposition (Cl. in B-flat 1).

2. The part must contain all tempo indications which appear at the top of the score, including retards, accelerandos, fermatas, and so forth.

3. All dynamics, including crescendos and diminuendos, must appear below the staff.

4. All expression marks and phrasing must appear in the part also.

5. A solo string instrument or a *divisi* section for strings should be written on a separate staff, bracketed together with the rest of the section.

6. All bar numberings which appear in the score *must* appear in the parts as well.

7. *Cues* should be written whenever an instrument has to rest for more than a few bars. Cues are lines played by other instruments which will be prominent in the orchestra, either in a neighboring section, in the same section, or in instruments of similar range (for example, try to cue oboe with flute, bassoons with trombone). The cues are written with smaller note heads above or below the rests in the part. The name of instrument must be placed at the beginning of the cue.

8. A diagonal slash with dots on each side indicates that a bar is to be repeated. When there are more than two or three of these indications, small numbers should appear above the bars to show how many times the bar is to be repeated so the player does not lose count. This symbol can extend over two bars which are to be repeated as well. (See Figure 31–2).

9. A rest of more than a bar can be indicated by a long, thick, horizontal line in the middle of the staff with diagonal slashes at the end and a large number written above to show the number of bars' rest, or, less commonly today, by more complex symbols (see Figure 31–1). These symbols cannot be used when, in the course of the rests, there is a change of tempo, fermata, double bar, change of key signature, or rehearsal number or letter. Then separate bars must be written so that any such change can be indicated in the part.

10. When the instrument does not play for an entire movement, the title of the movement appears and beneath it the word *tacet,* indicating that the player is to rest for that movement. Also, when an instrument has no more to play in a movement, the indication *tacet al fine* eliminates the necessity of writing out measures of rest to the end of the movement.

11. The abbreviation *V.S. (volta subito)* indicates that a page is to be turned rapidly because the player must play immediately over the page turn.

Figure 31–1

It is of paramount importance that the parts be checked as carefully as possible for any errors in order to save time at rehearsal. Many a piece has been thrown out at rehearsal because the parts were impossible. Most important is to make a *bar plan sheet* showing all bar numbers and tempo changes so that each part can be checked against it to ensure that it contains the right number of bars. A wrong note can usually be picked out and corrected at a rehearsal in a relatively short time, but a missing bar can necessitate a search of several minutes since it may not be obvious at first where the bar should be.

Orchestra parts may be copied by the performing organization (either *jobbed-out* to a professional copyist or done by the orchestra librarian) or a part of the commissioning fee for a work can include parts copying, which is then the responsibility of the composer. Since professional copyists are extremely expensive (a recent opera of mine cost the producing organization $17,000 for orchestra parts alone!), the composer must often copy his own or find students or other people who are willing and able to do the work cheaply. Quality of work should be the main criterion, however, since illegible parts are of no use to anyone. Figure 31–2 illustrates an orchestral part.

Figure 31–2

3. REHEARSAL

The luxury of extensive time for rehearsal is largely a thing of the past in professional music today, mainly because of the cost. The nine weeks of rehearsal alloted to *Robert le Diable* (partly at Meyerbeer's own expense) at the Paris Opera in the nineteenth century has few modern counterparts. Although the situation is somewhat better in Europe, an American orchestra is often lucky to get three rehearsals for a concert. The length of a rehearsal is established by union regulations at two and one-half hours with one ten- or fifteen-minute break. When the rehearsal time is over the union representative in the orchestra will come forward and stop the conductor should he go overtime by so much as a minute. If overtime is necessary, time-and-a half must be paid, an enormous expense for ninety-odd musicians. Sometimes entire operas are put together in as little as a week with three or even fewer orchestra rehearsals. Under these circumstances, flawless and perfectly legible parts are not merely desirable but mandatory. Also, the music must be practically written for the instruments. Performers know immediately whether or not the composer understands their instrument.

It is of utmost importance that the composer be present at rehearsals. As he hears his music being brought to life, he may find many sections which were miscalculated and do not sound as he imagined they would. This is the time for taking notes of corrections and improvements in the parts to be passed on to the players before the next rehearsal (and to the conductor as well so that he will not be surprised at the next rehearsal by what he hears from the orchestra).

Some conductors are more experienced than others in rehearsing new works, but the composer should listen to any suggestions for changes the conductor might make and act on them if he agrees. On the other hand, if he disagrees, he must be firm enough to stand up for his original conception. Most conductors will accede to the composer's wishes, though if the composer is unreasonable and a section just doesn't "sound," he may find that the conductor will take instruments down an octave, delete them, cut entire sections, or even reject the piece for performance entirely. In the best of circumstances, the composer will find that his bowings or wind phrasings have been changed, probably for the better. Certainly Toscanini's additions to Beethoven's horn and trumpet parts where Beethoven obviously would have continued a line except for the fact that the notes were not available on the natural instruments, and Solti's doubling of the woodwinds in the tutti sections of Beethoven's symphonies to balance with the modern orchestra's strings, a practice common in Beethoven's day in concerts with large string sections, are examples of justifiable realizations of the composer's probable intentions.

In rehearsal, the conductor may ask the composer whether he wants a wind passage slurred or tongued, a string passage legato or on separate bows, and on or off the string. When particular bars are referred to orally, expressions such as "the fourth bar of letter C," "two before D," and "bar 128" are used.

Finally, it should be kept in mind that many scores have not been performed because they called for an unusual number of instruments or an unusual type of instrument. In these cases, extra players must be hired, sometimes at prohibitive expense. Remember, an orchestra can always play the Beethoven Fifth instead of your piece.

4. PERFORMANCE

The orchestra traditionally tunes to the a^1 of the oboe. This tuning is done section by section and usually directed by the concertmaster, who can ask a section to retune if he is not satisfied. The effect of a piece can, of course, vary from performance to performance depending on the conductor, the orchestra, the acoustics of the hall, and the temperature and humidity in the case of outdoor performances. A little more than a second's reverberation in an almost-filled hall is considered ideal. Performances may have to be amplified, especially out of doors. This almost inevitably results in a certain amount of distortion and imbalance of the orchestra.

Most orchestras seat the woodwinds facing the conductor, first flute and first oboe in the center with the other players strung out on either side in the first row, first clarinet and first bassoon together in the center of the second row with the other players filling out the row. The brass are usually placed at the back of the orchestra: horns, trumpets, trombones, and tuba from left to right. The percussion are usually to the left at the back of the orchestra but may spread out along both sides in the case of works with much percussion. The first violins are placed in a double row, two players to a desk, with the concert-master in the first outside chair to the left of the conductor. In the next double row, upstage, are the second violins, with the principal second in the first outside chair. Usually cellos are to the conductor's right, violas upstage, principal players in first outside chairs. The double basses are to the far right in a row facing the conductor. Sometimes the violas are downstage of the cellos but then their f-holes point away from the audience and they are not heard as well. Figure 31–3 (page 414) gives an orchestra seating chart.

In the late nineteenth century it was usual for the first violins to be on the conductor's left, the seconds on the right, giving rise to a better separation for antiphonal effects between the violins. This effect has been sacrificed today for a better blend between the two sections.

In the pit, of course, the orchestra must be spread out more from left to right but usually a similar seating is used. Some conductors prefer a return to the seating popular in German opera houses in the nineteenth century, with winds grouped on one side, strings on the other. This seems to sacrifice an overall blend in the orchestra as heard in the audience (*out front* or *in the house*).

5. PUBLISHING

Finding a publisher is always a difficult problem for the beginning composer. He should choose a publisher large enough to have the facilities to promote and distribute his music. He should also look through various scores in music stores to find which publishers specialize in the type of music he writes. It would be silly to take a symphony to a publisher who specializes in instructional material, for instance. There is a considerable market for instructional material, band music, chorus music, and almost anything for flute, since there are so many flute players in America.

Once the publisher has sent a contract, the composer should have it read by a lawyer who specializes in contracts of this sort. Usually, the composer will receive a small percentage (say 10 percent) of the income from sales of sheet

Figure 31-3

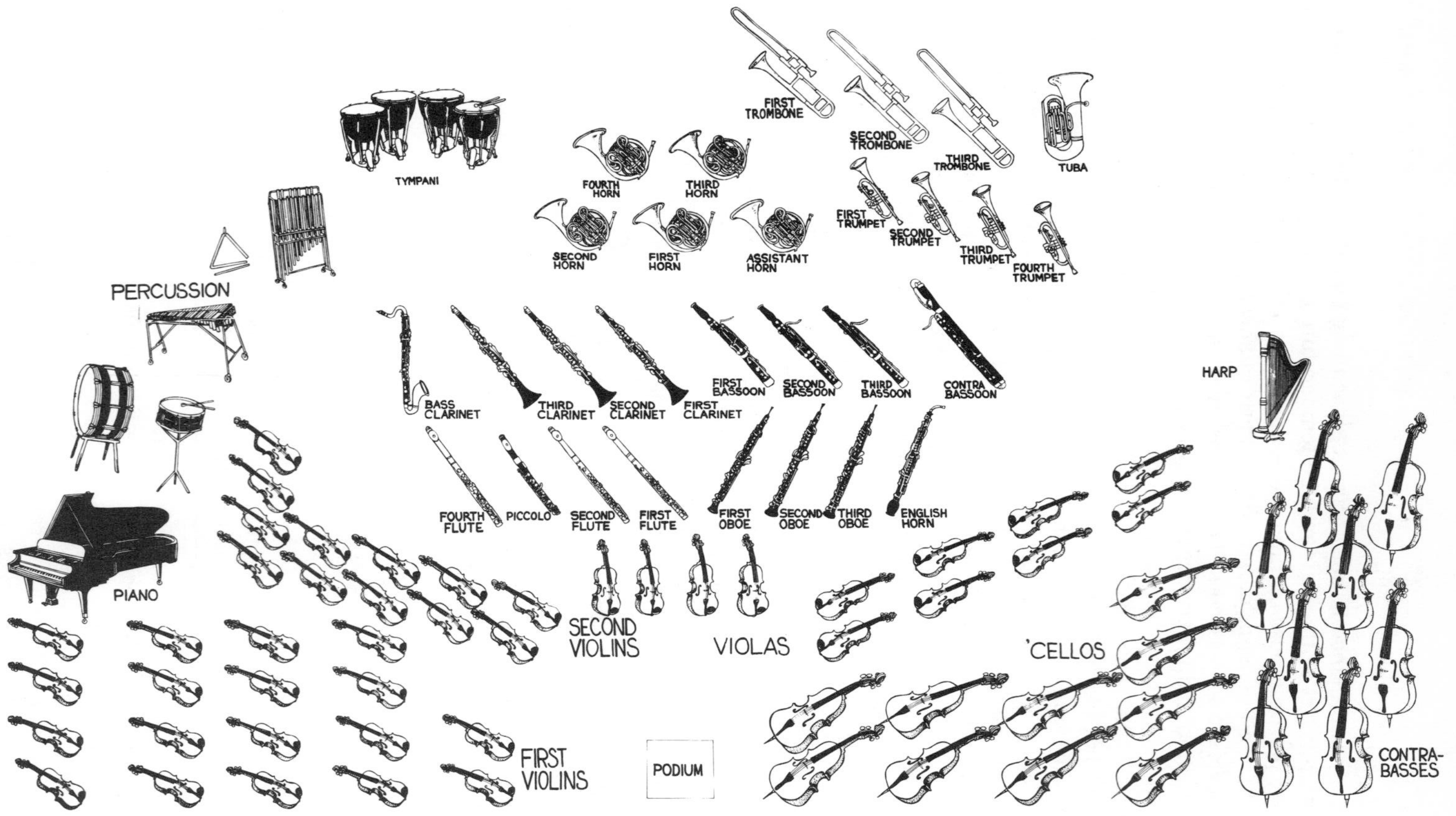

Reprinted by permission of the National Symphony.

music plus a certain performance royalty. The publisher will take care of copyrighting the piece. The composer can do this himself, but if he has proof of when it was written, he is legally protected and copyright is more of a formality than a necessity until the piece is printed. Publisher's contracts usually stipulate that they own the work and can arrange it in any way, promote it in any way, and otherwise do what they wish with it. Of course the rights to set texts not in public domain must be obtained.

Performance and broadcast royalties are paid through one of two organizations in the United States: ASCAP (American Society of Composers, Authors, and Publishers) and BMI (Broadcast Music Incorporated), both located in New York City. A composer joins either one or the other. He should carefully check to see which one it is to his benefit to join. Again, legal advice is recommended. Both organizations also encourage the composition of serious works by young composers and give annual awards. Most other countries have similar organizations (SESAC, GEMA, and others).

Recording of new music is so expensive today that records are usually arranged, if at all, through the performing organization, though there are a few so-called vanity labels which will record a work if the composer pays for it. One recording session with a major symphony orchestra costs many thousands of dollars.

There are many composition competitions both in the United States and Europe, with prizes ranging from a few hundred to several thousand dollars to promote new works for various combinations of instruments up to symphonic size. Publications such as *Musical America* (obtained through *High Fidelity*), *Music Educator's Journal, American Music Center Newsletter, Music Journal*, and others periodically carry information about these contests.

PART III

WRITING FOR BAND
AND OTHER ENSEMBLES

32

Band Instruments

Many common band instruments are found in the orchestra as well. Therefore this chapter describes in detail only those instruments not already described in Part I. Since instrumentalists in all but the best concert bands are usually not as technically adept as those in symphony orchestras, practical ranges are included which apply to all but virtuoso band music. The instruments are listed in order of their appearance in a band score. In addition to Figure 32–1, see also Table I on page 567 for a graphic presentation of the ranges of these instruments, as well as Appendix A.

1. *Piccolo*. Piccolos in the band may be either in C like the orchestral piccolo or in $D^\flat$. They both have the same written range but the $D^\flat$ piccolo sounds a minor ninth higher than written. The sound of the two instruments is not appreciably different, and the fingering and technique are the same. Practical range is from d^1 to a^3 (written) for both.

2. *Flute*. Also in C or $D^\flat$, sounding a minor second up. Practical range is from g^1 to c^4 (the lower range seldom has much use in the band). Flutes in $E^\flat$ are also to be found.

3. *Oboe*. Same as in the orchestra. Practical band range is d^1 to b^2.

4. *English horn*. Same as in the orchestra. Practical range is from d^1 to c^3 (written).

5. *Clarinet in $E^\flat$*. Same as in the orchestra. Practical range is e to d^3 (written).

6. *Clarinet in $B^\flat$*. Same as in the orchestra. Practical range is from e to d^3.

Figure 32-1

7. *Alto clarinet in E♭*. A clarinet built a fifth below the B♭ clarinet with a written range, in the treble clef, of e to c³, sounding a major sixth lower. Practical range is from e to g². In Europe they are sometimes built in F.

8. *Bass clarinet in B♭*. Same as in the orchestra. Practical range is from e to g².

9. *Contrabass clarinet in B♭*. An instrument found only in the largest concert bands, built an octave lower than the bass clarinet with the same written range, in the treble clef, sounding an octave lower than the bass clarinet (two octaves and a major second lower than written). It requires much wind, but has a rich, reedy tone and is capable of a wide dynamic range and fine support in the deep bass. A contrabass clarinet pitched in E♭, a fifth below the bass clarinet and transposing accordingly, also exists and is somewhat easier to play. It is sometimes seen in recording sessions for motion picture music. It has been used in the orchestra by Strauss and D'Indy.

10. *Bassoon*. Same as in the orchestra. Practical range is from D to g¹.

11. *Contrabassoon*. Same as in the orchestra. Found in large concert bands. Practical range is D to f¹.

12. *Saxophone* (Ital. *sassofone*, Ger. *Saxophon*, Fr. *saxophone*). A family of instruments invented by Adolphe Sax in 1840. Although never a standard member of the orchestra, it has been used in a number of works since 1844 and is in compositions by Saint-Saëns, Debussy, Berg, Britten, and many other twentieth-century composers. A quartet of saxophones has been used by Massenet, D'Indy, and Strauss (*Sinfonia Domestica*). The soprano saxophone appears in works by Ravel (*Bolero*) and Copland (*Piano Concerto*).

The saxophone is a stopped conical pipe of metal. Such a pipe acts like a cylindrical open pipe and therefore the saxophone overblows at the octave (see Appendix B). The saxophone has a single reed like the clarinet and is, in effect, a keyed brass instrument played with a reed like a woodwind. It has a wide dynamic range and surprising agility. The middle and upper range is surprisingly smooth and the lower range rich, though sometimes somewhat "honky," especially in the hands of a less-than-first-class player.

The written range, in the treble clef, is the same for all saxophones, b♭ to f³ (or f♯³ with an extra key). Any professional saxophonist plays an octave higher (to f⁴) in the *altissimo* range with comparative ease. A good practical band range is e¹ to c³. Following are the different sizes of saxophones and their transpositions:

A. *Soprano saxophone in B♭*. Sounds a major second lower than written. Though parts exist in band scores for the instrument, it is almost obsolete today, the parts being played on the alto sax.

B. *Alto saxophone in E♭*. Sounds down a major sixth. This is the most popular solo instrument of the sax family.

C. *Tenor saxophone in B♭*. Sounds a major ninth lower than written.

D. *Baritone saxophone in E♭*. Sounds an octave and a major sixth lower than written. Sometimes with low (written) a.

E. *Bass saxophone in B♭*. Sounds two octaves and a major second lower than written. Rare today.

A sopranino E♭ and a contrabass E♭ saxophone existed (sounding respectively a minor third higher and two octaves and a major sixth lower) but are now museum pieces. Continental saxes are sometimes pitched in F and C rather than B♭ and E♭ (the soprano sax in *Bolero* was written for soprano F sax but is played on soprano B♭ sax).

13. *Cornet in B♭* (Ital. *cornetto* or *cornetta*, Ger. *Kornett*, Fr. *cornet à pistons* or *piston*). An early nineteenth-century development from the Posthorn (see Chapter 12, section 1) with a system of piston valves like the trumpet but with a two-thirds conical bore, giving it a mellower and less brassy tone than the trumpet. It was originally used by composers such as Berlioz, Bizet, and Rossini to play chromatic parts before use of the valved trumpet became common. The cornet is found in many nineteenth-century ballet scores and works like Tchaikovsky's *Capriccio Italien* and Stravinsky's *Petrushka*. Older scores were written for cornets in C (or B and A with a slide mechanism which lowered the pitch a half step); the cornet in E♭, sounding up a minor third, is still common in Europe though rare in the United States.

The range, like that of the trumpet, is f♯ to c³, written in the treble clef. A good practical range is from a to b♭². The cornet in B♭ sounds a major second lower. The technique is like that of the trumpet. Muted cornets sound best from d¹ to g² since the sound becomes pinched in the high and the bell can rattle in the lower range. The solo cornet used to be a feature of much band music, though today these parts are usually played on the trumpet.

14. *Trumpet in B♭*. Same as in the orchestra. Practical range is c¹ to b♭² (written).

15. *Fluegelhorn in B♭* (Ital. *flicorno*, Ger. *Flügelhorn*, Fr. *bugle*). A larger bore instrument than the trumpet with a much mellower tone, somewhat like an alto cornet. Piston or rotary valves are used. The range, in the treble clef, is f♯ to b♭² (written) but the upper fourth of the range is seldom used since the unique quality of the fluegelhorn's sound is in the middle and lower range. Practical range is g to f². Though once popular in bands, it is almost never seen today except by some jazz trumpeters who sometimes prefer its mellower tone. It was used in the orchestra by Respighi (*Pines of Rome*) and Stravinsky (*Threni*). The alto fluegelhorn in E♭ exists in Europe. See also Appendix A.

16. *Horn in F*. Same as in the orchestra. Practical range is from g to g².

17. *E♭ alto horn* (Ital. *flicorno contralto, genis*, Ger. *Althorn*, Fr. *alto em mi♭, bugle alto*, Eng. *tenor cor*), Mellophone. The E♭ alto horn is shaped like a small tuba. It is half the length of the baritone horn (see below). Its range is f♯ to c³ (practical to f²) written in the treble clef and sounding a major sixth lower. It has pistons like the cornet or trumpet. It is used to reinforce or as a substitute for the French horn, especially in marching bands and school orchestras. It is easier to play than the French horn but has an inferior tone and for this reason is seldom found in concert bands of professional quality. Because of its shape, the left hand cannot be used in the bell as with the French horn. The mellophone is an instrument of the same range and transposition but built in the shape of a French horn. Both are also built in F and formerly in D in

Europe. Both are members of the *saxhorn* family, a group of instruments, including the cornet, fluegelhorn, tenor horn, euphonium, baritone, and tubas. The *mellophonium* is shaped like a trumpet.

18. *Trombone.* Same as in the orchestra. Practical ranges are: tenor, A to f¹; bass, E to f¹.

19. *Euphonium* (Ital. *flicorno basso*, Ger. *Baryton*, Fr. *basse à pistons*, *basse en si♭*) (see also Chapter 15), Baritone (Ital. *flicorno basso*, Ger. *Barytonhorn*, Fr. *baryton en si♭*, *corbasse ténor*, England *euphonium*). Both whole-tube 9-foot saxhorns in B♭ with three valves. Sometimes a fourth valve, extending the range down an augmented fourth, is used for more secure intonation. The additional range should not be used since not all instruments have the fourth valve and the additional range is of poor quality and intonation anyway. Some instruments have a fifth valve as well. These instruments can reach AA and, barely, the low FF pedal, which is of no practical use.

The euphonium is of wider bore and has an upright bell. In the baritone, the bell shapes forward and the tone is not as full as that of its larger-bore relative. Both have the range of the trombone, E to b♭¹, and both are written in the bass clef at pitch. The baritone is also written in the treble clef, a major ninth higher to facilitate playing by former trumpet or cornet players, who can use the same fingering. Parts are printed in both transpositions in band arrangements. The tone of both instruments is mellow and rich and they are surprisingly agile. They are built in C and formerly in A as well.

In the orchestra they are called on to play *tenor tuba* (see Appendix A) parts such as in Strauss's *Don Quixote*, Holst's *The Planets*, and Stravinsky's *Petrushka*.

20. *Bass tuba in E♭* (Ital. *tuba*, *basso tuba*, Ger. *Bass-tuba*, Fr. *contrebasse à pistons*, *tuba contrebasse*). The bass saxhorn in E♭ (the band version of the F tuba), commonly called simply the tuba or, in the band, the E♭ bass, has a range of AA to c¹ (practical from D to b♭). It is written in the bass clef at pitch. A fourth and at times a fifth valve are sometimes found for more secure intonation, extending the range down to EE. An old name for this instrument, still used in Europe, is the *bombardon*. The older instrument was often built in F and had three valves, with a range of DD to d¹.

21. *Double B♭ bass tuba, BB♭ bass tuba, Contrabass tuba* (Ital. *cimbasso*, *pelitton*, Ger. *Kontrabasstuba*, Fr. *contrebasse à pistons*). The band version of the orchestral contrabass (or just "bass") tuba in C, with a range of FF to b♭. A fourth valve, available on some instruments, lowers the pitch to DD. It is written in the bass clef, usually on the same staff as the E♭ bass, at concert pitch. The concert version is held in the lap and has an upright bell. The circular version, coiled around the body with a bell facing left, is called the *helicon*; these were built in F, E♭, C, and B♭. The *sousaphone*, John Philip Sousa's invention, has a forward-facing removable bell and is popular in marching bands.

22. *String bass.* Same as the orchestral double bass, used to solidify the bass

in some concert bands. Practical range is from E to g^1. On rare occasions, the cello is also found.

23. *Percussion.* Any percussion found in the orchestra can be found in the concert band. Commonly found are the following: marimba, chimes, bells, timpani (usually just two with a range of F to f, often without pedals), snare drums(s), field drums(s), tenor drum(s), bass drum, cymbals, triangle, wood block, *traps* of various kinds (whistles and other noise-makers).

Basic percussion in a school band might include: two snares, two to six parade drums, one bass drum, one or two marching bass drums, one concert cymbal, one marching cymbal, one suspended cymbal, orchestra bells, one pair timpani, xylophone, triangle, wood block, tambourine, castanets, whip, sleighbells, cowbell, temple blocks, ratchet, and possibly an extra timpano or two, bongo, various Latin instruments, chimes, tom-tom, drum set, marimba, vibraphone, and celesta.

24. *Other instruments.* Rarely, the alto flute, harp, accordion, piano, and voices are found with the band.

33

Writing for Band

1. ORIGIN OF THE BAND

Wind and percussion instruments have been used in association with the military since ancient times. Other predecessors of the modern band were the antiphonal wind ensembles of the Renaissance and the standard court band of the late eighteenth century consisting of two oboes, two clarinets, two horns, and two bassoons. Mozart, Haydn, Beethoven, Hummel, and Rossini wrote music for this ensemble. One of the first "modern" bands was the Band of the National Guard in Paris, founded in 1789, which contained 45 instrumentalists. By the middle of the nineteenth century the band had reached essentially its present-day form. Some of the rare serious works for band during the nineteenth century include Berlioz's *Grande Symphonie Funèbre et Triomphale* (1840) for 208 players and optional chorus (strings were added later), and works by Mendelssohn, von Weber, Wagner, Bruckner, Johann Strauss, Grieg, Saint-Saëns, Tchaikovsky, Meyerbeer, and Rimsky-Korsakov. During the nineteenth century in Italy, the term *banda* also referred to the brass and percussion in the orchestra.

Twentieth-century works for band include works by Holst, Grainger, Vaughan Williams, Florent Schmitt, Hindemith, Toch, Respighi, Roussel, Honegger, Prokofiev, Shostakovich, Schoenberg, Milhaud, Stravinsky and, in America, by William Schuman, Gould, Copland, Thomson, Piston, Mennin, Persichetti, Hanson, Moore, Ward, Beeson, Siegmeister, Barber, and Kubik.

2. TYPES OF BANDS

Today bands generally fall into one of the following categories:

1. Concert or symphonic bands
2. Wind ensembles
3. Military bands (which may be either symphonic or marching or both)
4. Marching bands
5. Brass bands
6. Drum and bugle corps

CONCERT OR SYMPHONIC BANDS

Concert bands vary in size from 25 to over 100 individuals. These bands perform in concert, they usually perform more original, serious, and difficult repertoire than other bands, and the players are generally quite skillful. These bands are found in the armed forces, large colleges, universities, and high schools, and, less commonly now than during the first half of the century, in large municipalities or even as independent organizations. The ratio of woodwinds to brass is generally up to the band director and may be equal or two to one. B♭ clarinets may constitute a third or more of the woodwinds. Following is a comparison of instrumentation in a typical 'basic' small concert band and a large or *full* concert band:

Small Band	**Large Band**
(*Wind Ensemble*)	(*Concert Band*)
	2 piccolos
1–2 flutes (with one doubling on piccolo)	6 + flutes (in two or three parts)
1–2 oboes (with one possibly doubling on English horn)	4 oboes (in one or two parts)
	1 English horn
possibly 1 E♭ clarinet	2 E♭ clarinets
2–6 B♭ clarinets (in two parts)	30 B♭ clarinets (in two or three parts)
	4 E♭ alto clarinets
possibly 1 bass clarinet	3 + bass clarinets
	1 contrabass clarinet
1–2 bassoons	4 + bassoons (in one or two parts with one doubling on contrabassoon)

Small Band	**Large Band**
(Wind Ensemble)	(Concert Band)
2 alto saxophones (in two parts, one possibly doubling on soprano)	2 alto saxophones (in two parts, one possibly doubling on soprano)
1 tenor sax	1 tenor sax
1 baritone sax	1 baritone sax
4 F or E♭ horns (in two or four parts)	8 + F horns (in 2 parts)
3 trumpets or cornets (in two or three parts)	6 + cornets
	4 trumpets (in two parts each)
2 trombones (in two parts)	4 + trombones (including one bass trombone, in two or three parts)
bass trombone	
1 baritone horn (or euphonium)	2 + baritone horns (or euphoniums)
1–2 bass tubas (possibly in E♭ and BB♭ in two parts)	5 + bass tubas in E♭ and BB♭ (possibly in two parts)
	1 string bass
3 percussion	6 percussion
possibly harp or keyboard	possibly harp, keyboard or other instruments

In addition, other instruments, such as alto flute, alto clarinet, contrabass clarinet, contrabassoon, bass sax, or any of the other band instruments mentioned in Chapter 32 may be found in the concert band. Sousa's band even included cellos and violas, and the U.S. Air Force band has used cellos. Piano and harp are not uncommon in large concert bands. Naturally, the smaller bands are to be found in smaller communities, colleges, high schools, junior high schools, and elementary schools.

High reeds are usually seated in front, high brass in the center, and low brass and percussion fill out the back of the band.

As should be obvious, an arrangement or original composition for concert band may sound quite different played by different size organizations of varying quality. Furthermore, published band scores must be extensively *cross-cued* so that if a particular instrument is missing, another instrument can play the part. This is different from orchestral cuing, which is there merely to give the player additional help in making his entrance. Band cuing is explained later in this chapter.

WIND ENSEMBLES

The wind ensemble can consist of anything from woodwind quintet or brass quintet (two trumpets or cornets, horn, trombone, tuba) to a small concert band of around 50 players such as the Eastman Wind Ensemble. These groups generally specialize in more difficult and serious music and are of high professional standards.

MILITARY BANDS

The military band can be either a concert band or a marching band and often players are called upon for service in both. The constitution of a military band varies from country to country.

MARCHING BANDS

The marching band, used for athletic events, parades, and various other festivities, can vary in size from 20 to 120. Instruments which are difficult or impossible to play while marching are omitted. Therefore there are often no oboes; alto, bass, or contrabass clarinets; or bassoons. E♭ alto horns may be used in preference to French horns, which are difficult to play on the march, and though timpani are occasionally found on mobile platforms, such instruments as chimes, marimba, harp, and piano are naturally not used. The drum section is considerably augmented, with snares, tenors, bass drums, cymbals, bell lyres, and triangles predominating.

Philip Lang [1] has suggested the following number of parts (which may be augmented by any numbers of instruments on each part); this instrumentation allows for a simpler, more effective arrangement of band music and has been accepted by many directors of marching bands.

D♭ piccolos—one part
B♭ clarinets—one or two parts
cornets or trumpets—one or two parts
horns (F or E♭ or both)—two parts
alto and tenor saxes—one part
baritone saxes and trombones—one part
baritone horns—one part
bass tubas (sousaphones)—one part
drums
bell lyres

Arranging for this ensemble is discussed later in this chapter. Traditional marching band scores include parts for flutes, saxes in four parts, trombones in two parts, and often parts for other instruments as well.

---

[1] Philip J. Lang, *Scoring for Band* (Belwin-Mills, New York, 1950).

BRASS BANDS

Brass bands, which originated in Prussia in the 1830's, were once much more popular in America than they are today. In Europe they are still common. A standard brass band contains the following instrumentation:

1 E♭ soprano cornet
8 B♭ cornets
1 B♭ fluegelhorn
3 E♭ tenor horns (see Appendix A)
2 B♭ baritone horns
2 B♭ euphoniums
2 B♭ tenor trombones
1 B♭ bass trombone
2 E♭ basses (bass tubas)
2 BB♭ basses

A typical university *Brass Ensemble* contains the following instrumentation:

3 trumpets
4 horns
3 trombones
2 baritone horns
tuba

DRUM AND BUGLE CORPS

The drum and bugle corps, associated with the armed forces, consists of cornets, trumpets, and percussion.

3. ARRANGING FOR BAND

Following are some general problems and considerations in scoring for band:

1. The band generally has greater powers of *forte* than the orchestra but less ability to play *piano.*
2. The preceding is largely due to the fact that more doubling must be used in the band than the orchestra. Without the help of strings, the winds can sound thin unless quite a few are playing at once.
3. Concert keys of from G to D♭ have fewer accidentals for the transposing band instruments. Written keys with more than two sharps should be avoided.
4. Melody, countermelody, accompaniment, bass line, and sustaining elements must be contrasted in color and carefully balanced.

5. The weaker woodwinds must be carefully balanced against the brass, especially in louder passages.
6. Solos, choirs, and sections must be balanced and contrasted with each other throughout the piece.
7. As with the orchestra, avoid close writing in the lower register. Double and fill octaves first, fifths second, then thirds, and so on through the overtone series.
8. Keep within the grade of difficulty for the type of band that you intend to have play your music.
9. Cuing is a special problem and is dealt with in section 5.

The woodwinds or *reeds* range from BB♭ to c⁵, the brass from EE to b♭². For this reason, but mainly because of their lesser power, the higher woodwinds are usually kept above the brass. Soprano ranges include the piccolo, flute, oboe, E♭ clarinet, B♭ clarinet, alto sax, cornet, and trumpet. Bass ranges include the bass clarinet, bassoon, baritone sax, trombone, baritone or euphonium, tubas, and string bass.

Following are some common uses of the woodwinds in the band:

Piccolo. Octaves with the flutes or clarinets, independent figuration or trills.

Flute. Solo in quiet passages, doubling at unison or octave with other woodwinds.

Oboe. Solo melody or countermelody, doubling with other woodwinds.

English horn. Solo or woodwind doubling.

E♭ clarinet. With flutes or high clarinets for added intensity.

B♭ clarinet. In unison or octaves for melody or countermelody, or, especially when present in large numbers, in two- or three-part harmony, especially in quiet passages.

E♭ alto clarinet. Occasional solos or with low clarinets or high bass clarinets.

Bass clarinet. Reed bass or occasional solos. It is best if there are several bass clarinets to balance the many higher-pitched reeds.

Contrabass clarinet. Since there are seldom parts written for this instrument, it is usually used to strengthen the bass. This is also true of the contrabassoon.

Bassoon. Reed bass and occasional solos. Also good in unison with low clarinets and other reeds.

Soprano sax. Almost obsolete. Parts are seldom written for this instrument, but it can be used to substitute for the first alto.

Alto sax. Solos, both alone and with the clarinets, or in harmony with the saxophone quartet.

Tenor sax. Harmony or doubling in unison or octaves with alto or baritone.

Baritone sax. Supports reed harmony, often doubles tubas an octave higher.

Bass saxophone. Rare, good for reed bass.

In general the saxophones provide a bridge between the woodwind and brass choirs. Typical *dance band* harmony can be created by doubling the sax harmony an octave higher in the clarinets.

Exercises in arranging for the reeds of the band are found in the workbook which accompanies this volume.

Following are some common uses of the brass and percussion in the band:

Cornet. First cornet often used as a solo instrument, often with woodwinds an octave higher or other brass an octave lower. Cornets can be used in unison or harmony as well and various mutes are employed (see Chapter 34). Often replaced by trumpets today.

Trumpet. Its more brilliant tone makes it suitable for more powerful passages, either alone or in unison with the cornets.

Fluegelhorn. Now rare, a mellower cornet useful for solos or as a lower part for the cornets.

Horns. Traditionally overused for offbeat rhythmic accompaniment, useful for solo passages with or without other brass and for sustained notes or intervals as in the orchestra.

E♭ alto horns. Simply an inferior version of the horn in F but easier to play.

Trombone. Solos, alone or an octave below cornets or trumpets, rhythmic or sustained harmony and heavy bass lines.

Baritone horn, Euphonium. Agile, mellow tone and good blend with other instruments. Good for solos alone or with any other brass or low reed.

Tubas in E♭ and BB♭. Bass line in octaves or unison. Occasional solos.

String bass. Arco or pizzicato to add homogeneity to reed bass or with full band.

Percussion. Every sort of rhythmic accent and background possible with the orchestra, though used more emphatically in the band. Also melodic doublings with bells and other definite pitch percussion instruments.

The harp and piano are usually used solistically. The cellos, like the string bass, are sometimes used to add smoothness to the bass line.

The brass are often treated as a double quartet, with the brighter cornets or trumpets (in two parts) and trombones (in two parts) juxtaposed with the mellower horns (in two parts), baritone and euphonium (one part), and basses (one part in unison or octaves).

The brass or reeds can be used for melody, chords, accents, sustaining elements, and rhythmic figures. One section can be used to outline a melody in another section, it can double at the octave or unison for increased strength and/or sonority, and the sections can be used independently or contrasted with one another.

Extreme care must be taken to balance instruments in the band, especially since numbers of instruments are by no means standard. For instance, in a large ensemble, a massing of trombones, horns, cornets, and saxes in the middle register can add enormous weight and a "tubby" sound to the arrangement.

Special effects such as woodwind trills, tremoli, fluttertonguing, glissandi, mutes, closed horns (hand in the bell), slap tongue saxes or clarinets, and offstage instruments can produce interesting variety if not overused.

4. NOTATION

The full band score consists of 25 to 30 staves with instruments in the order in which they were listed in Chapter 32. Flutes; oboes and English horn; clarinets; bassoons; saxophones; string bass; and basses are bracketed as sections. One staff is used for first and second flutes, one for first and second oboes, one for first and second trumpets, and so on except for the clarinet parts, which are written on separate staves. Older scores refer to the first clarinets as *solo clarinet*, the first cornets as *solo cornet*.

The basses are both written on the same staff. Single notes indicate they are playing in unison. Octaves indicate they are playing an octave apart; writing *a2* is not necessary. Single stems are used. Sometimes the number of basses is indicated.

A part which descends below the practical range for an instrument may be written in small notes with ordinary-size note heads an octave higher.

Percussion is notated on five-line staves or single lines. Snare and bass drum are often notated on one staff (Figure 33–1a and b), cymbals and triangle on another. The neutral clef should be used, though one still sees treble and bass clef employed for unpitched percussion. Sometimes x-, cross-, or diamond-shaped note heads are used for cymbals or other percussion (33–1c and d). Rarely, more than two percussion instruments are notated on a single staff (33–1d).

Figure 33–1

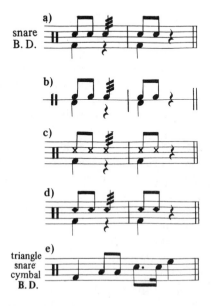

Often, in simpler band music, *compressed* scores of five to fourteen lines are used and several parts are written on each staff.

The *condensed* score is written on three staves. The top staff usually contains the high reeds, the second staff the cornets, trumpets, saxes, and horns, and the bottom staff the trombones, baritones, basses, low reeds, and, if they are playing low, the saxes and horns. Indications such as *col 8va* and *col 8vab* are used to show doublings at the octave above or below. Instrumentation is indicated by abbreviations of the instruments at their entrances (see Figure 33–2).

For marches and other extremely simple music, a *lead sheet* which contains the solo clarinet or cornet (*lead*) part and a few indications of countermelodies and other essential information is sometimes used.

In arranging for band, a *short score* of usually four staves (two for reeds, two for brass) is used. One plan for a tutti section would be to sketch out the melody and bass line in cornets or trumpets and basses; then go back and fill in the heavier brass, trombones, and baritones; add the horns and saxes; fill in alto clarinet, bass clarinet, bassoon; and finally add the high reeds and percussion. Of course there are many other approaches that could be used.

From this short score, parts can be directly copied if one has had much experience, but for the beginner it is best to derive a full band score, then copy parts. Paper is available already bracketed for band arrangements from most of the major music copying firms (see Chapter 31).

Examples of full band scores are found in Figure 33–5 at the end of this chapter.

5. CUING

As previously mentioned, cues for the band are meant to be played in case the instrument for which the part was originally written is missing. Let's say the arranger wished to write a solo for alto clarinet but knows that small bands may not have an alto clarinet. In this case he duplicates the part in the correct transposition for B♭ clarinet III or bassoon I or both, writing small note heads with the abbreviation *alto clar.* The cue may be bracketed. In a band with alto clarinet, the part will be played on the alto clarinet only. In bands without the alto clarinet, the band director will direct either the B♭ clarinet III or bassoon I to play the solo. Published scores generally have extensive cuing to enable the widest possible substitution of instruments and, therefore, sales of the music. Needless to say, this makes subtle artistic arrangements practically impossible if they are intended for commercial distribution. However, with no standardization of band instrumentation likely, it is a problem with which the arranger must deal with the greatest skill at his disposal.

Cross-cuing means that a particular part is cued for two different instruments. In the example above, if there were no alto clarinet and no bassoon, the cue could still be played by the B♭ clarinet III. The B♭ clarinet "has the alto clarinet cue" and the alto clarinet "is cued in the B♭ clarinet."

Some instruments are available in all bands and therefore need not be cued. They are the piccolo, flute, clarinet, saxes, cornet or trumpet, trombone, baritone, basses, and drums. All other instruments should be cued if not already sufficiently doubled in the arrangement. Third and fourth horn parts should be either harmonic filler or doubling which would not be missed in bands with only two horns. Otherwise they should be cued. Small bands often have no second cornet or third trombone. These must be cued as well. Parts of technical difficulty should be cued also. For instance, a difficult passage in the horns might be cued in the saxes.

The instrument(s) that are closest in range, dynamic power, and tone color and that are not otherwise employed at the moment should be chosen for cuing. For instance, muted brass might be cued with double reeds or vice versa. Since accompanying parts may be cued as well, all parts being cued at one time should be considered together for possible problems of balance or contrast. Following is a list of possible cuings. Naturally, the feasibility of any particular substitution depends on the range, dynamic, and color of the particular passage. These are only suggestions for possibilities.

Instrument	Cued In
oboe	flute, E♭ or B♭ clarinet, bassoon (if part is low), cornet, muted trumpet
English horn	oboe, alto clarinet, alto sax, bassoon, cornet, trumpet (muted), horn
E♭ clarinet	piccolo, flute, B♭ clarinet
alto clarinet	B♭ clarinet, bass clarinet, alto or tenor sax, horn
bass clarinet	alto clarinet (if part is high), tenor or baritone sax, bassoon, string bass
contrabass clarinet	bass clarinet, bass sax, string bass
baritone sax	bass clarinet, baritone, tuba
bass sax	baritone sax, bass clarinet, bassoon, string bass, tuba
bassoon	alto or bass clarinet, tenor or baritone sax, muted trombone, baritone, tuba
contrabassoon	bassoon, bass or contrabass clarinet, baritone or bass sax, baritone, tuba, string bass
third and fourth horns	alto or tenor sax, fluegelhorn, cornet, trumpet, trombone, baritone
cornet	trumpet
fluegelhorn	cornet, trumpet, horn, trombone, baritone
timpani	bass drum for rolls, tenor or snare drum for rhythmic figures
xylophone	bells, piccolo, flute, E♭ or B♭ clarinet, muted brass

marimba chords	woodwind chords with or without trills or tremoli
temple blocks	wood blocks
tom-tom	muffled snare, tenor drum
harp	piano
cello	string bass, tenor or baritone sax, horns, baritone, basses

Figure 33–2 shows cuing and cross-cuing in the E♭ clarinet, the bass clarinet, the tenor sax, the first horn, and the bass drum.

6. WRITING FOR MARCHING BAND

Naturally, music written to be played on the march outdoors must be louder and more rhythmic than music for concert band. It must also be in simple or compound duple or quadruple meter. There is usually little contrast of colors and much unison and octave doubling, especially on the melody. Simple rhythmic accompaniments and simple countermelodies or figuration are the rule.

Often, the proportion of instruments on each element is twice as many parts on the melody as the accompaniment or countermelody. Half the band will often be playing the rhythm. In a marching band of 50, there might be 20 cornets or trumpets in one or two parts. Trombones are also often written in two parts. High reeds may all double at the octave for melody or figuration. Horns, though traditionally playing afterbeats, are better for melody, countermelody, or sustaining elements. Solos are primarily in the cornets or trumpets, clarinets, or trombones. The main contrast comes dynamically between sections such as reeds predominating in the trio section of a march. Harmony is usually in the saxes, horns, baritones, and trombones. Typical marching band arrangements might have (1) the melody in the cornets and trumpets, doubled by the high reeds in octaves, with harmony or countermelody in the baritones and trombones; (2) the melody in the baritones and trombones in unison, with harmony in the cornets and trumpets and figuration in the high reeds; or (3) melody in the cornets and trumpets, harmony in the baritones and trombones, and figuration in the high reeds. The saxophones can work either with the reeds or with the horns or other brass with melody or harmony.

Percussion may constitute most of a marching band. Though there is no standard deployment, the percussion are usually in the middle or back of the band, behind the heavy brass. Even a small marching band needs a bass drum, cymbal, and two snares. These are augmented many times in a large marching band (see Chapter 32, section 23).

Figure 33–2   Arnold, *English Dances for Band*

Figure 33–2 (cont.)

Drum *cadences* are used to begin marching (*roll-off*), to stop (*halt*), and in between pieces when the band is marching but not playing (*marching cadence*).

Figure 33–3 shows some typical drum cadences.

Figure 33–4 shows a Sousa march in short score.

Figure 33–3

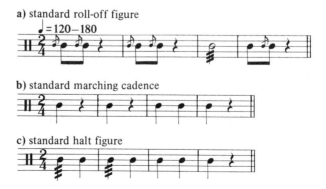

a) standard roll-off figure

b) standard marching cadence

c) standard halt figure

Figure 33–4

7. TRANSCRIBING ORCHESTRAL
MUSIC FOR BAND

Much literature for concert band consists of orchestral transcriptions. Much of the orchestral literature is difficult to transcribe effectively for band, especially that literature relying heavily on complex string writing. Therefore, appropriate material should be chosen. Orchestral music in sharp keys might be transposed up or down a step or half step to an easier key for band. The best transcriptions do not simply substitute band instruments for orchestral instruments but are true arrangements. Only familiarity with the orchestra and the band can lead to effective arrangements, but a few points might be mentioned.

Naturally, the prime difference between the two is that there are no strings in the band. Therefore appropriate wind writing must be substituted for all string writing. This may involve altering string figures, rearranging voices, doubling, filling, and even simplifying or elaborating the orchestral texture. It must be remembered that though the full band can play louder than the orchestra, it cannot play as softly. Very quiet sections can be obtained with reeds or muted brass in smaller numbers.

Though often referred to as the "strings" of the band, the clarinets are not at all directly comparable. The tone and fullness of texture of the strings are lacking, the clarinets cannot play as loud or with so strong an accent as the string section, winds must breathe, and lengthy staccato passages become tiring. Pizzicato in the lower strings can only be approximated by the staccato tubas or baritones, and though the clarinets can play arpeggios, the sonority of the string arpeggio is entirely lacking. Tremoli can only be approximated by a woodwind trill or snare roll. Basically, of course, the whole dimension of the string sound is missing. Wind instruments are simply quite different from string instruments. Therefore, a good band transcription must be rewritten to convey the original music effectively for winds. Though there are various types of additional winds in the band, the overall color and variety of texture are more limited than in the orchestra. This must be taken into account.

Direct substitutions for orchestral winds can be extrapolated from the list of possible cuings in section 5. The following band instruments often substitute for strings:

violin	B♭ clarinet, flute, E♭ clarinet, cornet, alto sax
viola	B♭ clarinet, alto clarinet, alto or tenor sax, horn
cello	bass clarinet, tenor or baritone sax, bassoon, baritone horn
double bass	contrabass clarinet, baritone or bass sax, tuba, string bass (usually in combination with other instruments since there is commonly only one in the band)

8. TRANSCRIBING PIANO MUSIC FOR BAND

Many of these problems have been dealt with in Chapters 16 and 29. Essentially they involve doubling and filling, transcribing broken intervals and chords, figuration, repeated notes, melody, and harmony. Accompaniment figures will often have to be changed or approximated and sustaining elements will be added. Care must be taken not to transcribe the technical difficulty of the piano part in the band score. In other words, difficult piano writing must be made simple band writing.

9. TRANSCRIBING OTHER MUSIC FOR BAND

The transcription of organ music for band is usually quite successful since the organ is, in a sense, a mechanical band anyway. Vocal music, especially choral music, often transcribes well with minimal changes in the music, since the voice too is a wind instrument.

There are few original pieces for solo instrument with band (Rimsky-Korsakov's *Concerto for Clarinet and Band* comes to mind). There is no reason why more such pieces shouldn't be written. The only problems are those of balance, especially with a soft solo instrument such as a clarinet, and the contrast of colors between soloist and band, especially with a wind instrument as soloist.

Chorus with band, though seldom heard, is effective and capable of exploitation since most schools have both a chorus and a band. The band can double the chorus and have independent accompaniment or do both at the same time. Doubling is useful if the chorus needs added sonority, if voices are in weak registers, if the music is complex or highly dissonant, and for climaxes.

Arranging popular tunes for band involves the writing of introductions, modulatory *bridge* passages and transitions, *endings* or codas, and even some variation or development of the musical material. Sections should be contrasted in color and should include alternation of solo choruses with sectional and full band instrumentation.

Figure 33–5 is an example of music written originally for band.

Figure 33–5   Hindemith, *Symphony for Concert Band*

34

Writing
For Jazz Band

---

1. ORIGINS

There is much disagreement as to what sort of music the term *jazz* actually implies. This text uses the term in its most general sense to cover a wide variety of styles which began to develop in the American Southeast during the nineteenth century and reached their culmination in much of the popular music of the twentieth century.

That the precursors of this style of music were already firmly entrenched is strikingly illustrated by Louis Moreau Gottschalk's Symphony No 1, *A Night in the Tropics,* which was written in the 1850's but could almost have been composed by George Gershwin. Gottschalk was a Creole, an educated, upper-class French-American living in New Orleans (the term *Creole* is often used, incorrectly, to refer to persons of mixed European and black ancestry). His music was highly influenced by the combination of Cuban rhythms and the work songs, gospels, and spirituals of the slaves. Though Gottschalk had great success in Europe with this new "American" music (he studied with Berlioz and his music was admired by Chopin), it was not until the rise of ragtime and dixieland during the early years of the twentieth century that this music began to be widely known in America.

2. INSTRUMENTATION

There is a remarkable similarity between late nineteenth- and twentieth-century ensembles for the performance of lighter music and the baroque instrumentation of the popular trio sonata. In the latter case, two instruments played melodic lines, a keyboard instrument (harpsichord) supplied the harmony, and one instrument (usually the viola da gamba) played the bass. In the Parisian *Salon Orchestra,* popular in the late nineteenth century for playing dance music and arrangements of popular operetta tunes, one or two instruments (originally violins, but later flute, cornet, trumpet, trombone, or sax in any combination with or without violins) played the melody and countermelody, a piano supplied the harmony, and a cello or double bass played the bass line. The only addition to the trio sonata format was a percussionist playing a variety of drums and other instruments. This combination, also popular in America in hotels and other public places (one might call it the beginning of Muzak), may have influenced the development of early jazz ensembles. Instrumentation varies with different styles, all of which are found today.

Dixieland   Popular from 1892 to about 1917, the dixieland band developed from the black bands who marched in funerals and other ceremonies. A typical band consisted of cornet or trumpet playing the melody, clarinet playing a countermelody or figuration above, a banjo playing harmony, a tuba playing bass, a trombone playing a *roving* bass line (a bass line with some melodic interest), and bass drum. When not played on the march, dixieland included a drum set, originally just a bass drum with foot pedal, a side drum or a pair of primitive tom-toms, and a suspended cymbal. Later piano was added.

Ragtime   Primarily a piano style developing at the same time as dixieland, it was played in Southern brothels. Ragtime is characterized by a steady alternation of bass octaves and chords in the left hand and syncopated melody in the right hand (from *ragged time*). The term *stride piano* refers to a later style involving wide leaps from the bass to the chords in the left hand (Jelly Roll Morton, Fats Waller). *Boogie-woogie* is a term applied to a piano style, popular during the 1930's, characterized by melody in the right hand and either chords or an ostinato bass line in dotted rhythm in the left hand. It was possibly derived from folk music for three guitars current at that time in logging and mining camps.

Chicago-style dixieland   This style was popular from 1917 to about 1933. Added introductions and endings, extensive solos, and $\frac{2}{4}$ time replaced "flat four" (the unaccented beat of early dixieland), as white musicians such as the Dorseys and Bob Crosby took up the dixieland style. The tenor sax was added under the cornet and the guitar replaced the banjo as the string bass did the tuba. More percussion was added including, not uncommonly, timpani and tam-tam.

Symphonic jazz This was a combination of serious musical form and jazz with a semi-symphonic sound, advocated by Paul Whiteman in the 1920's. His orchestra at one time included seven reeds (saxes and clarinets), six brass, two pianos, guitar, banjo, percussion (including timpani and gong), and seven violins. The *Rhapsody in Blue,* Gershwin's first symphonic jazz composition, was commissioned by Whiteman.

Swing The "Big Band" era, popular from about 1932 to 1942, was characterized by larger ensembles consisting of first and second alto sax, first and second tenor sax, baritone sax, first and second trumpet, third and fourth trumpet, first to fourth trombone, bass, guitar, piano, and drums. Some bands had only four reeds, three trumpets and three trombones, some even had five or six of each brass instrument, though these bands were rare. New instruments such as the flute (Guy Lombardo), accordion (Lawrence Welk), and vibes (Lionel Hampton) were added. Jazzmen such as Poggy Pogson experimented with pan pipes, African oboe, and other folk instruments.

Latin band Latin band was a group consisting of a large Latin rhythm section (see Chapter 21) and almost any combination of guitars, trumpets, saxes, violins, flutes, and other instruments.

Small combos Smaller ensembles consisting of just piano and bass, sometimes with guitar or other instruments, were used for work in more intimate surroundings such as night clubs. The Joe Daniels Sextet consisted of clarinet, trumpet, guitar, bass, piano, and drums.

Bop (bebop, rebop) A revolt against the big band style, bop developed in Harlem in the 1940's. It was characterized by the use of unusual melodic intervals, ninth, eleventh, and thirteenth chords, polychords, complex rhythm, the beat carried on the top (*ride*) cymbal, the introduction of the amplified guitar as a melody instrument, and *scat* singing (instrumental-style vocal improvisation on nonsense syllables exemplified by Ella Fitzgerald). Combos were any size.

Progressive Some big bands used bop innovations in their music (Stan Kenton).

Cool jazz A reaction to the tonal complexities of bop, cool jazz was popular in the early 1950's. The music was characterized by understatement, subtle sonorities, longer and more complex forms such as rondo and even fugue, and sometimes polyrhythms (Dave Brubeck). Three to eight instruments were used, sometimes including flute, French horn, oboe, cello, vibraphone, and the tuba, which had returned to jazz as a melody instrument. The usual rhythm section was always present, of course.

Funky hard bop A reversion to early jazz, this music was characterized by hard-driving rhythm, a basically vertical harmonic concept, open fifths and *blue notes* (flat thirds and sevenths). It could consist of piano alone to any size combo.

Third stream This attempt to combine jazz and classical principles sometimes resulted in works for jazz band and orchestra, like a concerto grosso (Rolf Lieberman, Dave Brubeck, William Kraft and others), jazz improvisations on classical pieces, or classical forms. Some of the works of Gunther Schuller are in this category.

Soul Soul music is an intense, gospel-oriented extension of the funky style.

Other developments Atonal improvisation, multiphonics (John Coltrane), the use of non-Western techniques such as the Indian raga (Don Ellis), and the introduction of unusual instruments have characterized later jazz.

Rock A style of music popular with youth in the 1950's and 1960's especially, it originated when white singers such as Elvis Presley took up *rhythm and blues,* a "low-down" funky style. It has gone through many stylistic periods (hard rock, acid rock, heavy-metal rock, the Beatles, punk rock, new wave, disco) encouraged by the commercial interests which it nourishes. Basic are the singer, amplified guitar(s) (Ger. *Schlaggitarre*), and drums. Electric piano, electric bass (a small instrument which does not need the large body of the string bass since the sound is amplified and can be played sitting down), and various winds and strings are also added, especially for recording. The resultant sound is more a matter of amplification, altering the recorded sound through electronic means, than it is instrumentation (see Chapter 39).

Country and western This is a commercialized form developed from folk music utilizing fiddles, guitars, banjos, and other instruments up to the size of the jazz band. It is characterized by simple melodies, harmonies, and forms.

Stage band The stage band originated in vaudeville and is used today for shows of various sorts, especially on television. It may be any size from the small combo to the big band.

Early Broadway pit orchestras In 1901 the Broadway pit orchestra reflected the instrumentation of the operetta, the popular form of the day, and consisted of one (each) flute, oboe, clarinet, bassoon, trumpet, horn, trombone, and tuba with a small string section and percussion. By 1915, pairs of winds were the rule.

The 20's Broadway pit With the arrival of the first black musical to Broadway in 1921 (Eubie Blake's *Shuffle Along*), the development of the American Musical Comedy began. The typical 1920's pit consisted of a string quartet, or double quartet, one or two trumpets, one or two trombones, eight to nine reeds of different types (with no doubling), banjo, piano, and drums.

The postwar Broadway pit The size of the pit since World War II is largely the result of the union rule requiring 26 musicians to be hired whether they play or not. Therefore, it is economically feasible to use 26 musicians but not many more. A typical pit orchestra consists of six violins, two violas, two cellos, a string bass (both *stand-up* [acoustic] and electric), two or three trumpets, two or three trombones, sometimes one or two horns, five reeds, all playing sax and all doubling on at least one other reed (such as flute, oboe, clarinet, or bassoon), piano (doubling on celesta, electric harpsichord, etc.), a trap drummer, and a percussionist who can play mallet instruments (xylophone, vibes, and the like). A harp is optional. Musicals with smaller instrumentation have also been written (*Threepenny Opera* for small jazz combo, *The Fantasticks* with harp and piano, for example).

3. NOTATION

Much jazz is, of course, improvised, but much music is written in score (or *chart*), especially for big bands or stage bands. For guitar and piano, however, chord symbols are usually written, leaving the voicing of the chords to the performer. Following are chord symbols used in jazz followed by their definition in traditional harmony. It should be noted that these symbols are often simplified, leaving it up to the player to determine the exact structure from the context and key of the music.

C	C major triad
C min	C minor triad
C+5 or C#5	C augmented triad
C−5 or C♭5	C triad with major third and diminished fifth
C°	C diminished triad
C⁶	C triad with added sixth
C⁷	C major-minor (dominant) seventh chord
C maj 7	C major seventh chord
C min 7	C minor seventh chord
C°⁷	C diminished seventh chord
C⁹	C major ninth chord
C maj 9	C with minor seventh as well as a major ninth
C+9 or C#9	C with minor seventh and raised ninth
C¹¹	C with minor seventh, major ninth, and perfect eleventh, third often omitted
C+11, C#11	C with raised eleventh, third often omitted
C¹³	C thirteenth chord, third often omitted

Vergules (diagonal slashes) are used to indicate the number of beats each chord is to be played (Figure 34–1). For further information on the guitar, see Appendix A. The piano can be written as illustrated here or with the double bass part in the bass clef with chord symbols above the staff. The pianist does not play the bass part but uses it to determine the spacing and rhythm of the

Figure 34–1

chords. Music with the melody written on one line and chord symbols above is known as a *lead sheet.* This is used by the solo pianist or the pianist accompanying vocalists as well as the pianist in a combo. A commercial piano part includes melody, complete but easily playable accompaniment and chord symbols.

4. THE DRUMS

The jazz (*trap*) drum set consists of a snare drum about 5 by 14 inches (13 by 35 cm), a bass drum worked with a foot pedal about 14 by 22 inches (35 by 56 cm), an 18-inch (46-cm) suspended cymbal, a 20-inch (51-cm) suspended *ride* cymbal, a hi-hat (two suspended cymbals about 14 inches (35 cm) in diameter which are struck together by means of a foot pedal), two tom-toms about 9 by 13 inches (23 by 33 cm) and 16 by 16 inches (40 by 40 cm), a cowbell attached to the bass drum, and various *traps* (see next paragraph). Snare sticks, wire brushes, marimba, and other mallets are used.

Traps include a wide variety of instruments, including washboard, saucepan lids, tin cans, spoons or bones clicked together (early jazz), triangle, tambourine, castanets, and sandpaper blocks.

Newer instruments include the ching-a-ring (a metal tambourine that fits on the hi-hat), the rock shaker stick (a stick with jingles), the slap hand or sock cymbals, the gong-like chinese cymbal, the sizzle cymbal (with metal rivets in holes around the edge), and the pang cymbal, a cymbal with flat edges and a brief ring.

Techniques include rolls, single-stroke rolls, paradiddles, rim shots with one or two sticks, dampening the cymbals with stick or hand (choke), and combining a circular motion of the brushes on a cymbal with the stick beating the rhythm.

Drum set notation consists of a simplified rhythmic outline on one staff, usually with bass clef (though the neutral clef would be more appropriate). The player amplifies on this rhythm, so that Figure 34–2a might be played like Figure 34–2b. Typical notation places the cymbals above the staff, often written with an x-shaped note head or an x within a circle. Here the former is used to designate the ride cymbal, the latter the smaller cymbal. The small and large toms are respectively on the first and third space from the top, the snare on the second space, the bass drum on the fourth (bottom) space, and the hi-hat below the staff (sometimes on the staff with an x-shaped note head). This system is fairly standard today. If a complex drum part is written out, two staves may be used. Latin rhythm sections use one staff for each player. Typical jazz drumming has bass drum on each beat, hi-hat on 2 and 4, and the rhythm on the ride cymbal as shown in Figure 34–2. A shorthand for improvised drumming is shown in Figure 34–2c. The drum set has also been used in the orchestra by William Walton (*Facade Suite No. 2*) and, in chamber music, by Stravinsky (*Histoire du Soldat*).

Figure 34–2

a) notation:

b) possible realization:

cymbal
small tom-tom
snare
large tom-tom
bass drum
high hat

c)

play 8 (saxes)   play 4 (brass)

The *cocktail drum*, used for convenience by traveling musicians, is a single drum 16 by 24 inches (40 by 60 cm) on legs. It has a foot pedal to beat the lower head like a bass drum while the upper head is played with sticks like a snare. A cymbal and cowbell are attached.

5. MUTES

Though the tuba uses one mute, and that rarely, and the horn two (transposing and nontransposing), the trumpet and trombone have several types in common; these were developed in the jazz era to balance and blend with the reeds in small ensembles and to use for special effects. Various types of mutes are being used increasingly in symphonic music.

Mutes change both the volume and tone color of an instrument. All brass mutes tend to sharpen the tone, and the player must compensate for this effect. Transposing notes alter the tone a half step but the notation is at pitch, the player making the adjustment. Mutes tend to be less effective in the extreme registers of an instrument. Following are the most common types of mutes.

Straight The basic orchestral mute, usually made of metal. In the *forte*, it has the characteristic acidic bite familiar in much twentieth-century music. In *piano*, it takes the edge off the trumpet or trombone tone but changes the basic color less than any other mute. Most players have several straight mutes, some of which are altered in that the felt which separates the mute from the bell is filed down in order to decrease the opening around the mute and therefore the stream of air in order to make a softer mute. The mute can also be *fanned* in and out (from *tight* to *loose*) with the left hand, creating a continuous change of tone between very muted and partially muted. Popular in the orchestra is the Leblanc Alessio-Vacchiano brand and, for solo work, the copper Tom Crown.

Cup Literally a cup-shaped mute, basic to jazz and big band. It is lined on the inside with some material such as felt, with rubber edging where it fits the bell. The tone is mellow, subdued, and echo-like but can be played *mezzo-forte* as well as *piano*. Cloth can be inserted into the mute for an even more subdued tone. Sometimes the best balance is obtained when the trumpets are playing with straight mutes if the trombones are playing with cups. Popular is the stone-lined Humes and Berg model.

Harmon A double mute with a removable stem in the center. Softer than the straight mute, it has a thin, metallic, and quiet tone. The stem can be removed entirely from the mute, creating the "cool" jazz sound (Miles Davis). The stem can also be used without the mute, or it can be tight or loose within the mute. When the hand is fanned over the mute, the typical *wa-wa* effect is obtained (which needs no explanation). The Harmon mute makes the instrument play sharper than any other and is not as effective on the trombone as on the trumpet. When trumpets use the Harmon mute, the trombones can use straight or cup mutes. Popular is the Ardsley model.

Plunger The original mute, the rubber end of a "plumber's helper" held in the left hand over the bell, is often still used. Commercial models are made by firms such as Humes and Berg. Like all hand-held mutes, it can be played tight or loose or fanned in and out. The plunger is not effective on the bass trombone below F.

Bucket A large mute which deadens the tone but creates intonation problems if not carefully controlled.

Derby Originally a derby hat, later made of metal and other materials, attached to a stand. The player plays into the derby and can vary the distance and therefore the degree of muting. It cuts the brilliance and softens the tone of the instrument much like the bucket. Held in the hand, the derby can be fanned to create the *doo-wa* or *wa-doo* sound.

Bag Simply a bag made of four to six layers of felt attached over the bell. The sound is distant and quite dull with few overtones. An extremely quiet sound is achieved by putting in the bag a trumpet already muted with a soft straight mute.

Solotone A mute with a nasal, echo-like tone, used in Latin music.

Whispa A very soft mute used for practicing or for very soft passages. The sound is as if the instrument were playing in the next room with the door closed.

Shastock A loud wooden mute which gives a rattling tone.

Other mutes There are also mutes for instruments such as the B♭ piccolo trumpet. The trombone can use the E♭ mellophone bucket mute effectively. One well-known symphonic trombonist has been known on more than one occasion to finish his coffee after an intermission, walk on stage, and use the styrofoam cup as a perfectly satisfactory mute.

6. SPECIAL EFFECTS

These techniques, derived from jazz, have found their way into some contemporary scores.

Slap-tongue A single-reed effect which produces an accent and slight percussive sound as the tongue is brought into contact with the reed on each attack. Good on the sax, all right on the clarinet, the effect is also written for oboe (Ferde Grofé) but is not effective on that instrument. The *quack,* produced by the oboist's forcing the tone, is also used.

The following effects are for brass:

Mute fanning   These effects, discussed in the last section, can be notated by a + over the notes with the mute tight, a ° over the notes with the mute loose or open. This and following effects are seldom notated. The *doo-wah* (*du-wah*) and *wa-wa* (*wah-wah*) sounds are onomatopoeic. Long sounds are indicated *wah, dah,* or *bah;* short sounds, *daht, aht, bop, vop, wap,* or *dop.* The growl can also be combined with fanning.

Trill, tremolo, and flutter   All used by the jazz player though less commonly than the vibrato.

Vibrato   Varies from wide to narrow, fast to slow, or no vibrato at all depending on the style of the music. It usually begins after the note is attacked and then accelerates. See Chapter 37 for ways of indicating vibrato.

Throw-away note   This, like several of the following effects, is achieved by use of half-valves (valves half depressed, ⊕). It is indicated by an x-shaped note head or note head within parentheses and the half-valve symbol above. It is a note of indefinite pitch.

Glissando   The following three effects are glissandi, either lip or with half-valves. The glissando between notes can be smooth (lip, Figure 34–3a) or *notey* with the pistons rapidly depressed in no particular order to create definite pitches between the two notes (Figure 34–3b). The notation is not standard for smooth or notey glissandi; both slurs and jagged lines are used for each, the choice being left to the taste (or lack of it) of the player.

Rip   The glissando up to a note (Figure 34–3c). The notation at Figure 34–3d indicates that the last few notes of the glissando should be emphasized.

Drop-off, Fall-off   Glissando from a note descending (Figure 34–3e).

Doit, Doik   Glissando up from a note (Figure 34–3f).

Bend   Movement up or down and back while playing a note, or chromatic movement between two notes (Figure 34–3g).

Shake, Wow   A rough lip trill, wide and slow (as much as a minor third, depending on the harmonic series), usually starting slow and accelerating Figure 34–3h).

Figure 34–3

Flip A rough turn, often occurring after a downward glissando between two notes. It consists in hitting the note, then the highest harmonic in the series with a glissando back down to the note (Figure 34–3i).

Growl Obtained by growling at the back of the throat while playing. Often used in conjunction with the plunger mute.

Altered rhythms In jazz, the performer will naturally alter simple meter to compound meter in the following ways:

1. Du-wop, du-daht (Figure 34–3j).
2. Shortened syncopations unless slurred (Figure 34–3k).
3. Kick beat (Figure 34–3l).
4. Du-wah (Figure 34–3m).

7. FORM

Arranging for jazz ensemble involves structural arrangement. Therefore, a few words on form are in order. The four-bar phrase and binary and ternary song forms have been remarkably consistent for centuries, and the *standard* or *popular* song in the twentieth century (including most rock) falls into a variant of this structure. Generally there is an introduction of about four bars, usually ending on a half cadence and based on motives from the *chorus* or *refrain* (originally sung by the chorus in early popular responsive vocal music). There follows a verse of about 16 bars and then a (usually repeated) chorus of about 32 measures with the usual sequence of phrases being *aaba* or *abac.* There may be an ending or *close* as well. The length of this form is somewhat determined by the length of time possible on a single record, between 2 minutes, 15 seconds, and 2 minutes, 45 seconds.

In jazz, the standard *blues* progression is 12 bars long (aab). A jazz composition based on the blues consists of the original statement of the blues by the ensemble and then anywhere from two or three to twenty or more improvisatory sections featuring solo instruments or, in a larger group, sections of the ensemble accompanied by the rhythm section. Each of these sections repeats the basic blues progression with improvisatory melodic lines above, much like a chaconne or passacaglia. At the end, the ensemble joins in for a final 12 bars. Some solos become so improvisatory that the periodic structure is disregarded and they may be extended indefinitely.

In instrumental pieces based on popular vocal numbers, the arrangement begins with an introduction, followed by an 8- or 16-bar chorus rendered by the ensemble, followed by repetitions of the chorus altered by variation, free improvisation, including nonperiodic solos, sometimes new thematic material, and alternation of instrumental combinations in each section, followed by a final (usually 16-bar) statement of the chorus by the entire ensemble with expansion and a short ending. This final section is often in a higher key. The sections can be connected by modulatory episodes or by *vamps,* accompaniment figures repeated ad libitum.

Another possible form, common when there is a vocalist with the combo or band, is the introduction and verse, followed by the chorus (all with vocalist and ensemble), then several sections leading to a chorus for the ensemble alone in a higher key, next a return to the vocalist, and finally a chorus for the vocalist and ensemble together.

Less commonly, a solo section can begin a number and build to the ensemble in the course of the number. In small combos, there are, of course, usually a series of solo sections, with the entire combo joining in at the end. After extended solos some cue (such as shake, growl, or flutter) is often used to alert the ensemble that the solo is at an end, much like the trill in the classical cadenza.

8. WRITING FOR JAZZ ENSEMBLES

Since one is dealing with wind instruments, it is most important always to leave places to breathe and in general to keep the arrangement transparent and clear.

Sections are usually used as a unit; in other words, trumpets and trombones are together as the brass section, saxes as the reeds. Generally a section doubles a line or plays in harmony together.

Harmony can be either *tight* or *block* (close position) or *spread* (open) and is usually in four parts. Generally the upper parts play in close position, the lower parts in open.

Parallel perfect consonances are acceptable in block harmony, especially with dissonant chords (sevenths, ninths, etc.), though they are generally avoided in triadic harmony and spread chords. The fifth voice (the lead alto sax with two trumpets and two trombones or four trumpets in four-part block harmony on top) will double the top line an octave lower in a full ensemble harmonization. The trombones will usually be in spread position, and the saxes, in a full ensemble, will pursue independent lines in spread position among the trumpets and trombones, softening their color. The lead alto is usually kept beneath the lead trumpet, and the baritone sax often doubles the lowest trombone. The rhythm section, of course, fills in its harmonies independently of the wind sections with a roving pizzicato bass in the string bass (usual range A to f^1).

The *foreground* consists of the melody either played solo, doubled at the unison, octave, or other intervals, or harmonized. The *background* is an independent part which can also be a single line or harmonized. Generally, if the brass has the lead or melody, the background will be in the saxes and vice versa. If the melody is active, the background will be sustained; if the melody is sustained, the background will move as a countermelody, single-line or harmonized, and be more active. The background can consist of sustained chords, countermelody, or rhythmic patterns in single lines or chords.

If the melody is a single line, the background can be a single line or chordal (Figure 34–4a). If the melody is harmonized, the background can be a single

Figure 34–4

line (Figure 34–4b) or chordal if the two elements are antiphonal (melody moving while background sustains, background moving when melody sustains) (Figure 34–4c). For intros, endings, or big choruses, the full ensemble can play in harmony (Figure 34–4d) or double each other at the octave for emphasis. In Figure 34, a short score in C is used. Drums are the same in each example.

A *stock arrangement* is one made on two staves which may be divided up for any size ensemble. Although sections are generally standard, sometimes instruments are combined, as with a "reed" section of alto, tenor, and baritone (or second tenor) sax and one trombone (the "gazelle" sound) or three tenors and baritone (the "four brothers" or "tenor band" sound).

9. OTHER INSTRUMENTS

The valve trombone is often used in place of the slide trombone, and such instruments as the alto and bass flutes, piccolo, mellophone, bassoon, and euphonium are sometimes seen. It should be noted that the jazz trumpet and trombone are narrower-bore instruments than their orchestral cousins.

Strings, though more characteristic of the 1920's and 1930's, are still found especially in recorded music. William Russo uses four cellos in his jazz orchestra and treats them like another section. They add a new dimension to jazz instrumentation. In the recording, television, and film studio, string *flurries* (rapid passages, flourishes), arpeggios, glissandos, and *rhubarb* counterpoint (a high obligato) are common effects. Usually three or four instruments are used to a section. Commonly, for economic reasons, *tape layering* (several recordings on top of one another) plus various electronic effects are used to make a small number of strings sound like a large symphony orchestra on the final recording (see also Chapter 39).

Voices are used solo for the melody and for scat singing. They are highly stylized in interpretation and make use of many vocal effects, some borrowed from the jazz trumpeter. Singing on vowel syllables, humming, sudden *fps*, crescendo and decrescendo, and sudden, accented cut-offs (notated with a tie to an eighth note with an accent), often with one voice sustaining after others have cut off, are common effects. These effects can also be used with chorus (often only three or four singers) or soloist plus chorus. Often the chorus is in two parts, women and men, who are used alternately and together.

Naturally it is not possible in a work of this scope to quote examples illustrating the many styles and ensembles current in jazz and popular music. William Russo's works (see Bibliography) are recommended for further study. Nothing, of course, can replace an intimate acquaintance with a variety of music in various styles.

35

Writing For School
And Amateur Ensembles

1. WRITING FOR SCHOOL
ORCHESTRAS

The high school orchestra may be of any size, from just a few strings up. In junior high school orchestras the strings are usually supplemented by piano, often playing from the piano reduction, which often serves as a score. *Youth orchestras,* consisting of young musicians from an entire area, exist throughout the United States, some of them of very high quality. They sometimes contain the full complement of orchestral instruments and take on scores by composers such as Wagner, Strauss, Copland, and Stravinsky.

Nevertheless, the average school orchestra is likely to be deficient in strings, especially violas; because of this, parts are occasionally supplied for Violin III, with the viola part written in the treble clef. Also, partly because of higher costs and partly out of indifference or ignorance, string programs are likely to be cut back or even abandoned by many school systems.

For these reasons, the music should be kept simple and technically undemanding. The following are some good guidelines:

1.   Avoid special effects such as harmonics or double stops. An exception may be
     made for occasional double stops with one open string, or for harmonics on
     the E string of the violin to facilitate execution of higher passages.

2. Avoid divided passages altogether if possible (there may be nothing to divide).
3. Keep to the first three positions as much as possible. Don't go beyond the fifth position or an octave above the highest open string.
4. Avoid difficult bowings, especially off-the-string bowings that require a certain degree of technical facility to be precise.
5. Avoid rapid (especially chromatic) passage work and difficult rhythmic passages.
6. Double the strings with the winds where possible; this may not be artistic, but it is practical and can achieve a much more pleasing overall effect where there are few strings.
7. Remember that the double basses seldom have an extension. Their lowest note is written E.
8. The ranges for school orchestras given in previous chapters apply (Figure 35–1).

Figure 35–1

The practical wind ranges listed in Chapter 32 apply to school orchestras and bands (arranging for school band has been dealt with in Chapter 33).

Repertoire should be carefully chosen with regard to the number and types of instruments in the ensemble and their technical level. Two of this writer's most excruciating musical memories are of community orchestras attempting Beethoven's Ninth Symphony and Wagner's *Dutchman* in uncut concert version. Much music exists from the baroque period, early classical period (much neglected, with delightful works by J.C. Bach, Michael Haydn, and others), and the twentieth century (Bartók *Pieces for Young Orchestra,* for example) which is suitable for small orchestra, is not of extreme difficulty, and is seldom performed by professional orchestras. The nineteenth-century repertoire is limited, though some works such as Wagner's *Siegfried Idyll* are possible. Small orchestra concerts might profitably include chamber music as well, with the players drawn from the better orchestra members.

2. ARRANGING FOR SCHOOL OR AMATEUR ORCHESTRA

Besides commercial reductions of works originally written for larger orchestra, it is often necessary to arrange music oneself. Music should be chosen which would be most effective for the particular ensemble. For instance, don't choose Mendelssohn's *Nocturne* from *A Midsummer Night's Dream* if there are no horns or they play badly. Instruments such as horns, violas, bassoons, or even oboes are often lacking. Horn parts can be played by trumpets, trombones, bassoons, or even saxophone, organ, or piano in a pinch (though the result is hardly aesthetic). The piano (solo, four-hands, or two pianos) can be used for reinforcing the bass line, for playing missing wind parts, and for supporting wind chords (see Figure 29–17c). A missing second flute or oboe can be replaced by a clarinet, a bassoon by a cello, etc. The main thing is to retain as much of the original color and balance as possible.

Orff *Schulwerk* instruments have also been used in conjunction with student ensembles of traditional instruments with good effect and an increased opportunity for more students to participate. Carl Orff developed a method to teach young children music through the use of simple instruments such as hand drums, claves (Ger. *Schlagstäbe*), triangles, cymbals and finger cymbals, sand blocks, wood block, coconut shells, tambourines in sizes of 10 to 20 inches (26 to 50 cm), rattles, maracas, sleighbells, and even timpani. Orff developed diatonic, one-row mallet instruments which could be played in keys other than C through substitution of bars tuned to sharps and flats for the natural bars. Of course, the instruments can be played in only one key at a time. They include soprano (sounding an octave higher than written) and alto glockenspiels; soprano (C^3 to g^4), alto (sounding an octave lower with a written range of C^1 to a^2), and bass (with a range of C to a^1) xylophones (Ger. *Trogxylophones*); and soprano, alto (sounding an octave lower), and bass metallophones with aluminum alloy bars. Also, simple music is played on recorders, cello, guitar, viola da gamba, ukulele (and baritone ukulele), autoharp, dulcimer, and other simple instruments. Slaps, claps, stamps, and leg-slapping (Ger. *patschen*) in rhythm are also used.

3. WRITING FOR SCHOOL AND AMATEUR VOICES

The main thing to remember in arranging music for school and amateur vocal groups is that one is dealing with untrained voices. Sight reading and vocal technique are not highly developed. Young voices often sound strained in *forte,* especially if sustained, though they can be trained to sing softly. Frequent rests should be written, as well as light accompaniment. Wide leaps and augmented and diminished intervals (especially if descending) are difficult. Unison, octaves, simple imitation, and simple harmony are the rule. The accompaniment can contain any necessary musical complexities. The arranger can make use of a *descant* (florid countermelody) on a neutral vowel or words of the text, solos (sung by a few voices if a good soloist is not available), humming, singing on neutral syllables, sustained chords beneath the melody, and speech either as rhythmic declamation, often accompanied by singing in the rest of the chorus, or as narration, and even clapping of hands and whistling.

Piano or instrumental accompaniment is possible. In *a cappella* (unaccompanied) sections, the piano part is always written doubling the chorus in small notes with the words, "for rehearsal only."

Ranges for children in the early teens (junior high school age) are shown in Figure 35–2. Extreme ranges, possible with training, are shown in parentheses. Nonsoprano boys range from b to d² or e² and are richer than the light but penetrating boy sopranos. Changing voices range from (g)f to c¹(a¹). Girls and boys in unison should be kept between b to c²(d²).

Ranges for children in the mid-teens (senior high school age) are given in Figure 35–3. The alto voice is light at this age. The extreme low bass notes are weak and useful only if doubled an octave higher.

Figure 35–2   *Figure 35–3*

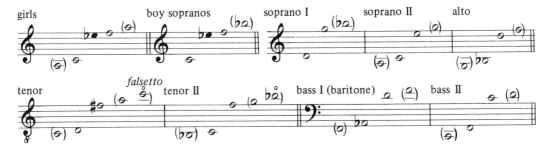

Mixed choirs of female with unchanged (treble) and changed male voices are common in high schools. Tenors are always scarce and altos often weak. Therefore, if parts are to be divided, it is best to divide sopranos or basses.

The tenors are often omitted in junior high school choruses, arrangements being made for SAB. At cadences the basses can be divided for complete chords, the additional part being written in small notes which are optional. The tenor part can be strengthened by the addition of altos if four-part arrangements are used. Two-part arrangements (SB) are possible for girls and boys or high and low voices. They usually need accompaniment and should be kept in the ranges shown in Figure 35–4.

Figure 35–4

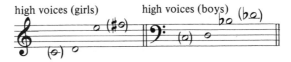

The treble chorus, or girls glee, has a small range and is lacking in variety of tone color, young girls' voices being rather shrill. The parts are treated as upper harmonic parts, the accompaniment supplying the bass. The usual arrangement is SSA. Two-part writing (SA) should not go above g² for the sopranos or below a for the altos. SSAA is unusual.

With both changed and unchanged male voices, the male choir contains more tonal variety than the female choir. In addition, falsetto offers a different quality for quiet passages. The tenors should not sing above g^1 (b^{b1} in falsetto), the basses not below F.

Barbershop quartets consist of two tenors, baritone, and bass. The melody is usually in the second (*lead*) tenor. The other voices improvise close chromatic harmony with typical cadence formulas. Portamento and rhythmic effects are common. Second tenor and baritone cross continually.

Other combinations of young men's voices include TTB or, more commonly, TBarBs. With two parts (TB), the tenors should not sing above $f^{\sharp 1}$, the baritones above d^1.

PART IV

TWENTIETH-CENTURY
TECHNIQUES
AND INSTRUMENTS

36

Instruments Found in Twentieth-Century Orchestral Scores

The use of unusual instruments in the orchestra is not a recent phenomenon but probably as old as the orchestra itself. During the eighteenth and nineteenth centuries unusual instruments appeared primarily in novelty pieces such as the toy instruments found in works by Leopold Mozart, Haydn, Sigmund Romberg, and others. Unusual percussion instruments began to appear in the late nineteenth century. The *terrophone* (Ger. *Terrophon*) was a Swiss instrument consisting of 44 tuned clay pots with a range of c to g³. A drum with a metal head appeared in 1871; the Paris Opera introduced the *codophone*, an instrument consisting of large bells played from a keyboard, in 1890; and in 1900 appeared the *aluminum harp,* an instrument consisting of tubes rubbed at the ends with rosined gloves. There was also a set of musical rattles tuned to definite pitches over two octaves and a set of musical coins which were spun on a marble table top. The carrying power of the latter instrument must remain open to question. The *Glocken-accordion* contained five to eight gongs or large bells tuned to definite pitches and operated from a console. Adolfe Sax, the inveterate inventor, even introduced a set of seven gong-timpani tuned to a scale.

The first use of artillery cannon in an orchestral piece was not in Tchaikovsky's *1812 Festival Overture,* written in 1882, but in a piece written by Rossini for the 1867 World's Exposition. The rifle was introduced into orchestral music in Berlioz's funeral march *Tristia,* although it and the pistol had long been used in the opera. The pop-gun (Ger. *Knallbüchse*) was popular in lighter music such as the champagne galop.

Other instruments common in lighter music such as galops, marches, polkas, and quadrilles at the turn of the twentieth century included the fire brigade horn, a small, one-valve trumpet built in different keys with a range from the second to sixth harmonic; various whistles imitating the nightingale, quail, turkey, duck, cock, pheasant, owl, partridge, snipe, blackbird, cricket, and cuckoo, the tin flute, locomotive whistle, and panpipe, (the seven-tube shepherd's pipe, pandean pipe, syrinx, or Papageno instrument).

The many percussive effects used in this music include *spurs* (Ger. *Sporen*) hung in a row and rhythmically beaten on a drumhead or box; the *railroad* (Ger. *Eisenbahn*), consisting of a sheet of tin hooked across the bass drum and beaten with a rod; the *rain machine* (Ger. *Regenmaschine*), a drum filled with peas or pebbles which is rotated; and sounds imitating the hissing of flame, sneezing, spitting, coughing, snoring, blowing one's nose, smacking the lips, ghosts (bags of glass and crockery dropped on the floor), snow (silkpaper confetti), and flowing water (a ball of strong paper rubbed on the floor).

Other effects included blowing rosin through a flame, rubbing feet on sand, rubbing paper over the bass drum head with a brush, hitting the floor with a stick or with two wooden shoes, and beating a funnel, plates, milk pails, glasses, bottles, fire tongs, tin covers, and stew pans. In his overture to *Il Signor Bruschino*, Rossini has the second violins tap their stands with their bows in rhythm.

Following are unusual instruments found in later twentieth-century scores. Other unusual orchestral instruments (organ, guitar, accordion, etc.) are found in Appendix A.

1. DRUMS

1. *Adufé.* The *tamborin,* a small, single-head frame drum played with a stick.

2. *African drum.* In twentieth-century scores, the term means a single-headed goblet or cup drum played with hands or sticks. Tom-toms can be substituted.

3. *Babylonian drum.* Used by Britten.

4. *Bangale drums.*

5. *Bombo (-i).* The *caxamba,* a small bass drum with foot pedal.

6. *Boo-bams.* A set of small (5 inch diameter) drums set in a row with resonators and played with beaters. The timbre, rich in overtones, sounds high and has the character of a slap-tongue clarinet. The range is chromatic from F to f^1.

7. *Chinese tom-tom.* Small drum with two pigskin heads and a lacquered shell. Also called Chinese clatter drum.

8. *Clay drums.*

9. *Cocktail drum.* Drum with heads of 16 inches (40 cm) and 24 inches (60 cm) diameter. The lower head is played by a foot pedal and the upper with

sticks, with or without snares. A cymbal and cowbell are attached. The drum is used by traveling jazz musicians. (See Chapter 34.)

10. *Cuica, String drum, Lion's roar* (Ger. *Waldteufel*). A friction or string drum with a single parchment head. A stick or string is attached to the center of the head and rubbed with wet or rosined hands to produce a deep gutteral sound. An African folk instrument, used in Europe until the nineteenth century for the celebration of Christmas and sometimes in the theater. Occasionally found in late twentieth-century scores of Varèse, Henze, and others. The Neopolitan *caccarella* (*cacavella*) is a tin friction drum.

11. *Darbuka, derabucca, derbaki, dumbeeki, dumberg, Greek drum, Miriam drum.* A clay goblet drum with a glued head. See also *Tabla*.

12. *Educational drums.* Bass, bongos, conga, cylindrums, drum sets, floor drums, hand drums, oriental drums, redonda, reverbo, rhythm, single-hand bongos, snare boy, snare, tenor, tiny tymps (10 and 12 inches), African tom-toms, American Indian tom-toms, Chinese tom-toms, floor tom-toms, Inca tom-toms, toy drums, tub drums, unibongo drums.

13. *Gongue.* Either a small drum or a single a-go-go bell.

14. *Hand drum* (Ital. *tamburello*, Ger. *Handtrommel*, Fr. *tambour*). Tambourine without jingles.

15. *Hebrew love drums.*

16. *Holzplattentrommel, Holz-tom-tom, Spierholzplatte* (Ger.), (Ital. *tamburo di legno-pelle*). Tom-tom with wood disc instead of membrane. Used by Luigi Nono in his *Diario Polacca 1958* to replace the slit or log drum. Also used by Karlheinz Stockhausen.

17. *Indian drum, American Indian tom-tom.* Single-headed wooden cup drum, usually in three sizes from 5 by 7.5 inches to 9 by 17 inches. Used by Hindemith, Ives, Chávez, Revueltas, and others.

18. *Paniero.* Latin tambourine covered with cloth.

19. *Provençal tambourine.* A tambourine with the shell longer than the diameter of the head. It is fastened to the right wrist, and the left hand plays a pipe. This is the pipe and tabor of southern France.

20. *Roc-o-rine.* Slats of wood on a ring.

21. *Roto-tom.* Tunable toms invented in 1968. They usually come in three sizes: 10 inches (c to c^1), 8 inches (g to g^1), and 6 inches (e^1 to e^2). The drums are tuned by rotating the rim. They are played with sticks, mallets, hands, or brushes.

22. *Schellenrassel, Stabpandiera* (Ger.). Two tambourine jingles on a stick. Used in Brazilian dance music and by Pierre Boulez (Fr. *cymbalettes*). The *Schellenreifen* (Ger.) is a tambourine without a head and is sometimes used in the orchestra in place of the tambourine when only the jingles are needed.

23. *Slit drum, log drum* (Ital. *tamburo di legno, tamburo africano*, Ger. *Schlitztrommel*, Fr. *tambour de bois, tambour à fente*). An African drum made of wood in the shape of a log with a longitudinal groove, usually from 20 to 28

in. long. Made in up to four sizes (as used by Luigi Nono). Tuned slit drums have been used by Henze (f^1 g^1 a^1 b^1 c^1 in *Voices*, one set of two-toned drums, a^b and d^b, c^1 and f^1, a^1 and d^2, a^{b2} and b^{b2} in *Compasses*, and e^1 f^1 a^1 b^1 in the *Violin Concerto No. 2*).

24. *Tabla.* Indian one-headed bowl-shaped drum tuned by sticks in straps which are around the drum head. Sounds like a high timpano. The Arabic version is egg-cup or hourglass-shaped and has a thinner tone (see *Darbuka*). Available tuned to a twelve-tone chromatic scale.

25. *Talking drums.* African drums of various pitches.

26. *Tamboo-bamboo drum.* Different lengths of stamping tubes, pounded on the ground.

27. *Tarole.* A very thin French military drum often used in jazz. Used by Varèse.

28. *Thunder drums.*

29. *Tibetan skull drum.*

30. *Toy drum.*

31. *Turtle drums.*

32. *Voodoo drums.*

33. *Water drum.* A gourd that floats in a tub of water and is beaten with sticks.

2. MALLET INSTRUMENTS

1. *Aluminophone.* A mallet instrument made of aluminum tubes. One exists with a microtonal compass of g^1 to b^4.

2. *Aluminum pipes.* Tuned pipes placed on the timpani heads and played with mallets. One set has a range of a^2 to e^4.

3. *Educational mallet instruments.* Sonant bars, glockenspiels, marimbaphones, marimbas, toy pianos, vibes, xylophones, xylophone-metallophones.

4. *Flapamba.* A series of bars suspended by the end with a range of c to c^2 and a long, sustaining tone not unlike that of the boo-bams. Invented by M. Brent Seawell.

5. *Marimbas.* Marimba eroica, bass marimba, diamond marimba, and bamboo marimba are lower-pitched marimbas developed by Harry Partch from 1946 to 1955. The marimba eroica, with a bar 2.5 meters long, has a low FFF. The resonator is 1.25 meters long. Deagan makes a bass marimba which has a range of C to f. A contrabass marimba is commercially produced with a range of GG to g. The octa-marimba or octa-rimba, invented in 1930, has a double row of bars which play octaves and has a range of c to c^4. The plastic marimba or piccolo boo-bams, invented by Emil Richards, is a row of plastic tubes with a range of g to c^3. The Partch instruments exist in the following ranges: c^1 to f^3, f to f^3, f to c^4, c to c^4, and A to c^4. There is also a bass marimba with a low AA.

6. *Marimbula, thumb (hand) piano, African harp, gypsy cymbal, sanza, mbira, kembe, kalimba, limba* (Ital. *arpa africano,* Ger. *Afrikanische Harfe*). A wooden resonator box with five to forty-five flexible, usually tunable, metal tongues which are plucked with the thumbs and fingers. Some have three manuals (keyboards). The tuning, which varies widely, is generally pentatonic, hexatonic, or heptatonic. Used in the orchestra by Henze and others.

7. *Melodic triangle beaters.* Different size beaters set in a box and played with other beaters. Not exact pitches but from about b^1 to a^2. Invented by Emil Richards.

8. *Resonaphone.* A series of gourd-resonated metal plates used by Percy Grainger.

9. *Steel drum, Trinidad steel drum* (Ital. *tamburo di latta,* Ger. *Stahltrommel*). A set of oil drums with the heads pressed into areas which give definite pitches. The number of notes per drum varies from 2 or 4 for the bass (boom) drum to as many as 32 for the treble (ping pong.) In between are the tenor (cellopan) and alto (guitar pan). A typical chromatic treble drum has a range of b to c^3, a diatonic pan from e^1 to c^3. Some go as high as f^3 or as low as F. They are played with rubber-headed beaters in "steel bands" of from 4 to 100 players and have been used in the orchestra by contemporary composers. A concerto exists by Vernon Evans.

10. *Tubophone.* A set of orchestra bells with tubes instead of bars.

11. *Vibraphones, microtonal.* Erv Wilson has constructed a *chromophone,* or vibraphone in which the octave is divided into 31 intervals with keys in five rows. There is also a 22-tone *transcelest* with brass tubes instead of bars and a range of f^1 to f^3. A 22-tone vibraphone has a range of c^1 to e^3.

12. *Wood blocks, tuned.* Range of c^3 to c^4 on one set.

13. *Xylophones.* A 22-tone microtonal xylophone with a range of f^1 to c^4 has been constructed. The *xylorimba* was used in the 1930's in popular music for solos. The range was c to c^5. The largest xylophone was a five-octave marimba-xylophone combination with a two-octave vibraphone, $10\frac{1}{2}$ feet long, constructed in 1931. The diatonic Orff bass xylophone has a range of C to a^1.

3. METAL INSTRUMENTS

1. *Artillery shell gong.* Used by Emil Richards.

2. *Bock-a-da-bock cymbals.*

3. *Boing gongs.* Adapted by Emil Richards from children's disc-shaped snow sleds, with ranges of from $b^\flat$ to c^1.

4. *Bottle cap shaker stick.*

5. *Brake drums* (Ger. *Bremstrommeln*). Automobile brake drums introduced by John Cage and Lou Harrison. Usually three to five of different pitches. Played with metal or marimba mallets.

6. *Chains.* Dropped on the floor or (Henze's Symphony No. 6) on the head of the timpani, bass drum, or wooden box (Varèse).

7. *Crescent.* Turkish metal rattle. See also *Sistrum.*

8. *Cymbal tree.* Up to seventeen cymbals mounted on a stand and played with a triangle beater or bowed.

9. *Educational metal instruments.* Metal castanets, cymbals, finger cymbals, pat cymbals, metal tap gong, nickel-plated gong, plate gong, rhythm gong, jingle clogs, double jingle taps, triple jingle taps, metal rhythm shakers, tambourines with or without jingles, triangles, tuning bars.

10. *Fishing reel.* Used for a less blatant ratchet.

11. *Flexatone.* A bent band of metal with wooden knobs. It is shaken, the thumb controlling the angle and pitch. Used by Khatchaturian and Schoenberg. Range about $c\sharp^2$ to d^5 in these works, but usually e^2 to g^3.

12. *Garbage can lids.*

13. *Gongs.* Balinese, Chinese, German, Indian, Italian, Japanese hand gongs, Javanese, Korean, Pakistani. The Javanese tuned gongs (Ital. *gong giavanese,* Ger. *Buckelgong,* Fr. *gong à mamelon*), used in the Gamelan orchestras, have as many as eight different pitches and are from 10 to 15 inches in diameter. They have deep rims and are played with various mallets. Tuned gongs have been used by many twentieth-century composers and as far back as Saint-Saëns, Puccini, and Strauss.

14. *Iron pipes.* Harrison and others have written for tuned pipes.

15. *Jingles.*

16. *Lujon.* Caribbean wood box divided into chambers with six to ten metal plates attached over openings. One instrument is tuned $A\flat$ $B\flat$ d f g a. Luciano Berio and others have used the instrument.

17. *Oil can poppers.*

18. *Paila.* Metal bowl played with mallets.

19. *Pang cymbal.* A cymbal with curved edges like a gong, used in jazz, with a rapid decay rate.

20. *Scissors.* Used by Ibert.

21. *Sistrum.* Modern version of the ancient Egyptian metal rattle. A wooden frame with four pairs of jingles or cup-shaped bells like a Chinese bell tree, used by Cage, Harrison, and others. One has a chromatic range of g^1 to g^3. Another, operated by a keyboard mechanism, is called a *celestette* and has a range of c^1 to c^3.

22. *Stainless steel salad bowls.* An Emil Richards invention.

23. *Steel plates.* Beaten with a hammer or clanked against each other.

24. *Twisted metal rod or autospring.*

25. *Vibra-slap.* A metal bell and flexible metal tongue with a ball on the end which is hit and vibrates.

26. *Water gong.* A gong played while being lowered into or removed from a tub of water, which alters the pitch. Used by Cage and Crumb.

27. *Washboard.* Played with metal thimbles, from early jazz.

4. BELLS

1. *Ankle bells.*
2. *Aporo bells.* A Congolese double bell hit with a stick.
3. *Bicycle bells.*
4. *Call bell.* See *Finger bell.*
5. *Camel bells.* Small iron bells attached to a rope.
6. *Carillon.* Used by Tchaikovsky in *1812 Festival Overture.*
7. *Carriage bells.*
8. *Chinese Confucian bells, Chung bells.* A tree of cup-shaped bells usually with microtonal ranges of from f to c³. They come in sets of three, five, seven, or nine. Other versions come from Japan, Pakistan, California missions, and other places.
9. *Corinthian tea bells.*
10. *Crank bell.* A bell continuously sounded by means of a turning key which operates a clapper.
11. *Death toll bell.*
12. *Dinner chimes.* Some exist in the following pitches: b♭ e♭¹ g¹ b♭¹ e♭² g².
13. *Dobači.* Large Japanese temple bell set on a cushion and hit with a cloth-covered stick. The tone sustains as long as three minutes and pitch is about e♭. Used by Henze.
14. *Educational bells.* Tuned bell blocks, chromatic bar bells, chromatic Swiss bells, diatonic bells, diatonic Swiss melody bells, resonator bells, song bells, step bells, tone educator bells, "Liberty" bell, brass Indo bells, camel bells in six sizes, cluster bells, cow, *Diwali,* hand rhythm bells, multi-cluster bells, rhythm bells, signal bells, sleighbells, sleigh wristlet bells, sweetmeat bells, Swiss hand bells, tea bells, temple bells, Turkish bells, Turkish hand bells, Turkish wrist bells, jingle bell stick.
15. *Elephant bells, sarna bells* (Ital. *campana da elefante,* Ger. *Elefantenglocke*). Used by Henze and others.
16. *Fight gong.*
17. *Finger bell, tap bell.* The service bell with tapper.
18. *Fire bell.*
19. *Foot bell.* Indian auto bell with two pitches. One has d² and f♯².
20. *Grelots.* Pellet bells.
21. *Hand bells.* Available in ranges from c¹ to e♭³. Used by Britten and others.
22. *Hawk bells.*
23. *Indian bells.* Like thick sleighbells.
24. *Microtonal bells.* Many sets exist. One, developed by Erv Wilson, divides the octave into 31 microintervals and has a range of c¹ to c⁴.
25. *Saw blade bells.* An invention of Emil Richards.
26. *School bells.*

27. *Ship bells.*
28. *Sleighbells.*
29. *Song bells.*
30. *Steeple bells.*
31. *Steeple tea bells.*
32. *Temple bells.*
33. *Water buffalo bells.* Like large American cowbells.
34. *Wood bells.*
35. *Wrist bells.*
36. *Yacht bells.*
37. *Yah bells.* Bronze Burmese bells.

5. WOOD INSTRUMENTS AND RATTLES

1. *Bean bag.* Hit on a metal plate with the fingers.
2. *Bowls.* Played with spoons or other mallets. Henry Cowell has a piece for tuned flowerpots.
3. *Caixa.* A bundle of sticks and wire brushes played with the hand.
4. *Coconut shells.* Half shells used to imitate the sound of horse's hooves.
5. *Conical gourd rattle.* See *trungonda.*
6. *Cylindrical wood block, wood cymbal* (Ital. *nacchera cilindrica,* Ger. *Röhrenholztrommel,* Fr. *bloc de bois cylindrique*). 4 to 6 in. cylinder with larger diameters on each end and tones a major third or perfect fourth apart.
7. *Educational wooden and gourd instruments.* Bones, finger, hand, and spring castanets, claves, small wooden cocktail shakers, guiros, maracas of gourd or wood, tubular maracas, rhythm sticks, musical spoons of plastic, tap-a-taps (pat-a-cakes), temple blocks in five pitches, tick tock blocks, Chino tone blocks, clave tone blocks, guiro tone blocks, tuned logs, wood blocks, two-tone wood blocks.
8. *Leather maracas.*
9. *Marching machine.* Wooden strips tied to a frame and stamped on the ground.
10. *Matraca.* A large cog rattle as large as $6\frac{1}{2}$ feet (2 m) in diameter with hammers that hit wooden slats when the wheel is rotated. Used by Henze.
11. *Mexican bean pod rattle.* 12 inches (30 cm) long with a sharper sound than maracas. Used by John Cage and Luciano Berio.
12. *Morache.* Indian rasp like the guiro. Used by Lou Harrison.
13. *Mugs.* Played with wooden spoons. Used by Britten.
14. *Pu-ili (pele) sticks.* A segment of bamboo cut three-fifths of the way down into thin slats. Shaken or struck against the hand or an object.
15. *Slit (log) drum.* Also known as the *wooden gong,* one foot to several feet

long (see *Wooden-plate drums, Teponatzli*). Ginastera has called for six of indefinite pitches, Stockhausen for several of definite pitch (f to d^2). One instrument has two pitches, $BB^\flat$ and $D^\flat$.

16. *Tap shoes.* Played with hands on a board.

17. *Teponatzli.* The South American slit drum. Used by Lou Harrison.

18. *Trungonda.* The conical gourd rattle used by Britten to imitate marching feet.

19. *Wobble board.* Large blackboard or masonite which is shaken. Invention of Emil Richards.

20. *Wooden hammer on plank.* Used by Mahler, Respighi, Berg, and Milhaud.

21. *Wooden plate drums.* $\frac{3}{8}$ inch (1-cm) thick piece of circular wood placed on a tom-tom head and played with mallets. Used by Puccini (*Turandot*) and revived by Karlheinz Stockhausen.

6. GLASS INSTRUMENTS

1. *Bottle and spoon.* Tuned to different pitches by different levels of water, with ranges of c^3 to c^4 or greater.

2. *Bottle tree.* A set of the top halves of bottles of different sizes mounted on a stand and played with various mallets.

3. *Bottle with marbles.* Shaken.

4. *Bouteillophone* (Fr.). A series of tuned bottles. Used by Satie and Honegger.

5. *Broken bottles.*

6. *Broken wine glass.* Used by Henze.

7. *Cloud chamber bowls.* Harry Partch instruments consisting of large half-bottles. Partch also invented instruments such as the 'spoils of war' and various low-pitched marimbas.

8. *Glasses.* Glasses tuned to various pitches with different levels of liquid have been used since Gluck wrote a concerto for 26 drinking glasses. Beethoven, Saint-Saëns, Glinka, and others wrote for glasses, as have such contemporary composers as Carl Nielsen and Carl Orff. They can be stroked with a wet finger or struck with mallets. Ranges are anywhere from c to c^5.

9. *Glass harmonica.* An instrument consisting of glass bowls of various sizes rotated in a trough of water. When fingers are brought into contact with the bowls, sounds of various pitches are produced. Mozart's famous music for the instrument was written for a version perfected by Benjamin Franklin. The instrument is also called the *glass euphonium, verrophone,* or *verrillon* (Fr.). Berlioz speaks of keyboard glass harmonicas with ranges of d^1 to e^3 and of a^1 to c^5.

10. *Glass harp* (Ital. *arpa di vetro*, Ger. *Glasharfe*, Fr. *harpe de verre*). A

twentieth-century instrument consisting of 46 glass bowls with short stems and a range of g to c⁴ or d to c⁴.

11. *Glass or china bell.* Used by Orff.
12. *Musical glasses.* See *Glasses*.
13. *Pop bottles.* See *Bottle and spoon*.
14. *Smashed glass.* A pane of glass smashed on the floor. Used by Henze and others.
15. *Tuned bottles.* See *Bottle and spoon*.

7. AEROPHONES OFTEN PLAYED BY PERCUSSIONISTS

1. *Auto horns.* Either bulb or electric. Gershwin writes for tuned horns in *American in Paris*. Also used by Bloch and Poulenc.
2. *Bamboo flute.* Used by Henze in *Voices*.
3. *Bengal flute.* In Henze's *Voices*.
4. *Bicycle horn.*
5. *Bosun whistle.* A slide whistle.
6. *Bullroarer* (Ger. *Schwirrholz*, Fr. *rhombe ronflaute*). A slat of wood on a string whirled around to produce a hum. Used by Henry Cowell.
7. *Compressed-air cylinder.* Used by Ernst Toch.
8. *Cyclone whistle.*
9. *Diesel horn.*
10. *Foghorn* (Ital. *sirena da battello*, Ger. *Nebelhorn*).
11. *Inca flute.* Used in Henze's *Voices*.
12. *Interurban whistle.*
13. *Kazoo.* Tube with a membrane covering a lateral hole. The player hums in the mouthpiece.
14. *Lotus flute.* In Henze's *Voices*; also called *swanee whistle*.
15. *Mama cry.* Player blows in tube and uses palm over opening.
16. *Mouth sirens.*
17. *Musical hose.* Whirled around creating harmonics three to six (about b¹ to b²).
18. *Nose flute.* Toy instrument from Africa.
19. *Ocean liner horn.*
20. *Panpipes.* A set of about seven pipes in a row.
21. *Police whistle.*
22. *Rugby whistle.*
23. *Siren.* Varèse writes for two of different pitch, hand-cranked with braking mechanisms.
24. *Slide whistle.* Used with glissando or vibrato. Range from g¹ to a².

Sometimes two pipes tuned to a minor third and a fingerhole for the cuckoo effect.

25. *Song whistle.* See *Slide whistle.*
26. *Steamboat whistle.* Two or three notes.
27. *Taxi horn.*
28. *Tin whistle.* Like a vertical flute with fingerholes. Used by Copland (*Billy the Kid*) with a range of a$^{\flat 1}$ to f^2.
29. *Train whistle.* Two or three notes.
30. *Tugboat whistle.*

8. BIRD (AND ANIMAL) CALLS

Ital. *richiamo di uccelli*   **Ger.** *Vogel-lockruf*

Antelope, baby, bear, bird, bobwhite, canary, cow, cricket, crow, cuckoo (see *Slide whistle*), curlew, deer, dog, dove, duck, elk, frog, goose, hen, jaybird, lark, lion, nightingale, peacock, plover, raccoon, rooster, skylark, snipe, squirrel, tiger, turkey, warbler, and even a wounded rabbit cry are commercially available.

9. MISCELLANEOUS INSTRUMENTS

1. *Abacus.*
2. *Bursting balloons.* Used by Nicolas Slonimsky and Henze (*Voices*)
3. *Bird-scare* (Ital. *ricciane*). A quieter version of the ratchet, like a New Year's ratchet. Used by bird-watchers and occasionally by percussionists.
4. *Boing box.* A monochord with a resonating box. A boing, bend, glissando, or wobble is possible. A variation of this instrument is an inverted metal tube with a wooden neck and one string.
5. *Buzz-imba.* Marimba with beads and enclosed resonators.
6. *Buzz rattles.*
7. *Cartophone.* Small cardboard boxes, with open ends covered with paper membranes, connected with cord; played with the hand. New instruments from the *"Groupe Instrumental à Percussion de Strasbourg."*
8. *Chimes.* Glass, metal (sometimes keys), shell, or wood pieces hung so that they can be hit together with various mallets or the hands. They can also be grasped to produce a "choke" effect. The bamboo chimes (Ital. *tubi di bambie*, Ger. *Bambus-Pendelrassel, hängende Bambusruhre*, Fr. *tubes de bambou*) are common in contemporary music. Made in Japan, they are commonly 8 in. long and consist of anywhere from 8 to 15 pieces of bamboo. Rustled in *pianissimo*, they sound like they are being moved by the wind. The "choke"

produces a sharp accent with some inevitable sound after the beat. The *water chimes* invented by Emil Richards are really small water gongs lowered and raised from a tank of water by an electric motor. The tone bends up and down a minor third. There is an underwater microphone to amplify the pitches.

9. *Ching-ring.* Set of small, bowl-shaped cymbals.

10. *Clavitimbre.* Keyboard metallophone with resonators.

11. *Dice.*

12. *Gear machine.*

13. *Jingle muffler on bass drum.*

14. *Lithophone* (Ger. *Steinspiel*). Rocks of various pitches such as are found in Chinese music. Porcelain bowls or even flowerpots (Henry Cowell) have been used. See also *Terrophone* in the introductory section to this Chapter.

15. *Marching machine.* See *Wood Instruments.*

16. *Music box.*

17. *Pan rattles.*

18. *Pop gun.*

19. *Prepared piano.* See Chapter 37.

20. *Radios.* John Cage has used radios tuned at random.

21. *Roulette wheel.* Used by Satie in *Parade.*

22. *Sandpaper blocks.* Used to imitate soft-shoe dancing. Hindemith used a box of sand which was shaken.

23. *Surrogate kithara.* An instrument of Harry Partch consisting of wooden resonators for eight strings stopped with a glass rod. The strings are hit with a stick.

24. *Tambura with mandola harp.* A modern lute drone with four plucked strings and seventeen strummed strings. The plucked strings are tuned a e^1 a a^1, the strummed strings diatonically from g to e^2.

25. *Ticking clocks.*

26. *Typewriter.* Used by Satie.

27. *Water splash.* Used by Satie.

37

Late Twentieth-
Century Techniques
And Notation

1. MICROINTERVALS

Although the existence of microintervals (intervals smaller than the minor second) has always been known, their use in Western European music began only in the twentieth century. Previously, their existence was considered only in relation to the pure or natural overtone series. The archicembalo, a keyboard instrument invented in 1555, divided the octave into 31 intervals, and made it possible to play the natural overtones of a number of pitches before the introduction of tempered tuning.

At the turn of the twentieth century the Czech Alois Hába and the Americans Charles Ives and Henry Cowell experimented with music utilizing microintervals. Ives even built a quarter tone (an interval half as large as a minor second) piano. Microintervals are possible on string instruments by means of fingering between the normal pitches and on wind instruments by means of special fingerings and lip and breath control. Keyboard instruments must be specially tuned. Unfortunately, no standard notation has been developed for this or many other new techniques. In Figure 37–1 are some of the many notations to be encountered. To avoid confusion, the two symbols shown in Figure 37–2 are recommended. Any pitch raised a quarter tone or lowered a quarter tone from a natural note can be indicated in this way. As with all nonstandardized notation, a note at the beginning of the score should clarify the meaning of the symbols. Intervals smaller than quarter tones are difficult to perform by most players and are seldom encountered today.

Figure 37–1

quarter tone sharp:

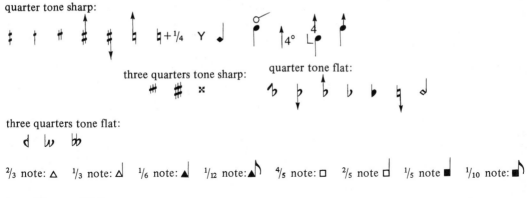

three quarters tone sharp: quarter tone flat:

three quarters tone flat:

$^2/_3$ note: △ $^1/_3$ note: ◬ $^1/_6$ note: ▲ $^1/_{12}$ note: ▲ $^4/_5$ note: □ $^2/_5$ note ▯ $^1/_5$ note ■ $^1/_{10}$ note: ♪

Figure 37–2

2. NEW NOTATION

In the 1940's and 1950's totally new notational methods were introduced but were soon found to be inferior to traditional notation (see Figure 37–3).

Figure 37–3

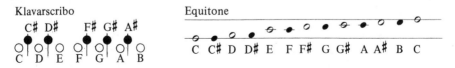

Klavarscribo

C♯ D♯   F♯ G♯ A♯

C D E F G A B

Equitone

C C♯ D D♯ E F F♯ G G♯ A A♯ B C

Figure 37–4 gives several common new methods of notation which have expanded rather than replaced standard notation. Many of these notations are *indicative,* that is, they do not refer to definite pitches or durations. When more than one notation is shown in the illustration, the first one given is the one recommended by the author.

Figure 37–4

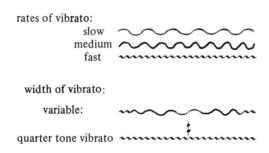

rates of vibrato:

slow

medium

fast

width of vibrato:

variable:

quarter tone vibrato

Figure 37-4 (cont.)

highest available pitch on instrument:

lowest available pitch:

indefinite pitch:

bend up or down a quarter tone:

scale or arpeggio on any notes:

rapid glissando (broken):

dampen the sound:

duration equals length of line:

duration equals distance between notes:

repeat the same pitch rapidly:

Figure 37-4 (cont.)

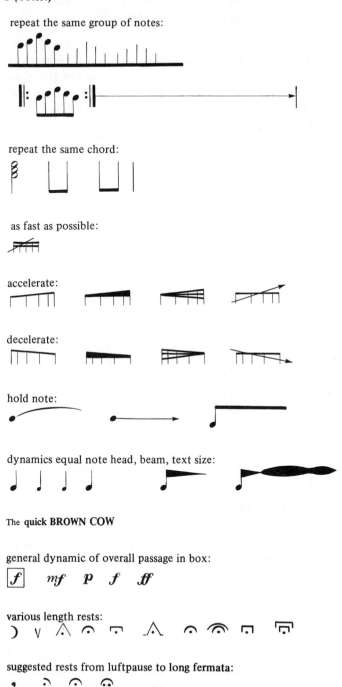

repeat the same group of notes:

repeat the same chord:

as fast as possible:

accelerate:

decelerate:

hold note:

dynamics equal note head, beam, text size:

The quick BROWN COW

general dynamic of overall passage in box:

$\boxed{f}$ *mf*   *p*   *f*   *ff*

various length rests:

suggested rests from luftpause to long fermata:

3. SCORE INDICATIONS AND ALEATORIC MUSIC

For convenience in score-reading, most contemporary scores are written in C (at concert pitch), except for the instruments which transpose at the octave. A note to this effect should be included at the beginning of the score.

Often staves are omitted when an instrument has nothing to play. When the instrument enters, the entrance is easy to see and easy for the conductor to cue (see Figure 37–5).

Sometimes meter is written as shown in Figure 37–6

Figure 37–5   *Figure 37–6*

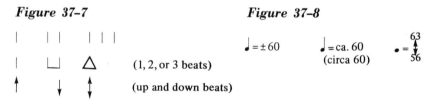

Composers occasionally notate the way a bar should be conducted (Figure 37–7), but this is best left up to the conductor, who will have his own system of marking the score if necessary.

A fluctuating meter or a meter within certain limits can be indicated as in Figure 37–8.

Figure 37–7   *Figure 37–8*

(1, 2, or 3 beats)

(up and down beats)

$\bullet = \pm 60$ $\bullet = \text{ca. } 60$ $\bullet = \begin{smallmatrix} 63 \\ \uparrow \\ \downarrow \\ 56 \end{smallmatrix}$

(circa 60)

Important melodic lines are often indicated as *Hauptstimme* or *voce maggiore*, secondary melodic lines as *Nebenstimme* or *voce secondaria* (see Figure 37–9).

Figure 37–9

H⌐‾‾‾‾¬   N⌐‾‾‾‾¬   √M⌐‾‾‾‾¬   √S⌐‾‾‾‾¬

Graphic notation shows proportional relationships or specific durations of notes (Figure 37–89 gives examples). Sections of a score within which the performers are allowed to perform in free rhythm can be indicated as in Figure 37–10. The conductor cues each section, which lasts for the indicated amount

Figure 37-10

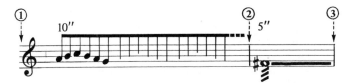

of time. Different groups of instruments can be cued to begin and end at different times so that sections overlap. This may require more than one conductor.

Music which allows such freedom of performance is called *aleatoric* (from the Assyrian goddess of chance, *Alea*) or *chance* music. This music may allow freedom of performance in any of the following ways:

1. Freedom of rhythm within limits.
2. Freedom of pitch choice within limits.
3. Freedom of dynamics, attack, performance medium, and so on.
4. Freedom of the order of performance of various *frames* or musical sections.
5. Freedom of where to begin within a cyclic framework.
6. Freedom to superimpose various musical elements in different combinations.
7. Freedom to perform from generalized graphic notation.
8. Total freedom to perform with little or no limits imposed—more or less total improvisation.

The choice of the above parameters may be made in advance or during performance by the conductor, players, or both. The players can react to one another or to a tape or can follow their own sequence independently.

In *frame notation,* the succession of musical sections can be preset, allowing the performer freedom within each frame, or individual parts may be set but may pursue their own sequence without synchronization of tempo, or there can be a combination of strict and free sections, or a sequence can be suggested or be left totally to the predilection of the performer.

The conductor can use an auxiliary score which shows only the general outline or schema for each frame, with which he has familiarized himself before the performance; in this way he can see at a glance the various possibilities and how they can be combined. Parts can have cut-out windows through which a frame is read or revolving strips which either show a frame or section or, if transparent, superimpose various elements on each other; or a long cyclic score can be rolled out and spread around the performer.

A box or brackets can contain one frame or musical event. The duration may be indicated above it. Possibly a choice of sequence will be indicated as well. The contents within a frame may be scattered. (See Figure 37–11). Staff lines moving up and down can indicate faster and slower tempi (Figure 37–12). A line, a series of headless stems, or a pitch band whose width indicates

Figure 37-11

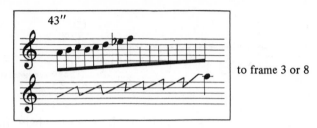

to frame 3 or 8

Figure 37-12

volume may be used to indicate approximate pitch and duration (Figure 37–13). A range can be indicated within which the performer selects one or more notes, or the performer may be asked to select as many tones as possible above or below a particular pitch (Figure 37–14).

Figure 37-13

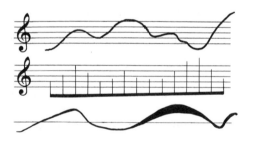

Figure 37-14

The parameters of extremely free music can be indicated by signs and symbols which are intended to convey to the performer some general characteristics of timbre, attack, sound complexes, manner of performance, dynamics, pitch, and even instrumentation. These symbols vary with the imagination of the composer, though whether this music can truly be considered *composed* is open to question. Frequency, duration, intensity, timbre, and various types of sound modification can be notated graphically for electronic music as well. This sort of graphic notation is necessary when an electronic tape and a performer must synchronize in live performance (see Chapter 39). Further notation will be considered under individual instrument types.

4. VOCAL TECHNIQUES

Schoenberg introduced the concept of *Sprechstimme* in his *Pierrot Lunaire* (1912). This is a form of vocal production halfway between speech and song: the words begin on definite pitches but rise and fall as in speaking. Today some composers make a distinction between *Sprechgesang* (*sung speech*) and *Sprechstimme* (literally, *spoken voice*), the former being closer to song. Figure 37–15 illustrates the various gradations between free speech and song. In the case of free speech, just the text and no notation is necessary. Any accompanying instruments either rest, hold a note or chord, or play without reference to the voice part, which is simply narration.

Figure 37–15

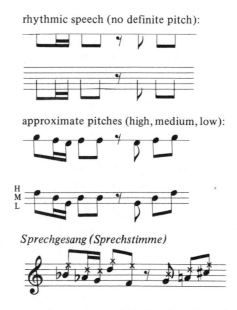

rhythmic speech (no definite pitch):

approximate pitches (high, medium, low):

Sprechgesang (Sprechstimme)

Figure 37–16 shows various ways of indicating *Sprechgesang*. As usual, the first method is that suggested by the author. Figure 37–17 shows the notation used by Schoenberg in *Pierrot Lunaire* for various vocal effects. *Sprechstimme*

Figure 37–16

Figure 37–17

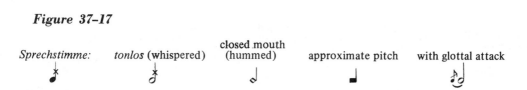

Sprechstimme:	*tonlos* (whispered)	closed mouth (hummed)	approximate pitch	with glottal attack

was taken up by Berg in *Wozzeck* and *Lulu* and became a standard vocal technique after the Second World War.

Besides traditional alterations of vocal technique such as *sotto voce* (beneath the voice or little voice), *mezzo voce* (half voice), *a piena voce* (full voice), the following techniques have been used: chanting (a sort of speech with melodization), head voice (nasal), chest voice (throat voice), falsetto, yodeling (Ger. *Jodeln*), an alternation of head and chest voice, shrieking (Ital. *gridando*), shouting, screaming, whispering (unvoiced, Ital. *sussurando*), breathy voice, inhaling (Ital. *aspirando*), exhaling, sighing (Ital. *sospirando*), moaning, whining, hiccuping, howling, heavy breathing, whistling, giggling, weeping, murmuring, breathing, gasping, sucking, crying, laughing (high and low), hissing sibilants (*s*, *sh*, or *f*), creaky voice, coughing, lack of resonance, tremolo, dental tremolo (with quivering jaw), trill with tongue against upper lip, glissando, fluttering sound, various widths and rates of vibrato, humming (mouth closed, Ital. *bocca chiusa*, Ger. *Mund zu*, Fr. *bouch fermée*), mouth slightly or half open (Ital. *bocca appena aperta*), lips rounded, glottal stop, mouth covered with hand, with cupped hand, half closed with hand, closed to open with hand (*wa-wa* effect), fingers tapped against oral cavity to produce sound, staccato articulation, explosive consonants, phonemes derived from text, rolled *R*, quickly repeated sounds, phonetic sounds with no relation to text, held consonants, and changing timbre on the same note. All these effects can change from one to another, merge, or in some cases, be combined.

The speaking tube or megaphone has been used since Wagner (for Fafner in *Siegfried*) to amplify the voice. All of the electronic alterations possible with amplified instruments can naturally be applied to the voice. John Cage has even used a contact mike at the throat to amplify sounds of smoking, drinking, and other such activities. The Roy Hart school of vocal production even includes multiphonics. Henze's *Essay on Pigs* gives the symbols shown in Figure 37–18.

Figure 37-18

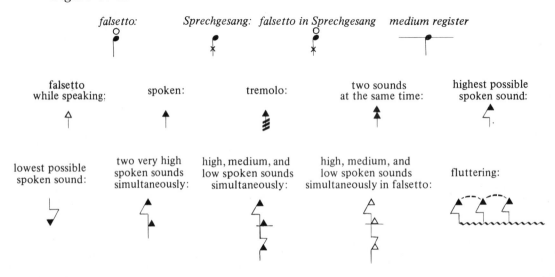

During the 1940's jazz musicians began singing while playing their instruments either in parallel intervals or simple counterpoint. This technique is used today, as are such effects as clapping hands, snapping fingers, rubbing feet on the floor, striking heel on the floor, tapping foot, the African tongue click (velar, not retroflex), the ordinary tongue cluck, popping lips, and kissing sounds. These may be performed by singers or instrumentalists, either while performing or alternately with vocal or instrumental performance.

In choral writing all of the above effects have been used, as have tone clusters (a group of several notes close together), aleatoric effects, microintervals, and the division of a line of text and/or melody among different sections of the chorus. The text may even be divided between syllables, in which case the proper order of the text is traced with a dotted or sometimes continuous line from one choral part to another. Many of these effects are illustrated in succeeding examples in this chapter.

5. STRING TECHNIQUES

Although the development of string technique up to the twentieth century was mainly confined to extensions of range, bowing techniques, multiple stops, and harmonics, occasional effects occurred such as Heinrich von Biber's seventeenth-century attempt to imitate the sound of a military drum by using paper on the strings of the violin in his piece *la Battaglia*. The following techniques have developed primarily since the Second World War.

CLUSTERS

Figure 37–19 shows three common ways to indicate tone clusters. In the first example, one staff shows the duration of the cluster while the lower staff shows the notes taken by each string instrument. Although clusters are also written

Figure 37–19

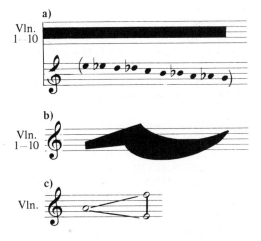

for other instruments (see Chapter 23), they are particularly suitable for the strings, with many performers in each section. Figure 37–19b shows approximate ranges of a changing cluster. Example c shows an expanding cluster. Composers such as Penderecki and Xenakis commonly employ such "clouds of pitches."

GLISSANDI

1. The string struck *col legno* and the left hand glissando to the bridge.
2. Pizzicato followed by glissando with the left hand (Figure 37–20).
3. Glissando with bouncing bow (a virtuoso solo technique).
4. The bow taken away or attacked *during* a glissando.
5. Glissando with the tuning peg.
6. Pizzicato tremolo with a glissando.
7. The bow sliding toward the bridge.
8. The fingernail scraping along the string.
9. Combination of bowed note with left hand pizzicato *and* glissando.

Figure 37–20

PIZZICATI

1. Besides the slap pizzicato mentioned in Chapter 5, the double bass can use the two- to four-finger pizzicato technique derived from jazz, but indicated as early as Monteverdi's *Il Combattimento di Tancredi e Clorinda* of 1627 and Franz Simandl's *Method* of 1869.
2. Thumb pizzicato for a darker sound on the bass and cello. The violins and violas use the thumb for quadruple stops in Berlioz's *Damnation of Faust* (1846).
3. Fingernail pizzicato or fingernail striking string.
4. Pizzicato with guitar pick.
5. Pizzicato *sul ponticello* or *sul tasto*.
6. Two to four notes (within the limit of a major third) under one pluck—the "slurred" pizzicato.
7. Pizzicato tremolo, first used in Elgar's 1910 *Violin Concerto*.
8. Finger-slap pizzicato.
9. Two-handed pizzicato on the bass.
10. Two fingers plucking the string on each side of the stopping finger, producing harmonics.
11. Pizzicato close to the stopped finger (*secco*).
12. A wooden sound created by the right hand's plucking the string as the left hand presses lightly on the string.
13. Thumb pizzicato between the nut and stopping finger.
14. Pizzicato with right hand as the left-hand fingernail stops the string for a guitar-like sound.

15. Left-hand pizzicato (indicated by +) while a second finger of the left hand stops a harmonic.
16. Left-hand pizzicato with arco.
17. Left-hand pizzicato as a counterpoint to the bowed line.
18. "Buzz" pizzicato on the bass produced by the plucked string's being touched by the fingernail.
19. Pizzicato behind the bridge.
20. Pizzicato in peg box.
21. Fingers flicked against or along string (*pizzicato gettato*).
22. *Pizzicato muto* on the double bass, guitar-like pizzicato harmonics. The thumb plucks as the palm dampens the string. Especially good on I and II.

MULTIPLE STOPS

1. Octaves are possible in the full range of the double bass in modern solo technique, especially from the fifth position up.
2. Double bass pizzicato on non-adjacent strings to the seventh position.

VIBRATO

Frequency and width of vibrato can be indicated as shown in Figure 37–4 of this chapter. A narrow vibrato with two fingers has also been indicated.

BOWING

1. Rapid or slow arpeggios ascending or descending (a straight line can be used for a rapid arpeggio, a wavy line for a slow one).
2. Off-string bowing with left-hand pizzicato.
3. *Col legno* with pizzicato.
4. Pizzicato with bowing *sul ponticello* or *sul tasto* or shifting between the two.
5. Shifting between *col legno tratto* and *battuto*.
6. Bowing directly on the bridge (Figure 37–21a), bowing on the tailpiece (section b), arpeggio on four strings between the bridge and tailpiece (c), or bowing between bridge and tailpiece (d).
7. Bowing between pegs and fingerboard, pizzicato between bow and bridge as bow is drawn (cellos and basses).
8. Reverse bowing under the strings, giving double stops on I and IV (bass).
9. Bowing above fingers of left hand (which can be indicated AF for "above fingers") for harmonics.
10. *Col legno battuto* with glissando to bridge in left hand.
11. *Col legno tratto* with bow moving to bridge or away from bridge.
12. *Col legno jeté.*
13. Diagonal bowing (bass) for groaning sound.

Figure 37–21

a) b) c) d)

14. Circular bowing for sighing sound.
15. Saltando along the length of the string while the left hand damps the string.
16. Ricochet *col legno* while left hand lightly stops the string.
17. Slack string.
18. Sawing with bow (Figure 37–22a), rubbing (b), scratching (c), or pressure resulting in a squeak or grunt (d).
19. Bowing on the wrong side of the left hand (bass).
20. Combining any non-mutually exclusive above techniques.

Figure 37–22

HARMONICS

1. Pulled harmonic—raising or lowering the pitch a half step.
2. Highest possible harmonic, indicated with a triangular note (see Figure 37–4).
3. Arpeggios or complex melodic lines to be played in harmonics by the bass. The examples in Figure 37–23 are to be played entirely in harmonics.
4. Natural harmonics from 1 to 8 on the bass on both halves of the strings (9 to 13 are rarely used and impossible on the E string). Notation is in the treble clef at actual pitch.
5. Natural harmonic double stops on the double bass. Figure 37–24 shows those available on III and IV. For II and III, transpose the list up a perfect fourth; for I and II, transpose it up a minor seventh.
6. Artifical harmonics on the bass of a fourth (sounding two octaves higher) or a fifth (sounding a twelfth higher), both possible from a minor seventh above the open string and higher. The third harmonic (sounding the seventeenth) is good from second position.
7. Artificial harmonic glissando.

Figure 37–23   Dragonetti (or E. Nanny), *Concerto for Double Bass*

Bottesini, *Lucia*

Figure 37–24

8. Natural harmonic pizzicato with *col legno battuto,* fingernail pizzicato, or *sul ponticello.*
9. Pizzicato harmonic on the bass, obtained by stopping the string with the left hand and touching it at the octave, twelfth or fifteenth with the right-hand thumb while plucking the string with a right-hand finger. The notation is suggested in Figure 37–25. Remember, since few of these notations are standard, a note in the score and part is mandatory.

Figure 37–25

SCORDATURA

Dragonetti tuned the solo bass up a step for added brilliance. A different set of harmonics can be obtained by tuning one or more strings to different pitches. In the 1950's many jazz bassists used the tuning CGDA.

MUTES

String mutes are made of rosewood, hard rubber, plastic, leather, ebony, aluminum, and brass. The heavy metal "practice" mute gives a ghostly, attenuated sound, but it is not used in performance.

PERCUSSIVE EFFECTS

1. Use of wood, coins, a rasp, fingernails, cloth, thimbles, metal, or plastic to pluck or scrape the string.
2. Knuckles, palm, fingertips, nails, cupped hand, or fist on the strings or body.
3. Playing with parts of the bow or any of the above on the ribs, neck, top, back, bridge, scroll, tailpiece, or fingerboard of instrument, or on music stand, chair, or other object. Especially effective with basses or celli.
4. Tapping strings with fingertips, left-hand tremolo without bow, or stroking strings with the hand.
5. Timpani stick, vibe mallet, maraca, or wooden spoon tapping or bowing string.
6. Paper between fingerboard and string for buzzing effect.
7. String player's playing other instruments.
8. Clapping and finger-snapping.
9. *Col legno* below bridge, like marimbula.
10. *Col legno* on bridge.
11. *Col legno* behind bridge with tip of bow.
12. Rubbing body of instrument with palm in circular direction or back and forth.
13. Rubbing body of instrument with rosined finger.

14. Fingers tapping strings—aeolian harp effect, harmonics.
15. Vocal effects (see section 4) by string player alone or with string effects

A second staff can be used to indicate the above effects.

MIXED EFFECTS

1. Changing sound generators, such as pizzicato, arco, *col legno* (pizzicato to arco, arco to *col legno*, arco to pizzicato tremolo, *col legno battuto* to arco or pizzicato tremolo, arco glissando to pizzicato tremolo, pizzicato tremolo to arco tremolo, pizzicato to arco to glissando, and so on.)
2. Combinations of arco with vocal, percussive, pizzicato, or rubbed sounds.
3. Combinations of pizzicato with vocal, percussive, or rubbed sounds.
4. Percussive with vocal sounds.
5. Left hand alone with vocal, rubbed, percussive, pizzicato, or arco.
6. Arco and vocal with percussive, rubbed, pizzicato, or left hand alone.
7. Pizzicato and vocal with rubbed, percussive, or left hand alone.
8. Slap pizzicato with knuckle or palm slap and other such combinations.
9. Combinations of four or five effects at the same time.

AMPLIFIED AND ELECTRONIC EFFECTS

Amplification of string instruments produces a higher ratio of noise (connected with bowing and other sounds) to music. The sound source is a standard instrument with a pickup microphone (FRAP, for "flat response audio pickup") or contact mike or an electronic instrument such as the electric bass. The sound goes to a pre-amp, an electronic effects control center, which alters the sound in various ways (see Chapter 39); it then goes through an amplifier and finally to a speaker system.

A magnetic pickup gives tone and isolation. The piezoelectric gives isolation. The FRAP (which is movable, attached to the instrument with wax) and Barcus Berry (fixed to the bridge) give wide frequency response and are hum-free.

Positioning of the pickup is important. If it is on the scroll, a blunt sound is obtained; if it is on the back or bass bar, a rich tone is achieved; and if it is on the bridge, a harsh, cutting sound results.

6. HARP TECHNIQUES

1. Playing *près de la table* (close to the sounding board). See Figure 37–26.
2. Left hand playing near sounding board, right hand playing normally.
3. Playing with the fingernails (Ital. *colla unghia*, Ger. *mit dem Nagel*, Fr. *sons d'onges*). See Figure 37–27.

Figure 37–26   **Figure 37–27**

4. Playing at the lower end of the strings, then sliding the fingers to the sounding board.
5. Damping the string in the middle and playing near the sounding board.
6. Playing near the screws.
7. Playing with a plectrum (Mahler, *Das Lied von der Erde,* Symphonies No. 3, 6, and 7).
8. Glissando with accelerando.
9. Playing on the string and sliding from the screw to the sounding board with or without damping.
10. Glissando by turning of the tuning key on a string.
11. Pinching the string (Stravinsky, *Symphony of Psalms*).
12. Right-hand thumb playing between the screw and grooves alternately in and out while the left hand plays the string normally. See Figure 37–28.

The following techniques (Nos. 13 to 47) were developed by Carlos Salzedo and published in 1918. They have since been widely used in solo harp music.

13. Using left foot for pedal on right side (Figure 37–29).
14. Using the same foot for two pedals (Figure 37–30).
15. Moving pedal without putting in notch, keeping foot on pedal (Figure 37–31).
16. Moving pedal during fermata (Figure 37–32).
17. Playing two strings with the same finger (notated with a slur).
18. Sliding along a string from center to top or vice versa (Fr. *glisser avec souplesse*) to connect two longer notes (Figure 37–33).
19. Glissando (Figure 37–34a) and flat, unbroken chord (Fr. *plaqué*) (Figure 37–34b).
20. Trill alternately in two hands (Figure 37–35).
21. Scordatura to extend the range downward (*Wozzeck* to low B♭ or to make

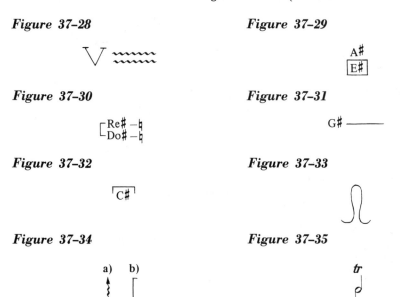

Figure 37–28

Figure 37–29

Figure 37–30

Figure 37–31

Figure 37–32

Figure 37–33

Figure 37–34

Figure 37–35

possible tunings to chords not possible with standard tuning. Not all strings of one pitch need be tuned to the same note.

22. Aeolian flux (Fr. *flux éoliens*), a sort of tremolo glissando with hands gliding up and down in different directions (Figure 37–36).

23. Aeolian rustling (Fr. *bruissements éoliens*), a slow glissando with fingertips close together (Figure 37–37).

24. Oboic flux (Fr. *flux hautboïstiques*), glissando near the sounding board; best *mf* and not too fast (Figure 37–38).

25. Falling hail (Fr. *flux en grêle*), glissando with the back of the fingernails ascending or descending; best *p* and rather slow (Figure 37–39).

26. Xyloflux, like falling hail but moving toward the sounding board (Figure 37–40).

27. Gushing chords (Fr. *accords en jet*), with strings tuned in chords, a brusque slide made from one note to another (Figure 37–41).

28. Snare drum effect (Fr. *effect de tambour militaire sans timbre*), the right hand playing gushing chords, with the left hand flat on the strings (Figure 37–42).

29. Aeolian tremolo (Fr. *trémolo éolien*) the flat of the hand rubbing rapidly between notes (Figure 37–43).

30. Ascending aeolian chords, two or three successive fingers strumming rapidly over a group of notes (Figure 37–44).

Figure 37–36

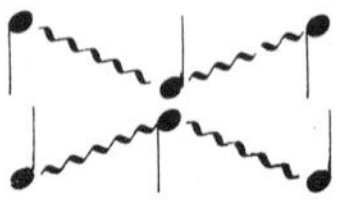

Figure 37–37

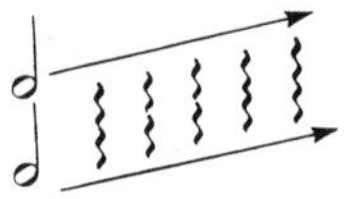

Figure 37–38

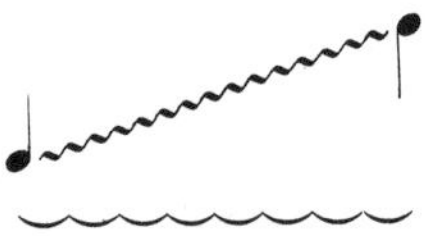

Figure 37–39

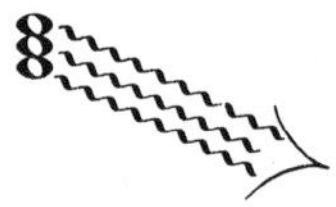

Figure 37–40

Figure 37–41

Figure 37–42

Figure 37–43

31. Thunder effect (Fr. *effet de tonnerre*), the finger sliding violently on the strings so that they strike each other (Figure 37–45).
32. Whistling sounds (Fr. *sons sifflés*), a lengthwise slide on all wire strings up or down with flat of the left hand (Figure 37–46).
33. Pedal glissando (Fr. *glissés de pédales*; Figure 37–47); can be combined with tremolo also.
34. Metallic sounds (Fr. *sons métalliques*), made with pedal halfway between notches (Figure 37–48.)
35. Tam-tam sounds (Fr. *sons de tam-tam*), striking the string with a hard stick; best between CC and FF♯. (Figure 37–49). Bartók's *Concerto for Orchestra* uses a glissando with a stick.
36. Guitaric sounds (Fr. *sons guitariques*), played very close to sounding board. Usual notation is same as for *près de la table*.
37. Playing from sounding board to center of string (Figure 37–50a) and vice versa (b).
38. Plectric sounds (Fr. *sons plectriques*), played near the sounding board with the fingernail (Figure 37–51).

Figure 37–44

Figure 37–45

Figure 37–46

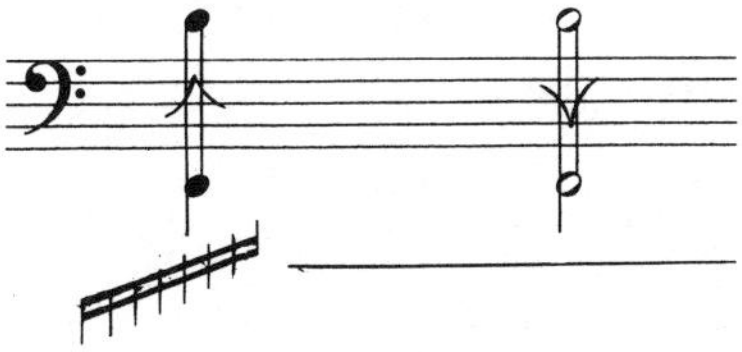

Figure 37–47

Figure 37–48

Figure 37–49

Figure 37–50

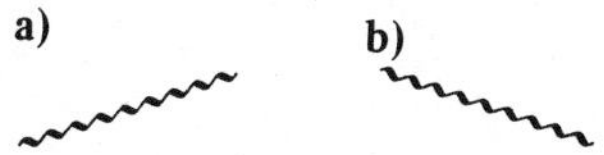

Figure 37–51

39. Timpanic sounds (Fr. *sons timbaliques*), fingertips of right hand tapping on sounding board as left hand plays normally (Figure 37–52).
40. Besides harmonics at the octave (written an octave below sounding pitch, see Chapter 6), twelfth harmonics, played a third above the center of the string are also possible. Salzedo's notation shows the string and resultant sound (Figure 37–53).
41. Xylophonic sounds (Fr. *sons xylharmoniques*), the harmonic being muffled as it is struck, or the left hand holding the lowest part of the string as the right hand plays in the center of the string (Figure 37–54).
42. Isolated sounds (Fr. *sons étouffés, étouffer*, Ital. *secco*), one finger stopping the previous string while playing the next (Figure 37–55).
43. Muffling individual notes or a group of notes, gradual muffling, or muffling a chord after playing (Figure 37–56).
44. Fluidic sounds (Fr. *sons fluidiques*), the left hand sliding the tuning key up and down the upper part of the string as the second finger of the right hand plays a repeated note at the lower end of the string (Figure 37–57).
45. Fluidic glides (Fr. *glissés fluidiques*), the same as 44 except with the tuning key gliding across several strings (Figure 37–58).
46. Rocket-like sounds (Fr. *sons en fusées*), the same as 45 but with as rapid a slide as possible.
47. Esoteric sounds (Fr. *sons ésotériques*), the pedal glissando, indicated by Salzedo as in Figure 37–59.

Figure 37–52

Figure 37–53

Figure 37–54

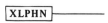

Figure 37–55

Figure 37–56

Figure 37–57

Figure 37–58

Figure 37–59

48. *Con sordino*, a $\frac{3}{4}$ inch strip of paper interlaced at the top of the strings, resulting in a sharp, harpsichord-like sound.
49. L. V., Fr. *laisser vibrer* (Ital. *lasciare vibrare*, Ger. *klingen lassen*), meaning let vibrate, do not dampen.
50. Interrupting the time in the middle of a phrase (Figure 37–60).
51. A breath (Ger. *Luftpause*) or a longer breath (Figure 37–61).
52. Shorter and longer fermatas (Figure 37–62).

Figure 37–60   *Figure 37–61*    *Figure 37–62*

7. OTHER STRING TECHNIQUES

The mandolin has been played with a glass rod or metal plectrum. Many harp techniques can be applied to the guitar, such as playing with a plectrum, fingernail, hitting with sticks or mallets, playing on the body, glissandi up and down the strings with a stick.

8. KEYBOARD TECHNIQUES

Some of the following techniques can be applied to keyboard instruments other than the piano as well as to the harp.

1. Glissandi can be made in both directions simultaneously.
2. Attack or stress can be indicated in detail. Staccato marks, slashes, slurs, arrowheads, and wedges are used separately or together. Sometimes composers invent other notations.
3. A staccato attack followed immediately by the engaging of the damper pedal produces an echo. A violently depressed pedal produces a ring, and a violently released pedal a bang. Gradual depressing or releasing of the pedals can be indicated for the una corda, sostenuto, or damper (Figure 37–63).
4. Clusters (see also Chapter 23), first used by Henry Cowell in 1911, can be for all keys between certain definite or indefinite limits (Figure 37–64a), for white keys only (example b), or for black keys only (c). A cluster glissando

Figure 37–63

Figure 37–64

Figure 37–64 (cont.)

can begin with lower notes and move up (d), begin with upper notes and move down (e), or release from upper to lower (f) or lower to upper (g). Clusters can be played with fist, fingertips, palm, side of hand, forearm, or a board (4 feet long to cover all the keys), which can be rolled back and forth from white to black keys.

The following techniques are applied directly on the strings within the piano. This technique was first used by Rued Langgaard in his 1918 *Music of the Spheres.*

5. Playing on the strings (Ital. *sulle corde,* Ger. *auf den Saiten,* Fr. *sur les cordes*). Since the metal frame divides the interior of the piano into four sections, a glissando all the way up and down the strings is not possible. The section of the frame should be indicated (I, II, III, and IV from top to bottom). These glissandi can be made with or without pedals. The strings can be stroked, struck, or rubbed with fingertips, fingernails, sticks of soft yarn, triangle beater, brushes, wood, metal, coins, picks, hard rubber, forks, or other objects, *pp* to *ff.* A ruler can be used to stroke or scrape several strings at once. Strings can be stroked up and down or lengthwise. The hand can be flung across the strings for a *glissando gettato.*
   Soft sticks produce a gong-like boom on the lower strings, hard sticks a thin and metallic sound. The sound near the pegs is harsh; in the center, soft, being less rich in harmonics.
   Graphic notation shows the direction of the glissando, with a straight line slanted up or down. A separate staff (for playing *within* the piano) should be used.
6. Plucked notes within the piano, like all such effects, are not very loud and therefore are generally suitable only for chamber music or quiet passages unless amplified. Notes can be plucked with fingernail or pick. The pianist Aloys Kontarsky has used the symbols in Figure 37–65a, for either plucked or muted strings. The additional symbols in Figure 37–65b are used for plucked strings, and in c for muted strings. Example d shows a cluster pizzicato and e a snap pizzicato.

Figure 37–65

Figure 37–65 (cont.)

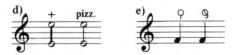

7. Harmonics can be played by touching a string at a node (marked with chalk in advance) and setting the string in vibration by any method. Octave, twelfth, and fifteenth harmonics (in the center, a third or a fourth the length of the string) are practical. Figure 37–66 suggests the notation.

8. The keys can be depressed silently (Ital. *sostenete le taste tacitamente,* Ger. *Tasten tonlos (stumm) niederdrücken,* Fr. *baissez les touches sans sonner*) with or without the damper pedal prior to performance within the piano. With no pedal, the raised dampers show the performer what strings to play within the piano. Figure 37–67 shows the notation.

9. Strings can be muted with one hand, a cloth, rubber, a book, plasticine, wood or metal rulers (especially near the hammers), fingernails, or other means. They can be dampened before or after playing, producing harmonics. Muting can be combined with playing on the keyboard, or playing on the strings in any of the above-listed ways. One notation is suggested in Figure 37–68.

Figure 37–66   **Figure 37–67**   **Figure 37–68**

10. Other techniques which have been used include dropping a box, marbles, or tennis balls (Henze, *Voices*) on the strings, a glissando with fingernail on the keyboard or tapping the keys without depressing them, slapping or slamming the lid, rapping the case, rapping the sounding board with knuckles or open palm or an object such as a mallet, rubbing with a rosined finger, playing an instrument into the piano for the resulting sympathetic resonance, playing on the surface of the instrument or the sounding board with sticks or mallets, playing on the cover with a coin (Krenek), pulling a rod along the wrest pins, or pushing the piano into the orchestra pit (at Darmstadt), an expensive technique.

11. All these effects can be amplified with various microphones and the resulting sound varied in the ways described in Chapter 39. The microphone (an inexpensive one is recommended) can also be used to rub, scratch, or beat the instrument.

    If only one player is to perform both at the keyboard and within the piano, a few moments must be allowed for him to stand up and prepare for the new performance method.

12. The *prepared piano* was introduced by John Cage in the 1940's. Materials are placed on or between the strings to change the tone color. Either some or all of the strings may be prepared in the same or different manners. Screws or bolts placed between strings result in a metallic twang. With nuts and washers a jingle or buzz results. Rubber strips may be threaded between the strings at the nodes to produce a dull thud and a pure harmonic. Rubber

wedges, felt, wood, and other materials can be used for a soft sound. It takes time to prepare the piano, so it should not be done in performance. If both prepared and ordinary pianos are to be used, it is best to have two pianos available.

13. A tambourine has been placed on the low strings of the piano and played with fingers or mallets. The keyboard can be used in this manner as well.

9. PERCUSSION TECHNIQUES

MALLET INSTRUMENTS

1. Glissando over the resonators with stick or cane.
2. Dampening and striking simultaneously.
3. Striking with cymbal.
4. Striking frame.
5. Sustaining pitch by humming or singing.
6. Holding mallet at node, striking bar, and moving mallet to center (vibraphone).
7. With the motor off, moving the fan from closed to open after playing, creating a crescendo (vibraphone).
8. Striking with soft mallet and drawing hard mallet two inches in toward the end of the bar, creating a bend downward of about a quarter tone (vibraphone).
9. Bowing the bar.
10. Hitting a suspended orchestra bell on the side to get a harmonic about a sharp major ninth above.
11. Striking and shaking a suspended orchestra bell, producing a vibrato.

DRUMS

1. Playing any drum like a string drum by placing the end of a stick in the center of the head and rubbing the stick with rosined fingers or a cloth.
2 . Fingers on drumhead.
3. Fingers on the rim.
4. Fingernail flicked on vellum.
5. Glancing blow.
6. Rotating blow.
7. Successive fingers striking head.
8. Pressing head to raise pitch, or glissando (while playing).
9. Pushing thumb or finger across head (friction drum).
10. Using fingertips or fingernails, knuckles, or side or flat of hand.
11. Slackening heads for booming tone and *scoop* in pitch (*Rite of Spring*, cannon in *Tosca*).
12. Rotating a stick on the head.
13. Bouncing a stick on the surface.
14. Indicating speed of roll.
15. Striking frame.
16. Striking drum with object.

17. Wire brushes on timpani or bass drum.
18. Snare stick on timpani.
19. Using maracas as timpani mallets (Leonard Bernstein's *Jeremiah Symphony*).
20. Dropping coins on drumhead.
21. Dropping chains on drumhead (Henze's Symphony No. 6).
22. Blowing horn into drumhead.
23. Placing tambourine on a drumhead and playing tambourine or drum with mallets.
24. Strumming snares on snare drum.
25. Tuning the two heads of the bass drum differently (as in Scotch drumming).
26. Tuning the bass drum to C (Gunther Schuller).
27. Rubbing drumhead with rubber or finger.
28. Playing timpani on the shell, rim, or head with stick handles.
29. Playing timpani with triangle sticks.
30. Playing timpani or other drum with two different sticks at once.
31. Sweeping wire brush around timpani head near rim.
32. Playing with coins near rim for *pp* trill (Elgar's *Enigma Variations*).
33. Playing with cork mallets (Ital. *campalline di sughero*).
34. Deadening the vibrations with mutes consisting of a soft cloth placed on the head and held in place by a heavy block (or a cloth-covered block) (Berlioz, Liszt, Stravinsky, Copland, and others). Three such mutes placed at the angles of an equilateral triangle around the head give a very muted effect not unlike the sound of a small drum.

CYMBALS

1. Placing a coin to the bow of the cymbal after playing for sizzle effect.
2. Shaking cymbal after playing for vibrato.
3. Choking and holding cymbals together.

HI-HAT

1. Attaching tambourine to hi-hat.
2. Playing on cardboard held between closed cymbals with snare sticks (sounds like maracas).
3. Striking with stick.
4. Playing with foot pedal.
5. Leaving half open and striking with stick for rattle.
6. Slamming pedal closed.
7. Clashing together and immediately releasing.
8. Leaving closed and striking with stick.
9. Leaving closed, striking with stick, and opening immediately.

OTHER

1. Three-note clash on chimes with side of mallet.
2. Shaking triangle after striking for vibrato.
3. Shaking crotales after striking for vibrato.
4. For bowed gong, bowed cymbal, water gong, see Chapter 20.

UNUSUAL MALLETS

The following objects may be used as mallets: iron comb, hairbrush, wood cluster stick, metal cluster stick, wood or metal hammer, knife (for scraping), knitting needles, porcelain mallets, bundle of nails, plectrum, thimble, tuning fork.

NOTATION

Ambivalent abbreviations such as *mar.*, which could mean *maracas* or *marimba*, should be avoided. In preference, use *mrcas.* or *mrb.* (this could be confused with *marimbula*, but since that is an uncommon instrument, there would be no confusion unless it also happened to be used in the particular score).

Many contemporary composers prefer to use symbols rather than abbreviations for the instruments of percussion. This practice is often more of a hindrance than a help to the player since these symbols are not standardized and one symbol can represent more than one instrument. Figure 37–69 shows some of the more common symbols which have been accepted by an International Conference on new notation held in Ghent in 1974. Whether composers and percussionists will universally accept them remains to be seen. A note in the score and parts is still required to explain the symbols.

Figure 37–69

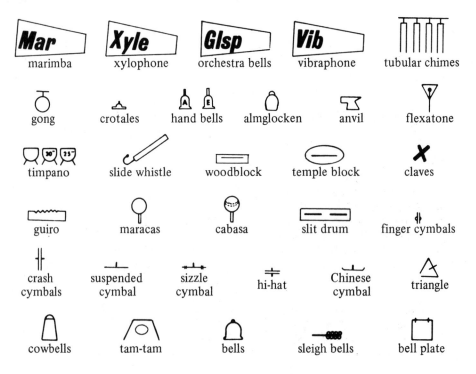

Figure 37-69 (cont.)

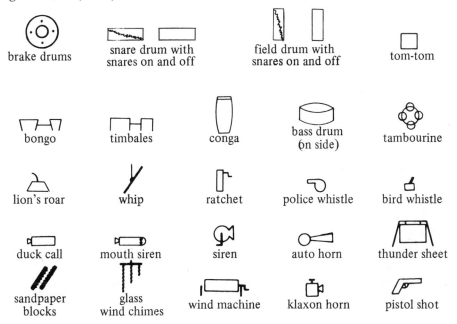

Naturally, symbolic notation is more prevalent in Europe, where a piece may be performed by orchestras in several countries, so that players speak different languages and abbreviations in one language might be incomprehensible in another. Figure 37–70 shows some of the more common indications for various mallet types.

Figure 37-70

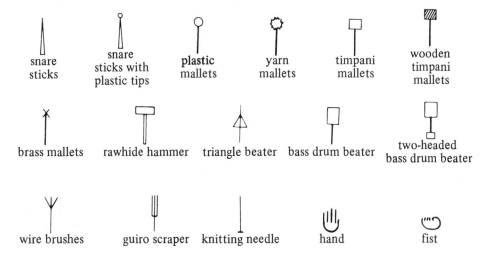

Figure 37–70 (cont.)

fingernail   coin   handle   hard   medium   soft

Following is a list of written notations for various methods of performance (see also Chapters 17–22):

> in the center (of the membrane of a drum or the dome of a cymbal) (Ital. *sul mezzo, sulla cupola* [dome], Ger. *In der Mitte, Auf die Kuppel* [dome], Fr. *au milieu, sur la protubérance* [dome])
>
> at the edge (Ital. *all'estremità, in margine, sul bordo,* Ger. *am Rand,* Fr. *au bord, blousée, a la jante*)
>
> on the shell (Ital. *al fusto,* Ger. *an den Aussenseiten,* Fr. *sur le cadre*)
>
> with the fingers (Ital. *con le dita,* Ger. *mit den Fingern,* Fr. *avec les doigts*)
>
> with the hands (Ital. *con le mani,* Ger. *mit den Händen,* Fr. *avec les mains*)
>
> with a bow (Ital. *coll'arco,* Ger. *mit einem Bogen,* Fr. *avec l'archet*)
>
> muffled stroke (Ital. *sordinato,* Ger. *gedämpfter Schlag,* Fr. *en sourdine*)

Figure 37–71 shows some symbols used for various methods of playing. None of these has become standard. Besides the various symbols for different modes of attack in Figure 37–71, an additional staff line can be used just to indicate the mode of attack.

Figure 37–71

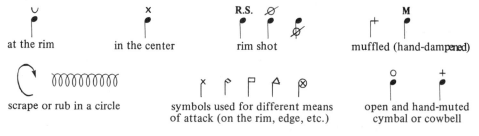

at the rim   in the center   R.S.   rim shot   M   muffled (hand-dampened)

scrape or rub in a circle   symbols used for different means of attack (on the rim, edge, etc.)   open and hand-muted cymbal or cowbell

Snare rolls may be indicated as press or crush rolls with two sticks, as multibounce rolls (LLLRRR or LLLLRRRR) for more saturation, or as parade rolls (LLRR); however, it is usually wiser to leave it up to the player.

10. WOODWIND TECHNIQUES

Since woodwind technique up to the twentieth century was oriented toward producing secure intonation and an even tone throughout the range, many other possibilities, including the production of chords (multiphonics) by a single woodwind instrument, were ignored until the search by composers for new sonorities in the 1960's led to the codification of other sounds.

Jazz musicians produced several innovations that have now been taken up by symphonic composers, such as the *slap tongue* technique, in which the tongue strikes the reed. Figure 37–72 shows three ways of indicating slap tongue (a,b, and c); example d indicates slap tongue without a pitch being produced (see also Chapter 34).

Figure 37–72

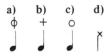

Extensions of normal technique include rapid or slow trills, half-hole fingering, breathy tone, short or long breaths, notes held as long as possible, extreme high registers such as the clarinet's playing to written e^4 and the *altissimo* register of the saxophone up to f^4. Attack can be indicated as sharp or soft (throat) or even more precisely as follows:

tu – sharp tongue attack
du – sostenuto tongue attack
hu – no tongue (breath or throat attack)
tah – release breath
taht (*tah-t*) – stop tone with tongue

Tone clusters can be indicated for a group of winds as in Figure 37–73.

Figure 37–73

QUARTER TONES

Quarter-tone clarinets were built in the early twentieth century, though it was later discovered that normal clarinets could produce quarter tones quite well with unusual fingerings. These fingerings consist largely of *cross fingerings*: one or more closed holes below an open hole with open holes below that produce quarter tones as well as wide variations in timbre, generally of a darker tone with fewer overtones. The notation of quarter tones has already been discussed. Also possible are bends up or down a quarter tone (Ital. *nota flessuosa*) quarter-tone trills, expanding trills, harmonics from a quarter-tone fundamental, and yet smaller intervals. Although many treatises and some books on woodwind technique list fingerings throughout the range of the instrument, individual players who study these techniques choose the fingerings which work best with their technique and individual instrument (see Bibliography).

TIMBRE VARIATION

Besides fingerings, other elements affect timbre. Bruno Bartolozzi has suggested the symbols in Figure 37–74 for indicating these variables, and they are generally accepted today.

Bartolozzi describes timbre variants as closed, closed-dark, light, open-light, closed-light, open-dark, dark, and open. Timbres can be changed while a note is being played. Alternate fingerings can produce artificial harmonics. A natural harmonic series can be produced with the help of a mute (Figure 37–75).

The reed can also be moved in and out, the flute can blow to the opposite

Figure 37–74

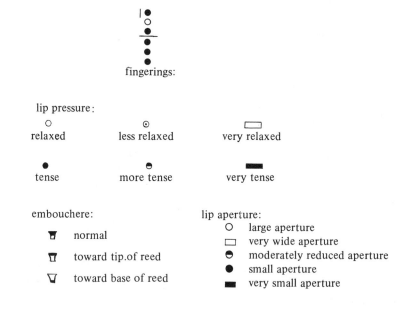

fingerings:

lip pressure:

| O | ⊙ | ▭ |
| relaxed | less relaxed | very relaxed |

| ● | ◓ | ▬ |
| tense | more tense | very tense |

air pressure:
- **N. Pr.** — normal
- **M. Pr.** — much
- **P. Pr.** — little
- **A. Pr.** — augment
- **D. Pr.** — diminish

embouchere:

- ♉ normal
- ♉ toward tip of reed
- ♈ toward base of reed

lip aperture:

- O large aperture
- ▭ very wide aperture
- ◓ moderately reduced aperture
- ● small aperture
- ▬ very small aperture

Figure 37–75

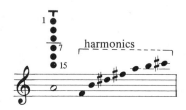

side of the mouthpiece, and the oboe can overblow (Fr. *cuivrez*). The pedal key on the clarinet and saxophone can produce different timbres as well.

The "whistle tones" of the flute are soft, high, clear harmonics (fifth to tenth partials) of the fundamentals b, c^1 and $c\#^1$. Alternate fingerings on the flute can produce a harmonic as low as $d\#^1$. Pulling out the head joint can lower the harmonic series still further.

Since the tone is richer in the lower register of the instruments, greater variation in timbre is possible in that register. Timbre trills are possible with key vibrato, which changes the timbre but not the pitch.

VIBRATO

Slow to fast as well as narrow to wide vibrato and their notation have already been discussed in this chapter. Jaw vibrato affects pitch, and air pressure alteration creates an intensity vibrato, which can be measured or unmeasured. Rapid single tonguing, measured or unmeasured, can be considered a sort of tongued tremolo. *Vib.* or just *v.* can be used as the notation; *non* (*senza*) *vib.* or *n. v.* (*s. v.*) means no vibrato. Six to eight fluctuations per second is about the limit. Sometimes the width of the vibrato is indicated (quarter tone, for instance).

GLISSANDO AND PORTAMENTO

Though often used interchangeably, the glissando can mean a fingered chromatic scale as opposed to the lip slide or portamento. The latter is best over a small range, aided by fingering. A wavy line can be used for glissando, a straight line for portamento.

Attack and release can involve glissando or portamento. In jazz, these techniques are known by the terms *fall-off, drop-off, spill, plop, doink,* and others. Figure 37–76 shows the notation (see also Chapter 34).

A glissando can be made on the flute by withdrawing the finger from the head joint.

Figure 37–76

FLUTTER TONGUING

Flutter can occur at the tip of the tongue or at the uvula, on a rolled R, without definite pitch, in conjunction with humming, or by means of the jazz "buzz." The base of the tongue against the soft palate produces the "growl." Also, the aperture of the flute can be covered with the lips and flutter tonguing produced that way.

SMORZATO

Smorzato is a sort of intensity vibrato in which the attack and release of the sound are accomplished through embouchure pressure rather than the tongue. The air pressure is maintained and the reed alternately squeezed with the lips. See Figure 37–77. This can also be performed with multiphonics (see below).

Figure 37–77

OTHER EFFECTS

The sound envelope of attack and decay can be reversed with a soft breath attack at the start of the tone, then a crescendo, and an abrupt tongue release. Figure 37–78 shows one notation.

The *subtone* or *echo tone* is produced when the tongue touches the reed and produces a subdued tone. It is possible without definite pitch as well. The lower register is best. Figure 37–79 shows one notation. Naturally, those effects which involve the reeds are not possible on the flute.

Figure 37–78   **Figure 37–79**

MULTIPHONICS

John C. Heiss (in 1966) and Bruno Bartolozzi (in 1967) were the first to publish texts illustrating multiphonic possibilities on the woodwinds. Multiphonics seem to be produced by the air column's vibrating over its entire length as well as the distance from the end to the open hole(s). They can be produced by unusual fingerings alone or by a combination of fingerings and altered tone production (air pressure, for example). They can also be produced by a combination of normal tones and humming while playing, especially while playing in the lower register. They can be combined with glissando or without the reed's vibrating. The hummed part should be written on a separate staff, or, if it is simple enough, on the same staff with stems in the opposite direction, crosses under the notes, and the notation "hummed." The *buzz* tone of jazz is produced in the same way.

Normal fingering plus an adjustment of the oral cavity, breath pressure, and/or embouchure produces multiphonics as in Figure 37–80. The production of a fundamental and a note in the upper octave is shown in Figure 37–81.

The position of the tongue is also important. If it is held high in the mouth, an *e* sound results; when it is held down, a more open *o* sound is produced.

A series of homogeneous multiphonics is also possible (Figure 37–82).

Figure 37–80

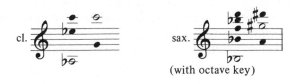

(with octave key)

Figure 37–81

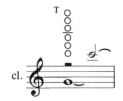

Figure 37–82

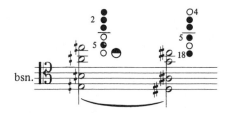

A single note can be connected to a multiphonic with only a change of lip or air pressure or with fingering changes (Figure 37–83).

Multiphonic trills are possible where there is an easy fingering change between two multiphonics or where one. fundamental key can be opened and closed to produce the multiphonics in succession (Figure 37–84).

A general characteristic of multiphonics is the creation of *beats*, resulting

Figure 37–83

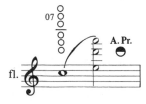

Figure 37–84

from the sum and difference of different pitches, and *rolling tones*, which are slower beats. Some control of the rate of these beats is possible.

Aleatory fingerings (not available on the flute) produce unpredictable results. In fact, most multiphonics depend on the player and his own technique. Lists published in various books do not agree and the composer had best work out multiphonics with a performer who has studied these effects. It is also a good idea to publish an alternate version of the composition, or an ossia without multiphonics.

Figure 37–85 shows (a) a smorzato effect with chords and (b) a hummed note with multiphonics.

Figure 37–85

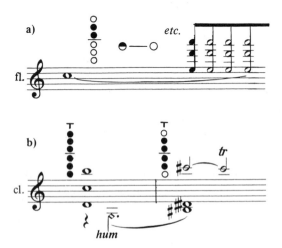

Multiphonics can consist of two to five notes (Bartolozzi postulates more but these are detectable only through electronic means and not with the human ear); these notes are within the following approximate ranges of upper and lower notes:

	lower	upper
flute	$c^1 - e^3$	$b^1 - b^{\flat 3}$
oboe	$b - d^{\sharp 2}$	$e^2 - f^3$
clarinet	$a^\flat - g^\flat$	$f^2 - f^3$
bassoon	$BB^\flat - F$	$b - a^1$
saxophone	$d^1 - f^{\sharp 2}$	$d^2 - g^{\sharp 3}$

PERCUSSIVE EFFECTS

Following are various percussive effects that are possible on woodwinds.

Key Clicks   Keys can be rattled or trilled at random (Ital. *colpo di chiave*). This can be combined with air sounds (Figure 37–86).

Figure 37–86

Key Pops or Key Slaps   The key is forcefully depressed on a given pitch with or without air. This can be combined with normal tone production. Varèse first used this technique in his *Density 21.5*. With air it is best in the lower octave of the instrument. When the lower lip covers the blow hole on the flute, the instrument acts like a closed pipe and sounds an octave lower. Figure 37–87 shows the above techniques as well as a normally sustained note with key slap attack.

Figure 37–87

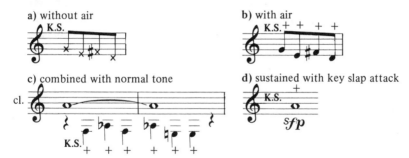

Hand Pops   A pitched sound is produced when the opening of the barrel is slapped with the palm. The mouthpiece can be removed and the other hand can finger certain limited pitches. The notation is the same as for key slaps without air (an x-shaped note head) with the abbreviation *H. P.* As with other effects, a footnote describing the performance technique and notation is obligatory.

Tapping   The body or mouthpiece of the instrument can be tapped with fingers, fingernails, or an object. The notation should be simple rhythmic notation with a footnote to indicate the manner of tone production.

Air Sounds   With a weak airstream or loose embouchure or both, the reed will not vibrate. The mouthpiece can also be removed and the instrument played directly. Air can be blown without producing a tone but only a "white sound" (or random sounds, like the rush of air), and a white noise glissando or rapid overtones can be played in this manner. These techniques can also be combined with flutter tonguing.

If the embouchure of the flute is played like a brass mouthpiece, notes below b are possible. Villa-Lobos used a jet whistle effect in 1953, performed by closing the mouth over the blow hole of the flute and producing a sudden burst of air on the note b.

Tone can alternate from air sounds to a normal tone and back again and be combined with key pops or clicks. Notation is the same as above, normal notes with crosses above for definite pitches, x-shaped note heads for air sounds without tone.

VOCAL SOUNDS

It is possible to hum and play simultaneously, with or without glissando and with or without the reed's vibrating.

MOUTHPIECE ALONE

The mouthpiece (clarinet and saxophone) or reed (oboe and bassoon) can be played alone. A range of a sixth to an octave is possible. A larger range can be obtained with the cupped hand over the end. This can be combined with portamento (lip glissando) or indefinite pitches over a wide dynamic range.

LIP BUZZ

With the mouthpiece removed, the lips can produce a buzz, the pitch being controlled with the embouchure. Indefinite pitches should be written, as it is difficult to obtain specific pitches with this technique.

MUTES

The handkerchief is often used to mute woodwinds, though circle mutes which can be inserted full or halfway are available for saxophone. Both types of circle mute remove overtones and take the edge off the tone.

11. BRASS TECHNIQUES

Many of the woodwind techniques, including multiphonics, can be applied to the brass as well, but are, as yet, less common. Gluck's experiment with two horns being played with their bells held together is an early example of unusual brass effects. Some contemporary effects follow:

1. Playing on mouthpiece.
2. Playing on mouthpiece into clenched fists.

3. Slapping mouthpiece.
4. Tapping mouthpiece.
5. Blowing in instrument without mouthpiece.
6. Reversing mouthpiece, holding it against the end of the pipe and blowing for a white noise effect.
7. Striking the opening with the hand.
8. Blowing into the instrument without definite pitch.
9. Sucking in air through the mouthpiece.
10. Half-valve glissando or bending of pitch.
11. Changing fingering while maintaining pitch, for changes in timbre.
12. The use of mutes, already described in Chapter 34. Mutes can be in or out, changed gradually from in to out or vice versa, or half stopped (Figure 37–88). Mutes can also be inserted or removed by a second player while the first is playing normally.

Figure 37–88

stopped +   open ○   change gradually +———○, ○———+   half stopped ⊕

13. Tapping bell.
14. Slapping hand on embouchure.
15. Striking valve with finger and blowing.
16. Striking valve with finger and not blowing.
17. Depressing valves, slapping valve.
18. Fluttering or rolling *R*.
19. Uneven fluttering.
20. Fluttering without pitch.
21. Blowing air and fluttering without pitch.
22. Fluttering with mouthpiece enclosed in lips.
23. Slapping tongue.
24. Tonguing without definite pitch.
25. Sounding at back of throat (growl).
26. Articulating different consonants while playing.
27. Humming and playing at the same time.
28. No vibrato to wide vibrato or vice versa.

12. MUSICAL EXAMPLES ILLUSTRATING CONTEMPORARY TECHNIQUES

Figure 37–89 shows *Sprechstimme* (example a); highest notes on the instruments, varying vibrato, and graphic durational notation (example b); humming (notated *b.ch.* = *bocca chiusa*), indefinite duration, and clusters (c-1); vocalization on different vowels (c-2); unsynchronized polyrhythms and indefinitely repeated figures in free rhythm (c-3); and quarter tones and multiphonics (d).

Figure 37–89

a)

b)

Penderecki, *Threnody*

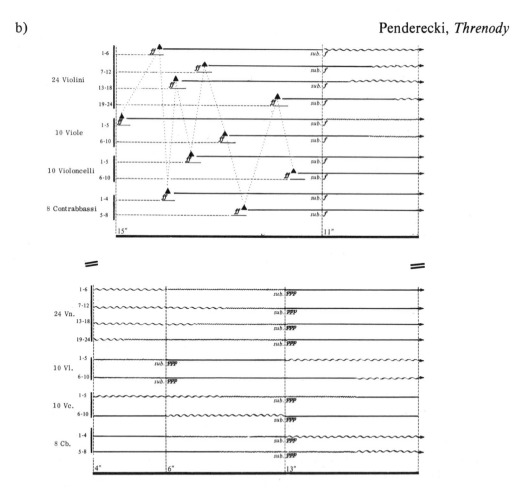

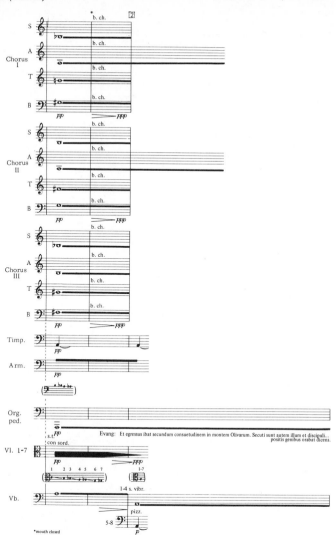

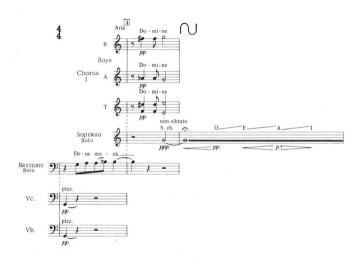

Figure 37–89 (cont.)   Penderecki, *St. Luke Passion*

Figure 37–89 (cont.)

c-3)

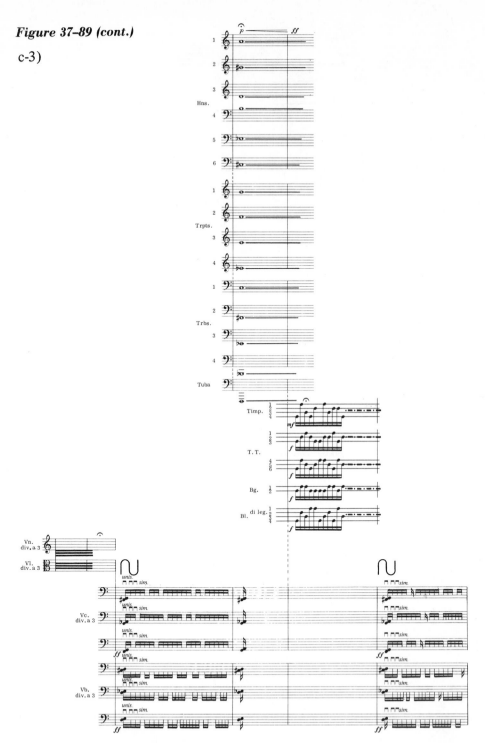

Figure 37–89 (cont.)   Burton, *Three Poems*

d) **Molto lento e liberamente**

38

Writing Background Music
and Recording

This chapter can be nothing more than a brief introduction to a highly skilled and specialized profession, that of the film composer. Certain general observations may be of use, however, especially to the young person starting out in this field.

In the days of silent films, whole orchestras were hired to play and prominent composers commissioned to write music for the performance of silent films in the more expensive theaters. In less well-to-do establishments this ensemble was reduced to a stage band or just an organist or pianist improvising or playing appropriate excerpts from "the classics." This "stock" music included Beethoven's *Moonlight Sonata*, the *William Tell Overture*, the wedding marches from *Lohengrin* and *A Midsummer Night's Dream*, and others.

With the advent of sound, scores were composed after the final editing of the film; they were recorded in a studio and then dubbed into the sound track. Naturally, timing became the prime consideration since the music had to fit exactly with the predetermined sequence of the film. This made the use of extended, complex musical forms impractical except in those rare instances when the director oriented the film editing to the musical score (Sergei Eisenstein's probably unique arrangement with Sergei Prokofiev in *Alexander Nevsky* being the only case that comes to mind) or when a piece of music was choreographed for film (such as *An American in Paris*). Walt Disney's *Fantasia* is an early and rare example of animation following a preconceived musical score.

Since music is generally a subsidiary element in most commercial films oriented toward a mass market, the premium on originality and musical interest is not very high in most cases. Indeed, it would be incorrect and ineffective to compose a score of intrinsic musical interest where the purpose is only to enhance the mood or punctuate the action of a film and not to detract from the audience's concentration on visual or plot elements.

A wide variety of styles from classical to pop to avant garde are to be found, sometimes side by side in the same film. Simple forms based on ostinati, repeated melodic phrases, and so on are common. So is the use of *leitmotifs* (leading motives) to represent various characters, moods, and other elements. Sometimes a *title song* and phrases derived from it fulfill this function. Cliches, such as the use of *tremolo sul ponticello* to illustrate tension, should be avoided.

In general, background music should be just that—subliminal. There is an old saw that background music should be felt and not heard. Any too-prominent musical interest during dialogue, for instance, can destroy the focus of a scene. Music can also fill pauses between dialogue. It can illustrate locale, weather, or other things by using a flute for birds, a horn for the mountains, rain with the staccato of piano and woodwinds, pizzicato, trills and figures, a gale with chromatic scales on the strings, and so forth. Most important is that everything in the music must be motivated by something visual or spoken in the film.

Since the volume of the music is regulated by recording engineers, subtle dynamic gradations in the score are likely to be lost in the final sound track of the film. On the other hand, a great refinement of balance within the ensemble can be obtained by electronically regulating the several recording tracks, allowing effects that are not possible in the concert hall, such as solo flute carrying melodic interest against the rest of the orchestra *ff*.

Music often comes into its own only during the titles and at the close. Here more scope for pure musical development is possible, though on a limited scale, and here the *tunes* can predominate and be of interest.

The symphonic scores of the midcentury are economically feasible only for the highest budget films. Most film composers must content themselves with a small orchestra at best, or sometimes only a few musicians. This limitation is somewhat compensated for by the fact that studio musicians today are of high caliber, can read anything at sight, and double on any number of common and uncommon instruments such as bass flute, baritone oboe, Heckelphone, E♭ contrabass clarinet, harmonica, soprano sax, mandolin, and others (see Appendix A).

The composer is usually the conductor of the recording session, during which the film is projected and the composer-conductor, guided by his previous knowledge of the film in its edited form and copious cues in the score itself, attempts to synchronize the musical performance perfectly to the film. It is not economically possible to make very many takes and often the recording must be completed in one session. The value of fermatas, vamps, ritards, and the like at transitional sections when one must wait for a cue from the screen will easily be appreciated by the reader. Each bar of the score should be numbered to save time should a retake be necessary.

Any number of sound effects, either produced in the studio or prerecorded, as well as synthesized sound are available to the film composer (see Chapter 39). Early examples of experiments with instruments impractical in the concert hall were the two steel girders hung from the ceiling in Sir Arthur Bliss's score for *The Shape of Things to Come* and gigantic metal tubes used for the bells of Saint Petersburg in *Anna Karenina.*

Vocal music is almost inevitably dubbed. That is, the music is prerecorded and then the film or tape is shot with the singer mouthing the words. This not only simplifies production (any sounds made during filming are not picked up since the sound track is already made, the singer and orchestra having been recorded in advance under ideal conditions) but also makes possible an exterior (out-of-doors) sequence with full orchestra. Furthermore, this method obviates the sometimes grotesque facial contortions that singers necessarily produce, which are of no import in the opera house but in a close-up can be unpleasant to look at.

In recording a work for broadcast or commercial release where no visual considerations intrude, the primary consideration is time because of the vast expense of recording, especially with symphony orchestras today. The recording should be carefully planned so that at least one acceptable take is made of each section of the work before time runs out. Then, in any time remaining, questionable sections can be repeated. Since several takes of the same section may be made in a short period of time, any trying vocal or solo instrumental sections which require particular stamina should take place at the beginning of the session because the soloist may not be able to perform adequately later on.

Which sections are to be retaped is a joint decision of the conductor and recording engineer. The latter controls the session from the master booth, sometimes with only microphonic communication with the podium. If there is only one session, all discussion and decisions must occur during the break. Recording can be done with two microphones or many, and in the latter case the conductor may find the orchestra has been substantially rearranged spacially to facilitate separation of the sound tracks.

With commercial music, the recording engineer plays the console like an instrumentalist, adjusting balance and sound modification. The result, including length and order of numbers, is largely a matter of this electronic manipulation. It is for this reason that much late twentieth-century popular music is not as effective in live performance as through electronic reproduction. Electronic effects largely take the place of melody, harmony, and other structural principles in the appeal of much of this music.

39

Electronic Music

---

1. THE DEVELOPMENT OF ELECTRONIC MUSIC

The ancient *Hydraulos* of the Greeks is an example of one of the earliest mechanical instruments. The nineteenth century saw the development of a steam computer for composing music; this mechanism, which stored encoded information, was impractical. In 1897 the piano roll (pianola) was invented. The year 1906 saw the invention of the vacuum tube and the next year Busoni postulated electronic music. During the early years of the century the *color organ* (Ital. *tastiera per luce*, Ger. *Farbenklavier*, Fr. *clavier à lumières*) was invented; it produced color, originally mechanically by such means as colored tapes and later electronically. Scriabin wrote *Prometheus* for such performance, though it was performed only once in its originally intended form, in New York in 1915. In 1924 came reflected light compositions in Berlin and Vienna, and Respighi first used the phonograph with orchestra in *Pini di Roma* for the sound of the nightingale. In 1926 came George Antheil's *Ballet Méchanique* for auto horns, airplane propellers, saws, and anvils. That year also saw the invention of the *theremin*, one of the earliest electronic instruments, capable of 1,200 divisions in the octave. The sound was generated electronically and altered in pitch by means of a keyboard or a metal ribbon which, when touched with the finger, produced different pitches at different points, producing a glissando. Succeeding years saw the invention of other instruments such as the sphereophone, electrophone, kaleidophone, partiturophone, emicron, thyratone, and helerion.

In 1928 Maurice Martenot invented the *Ondes Martenot,* which is operated by a keyboard with the range of the piano or by a ribbon. It has been used by such composers as Honegger, Milhaud, Messiaen, Jolivet, Koechlin, Varèse, and Canteloube. The same year, the *dynamophone* was invented and Frederich Trautwein invented the *Trautonium,* an instrument similar to the Ondes, also capable of multiphonic sounds, with music usually written on three staves. Hindemith and Egk have written for the instrument. The year 1929 saw the first synthesis of sound from electronic oscillators, as well as the introduction of the Hammond electronic organ. The Hammond Solovox, which produced sounds through a master *oscillator,* had octave doublings, vibrato, and dynamic control. The Compton organ had an *envelope* device (see section 2) and over 32 harmonics. The tone was produced by an electrostatic tone generator and scanning discs. Transistors generate the tone in the Baldwin organ. The tone is achieved by subtraction from sawtooth and square waves by filters (see next section). There is an echo effect as well. The Allen organ has a transistor oscillator and rotating speakers. Pitches slightly out of phase imitate the sound of a pipe organ. The Conn-Wurlitzer used a feedback system of tone generation. The Wurlitzer organ is entirely electronic except that brass reeds generate the original sound.

The 1930's saw the invention of the Rhythmicon by Leon Theremin, an instrument suggested by Henry Cowell; the *croix sonore;* the melodium; the microtonal ondes; and, in 1935, the tape recorder (magnetophone), which had first been envisioned in 1889.

In the 1940's the ondioline and melochord were invented, the tape recorder was first used in conjunction with oscillators, Percy Grainger devised a system of graphic notation for sounds produced from oscillators, the *Mixturtrautonium,* an improved trautonium, was developed and later used by composers such as Henze and Orff. The year 1948 also saw the birth of the term *"musique concrète"* for music produced from natural sounds or from conventional musical sounds by manipulation of a tape recording. This is still an important technique in electronic music. The original sounds can be altered by speeding up or slowing down the tape, splicing, overlaying more than one sound, playing backwards, using a repeating tape loop, and varying intensity and tone (through filtering, distortion, and other means).

During the 1950's electronic studios were established at Cologne, Paris (RTF), Milan (RAI), Tokyo, Warsaw, Brussels, Delft, Tel-Aviv, and Toronto, and at Columbia and Princeton Universities in the United States. During the early 1950's Karlheinz Stockhausen produced the first electronic music from synthesized (electronically generated) sounds, American composers such as Otto Luening and Vladimir Ussachevsky were working with tape. Henze used electronic sounds in his opera *Das Ende einer Welt,* and Varèse used electronic sounds with orchestra in *Deserts*. In 1956 the first piece produced by computer appeared.

The 1960's saw the birth of the Syn-Ket, an instrument with rows of keys which was an early, playable synthesizer. The introduction of the modular design concept and of voltage control, where sound generation and alteration could be controlled by electric current rather than mechanically by dials, made possible the development of practical synthesizers by Robert Moog and Donald Buchla and the popularization of electronic music by Walter Carlos and many film and television composers.

2. HOW ELECTRONIC MUSIC IS PRODUCED

In electronic music studios, oscillators (signal generators) produce sine waves (smooth curves which yield pure tones), sawtooth waves (which contain all the harmonics as well as the fundamental), and square or pulse and triangle waves (which contain the fundamental and odd harmonics only). Random noise generators produce white noise, that is, randomly generated pitches; pure white noise sounds like static, which, in a sense, it is. These sounds are then filtered and modified. Example 39–1 shows the waveforms as they appear graphically.

Figure 39–1

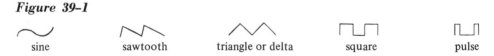

| sine | sawtooth | triangle or delta | square | pulse |

The frequency, volume, timbre, duration, and *sound envelope* (attack and decay profile) can all be controlled by voltage. There is a voltage-controlled oscillator (VCO), voltage-controlled amplifier (VCA), and voltage-controlled filter (VCF). Dials, a keyboard, a metal ribbon, a *sequencer* (see below) which produces a pattern of voltages, and a random voltage source can all be used to control various elements of the sound *event* (the sound in all its dimensions). The resulting sound can be recorded on tape recorders with all the modifications possible with *musique concrète*. Recorders may be half- or quarter-track or multi-track, and erase heads may or may not be activated in order to layer several separate recordings.

A *filter* is a sound modifier which attenuates or emphasizes certain frequencies. A high-pass filter allows high frequencies to pass through, a low-pass filter, low frequencies. A band-pass filter allows only a certain, adjustable width of frequencies to pass through. A band reject filter rejects a certain band width. The cut-off frequency is the border between the frequencies which are passed and rejected. Sound may be filtered several times.

Voltage control can alter both the frequency and *amplitude* (strength) of the sound. A *mixer* combines signals. A *voltage inverter* changes the direction of the voltage. A *trigger* sets the sound event in motion. A *gate* controls the amplitude of the signal. An *equalizer* increases or decreases signal strength. A *reverberation unit* creates close echos of the sound event. A *sequencer* is a voltage control source which can be preset to different voltages at different points and repeats continuously. A *frequency follower* converts pitch to a proportional voltage control source which may be used to modify any element of the sound event. An *envelope follower* does the same with the amplitude of the event. An *envelope generator* creates the sound envelope for the event.

Ring modulation modifies one signal with another. The output of the modulator equals the sum and differences of all the input frequencies. This produces a harmonically complex sound consisting of dramatically altered frequencies, durations, amplitudes, and timbres. *Double-ring modulation* is produced by two ring modulators controlled by two VCO's. *Triple-ring modulation* produces even more complex sounds.

Popular synthesizers are produced by Moog, Arp, and Buchla in price ranges of from a few hundred to several hundred thousand dollars.

Computers can be used to store material, edit it by a preprogrammed set of rules, or create it at random or according to programmed rules. The result can be synthesized directly by the computer or translated into conventional notation for performance by instruments. Computer music has not found a wide human audience.

One or more live performers can perform with a taped piece of electronic music. The live performers can also be recorded, the sound altered and played back during performance while the players continue to perform. Electronic music can also be synthesized directly in the concert hall. John Cage's use of twelve radios tuned at random was an early use of electronic sounds with live performers. Today when there is a combination of tape and instruments, the performer usually has a graphic score of the sounds that are on the tape, so he can synchronize with the recorded sounds.

3. ELECTRONICALLY AMPLIFIED INSTRUMENTS

One of the earliest applications of electronic amplification was to electrically operated carillon systems in churches. The electronic piano can simply be an amplified conventional piano or an instrument which synthesizes a piano-like tone which is then amplified, much like an electronic organ. *Contact* microphones can be attached to the body of various instruments, where they amplify bowing and other noises as well as the musical sounds produced by the instrument. Any instrument may be amplified. Henze even uses an amplified yo-yo in *Voices*. The electric bass can be either a normal (acoustic) bass with a contact mike or an electric bass with a vestigial (because unnecessary) body. The same is true of the Spanish and Hawaiian electric guitars. The placement of the *pickup* (microphone) determines the quality of the sound. (See Chapter 37.)

Besides amplification of sound, the following modifications are available on commercial electronic equipment:

1. *Tremolo.* Fluctuating volume level.
2. *Vibrato.* Variable control of frequency variation up to a quarter tone.
3. *Reverberation.* A delay of about .0004 second added to the signal.
4. *Echo.* A longer reverb.
5. *Fuzz.* Distortion added to the signal.
6. *Wah-wah.* A sharp cut-off low-pass filter.
7. *Tone extender, sustain control, expander, automatic gain control (AGC).* A device that sustains the level indefinitely according to the setting.
8. *Ring modulation.* Described above, operated with a pedal control.

Feedback is a phenomenon which results from sound from the speakers being picked up by the microphone and cycling through the system.

The electronic rhythm box produces various rhythmic combinations with synthesized, percussive sounds. Electronic metronomes are available which can play up to three different tempi on three different pitches simultaneously.

Afterword

It seems appropriate to conclude this work with some comments on the state of the orchestra at the time of this writing. Leonard Bernstein's famous comment that the symphony orchestra is dead has been heatedly debated during the last decade and he himself explained at the 1980 conference of the American Symphony Orchestra League in New York City that that statement has been misinterpreted and taken out of context. The truth of the matter is that the symphony orchestra, as well as the opera and ballet orchestra, are alive and well and doing better than ever before. Last year there were over 50 million paid admissions to symphony concerts, opera, and ballet in the United States. More Americans attended ballet than attended professional football and more money was spent on classical recordings than on tickets to professional baseball. Hundreds of performances of works by American composers were given by the thirty "major" (budgets over $2.5 million per year each) American orchestras, in addition to the other 1,500 orchestras in this country. According to Opera America and the Central Opera Service, more than a thousand opera companies, from the Metropolitan with its $40 million annual budget to university opera labs, gave performances including over 3,000 performances of American works. Audiences for ballet and opera have doubled in just a few years. In addition, there are the fields of chamber music, Broadway, popular music, and jazz, all of which employ instrumental ensembles from orchestral size down. Outside of this country are many more performing organizations, including Germany's 98 full-season opera houses and the hundreds of European orchestras.

In light of the above, it seems safe to say that more people are performing and listening to live music, "serious" and "popular" (unfortunate terms), new and old, than ever before. With the advent of recording and radio and television broadcasting, that audience has multiplied many fold. While there is always a debate about how much new or American music is being performed in comparison with music of the past, the art of orchestration remains a vital, ever-changing, and fascinating element in the creative life of this country and the world.

Stephen Douglas Burton
New York City, December 18, 1981

Appendix A

Miscellaneous Instruments

In this Appendix are listed unusual orchestral instruments, folk instruments occasionally used in the orchestra or band, and obsolete instruments still to be encountered in orchestral scores.

Besides the varieties of instruments already encountered and those listed below, common wind instruments built in unusual pitches are sometimes to be found. Today these parts are played on the more common instruments, the players transposing at sight or the part being copied at the pitch of the modern instrument. Military piccolos in E♭, flutes in A♭, B♭, F, and E♭ are to be encountered in older European band music. The *flauto d'amore* was in A and sounded a minor third lower than written, the *Terzflöte* (Ger.) was in E♭ and sounded a minor third higher. Oboes were built in E♭ (like the E♭ clarinet) and B♭ (like the B♭ clarinet), and a double bass oboe existed. See also the *oboe d'amore* and *oboe da caccia*, the baritone oboe and bass oboe. Clarinets in C were common in Mozart's time and existed in bands until the end of the nineteenth century. Besides the small clarinets in E♭ and D, sopranino clarinets in A♭ and D♭ and larger clarinets in A♭, G, and F existed. There was also a contrabass clarinet in E♭ (still found today) as well as a *clarinetto d'amore* in G with an in-curved bell and a mellow tone. Bassoons in B♭ were built, as was an E♭ contrabassoon, a soprano bassoon (an octave above the ordinary instrument), and the tritonicon, a sub-contrabassoon built an octave below the contrabassoon. French horns were built in high F and C according to Strauss, and trombones existed in B♭, G, F, and E♭ basso. Many unusual instruments are found in studio recording sessions today.

1. **Accordion** (Ger. *Ziehharmonica*). An instrument consisting of two handboards connected by a bellows operated by the arms. Inside the headboards are free-beating reeds which are set in action by the bellows. The right hand plays a vertical keyboard like a piano keyboard; the left hand operates up to 120 buttons. The first two rows of buttons produce bass notes. Four additional rows give major and minor triads and seventh chords at the octave or two octaves above and bass notes up to five octaves (C to c³). A unison or *chorist* coupler doubles at the octave below and a *tremulant* adds reeds tuned slightly off-pitch for a "beating" effect. A vibrato effect can also be obtained with the bellows. When they are half-closed and worked in and out over a short distance, a muted effect is obtained (see Figure A–1).

Figure A–1   Creston, *Concerto for Accordion and Orchestra*

2. **Albisiphone.** See **Bass flute.**

3. **Alpenhorn, alphorn.** Long, straight wooden trumpet in D or D♭ used for signaling in mountainous locales of Europe. The instrument used in Bayreuth to play the famous offstage solo in the third act of *Tristan* is modeled after this instrument, by Wagner's own direction, despite the indication in the score that the part should be played on an English horn. The Alpenhorn is not to be confused with the Swiss herdsman's horn (Ger. *Kuhhirtenhorn*), which is merely a goat's horn.

4. **Alto trombone.** Small trombone replaced by a first tenor trombone in the nineteenth century. The range was A to f². See also Chapter 14.

5. **Arpeggione.** A cello-sized instrument with a guitar-like body and six

strings tuned like those of the guitar. Invented in 1823. Schubert's famous sonata for arpeggione and piano is the only extant work written for the instrument.

6. **Bagpipe** (Ital. *piva, zampogna,* Ger. *Dudelsack, Sackpfeife,* Fr. *musette*). An instrument with a windbag which provides air for one or more single or double reed pipes. One pipe is the *chanter,* with finger holes to play the melody. It overblows at the octave. The other pipes are *drones,* which produce continuous notes at the octave or fifth. Older, Eastern bagpipes, have all single reeds. In Italy and parts of France all are double reeds, while in Scotland (the Highland bagpipe), Ireland (the Uilleann pipes), and Brittany the drones are single reeds and the chanter a double reed. The wind in the bag is supplied from the mouth through a blowing pipe except in the Northumbrian bagpipe, the modern Irish bagpipe, and the French musette, the latter having two chanters, pitched high and low.

7. **Banjo.** A long-necked guitar-like instrument with a small round body consisting of a single-headed drum. It has a light, twangy tone. The banjo may have from five to nine strings. The compass is from g or a to d³ or g³. Tuning is not standardized. One common tuning for the popular five-string banjo is the "G" tuning: g² d¹ g¹ b¹ d². This is convenient for playing in the key of G and related keys. The "C" tuning is g² c¹ g¹ b¹ d². Other common tunings are a e¹ g♯ b¹ e², and c¹ g¹ b¹ d² f². The six-string banjo is often tuned g d¹ g¹ b¹ d² g². The banjo has 22 frets.

The basic banjo strum consists of a stroke with the index finger followed by a nail brush over the strings and a strum with the thumb on the fifth string after it hits the drumhead. Common effects include the "pull off," the left hand leaving the stopped string after it is plucked; the use of a *capo* (Ital. *capotasto,* Ger. *Kapodaster,* Fr. *barré*), which is attached at a fret across the strings and acts as a temporary nut; "double-thumbing," the thumb playing on more than the fifth string; "frailing," the first beat being strummed with the nail of the second finger for a more percussive effect; the "blues shuffle," a dotted rhythm alternating three down strokes with the fingernails followed by an up stroke with the index finger; "finger-picking," arpeggiating chords or figures by plucking each string in succession; and the slide of the left hand from one fret to the next after the right hand plucks the string. Like the guitar, the banjo commonly uses chord symbols except when it has the melody. The *long-necked banjo* has three extra frets, which facilitate playing in some keys.

8. **Baritone oboe.** See **Heckelphone.**

9. **Basset Horn** (Ital. *corno di bassetto,* Ger. *Bassethorn,* Fr. *cor de basset*). Late eighteenth century, originally crescent-shaped, narrow-bore alto clarinet with a brass bell. It is pitched in F with a range of c to g³. The basset horn was often used by Mozart and once each by Beethoven, Mendelssohn, and Strauss. The parts today are usually played on the alto clarinet in E♭, an instrument of distinctly less incisive tone. The name originally meant "little bass clarinet

(basset) made by Horn." Horn is the name of the inventor, a fact leading to lasting confusion.

10. **Bass flute** (Ital. *flauto basso*, Ger. *Bassflöte*, Fr. *flûte basse*). Really a tenor flute and sometimes mistakenly called the contrabass flute, it was, in the sixteenth century, an unwieldy instrument with a 1-inch (5-cm) bore, 43 inches (110 cm) long. An improved, L-shaped version, with a loop in the pipe to decrease the length and with the addition of the Boehm key system, was developed in 1911 by Abelardo Albisi; it is sometimes called the *Albisiphone*. It has a range of B to f$\sharp^2$. Although almost never found in the orchestra, it is used in some jazz, film music, and contemporary chamber music. The tone is breathy and it has limited dynamic power. In 1932 a real bass flute which allegedly could descend to C was invented.

11. **Bass oboe.** See **Heckelphone.**

12. **Bass trumpet** (Ital. *tromba bassa*, Ger. *Basstrompette*, Fr. *trompette basse*). There are two types, the bass trumpet in E$\flat$, which, with the addition of a fourth valve, sounds a major sixth lower than the written range of the C trumpet, and the bass trumpets in C and B$\flat$, which sound, respectively, an octave and a major ninth lower. This instrument is in effect a valve trombone and is played with a trombone mouthpiece by trombonists. This is the instrument used by Wagner and Strauss. Wagner experimented with bass trumpets in E, E$\flat$, D, and low C.

The eighteenth- and nineteenth-century F trumpet, which is still to be found in Stravinsky's *Rite of Spring*, is a similar instrument to the E$\flat$ bass trumpet. Rimsky-Korsakov invented a larger bore *tromba contralto* in F, found in many Russian scores.

13. **Bugle.** Usually pitched in B$\flat$, C, or E$\flat$, the only notes possible are in the natural overtone series. The fundamental c is hard to obtain and only c^1, g^1, c^2, e^2, g^2, b$\flat^2$, and sometimes c^3 are of any use. The primitive tone of this instrument has kept it from any musical use except in drum and bugle corps.

14. **Bull's horn.** See **Cowhorn.**

15. **Cimbalon** (Ital. *cimbalo*, *salterio* (*-ongarese*), Ger. *Cimbal*, *Hackbrett*, Fr. *cimbel*, *cinbalon*, *tympanon*). Large Hungarian dulcimer with a shallow, trapezoidal sound box and 49 strings, played with two flexible mallets and used in gypsy music as well as some orchestral compositions by Hungarian composers. The range is chromatic from E to e^3. It is written on one or two staves in treble and/or bass clefs and is surprisingly agile in technique in the hands of a good player.

16. **Concertina, Melodium.** Small, hexagonal accordian with buttons for both hands and a range of about g to c^4. Concertinas in bass and alto were once manufactured. The older ones are not tempered and the buttons alternate on each side for every two notes of the chromatic scale. Doubling in thirds and sixths, simple two part writing, and chords of six or more parts are possible. Tchaikovsky used the instrument in his *Orchestral Suite Op. 53*.

17. **Cowhorn.** Simply the horn of a cow with one or two overtones possible around c^1. Used in Wagner's *Ring* and in Britten's *Spring Symphony*.

18. **Double bass oboe** (Fr. *hautbois contrebasse*). An instrument reputedly an octave below the bass oboe. See **Heckelphone.**

19. **Double bass trombone** (Ital. *trombone contrabasso*, Ger. *Kontrabass-posaune*, Fr. *trombone contrebasse*). Instrument introduced by Wagner in his *Ring*, written at pitch but built in B$^\flat$ or C and with a range of EE to d^1.

20. **Dulcimer.** A folk instrument derived from the German *Scheitholt* and the Swedish *hummel*. Popular in the Southern Appalachian Mountains of the United States. It consists of a long box with a fretted fingerboard. In a three-string instrument, one string will be tuned to the tonic and the melody will be played on this string, traditionally with a goose quill. The other strings are tuned to the dominant and act as drones.

21. **Dulcitone, Typophone.** An instrument like the celesta but with small tuning forks instead of metal bars. Vincent d'Indy wrote for it in his orchestral scores. It comes in small (f to c^4), medium (c to c^4), and large (A to a^4) sizes.

22. **Flageolet.** A small beak flute which was replaced by the recorder but which, with the addition of keys, survived into the nineteenth century. It had a written range of c^1 to d^3, sounding up a twelfth, and was used instead of the piccolo by Handel, Gluck, and Mozart.

23. **Glass harmonica.** An instrument consisting of glass bowls of increasing size fitted to a spindle and set in a trough of water. A foot pedal rotates the glass bowls, which are made to sound various pitches when touched with the fingertips. This mechanical model was invented by Benjamin Franklin in 1763 and was used by Mozart (K. 356 and 617) and Strauss (*Die Frau Ohne Schatten*). See also Chapter 36.

24. **Guitar** (Ital. *chitarra*, Ger. *Guitarre*, Fr. *guitare*). A six-string instrument tuned to e a d^1 g^1 b^1 and e^2. The range is e to a^3. The guitar is written on one staff in the treble clef an octave above true pitch. In classical style, chords are written out and each string plucked by a separate finger. In popular styles, strumming across the strings is more common and chord symbols are used. A *capo* can be used across the strings to act as a temporary nut, or, in the technique of *barrage* (Fr. *barré*), the fingers of the left hand can perform the same function with greater alacrity. Keys of C to E are easiest, the flat keys more difficult. Chords should be written with no more than a fifth or sixth between notes. Thirds, sixths, or octaves in sequence are usually relatively easy. Repeated notes and arpeggios are common. Complex part writing is not in the nature of the guitar. A slide or a slur over one fret up or down is a common technique. Harmonics are good to the fifth overtone (giving the notes e a b d^1 e^1 and g^1 chromatically to a^3 with the exception of the notes a$\sharp^1$ c^2 d$\sharp^2$ f^2 g$\sharp^2$ and a$\sharp^2$). Artificial harmonics are possible when the left hand stops the string and the right hand both lightly touches the string at the node and plucks it.

The guitar was first used in the orchestra by Rossini and later by Weber, Berlioz (who played it), Verdi, Mahler, and, since Schoenberg, by virtually every twentieth-century composer. Percy Grainger wrote for several guitars tuned to different chords in his orchestral music. Unless one plays the guitar, one should consult with a guitarist when writing for the instrument.

25. **Harmonica, mouth organ** (Ital. *armonica a bocca*, Ger. *Mundharmonika*, Fr. *harmonica à bouche*). Invented in 1829 by a Sir Charles Wheatstone and raised to the status of an orchestral instrument by Larry Adler through his commissions and astounding technique. The harmonica is a metal box with openings along the side through which the player inhales and exhales to set pairs of reeds in vibration. Exhaling on one side produces chords of the tonic; inhaling, the diminished triad on the seventh degree. Exhaling and inhaling on the other side produces the same chords a third lower. Ranges vary by manufacturer, but g to f³ is common (see Figure A–2).

Figure A–2   Chagrin, *Roumanian Fantasy*

26. **Harmonium, melodium, American organ.** Originally, in the nineteenth century, a small organ with one keyboard (manual) and no pedal keyboard. Two foot-pedals operated the bellows, which also produced crescendo and decrescendo. The unique sound of the harmonium is due to metal tongues being used in the pipes instead of reeds. The range is C to c⁴ but is expanded by the use of stops. In the right hand, the ½-foot flute stop is common, and clarinet, fife, oboe, and musette stops are often found. The left hand always includes English horn and often bourdon, clarion, bassoon, and cello stops. A stop called *piano des basses* lowers the bass dynamic, the *grand jeu* opens all stops, and the *expression* adds a tremulous sound to the tone. In all, seven octaves (CC to c⁵) are obtained with the stops (see also *Organ*). Knobs and levers worked by hand or knee activate the stops. On the original harmoniums there were only single and double octave stops, no mixture stops. Later, harmoniums with two keyboards and up to 34 registers were developed. The harmonium has been used in the orchestra by Tchaikovsky (*Manfred*), Mahler (Symphony No. 8), Strauss (*Ariadne auf Naxos*), and Shostakovich (*Golden Age*), among others.

27. **Harpsichord** (Ital. *clavicembalo, cembalo*, Ger. *Cembalo, Kielflügel*, Fr. *clavecin*). A baroque instrument, it was the forerunner of the piano, with strings plucked by a plectrum instead of struck with a hammer. Therefore,

dynamic gradations are possible only through couplings of other ranks of strings producing octave doublings above and below (4, 8, and 16 feet). This is accomplished by a system of pedals. There is also a *lute* or *sordino* stop on some instruments which mutes the tone. Large instruments have two keyboards and a range of from FF to f³. The harpsichord survived into the early nineteenth century to accompany recitatives in the opera and was not revived in the orchestra until Strauss. The instrument has been prominently used by composers such as de Falla, Poulenc, Martin, Carter, and others.

28. **Heckelclarind** (Ger.). An instrument invented by Wilhelm Heckel specifically to play the Alpenhorn solo in *Tristan*. It is in B♭ with a written range of b to f³.

29. **Heckelphone.** A baritone oboe with a wide, tapering bore and a globular bell with an air outlet in the side, invented by Wilhelm Heckel in 1904. Its range is a to g³ sounding down an octave. The tone is full and reedy. It was used by Strauss and Delius and is sometimes to be met with in commercial film scores. A piccolo Heckelphone also existed.

The Heckelphone is not to be confused with the eighteenth-century *baritone oboe,* which also had a *d'amore* version sounding down a minor third. It is unclear if this is the instrument referred to by Berlioz and others as a double bass oboe. The term "bass oboe" is sometimes applied to this instrument, as it is to the Heckelphone.

30. **Hurdy-gurdy.** A medieval stringed instrument in which the strings were set in vibration by a rosined wheel set in motion by a crank. Haydn wrote concertos and nocturnes for a pair of these instruments, which he called *lyras.*

31. **Jew's harp, Jaw's harp, Trump** (Ger. *Maultrommel, Brummeisen,* Fr. *Guimbarde*). A strip of metal attached to a curved frame held between the player's teeth. The metal strip is plucked and thus vibrates. Changes in size of the oral cavity produce different pitches. Used as a solo instrument in the eighteenth century and by twentieth-century composers such as Charles Ives.

32. **Keyed bugle, Kent bugle.** A bugle with keys like a saxophone. The range was from b chromatically to g♯² or as high as c³. It was usually built in B♭ or A and was used by Meyerbeer and in Italian orchestras throughout the nineteenth century.

33. **Mandolin** (It. *mandolino,* Ger. *Mandoline,* Fr. *mandoline*). A smaller, pear-shaped version of the obsolete *mandola,* with four double strings generally tuned g d¹ a¹ e², with a range up to e³ or sometimes a³, written in the treble clef on one staff. It is played with a pick or plectrum. Although four-part chords are possible, it is primarily a melodic instrument. The tremolo on a pair of strings is a typical technique. The mandolin has been used orchestrally by Mozart (*Don Giovanni*), Verdi, Mahler, Respighi, Schoenberg, Stravinsky (*Agon*), and others.

34. **Mouth organ.** See **Harmonica.**

35. **Natural horn, Hunting horn** (Ger. *Jagdhorn*). Usually in D or E♭ playing from the second to fourteenth overtone (c g c¹ e¹ g¹ b♭¹ c² d² e² f² g² b♭² c³). See also **Posthorn.**

36. **Natural trumpet.** See **Bugle, Posttrumpet.**

37. **Oboe d'amore** (Ger. *Liebesoboe,* Fr. *hautbois d'amour*). A mezzo-soprano oboe with a range of b to f³ sounding a minor third lower. Popular with Bach, the instrument was revived by Strauss (*Sinfonia Domestica*), Debussy (*Gigues*), and Ravel (*Bolero*).

38. **Oboe da caccia.** Curved (hence the name) forerunner of the English horn in F with a range of c¹ to d³ sounding down a perfect fifth. Often used by Bach.

39. **Ocarina.** Globular whistle-flute with a number of holes. Used in folk music and in the orchestra by Henze.

40. **Ophicleide.** A keyed serpent (from the Greek *ophis* and *kleis*). Though formerly built in alto ranges, in F and E♭, it was the bass ophicleide (usually in B♭ but also in C and A♭) which was used during the early nineteenth century to play the brass basses in the orchestra and band. The written range was from BB to c² and the instrument was used by Mendelssohn, Berlioz, Schumann, Meyerbeer, Verdi, Wagner, and others, though around 1850 the tuba, with its better tone and technique, quickly replaced the ophicleide in the orchestra. It survived in bands in Europe and South America until the turn of the century. A contrabass ophicleide, 8 feet long with a range down to DD, was built in 1843.

41. **Organ** (Ital. *organo,* Ger. *Orgel,* Fr. *orgue*). Any keyboard wind instrument. The ancient Roman *Hydraulos* was worked by a primitive keyboard, which was rediscovered in the Middle Ages. Large church organs sometimes required up to 70 men to work the bellows, though small portable *positives* (organs without pedals) and *portatives* (for which one hand worked the bellows) were popular. *Regals* were small reed organs. *Chamber organs* were popular through the baroque period. The Renaissance saw the introduction of multiple stops, and organ building reached its height in the baroque period. During the nineteenth century the old *tracker action* gave way to *pneumatic* organs worked by air pressure and, finally, in the twentieth century, to electro-pneumatic organs, in which the air was controlled by electric mechanisms, making possible instantaneous reply from console to pipes and a console physically removed from the rest of the organ. Organs for which the sound is produced electronically are treated in Chapter 39.

The organ consists of different ranks of pipes of different range, timbre, and volume. The basic pipes are *flue* pipes, where the sound is produced by the air's being directed over an opening. These pipes have weak overtones and are flute-like in sound. *Reed* pipes employ reeds to produce the sound and are richer in overtones. Narrow-bore pipes are richer in harmonics, wider-bore weaker. Pipes are open or closed, cylindrical or conical, with the corresponding effect on pitch and timbre as with any wind instrument. *Voicing* can be forward, producing an explosive attack and rich overtones, or mild, producing a reticent attack and weaker overtones. The various types of pipes produce a wide variety of tone colors.

The organ has up to five *manuals* (keyboards) which are named principal, great, choir, positive, and echo. They all can be connected to different ranks of pipes by *stops,* which are controlled by keys or, on older organs, knobs above and to the sides of the keyboards and which turn various registers on or off. The manual keyboards represent successively fewer stops and less power as they ascend from the principal. All are based on the 8-foot tone, meaning that in this rank the largest pipe is 8 feet long and represents the note C. With this rank, the keyboard plays at its written range, C to c⁴. With 4-foot stops engaged, it sounds an octave higher. Pipes of 32, 16, 8, 4, 2, and 1 feet give other octaves and are called *foundation* stops. The pedal keyboard has a range of C to g¹ and is based on the 16-foot pipes.

Stops of $1\frac{1}{3}$, $2\frac{2}{3}$, $5\frac{1}{3}$ and $10\frac{2}{3}$ feet give fifths above the fundamental and $3\frac{1}{5}$-foot pipes give thirds. These are called *mutations* and are used in combination with the foundation stops to produce *mixtures* (more than one stop), whereby an entire chord is sounded by pressing one key and obtaining the fundamental, fifth, and third with any octave doublings. The *diapason* or *principal* stops are open pipes used as the basis of most *registration* (combinations of stops) on the organ.

Dynamics are regulated by adding and subtracting stops, which is facilitated by *couplers,* which combine different manuals, and by *combination stops,* which can preset any combination of stops and be instantly engaged by the player during performance. The *Venetian swell* consists of shutters over some ranks of pipes which can be opened and closed by motors during performance. The *crescendo pedal* adds or subtracts stops consecutively. The *tremulant* adds vibrato.

The technique of the organ is like that of other keyboard instruments except that gradations of dynamics and attack cannot be obtained on the keyboards and legato is possible only with finger technique since there is no equivalent of the piano's damper pedal. Three staves are used, two with treble and bass clefs as with the piano, and a third staff below for the pedals, written in the bass clef. On occasion, three staves may be necessary for the manuals. The large theater organs of the early twentieth century, represented by a few Wurlitzer models still in existence, contained a bewildering variety of stops and sound effects.

The organ has been used with the orchestra from the earliest times, with particularly noteworthy works by Bach, Handel, and Mozart. In the nineteenth century the organ was used with the orchestra in large choral works to add volume and brilliance and to support extremely low or full passages. Gounod, Verdi, Mahler, Strauss, Saint-Saëns, Respighi, Holst, and Honegger have used the instrument in this manner.

Following are common stops:

I. *Diapason*

16 feet: contra dulciana, contra salicional, double open diapason, open metal, open wood, quintaton

8 feet: dulciana, open diapason (also 16 feet), salicional, voix celeste

4 feet: dulcet, octave, principal (prestant), salicet

2 feet: fifteenth (doublette), superoctave

II. *Mixtures and Mutations*

Acuta, carillon, cornet, cymbal, dulcet twelfth ($2\frac{2}{3}$ feet, echo cornet, full mixture, furniture, mixture (plain jeu), quint ($10\frac{2}{3}$, $5\frac{1}{3}$, $2\frac{2}{3}$ feet), septieme ($1\frac{1}{7}$ feet), sesquialtera, sharp mixture, tierce ($1\frac{3}{5}$ feet), twelfth ($2\frac{2}{3}$ feet)

III. *String Stops*

16 feet: contra geigen, contra viola, violine

8 and 16 feet: celeste, gamba

8 and 4 feet: geigen, viola

8 feet: geigen principal, viola da gamba, viole d'orchestre, violoncello

IV. *Flute Stops*

32 feet: sub-bourdon, sub-bass

16 feet: bourdon, contra-bourdon, grosse flote, sub-bass

8 feet: bass flute, clarabel, cor de nuit, gedact (Gedackt), hohlfloete, lieblich gedact, quintadena, stopped diapason, suabe flute

8 and 4 feet: rohr flute, spitzfloete

4 feet: flauto traverso, flute ouverte, gemshorn, harmonic flute, stopped flute, waldflote

2 and 1 feet: flageolet

2 feet: flautina, harmonic piccolo, piccolo

$1\frac{1}{3}$ feet: larigot

$5\frac{1}{3}$ and $2\frac{2}{3}$ feet: nazart (nassard)

V. *Reed Stops*

16 feet: bombarde, contra fagotto, contra posaune, contra tromba, double clarinet, double oboe, double trumpet, fagotto (bassoon), ophicleide, trombone (posaune)

16, 8, and 4 feet: tuba

8 feet: clarinet (clarionet), cor anglais, cornopean, cromorne (krummhorn), horn, oboe, orchestral oboe, posaune, tromba, trumpet (trompette), vox humana

4 feet: clarion (clairon), schalmei

The *vox celeste* consists of two pipes slightly out of tune producing beats. An older stop, the *unda maris,* consisted of two pipes slightly out of tune at the octave. The *aeolina* was an extremely soft stop. *Chimes* are often attached to the organ and can be operated by the keyboard. All these stops must be heard for their timbre to be understood. Needless to say, each organ is different and stops can only approximate the sound of the instruments after which they are named.

42. **Posthorn.** A natural horn 4 feet long with a small conical bore, used during the nineteenth century to signal the arrival of the mail coach. It was usually in B♭ or C and played the second to sixth or eighth overtones (c^1 g^1 c^2 e^2 g^2 etc.). Mozart, Beethoven, and Mahler wrote for it.

43. **Posttrumpet.** A natural trumpet in G or F with one hole which stops the tone up a fourth. The notes are (written) c g c^1 e^1 g^1 $b♭^1$ c^2 d^2 e^2 g^2.

44. **Recorder** (Ital. *flauto dritto,* Ger. *Blockflöte,* Fr. *flûte à bec*). A beaked flute with a wide, tapering bore. Widely used in the baroque period and re-

cently revived for educational purposes and the performance of older music. The modern recorder comes in six sizes as follows, the largest being 4 feet long:

sopranino	$f^2 - g^4$
soprano	$c^2 - d^4$
alto	$f^1 - g^3$
tenor	$c^1 - d^3$
bass	$f - g^2$
low bass	$c - d^2$

45. Sacred horns. Large-bore natural horns built for Rimsky-Korsakov's *Mlada*.

46. Sarrusophone (Ital. *sarrusofone*, Ger. *Sarrusophon*, Fr. *sarrousophone*). A family of double-reed brass instruments invented by Sarrus, with a wide conical bore, a penetrating tone, and a saxophone-like key system. Originally they came in six sizes from sopranino to contrabass, alternating in the keys of E^b and B^b like the saxophones and, like the saxophones, written in the treble clef with a range of b^b to g^3. The only instrument commonly used was the contrabass, which came to be written in the bass clef an octave above its true pitch. The written range was therefore BB^b to g. Ravel wrote for the sarrusophone in *Rapsodie Espagnole* and it was often used in the orchestra as a substitute for the contrabassoon.

47. Saxhorn. A family of valved, bugle-like instruments invented by Adolphe Sax. Like the saxophones, they came in alternate sizes in E^b and B^b with written ranges in the treble clef of $f\sharp$ to c^3, beginning with the sopranino in E^b sounding up a minor third to the tenor in B^b sounding down a major ninth. A bass in E^b and a contrabass in B^b sounding down a thirteenth (an octave and a major sixth) and a sixteenth (two octaves plus a major second) respectively, had written ranges of c to c^3. Strauss writes of contrabass saxhorns an octave below the two preceding instruments as well as a subcontrabass instrument in low E^b and a drone in B^b sounding four octaves and a major second below the written notes (perhaps a mistake in octave register)! The lower notes on the last two instruments were apparently unusable. The higher instruments are comparable to fluegelhorns, euphoniums, and baritones, the lower instruments essentially tubas. There was also a piccolo saxhorn in C or B^b which was similar to the cornet. The saxhorns are still used in some bands.

48. Saxtrombas. A family of valved, trumpet-like instruments with a bore narrower than that of the saxhorns but larger than that of the trumpets. It has the same range and transposition as the saxhorns, from the soprano in E^b to the contrabass in B^b. One was built in F as a substitute for the French horn.

49. Saxtubas. Larger-bore saxhorns with the same range and sizes as the saxtrombas.

50. Serpent. A bass cornet curved in an S shape, made of wood, covered in leather, and played with a mouthpiece. It appeared in the sixteenth century and was in use until the nineteenth. Rossini, Mendelssohn, Wagner, and Verdi wrote for the serpent, though its poor tone and intonation led to its rapid replacement by the ophicleide and shortly thereafter by the tuba. It was in B♭ with a written range of BB to c². Related to the "Russian Bassoon."

51. **Slide trumpet** (Ital. *tromba da tirarsi*, Ger. *Zugtrompete*, Fr. *trompette à coulisse*). A trumpet with a slide like that of the trombone. Bach's *corno da tirarsi* was probably the same instrument. The range was A to c². The discant trombone, still used in European churches, is a similar instrument with a range of e to b♭².

52. **Steel guitar, Hawaiian guitar.** A horizontal, six-string guitar with a large bridge. The right hand plucks the strings with a plectrum while the left hand slides a bar along the strings to produce a portamento effect. The instrument is usually electronically amplified.

53. **Stierhorn.** See **Cowhorn.**

54. **Strumento d'acciaio.** The instrument indicated by Mozart in *Die Zauberflöte*. Probably a set of bells played from a keyboard (not the celesta on which the part is played today).

55. **Tarogato** (Ger. *Holztrompette*). Hungarian double-reed wooden saxophone-like instrument used in Paris at one time to play the Alpenhorn part in *Tristan*.

56. **Tenor horn, B♭ tenor** (Ital. *tenore in si♭*, Ger. *Tenorhorn*, Bavaria *Althorn*, Austria *Bassflügelhorn*, Fr. *bugle ténor*, *bugle basse*, England *baritone*). A valved brass instrument of the cornet family occasionally found in the band. It has a conical bore and three valves. It is in B♭ (occasionally C or A) and has a range of E to b♭¹.

57. **Tenoroon** (Ital. *fagottino*, Ger. *Quint, Tenor-fagott*, Fr. *basson quinte*). Small bassoon sounding a perfect fifth above the ordinary bassoon (written range BB♭ to b♭¹), in use until the early nineteenth century. The *Quartfagott* (Ger.) sounded a perfect fourth below the ordinary bassoon.

58. **Tromba da tirarsi, Tromba spezzata.** See **Slide trumpet.**

59. **Ukelele, Ukulele.** Small four-string Hawaiian guitar with a long fingerboard. Usually tuned d¹ f♯¹ a¹ b¹ or g¹ c¹ e¹ a¹.

60. **Valve trombone** (Ital. *trombone a cilindri* [*ventili*], Ger. *Ventilposaune*, Fr. *trombone a pistons*). A valved trombone with a range of BB or AA♭ to b♭¹ or d². It is written in the bass clef at pitch and is used in some bands but, because of its inferior tone, never in the orchestra.

61. **Viola alta** (Ger. *Alt-Geige*). Larger viola built in 1875 by Karl Adam Hörlein and used by Wagner in the 1876 performance of the *Ring* at Bayreuth in place of ordinary violas because of its richer tone. It sometimes has a fifth string, tuned to e².

62. **Viola d'amore** (Ger. *Liebesgeige*, Fr. *viole d'amour*). An instrument larger than the viola and with a sweeter tone. It has seven strings, tuned d f♯ a d¹ f♯¹ a¹ d², and seven sympathetic strings tuned to the same pitches. The range is to a³ and it is written in the alto clef. Because of the tuning, chords of four or more notes are characteristic of the instrument, as long as the intervals be-

tween strings are confined to thirds or fourths and no open strings are used. Although primarily a baroque instrument, it has also been used by composers such as Haydn, Meyerbeer, Puccini, and Hindemith, who wrote a concerto for the instrument.

63. **Wagner tuba, Bayreuth horn or tuba** (Ital. *corno tube,* Ger. *Bayreuthtuben, Waldhorntuben*). Modified horns built for Wagner's *Ring* in an attempt to extend the range of the brass bass. These are played by the fifth to eighth hornists as alternate instruments. They have the half-conical bore of the horns with the wide bore of the tuba and are played with larger horn mouthpieces. Wagner used two tenor tubas, two bass tubas, and a contrabasstuba (see Chapter 15) as a quintet. The tenor tubas have a range of C to g^2 and are usually written in B♭. The bass tubas have a range of F to g^2 and are usually written in F. Following are the various transpositions used in the major works employing Wagner tubas (treble or bass clefs are used):

    I.   Wagner, *Das Rheingold and Die Götterdämmerung, Sc. 1:*
          Tenor tuba in B♭ written a major second above pitch
          Bass tuba in F written a perfect fifth above pitch
   II.   Wagner, *Walküre, Siegfried* and the rest of *Götterdämmerung:*
          Tenor tuba in E♭ sounding down a major sixth
          Bass tuba in B♭ sounding down a major ninth
  III.   Bruckner, *Symphony No. 9:*
          Tenor tuba in B♭ sounding down a major second
          Bass tuba in F written in bass clef sounding up a perfect fourth
  IV.   Bruckner, *Symphony No. 7* and Strauss, *Elektra:*
          Tenor tuba in B♭ sounding down a major ninth
          Bass tuba in F sounding down a perfect twelfth

64. **Zither** (Ital. *cythare,* Ger. *Zither,* Fr. *cythare*). Austrian and Bavarian folk instrument consisting of a wooden soundbox and four or five fretted strings tuned a^1 (or e^2) a^1 d^1 g c. These are plucked with the right thumb with a plectrum and stopped with the left hand. Accompaniment strings, tuned to $a^{♭2}$ $e^{♭2}$ $b^{♭1}$ f^2 c^2 g^1 d^2 a^1 e^2 b^1 $f^{♯1}$ $c^{♯2}$ and $g^{♯1}$, are strummed with the other fingers of the right hand, as are bass strings tuned to $e^{♭1}$ b♭ f^1 c^1 g d^1 a e^1 b^1 f♯ $c^{♯1}$ and g♯. The zither is written on two staves in the treble clef an octave above pitch but the bass strings are sometimes written in the bass clef at pitch. The range of the melody strings is c to d^4. The 40-string zither has a total combined range of AA to d^4 including contrabass strings. The instrument was used in the orchestra by Johann Strauss. The tremolo is characteristic of the instrument, as are natural and artificial harmonics. A bowed zither with four strings like the violin also exists.

Though they are not often met with today, it seems appropriate to include here a brief list of older string instruments occasionally encountered in the performance of old music and sometimes in contemporary scoring.

Violino piccolo. Tuned a fourth or fifth above the violin. Used by Bach.

Quinton. A five-string violin tuned g d¹ a¹ d² g².

Contralto violin. A larger violin tuned a step below the ordinary instrument.

Viola pomposa. A five-string alto violin tuned c g d¹ g¹ c².

Viola da spalla. A small cello with standard tuning, carried with a shoulder strap.

Violoncello piccolo. A small five-string cello tuned C g d a e¹ (possibly Boccherini's *violoncello alto* or Bach's *violoncello a cinq acordes* (sixth cello suite).

Octobass. A three-string bass tuned CC GG C and written an octave higher with a range to written g. Levers and foot pedals operated the instrument.

Tenor violin. Tuned to G d a e¹ and played by cellists.

The following instruments are members of the viol family:

Double bass viol (violone). Tuned DD GG C E A d.

Bass viol (viola da gamba). Tuned AA (sometimes absent) D G c e a d¹.

Tenor viol. Tuned G c f a d¹ g¹.

Alto viol. Tuned c f a (or b) d¹ g¹ c².

Treble viol. Tuned d g c¹ e¹ a¹ d².

Division viol. A small solo gamba.

Pardessus. Tuned a fourth above the treble viol.

Lyra viol. A high viol with variable tuning.

Appendix B

Acoustics and
How Instruments Work

THE NATURE OF SOUND

The study of sound is the province of *acoustics*, a branch of physics. The fluctuation in the density of air molecules striking the tympanic membrane (eardrum) is transmitted to the brain, where it is perceived as sound. These fluctuations in the density of molecules are usually produced by some vibrating object which sets the molecules in motion, alternately compressing and decompressing them. This movement creates *sound waves* which travel outward in all directions from the vibrating body.

When these vibrations occur at a regular rate, a *pitch* is produced. In scientific terms, this is the *frequency* of the sound, or the number of vibrations or cycles per second (vps, cps, or *Hertz*). A complex series of vibrations, in which no definite pitch is discernible, is called *noise*. While most musical instruments produce sounds of definite pitch, others produce sounds of indefinite pitch, notably certain percussion instruments. Sound waves can be illustrated by a graph in which a horizontal line indicates the average density of the air, the top of the curve the point of maximum compression, and the bottom the point of maximum decompression (Figure B–1). The points at which the curve intersects the line are called *nodes;* the high and low points of the curve are *antinodes* (wave crests). Such a pitch, produced by a body vibrating over its entire length, is called the *fundamental.*

Figure B–1

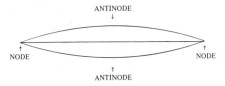

For a good graphic example of a sound wave, imagine the horizontal line as a string held under tension at both ends and then set in vibration by bowing (the violin), plucking (the harp), or striking (the hammers of the piano). The string then vibrates above and below its original position as indicated in Figure B–1, producing sound waves. Rapid fluctuation produces *high* frequency, perceived by the mind as *high* pitch, and relatively slow fluctuation produces *low* frequency, perceived as *low* pitch. The more molecules set in motion, the greater the distance between antinodes and the greater the *amplitude* or *volume* of the sound. The human ear responds to sounds between about 20 and 20,000 vps.

HARMONICS

Besides vibrating over its entire length, a string, column of air, or other vibrating body also vibrates in simple fractions of its own length: $\frac{1}{2}$, $\frac{1}{3}$, $\frac{1}{4}$, $\frac{1}{5}$, $\frac{1}{6}$, and so on (see Figure B–2). These vibrations all occur simultaneously in any vibrating body. Therefore, other, higher pitches are being produced at the same time as the *fundamental*. These additional pitches are known as *overtones* or *partials*. *Harmonics* are tones which include both the fundamental and the overtones. All sounds, whether produced in nature or produced by musical instruments, generate overtones.

Figure B–2

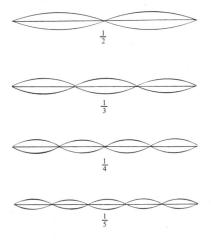

The relation of the overtones to the fundamental is always exactly the same, no matter what pitch that fundamental has. In other words, exactly the same overtones are always produced relative to the fundamental, creating the same *intervals* (differences in pitch).

It will be noticed (Figure B–3) that the first overtone, produced by a string or any other body vibrating in halves, is exactly twice the frequency of the fundamental pitch. The following table shows the ratio of the lengths into which a vibrating body is divided and the corresponding musical intervals produced above the fundamental.

"perfect" consonances	octave	2:1
	perfect 5th	3:2
	perfect 4th	4:3
"imperfect" consonances	major 3rd	5:4
	major 6th	5:3
	minor 3rd	6:5
	minor 6th	8:5
dissonances	minor 7th	9:5
	major 7th	15:8

Figure B–3

Overtones:	1	2	3	4	5	6	7	8	9	10	11	12	13	14	15
Harmonics: 1	2	3	4	5	6	7	8	9	10	11	12	13	14	15	16

Fundamental
VPS: 65 131 196 262 327 392 458 523 589 654 719 785 850 916 981 1046

Musical intervals which we hear as consonant have the simplest ratio of frequencies to each other; those we hear as dissonant have more complex ratios. During the Middle Ages, the early centuries of *polyphonic* music (music in more than one part), only the perfect consonances were heard as being agreeable and written as harmonic intervals. By the sixteenth century the imperfect consonances had become acceptable as pleasing sounds, and since the late nineteenth century the dissonances have been used in increasingly independent ways (not requiring resolution to a consonance).

The frequencies given in Figure B–3 are all *pure* or *just* pitches. Pythagoras discovered the relations between intervals in the sixth century B.C., setting the basis for Western musical theory.

These natural harmonics, however, do not lend themselves to the system of major and minor scales used in Western music since if one tunes an instrument according to pure pitch, some keys are "in tune" to our ears and others are drastically "out of tune." Therefore, in the eighteenth century a compromise system of *equal temperament* was devised whereby the notes of each scale would be in the same relation to one another with equal semitones. Bach's *Well-tempered Clavier,* with preludes and fugues in each major and minor key, was written for instruments tuned in this fashion. The pitches marked with a cross in Figure B–3 are slightly different in pitch from the pure harmonics.

In addition, pitch has changed over the centuries. In the early eighteenth century, pitch was generally a half step lower for any particular written note than it is today. At one time some orchestras in the United States tuned to a pitch a half step higher than today. In 1834 a conference in Stuttgart set standard pitch at 440 vps for the A above middle C, though slight differences in pitch are still to be found in different countries.

The presence of overtones can be easily demonstrated at the piano by one's silently depressing the keys corresponding to the natural overtone series of any note, thereby removing the dampers from the strings tuned to those pitches and leaving them free to vibrate. Then by loudly and briefly depressing the key corresponding to the fundamental pitch, one will hear the upper pitches "ring" after the lower key has been released. These *sympathetic vibrations* or resonance results because the sound waves produced by the overtones of the lower string set in vibration the upper strings tuned to the same pitches. If the experiment is tried with notes not in the overtone series of the fundamental (assuming the piano is in tune), no sympathetic vibration will result and no sound be heard except the fundamental.

Resonating chambers are used on many instruments to strengthen the volume and alter the *tone color* (see next section) of the sound produced. Examples are the bodies of string instruments and the resonators of the marimba.

Beats are a phenomenon produced by two different sources of the same pitch which are slightly out of synchronization with each other. An audible periodic variation in intensity of sound is produced by the different sources reinforcing each other or cancelling each other out.

TONE COLOR

In 1862 Helmholtz discovered that the differences in quality of a musical sound, which we refer to as *tone color* or *timbre,* and by which we distinguish between the sound of a trombone or cello, flute or human voice, *is dependent solely on the relative strength of the harmonics produced by a particular instrument.* This can be demonstrated by electronically removing the overtones of the same fundamental played by different instruments. As more overtones are removed, the sound becomes less and less characteristic, until, when the fundamental tone is isolated, all instruments produce the same colorless hum. Absolutely "pure" fundamentals without any overtones rarely occur in nature but can be produced by electronic means.

STRING INSTRUMENTS

A string produces a frequency in inverse proportion to its length: string instruments of high pitch are small, instruments of low pitch large. The length of the body must correspond in size to the length of the string to resonate properly. The tone color can be altered through different methods of bowing, bowing at different points on the string or on different strings, plucking, and the use of mutes. Different registers also have overtones in varying ratios of strength. *Vibrato* is a slight fluctuation in pitch produced by a rapid vibration of the finger on the string.

WIND INSTRUMENTS

Pitches can be generated directly in a volume of air by creating regular disturbances which produce a definite pitch. The primitive "bull-roarer," an instrument consisting of a piece of wood on a string which is twirled rapidly in a circle, illustrates this type of sound, known as an *aeolian tone*. A telephone wire can produce a definite pitch by sympathetic vibration if the disturbances in the air around it are at the same frequency.

These means of production are impractical for a musical wind instrument, however. Instruments utilize a column of air confined in a *tube* or *pipe*. Tubes open at both ends are known as *open* pipes, tubes closed at one end as *stopped* or *closed* pipes. Density changes in an open pipe operate from both ends, producing a node in the middle of the pipe (see Figure B–4). Therefore, the fundamental or lowest pitch is one in which the distance from one end of the pipe to the other is the distance from one antinode to the next of the sound wave.

Since sound travels at a relatively steady rate, in sounds of higher frequencies the distance from one antinode to the next (*wavelength*) is less than in sounds of lower frequencies. Therefore, to produce higher pitches, wind instruments need only short columns; to produce lower pitches, they need longer columns. An open pipe of 2 feet (61 cm) is required to produce middle C. To produce a note an octave lower, a 4 foot (122-cm) pipe is required.

A stopped pipe, closed at one end, such as some organ pipes, produces a fundamental an octave lower than an open pipe of the same length since the closed end acts as a node and therefore the entire length of the pipe is available to produce the distance from node to antinode, rather than half the length as in the case of an open pipe.

In Figure B–4 the total wavelength of a vibration, or cycle, includes two successive antinodes, the first designating maximum compression, the second maximum decompression. It can be easily calculated how long each wave will be for a given frequency by dividing the speed of sound in feet per second by the number of vibrations per second. The wavelength of middle C is about 4 feet. Since only one-half the cycle need be present in a column of air in an open

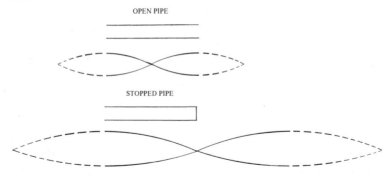

OPEN PIPE

STOPPED PIPE

pipe to produce that pitch, only a two-foot pipe is necessary. A stopped pipe need be only as long as one-quarter the entire wavelength. The wavelength of a frequency twice as rapid, that is, a pitch an octave higher, will require a pipe only half as long since the wavelength will be half as long.

An open pipe produces all the overtones, but a stopped pipe produces only odd-numbered harmonics since an antinode would have to be present at both ends of the tube to produce even-numbered harmonics (with the air column vibrating in halves, fourths, etc.). For this reason, the tone color of an open pipe is richer and brighter than that of a stopped pipe. All orchestral wind instruments except the clarinets are open pipes. Blowing across the end of a bottle illustrates the sound of a stopped pipe.

The *flue* (flute) pipes of an organ are set in vibration by air's being directed against the edge of an opening in the end of the pipe. This is called an *air reed, free reed, aerial reed,* or *nonreed.* The flute is also an air reed. It is an open pipe 2 feet (61 cm) long, producing a fundamental middle C. By means of holes covered by fingers or keys, the effective length of the air column is shortened and higher pitches can be produced. The flute *overblows* at the octave; that is, if the force of the air against the opening is increased, the first overtone is produced more strongly than the fundamental. With various fingerings and further overblowing, a chromatic range of three octaves is obtained. The piccolo, being half as long as the flute, has a fundamental an octave higher.

Reed instruments (including the organ reed pipes and the accordion and mouth organ) set the air column in vibration by means of one or two elastic pieces of thin reed which are fixed in one end of a pipe. The clarinet is a single-reed instrument which is almost a closed pipe but has some weak even-numbered harmonics. Since it acts as a closed pipe, though it is little longer than the flute, it produces a fundamental an octave lower. It overblows at the twelfth, that is, the second overtone can be played by dividing the air column in three parts. This is facilitated by a "speaker key" which opens a hole in the instrument a third of the way up, thereby emphasizing the node necessary for the second overtone and allowing it to "speak" or sound.

The *bore* is the inside area of the pipe. A distinction is made in open pipes between so-called *whole-tube* (wide-bore, that is, large diameter in relation to tube length) instruments in which the entire air column vibrates and easily produces the fundamental and *half-tube* (narrow-bore) instruments in which the fundamental is difficult or impossible to obtain but the first overtone is produced with ease. Although narrow-bore brass instruments, such as trumpets, horns, and trombones, are theoretically half-tube instruments, the fundamental is obtainable by skilled players on the trumpet and in the upper slide positions by trombonists.

Both the flute and clarinet are cylindrical pipes. The saxophone, however, is an example of a reed instrument with a conical bore. A stopped conical pipe acts the same way as an open cylindrical pipe of the same length. Therefore it must be twice as long as a cylindrical pipe to produce the same fundamental, but all the overtones are present.

The oboe has a double reed, the two ends of which vibrate together, and is a slightly conical stopped pipe. The bassoon is also a double-reed instrument with a conical bore about 8 feet (244 cm) long and therefore pitched two octaves below the oboe. Its fundamental is weak.

With brass instruments the lips act as a double reed. Most brass instruments are conical for at least part of their length. The flaring bell allows the sound to emerge more efficiently and directly in spherical waves and adds intensity to the upper partials. Most brass instruments have a narrow bore, making the fundamental difficult to produce. The deep, conical mouthpiece of the horn results in its smooth and mellow tone; the shallower, cup-shaped mouthpieces of the trumpet and trombone, emphasizing the upper partials, cause their brighter tone. The horn has a strong fundamental in its upper register but a weak fundamental in its lower range. The tuba, with its wider bore, can easily produce the fundamental. The fact that some wind instruments are pipes curved back on themselves for convenience in no way affects the sound of the instrument.

In the human voice, a wind instrument, the *glottis* or opening between the two muscles in the larynx acts as a double reed. The oral, nasal, and sinus cavities resonate the sound. The size and shape of the oral cavity can be altered to change the tone color by emphasizing different combinations of overtones.

PERCUSSION INSTRUMENTS

Membranes, plates, and bars can be made to vibrate by striking. Bars (as in the xylophone) produce more or less detectable definite pitches but also many *nonharmonic* overtones (not part of the natural harmonic series) which tend to give them the tone color of indefinite pitch instruments as well. Plates (cymbals) usually produce a complex of nonharmonic overtones resulting in indefinite pitch. Membranes (drums) can produce sounds of definite (timpani) or indefinite (snare) pitch, depending on their construction.

Bells usually produce a fundamental and overtones of a strong perfect fifth and minor third. The fundamental is known as the *strike tone* and is what we associate with the audible pitch of the bell. There are also a multitude of nonharmonic overtones, which are responsible for the brightness of a bell's tone, as well as a *hum tone,* an additional note located about a major sixth below the fundamental and responsible for the vibrant sound with its resultant beats and dissonances occurring after the bell has been struck. This complex of harmonics is due to the material out of which the bell is made as well as its shape. See also Chapter 19.

Bibliography

This bibliography is not intended to be comprehensive, and many more volumes were consulted in the preparation of this text. Included here are those books most likely to be of interest to the general student of orchestration. The Harvard and Grove's Dictionaries have valuable information in condensed form. Dates are of the latest revised edition, not of the latest printing.

Avgerinos, Gerassimos, *Handbuch der Schlag- und Effect-Instrumente.* Frankfurt: Verlag der Musikinstrumente, 1967.

Baines, Anthony, *Woodwind Instruments and Their History.* New York: W.W. Norton, 1962.

Bartolozzi, Bruno, *New Sounds for Woodwind,* trans. Reginald Smith Brindle. London: Oxford University Press, 1967.

Berlioz, Hector, *Treatise on Instrumentation,* ed. and enlarged by Richard Strauss, trans. Theodore Front. New York: Belwin-Mills, 1904.

Blades, James, *Percussion Instruments and Their History.* New York: Praeger, 1970.

Boretz, Benjamin, and **Edward T. Cone,** eds. *Perspectives on Notation and Performance.* New York: W.W. Norton, 1976.

Brindle, Reginald Smith, *Contemporary Percussion.* London: Oxford University Press, 1970.

Carse, Adam, *The History of Orchestration.* New York: Dover, 1964.

———, *Musical Wind Instruments.* New York: Da Capo, 1965.

Casella, Alfredo, *La Tecnica dell'orchestra contemporanea.* Milan: Ricordi, 1974.

Donington, Robert, *The Instruments of Music.* London: Methuen, 1970.

Erpf, Hermann, *Lehrbuch der Instrumentation und Instrumentenkunde.* Mainz: Schott's, 1959.

Forsyth, Cecil, *Orchestration.* New York: Macmillan, 1914.

Galpin, Francis, *Textbook of European Musical Instruments.* New York: Greenwood Press, 1956.

Gavaert, F., *Nouveau Traite d'Instrumentation.* Paris: F. Lemoine, 1885.

Harrison, Frank, and Joan Rimmer, *European Musical Instruments.* New York: W.W. Norton, 1964.

Hunter, J. J., and **D. I. Crecraft,** *Instrumentation.* New York: British Book Center, 1976.

Jacob, Gordon, *The Elements of Orchestration.* New York: October House, 1966.

——, *Orchestral Technique: A Manual for Students.* London: Oxford University Press, 1940.

Karkoschka, Erhard, *Notation in New Music,* trans. Ruth Koenig. New York: Praeger, 1972.

Kennan, Kent, *The Technique of Orchestration.* Englewood Cliffs, N.J.: Prentice-Hall, 1952.

Kling, H., *Modern Orchestration and Instrumentation,* trans, Gustav Sänger. New York: Carl Fischer, 1902.

Kotonski, A., *Schlag Instrumente in Modernen Orchester.* Mainz: B. Schott's Söhne, 1965.

Kunitz, H., *Die Instrumentation.* Leipzig: 1960.

Lang, Philip J., *Scoring for the Band.* New York: Belwin-Mills, 1950.

Leibowitz, Rene, and **G. Maguire,** *Thinking for Orchestra.* New York: G. Schirmer, 1960.

Leidzén, Erik, *An Invitation to Band Arranging.* Bryn Mawr, Penn.: Theodore Presser, 1950.

Marcuse, Sibyl, *Musical Instruments: A Comprehensive Dictionary.* New York: W.W. Norton, 1975.

——, *A Survey of Musical Instruments.* New York: Harper & Row, 1975.

McKay, Gardner, *Creative Orchestration.* Boston: Allyn & Bacon, 1963.

Peinkofer, Karl, and **Fritz Tannigel,** *Handbuch des Schlagzeuges.* Mainz: B. Schott's Söhne, 1969.

Piston, Walter, *Orchestration.* New York: W.W. Norton, 1955.

Practical Orchestration: A Method of Arranging for School Orchestras. New York: Robbins Music Corp., 1963.

Prout, Ebenezer, *The Orchestra.* London: Augener, 1887.

Rauscher, D., *Orchestration.* New York: The Free Press, 1963.

Read, Gardner, *Music Notation.* Boston: Allyn & Bacon, 1964.

——, *Thesaurus of Orchestral Devices.* New York: Greenwood Press, 1969.

Richards, Emil, *Emil Richards' World of Percussion.* Los Angeles: Gwyn.

Rimski-Korsakov, Nikolai, *Principles of Orchestration,* ed. Maximilian Steinberg, trans. Edward Agate. New York: Dover, 1905.

Risatti, Howard, *New Music Vocabulary: A Guide to Notational Signs for Contemporary Music.* Urbana: University of Illinois Press, 1975.

Rogers, B., *The Art of Orchestration.* New York: Appleton, 1951.

Russcol, Herbert, *The Liberation of Sound: An Introduction to Electronic Music.* Englewood Cliffs, N.J.: Prentice-Hall, 1972.

Russel-Smith, Geoffrey, *Sound Sense: The Instruments of the Orchestra and How They Work.* London: Boosey & Hawkes, 1965.

Russo, William, *Composing for the Jazz Orchestra*. Chicago: University of Chicago Press, 1961.

————, *Jazz Composition and Orchestration*. Chicago: University of Chicago Press, 1968.

Salzedo, Carlos, *Modern Study of the Harp*. New York: G. Schirmer, 1921.

Spohn, Charles, and **John Tatgenhorst,** *The Percussion*. Boston: Allyn & Bacon, 1971.

Turetzky, Bertram, *The Contemporary Contrabass*. Berkeley: University of California Press, 1974.

Wagner, Joseph, *Band Scoring*. New York: McGraw-Hill, 1960.

————, *Orchestration: A Practical Handbook*. New York: McGraw-Hill, 1959.

Widor, C., *The Modern Orchestra*. London: J. Williams, 1906.

Glossary

Not included here are the names of individual instruments and vocal types. Also omitted are terms dealing with Salzedo harp techniques, jazz styles, and electronic music, none of which is likely to be encountered out of context and all of which are treated in their respective sections. These terms are to be found in the index.

A

Abstrich (G.)—downbow

a cappella (It.)—unaccompanied (e.g., a chorus)

accompanied recitative—recitative with orchestral accompaniment

accordez (F.)—tune

a due, a2—a unison of two instruments (e.g., woodwinds)

aerophones—wind instruments

agilità (It.)—the ability of a singer to perform rapid, difficult passage work

agitare (It.)—to shake, as a rattle (*agitato means* [play] in an excited manner)

agité (F.)—same as *agitato* (see **agitare**)

air sounds—sounds made on a wind in-

strument without production of a definite pitch

a la jante (F.)—at the edge (of a cymbal or drumhead)

a la pointe (F.)—with the tip of the bow

al centro (It.)—in the center (of a cymbal or drumhead)

aleatoric fingerings—fingerings which produce unpredictable sounds on woodwind instruments

aleatoric music—music which is left partly to chance by the composer

al fusto (It.)—on the shell (of a drum)

alla campana (It.)—on the dome (of a cymbal)

alla metà (It.)—in the middle (of a cymbal or drumhead)

alla punta (It.)—with the tip of the bow

all'estremità (It.)—on the edge (of a cymbal or drumhead)

al margine (It.)—at the edge (of a cymbal or drumhead)

al tallone (It.)—at or near the frog of the bow

ambedue bacchette (It.)—with both sticks

am Frosch (G.)—with the frog of the bow

am Griffbrett (G.)—(bow) at or near the fingerboard

am Rand(e) (G.)—at the edge (of a cymbal or on the rim of a drum)

an den Aussenseiten (G.)—on the outside (i.e., the shell of a drum)

an der Spitze (G.)—at the tip of the bow

aperto (It.)—open (e.g., a brass instrument with mute removed)

a piena voce (It.)—full voice

arcata in giù (It.)—upbow

arcata in su (It.)—downbow

archet (F.)—bow

archetto (It.)—bow

arco (It.)—with the bow

armonico (It.)—harmonic

arpeggiando (It.)—(play) as broken chords

arrange—to adapt music for a different ensemble than that for which it was originally written

artificial harmonic—a harmonic played by stopping a string with one finger and touching it at a node with another

aspirando (It.)—inhaled

assistant first chair—a player who sometimes substitutes for the first chair player

associate first chair—a player who shares more or less equally with another the first chair duties

attack—the manner of initiating a tone on an instrument

au bord (F.)—at the edge (of a cymbal or drumhead)

au centre (F.)—at the center (of a cymbal or drumhead)

auf beiden Fellen (G.)—on both drumheads

auf den Holzrand (G.)—on the rim

auf dem Steg (G.)—at (or near) the bridge

auf den Saiten (G.)—on the strings

auf der (A) Saite (G.)—on the (A) string

auf die Kuppe(l) (G.)—on the dome (of a cymbal)

Aufstrich (G.)—upbow

au milieu (F.)—in the middle

auxiliary instruments—instruments in the same family as a primary orchestral instrument with similar techniques, fingerings, and so forth, as the English horn is to the oboe, for instance

avec cordes (F.)—snares on

avec l'archet (F.)—with the bow

avec le pouce, doigts, mains (F.)—with the thumb (i.e., the thumb roll on the tambourine), fingers, hands

avec sourdine(s) (F.)—with the mute(s)

B

bacchette (It.)—sticks: *molle* (soft), *dure* (hard), *di legno* (wooden)

back—that part of a string instrument which is opposite the belly or, in the case of the harp, opposite the neck

background—music to accompany a drama or film; also that material other than primary melodic material in a jazz arrangement

bag mute—literally a bag hung over the bell of a wind instrument

baguettes (F.)—sticks: *molles* (soft), *dures* (hard), *de bois* (wooden)

baissez les touches sans sonner (F.)—depress keys silently

balais métalliques (F.)—jazz brushes

balance—the relationship in relative volume (loudness) between different instruments in an ensemble

band—a group of wind instruments, usually with percussion

banda (It.)—a band; also (in Italy) the winds and percussion in the orchestra

bariolage (F.)—the technique of bowing broken chords across the strings

bass bar—a strip of wood which reinforces the belly of a string instrument

basso continuo (It.)—a bass instrument (usually string) playing the bass line with a keyboard instrument filling in the chords

bel canto (It.)—a type of singing characterized by facile and florid technical ability

bell—the flare at the end of a wind instrument; the dome of a cymbal; also a metallophone (see Chapter 19) of definite pitch

belly—the sounding board of a string instrument

bend—a fluctuation up or down in pitch, returning to the original note.

bisbigliando (It.)—a rustling tremolo on the harp

blousée, blousez (F.)—at the rim or edge

bocal—the curved tube connecting the reed to the bassoon

bocca aperta (It.)—mouth open

bocca appena aperta (It.)—mouth less open

bocca chiusa (It.)—mouth closed (humming)

Bogen (G.)—bow

bouché (F.)—stopped (as a horn)

bouche fermeé (F.)—mouth closed (humming)

bow—the device with which strings are set in vibration on a string instrument; also the section of a cymbal between the bell and the edge

bowed cymbal (gong)—a cymbal (or gong) played with a bow on the edge, producing a harmonic

bowed tremolo—a tremolo produced by rapidly alternating up and down bows

bowings—the various techniques of addressing the strings with the bow

boy soprano—a young, unchanged male voice

brass—the wind instruments made of metal and played with a mouthpiece

brass band—a band consisting primarily of brass and percussion

break—the place in the range of the voice or any wind instrument where there is a change of register; the break in the clarinet occurs between the twelfth above the fundamental and the first overblown note

brushes—wire brushes used on a drum, cymbal, and the like, also known as *jazz brushes*

bucket mute—a mute with a large concavity

buzz tone—tone produced by humming while playing a wind instrument

C

cadence—the harmonic resolution at the end of a musical phrase; also the drum rhythm in a marching band

cambio d'arco a piacere (It.)—change of bow at will

campalline di sughero (It.)—cork mallets

campane in alto (It.)—bells up (for winds)

castrato (It.)—a high male voice produced by castration before puberty

chamber music—music for from one performer to a chamber orchestra

chance music—see aleatoric music

change en, changez (F.)—retune; also, take another instrument

chest voice—that part of the vocal range which resonates in the chest

chiuso (It.)—closed

choke—to dampen suddenly with the hand

chordophones—string instruments

chorus—a group of voices; the main melody (usually repeated) of a song

chromatic—involving tones other than those of a mode or scale; also describing a scale formed of half steps

circle mute—a type of mute manufactured for saxophone

clarino (It.)—a type of performance utilizing the upper portion of the overtone series on a brass instrument

close—the coda of a jazz or popular arrangement

closed vowels—vowels pronounced with a constricted mouth and throat (ee)

close position—the disposition of notes in a chord whereby the upper voices are as close together as possible, there being no gaps in the chord

clusters—groups of several notes separated by steps or half steps

coll'arco (It.)—with the bow

colla unghia (It.)—with the fingernail

col legno battuto (It.)—beaten with the wood of the bow

col legno tratto (It.)—bowed with the wood of the bow

colpo di chiave (It.)—see **key clicks**

col pollice (It.)—with the thumb

column—the cylindrical support at the front of the harp

come un eco (It.)—like an echo; echo tone

compressed score—a band score utilizing five to fourteen staves

comprimario (It.)—a supporting role in opera

concert band—large, seated band used in concert

concertmaster—the first chair violinist who leads the firsts in an orchestra

concert pitch—actual pitch as opposed to the written pitch of transposing instruments

concert score—a conductors's score written at actual pitch

con corde (It.)—with snares

condensed score—a band score on three or four staves

conductor's score—the full score

con la dita (It.)—with the finger

con la mano (It.)—with the hand

con sordino(i) (It.)—with mute(s)

contre le pupitre (F.)—on the rim

coperto (It.)—muted, covered

countermelody—a secondary melodic line

coups d'archet (F.)—bowings

crook—an additional length of tubing to change the pitch of the old hand horn; also another name for the bocal

cross-cuing—a method used in band arranging: any part for an unusual instrument is written in the part of a common instrument so that if the first instrument is not available, the part

can be played by the other instrument

cross-hammering—a mallet technique whereby a passage is played with alternating mallets

cue—another instrument's part written in small notes during the rests of an instrument to facilitate following the progress of the music and to alert for the next entrance; see also **cross-cuing**

cuivré (F.)—brassy

cup mute—a lined, cup-shaped mute with rubber edging and a mellow tone

D

dalle due parti (It.)—on both heads (of a drum)

damp—to mute the sound

damper pedal—the pedal that raises the dampers on a piano and allows all the strings to vibrate freely

dämpfen (G.)—to mute the sound

decay—the gradual diminution of sound from a vibrating body

dental stops—consonants produced by the tongue against the teeth (d, t)

derby mute—a hat placed over the bell of a brass instrument

desk—a music stand; also the players reading from that part

détaché (F.)—separate bows

diatonic—music consisting of the notes of a scale

die Hälfte (G.)—half (of a string section)

divisi, div. (It.)—divided (string section)

doink, doit, dork—jazz terms for a glissando up from a note as an embellishment

dome—the raised bell in the center of a cymbal

double-action harp—the modern harp with foot pedals to change the pitch of the strings

double stop—two adjacent strings bowed simultaneously

double tonguing—technique used for rapid passage work (tu-ka, tu-ka) on a wind instrument

doubling—having more than one instrument play a line; also, playing more than one instrument in the course of a piece

downbow—the bow stroke from frog to tip

drag—in drum technique, two or more grace notes on a beat

Drahtbürste (G.)—jazz brushes

drop-off—jazz term for a glissando down from a note as an embellishment

drum and bugle corps—a military band made up of cornets, trumpets, and percussion

du-daht, du-wah, du-wop—jazz terms referring to the addition of syncopation in performance to lines written in regular rhythm

dub—to record over a prerecorded sound track or film

du talon (F.)—at the frog of the bow

E

écho (F.)—like an echo; echo tone

Echoton (G.)—echo tone

echo tone—a sound produced on the clarinet by touching the tongue to the reed while playing

electrophones—instruments which produce sound electronically; synthesizers

elevations—those angles of the bow which put it in contact with particular strings

embouchure—the lip position of a wind player or the mouthpiece of the instrument

étouffer, étouffés (F.)—dry, dampened sound, especially on the harp

extension—a device which enables the double bass to extend its range from EE down to CC

F

Fach (G.)—the voice type

fall-off—jazz term for a glissando down from a note as an embellishment

falsetto—the high, thin register of a man's voice produced like the overblown octave of a wind instrument

f-holes—the openings in the belly of a string instrument

fingerboard—place where the string player's left hand presses down the strings to create different pitches

fingered tremolo—a rapid alternation of pitches on a string instrument, produced by the alternation of the fingers of the left hand; if the interval is larger than a major second, it is called a *fingered tremolo*; a major or minor second is simply called a *trill*

fioritura (It.)—the vocal technique of florid passage work

first chair—the leading player in any orchestral section who also plays the instrumental solos

Flageolett (G.)—harmonic

flam—a two-stroke drum figure

Flatterzunge (G.)—flutter tonguing

flautando (It.)—on the fingerboard; also, "harmonic-like"

flip—jazz term for a rough turn

flutter glissando—simultaneous flutter tonguing and glissando on the trombone; introduced by John Marcellus

flutter tonguing—a roll with the tongue while one is playing a wind instrument

foreground—the main melodic material in a jazz arrangement, sometimes doubled in harmony

frame notation—segments or "frames" of music being juxtaposed in various ways in aleatoric music

frequency—the rate of vibrations of a pitch in vibrations per second, which is the same as cycles per second or Hertz, Hz.

fricatives—consonants produced by releasing air under pressure as a hiss (s, *f*)

frog—the part of the bow held in the hand

frottées (F.)—a two-plate cymbal roll

frulando (It.)—flutter tonguing

fundamental—the basic tone produced by an instrument from which the overtones are produced

G

gedämpft (G.)—muted

gedämpfter Schlag (G.)—muted stroke

Generalpause, G. P.—a rest for the entire orchestra

geschlagen (G.)—beaten (as in *col legno battuto*)

gestopft (G.)—stopped (as the hand in the bell of a horn)

gestossen (G.)—*sautillé* (q.v.)

gestrichen (G.)—bowed or drawn (as in *col legno tratto*)

geteilt (G.)—*divisi* (q.v.)

gewöhnlich (G.)—in the usual manner

glissando (It.)—a slide from one note to another

grand (F.)—large

grand détaché (F.)—a *détaché* made with a long bow stroke, often indicated with dashes over each note

grande (It.)—large

graphic notation—notation giving approximate pitches, durations, and other indications

gridando (It.)—a shriek

gross (G.)—large

group staccato—two or three notes on each bow off the string

growl—jazz term for playing a wind instrument while growling in the throat

guttural consonants—those produced at the back of the mouth (g, k)

H

half tie—a tie from a note into a rest to indicate that the sound should not be dampened

half tube—a narrow-bore wind instrument which lacks the fundamental

half valve—a brass instrument technique used in jazz to create glissandi and other embellishments

halt cadence—a drum rhythm used with marching bands to bring the band to a halt

hand pops—a percussive sound created with the palm of the hand on the mouthpiece of a wind instrument

harmonic—an overtone; created on string instruments by lightly touching a string at a node

harmonique (F.)—harmonic

harmon mute—a mute with a removable stem

harte Schlegel (G.)—hard sticks

Hauptstimme (G.)—main voice, primary melodic line

head—the membrane of a drum

head voice—the upper range of the voice which resonates in the cavities of the head

heel—the frog of the bow

Holzschlegel (G.)—wooden sticks

homophones—two harp strings tuned to the same pitch enharmonically

hum—to vocalize with the mouth closed

I

idiophones—instruments of solid material which produce sound when set in vibration by striking or in some other way

in der Mitte (G.)—in the center (of a drumhead or cymbal)

indicative notation—see *graphic notation*

in margine (It.)—on the edge

in modo ordinario (It.)—in the normal manner of playing

J

Janitscharrenmusik (G.)—Janizary music

Janizary music—the music which accompanied the royal progress of the eighteenth-century Turkish sultan with enormous numbers of percussion instruments

Jazzbesen (G.)—jazz brushes

jeté (F.)—a bowing whereby the upper third of the bow is thrust against the strings on a downbow encompassing from two to ten notes

jeu ordinaire (F.)—the normal manner of playing

Jodeln (G.)—yodeling

K

key clicks—rapid depressing and releasing of the keys of a woodwind instrument without playing

key pops—forceful depressing of the key of a woodwind instrument on pitch, with or without release of air through the reed

key slaps—slapping of the keys of a woodwind instrument with the palm

kick beat—jazz term for the addition of a syncopated accent to an otherwise regular rhythm

Klangfarbenmelodie (G.)—a melody consisting primarily of variation in tone color produced by its being passed from one instrument to another

klein (G.)—small

klingen lassen (G.)—let vibrate

L

laisser vibrer (F.)—let vibrate

la metà (It.)—half (of a string section)

lasciare vibrare (It).—let vibrate

leading motive—a motive or theme used to identify a character, idea, etc. which appears in varied forms throughout a composition

lead sheet—written music consisting of a melody and chord symbols

legato (It.)—slurred; also combining more than one note under each bow

leggio (It.)—desk or stand

Leitmotif (G.)—leading motive

ligature—the screw clip on a clarinet or saxophone mouthpiece

lip buzz—buzzing with the lips on the mouthpiece

lip slur—technique used on brass instruments to play up or down the overtone series of one valve or slide position

lontano (It.)—distant, echo-like

louré (F.)—an expressive bow stroke involving a slight push on each note

Luftpause (G.)—literally a catch breath; used to indicate any brief pause for articulation and phrasing

M

mailloche (F.)—double-headed bass drum beater

mallet percussion—instruments, such as the orchestra bells, xylophone, marimba, and vibraphone, which are played with mallets

manuscript score—the composer's original hand-copied score

marcato (It.)—strongly accented; this term also refers to the *martelé* bowing

marching band—the band used for military, athletic, and festive events; it includes only those instruments which can be conveniently carried

marqué (F.)—*martelé* (q.v.)

martelé (F.)—an accented bowing whereby the bow is alternately drawn and stopped on the string for each note

martellato (It.)—*martelé* (q.v.)

measured tremolo—a bowed tremolo in specific note values

medio (It.)—medium

membranophones—drums

mezzo-carattere (It.)—a voice which lies in between or includes two normal voice classifications

mezzo voce (It.)—half voice

microintervals—intervals smaller than a minor second

military band—a marching or concert band connected with a military service

miniature score—the small version of the orchestra score for study purposes

mit beide Schlegel (G.)—with both sticks

mit Dämpfer(n) (G.)—with mute(s)

mit dem Bogen geschlagen (G.)—beaten with the bow on the strings

mit den Daumen (G.)—with the thumbs

mit dem Nagel (G.)—with the fingernail

mit den (einen) Bogen (G.)—with the bow

mit den Fingern (G.)—with the fingers

mit den Händen (G.)—with the hands

mitte (grosse) (G.)—medium (size)

mit Verscheibung (G.)—with the damper pedal

moyen (F.)—medium

multiphonics—chords played on wind instruments

Mund zu (G.)—mouth closed, humming

muta (in) (It.)—change (to) another instrument; retune (to) another note

mute—a device placed on the bridge of a string instrument or in the bell of a wind instrument which dampens the tone by slightly decreasing the volume but primarily by removing overtones and changing the timbre

mute fanning—the technique of alternately removing and inserting the mute in the bell of a wind instrument while playing

N

natural harmonic—a harmonic on an open string

naturel (F.)—in the normal manner of playing

Nebenstimme (G.)—secondary voice or melody

neck—the section of a string instrument between the pegbox and the body

nehmen (nimmt) (G.)—take(s)

nel mezzo (It.)—in the middle (of a drumhead)

neutral clef—two vertical lines indicating that indefinite pitches are being notated (for percussion)

nicht vibrierend (G.)—do not let vibrate; without vibrato

non vibrato (It.)—without vibrato

Normal (G.)—in the normal manner of playing

normale (It.)—in the normal manner of playing

nota flessuosa (It.)—a bend on a pitch

O

obligato (It.)—an important melodic accompanying part

Obertonkontrolle (G.)—a pad inside the snare drum which is engaged by a lever to mute the drum

offen (G.)—open (as a horn with hand out of the bell)

off the string—bowings with the bow bouncing off the string

ohne Dämpfer(n) (G.)—without mute(s)

on the string—bowings with the bow maintaining contact with the string

open—primarily used to refer to a wind instrument without mute or hand in the bell

open position—chords spread so that there are other possible chord notes which are not filled in or doubled in the upper voices

open vowels—those vowels pronounced with relatively open throat (*ah*)

ouvert (F.)—open

overblowing—playing above the fundamental octave (or, in the case of the clarinet, the twelfth) of a wind instrument; also blowing with great pressure to create a brassy effect

overtone—one of the higher pitches created when any object is set in vibration

P

paradiddle—a drum roll in which two successive beats are taken on each stick for a more rhythmic roll

parlato (It.)—a rapid, wordy style of vocal writing; spoken

parts—the music copied from the score for the individual players to read

passaggio (It.)—florid vocal technique

Patschen (G.)—leg slapping

pavillons en l'air (F.)—bells (of a wind instrument) up

Pedalton (G.)—pedal tone

pedal tone—the fundamental of an instrument; also any long-held note in an arrangement

percussion—instruments that can be set in vibration by beating

petit (F.)—small

piccolo (It.)—small

pitch—the frequency of a note

pit orchestra—the orchestra to accompany dance or musical theater

pizzicato (It.)—plucked

pizzicato gettato (It.)—the fingers flicked over the strings

pizzicato muto (It.)—notes plucked and dampened with the palm (double bass)

plop—jazz term for an embellishment consisting of a glissando from a note

plunger mute—hand-held mute used for fanning, often still made from a "plumber's helper"

pocket score—a study score

portamento (It.)—a smooth slide from one note to another; usually refers to small intervals, *glissando* to larger intervals

portato (It.)—*louré* (q.v.)

position—the placement of the left hand on the fingerboard of a string instrument; also the positions of the trombone slide

poussé (F.)—upbow

prende (It.)— take (another instrument or beater, etc.)

prendre (F.)—to take

prepared piano—a piano with various materials attached to the strings to change the timbre

près de la table (F.)—near the sounding board (of the harp)

près du chevalet (F.)—at or near the bridge

primo, I° (It.)—first player (winds)

principal—leader of a string section

Pult (G.)—desk

pupitre (F.)—desk

Q

quadruple stop—a four-note chord played across the strings

quarter tone—one half of a semitone

R

Randschlag (G.)—rim shot

range—the total compass in pitch of an instrument; the compass in pitch of a part written for an instrument

recitative—vocal writing in which the music is subjegated to the words

recitativo accompagnato (It.)—a vocal recitative accompanied by orchestra

recitativo secco (It.)—recitative accompanied only by sporadic chords on a keyboard instrument (usually harpsichord)

refrain—the repeated chorus of a song following the verse

register—a particular portion of an instrument's range

register key—the key on the clarinet or saxophone which allows the air column to vibrate in thirds

rehearsal—the time when an ensemble practices together

rehearsal letters (or **numbers**)—indications in the score and parts to designate particular bar numbers for ease in beginning in the middle of a piece at rehearsal

relâchées (F.)—without snares

ricochet (F.)—*jeté* (q.v.)

ride cymbal—the cymbal used to beat a repeated rhythm in the jazz ensemble

rim—the edge of a drum or cymbal

rim shot—a sharp accent obtained by placing one stick across the rim and head of a drum and striking it with the other

rip—a jazz term for a glissando up to a note

roll—a rapid alternation of drumsticks on the head

roll-off—a drum cadence for beginning a march or piece in the marching band

ruff—a drum stroke with two or more grace notes on a beat

Ruthe (G.)—a bundle of sticks used on the bass drum

S

saccade (F.)—the technique of bringing three strings into a plane by the pressure of the bow to play a triple stop simultaneously

saltando, saltato (It.)—*sautillé* (q.v.)

sans vibrer (F.)—without vibrato

sautillé (F.)—a light, bouncing, off-the-string bowing

Schalltrichter auf (G.)—bells up

Schlegel (G.)—sticks: *weiche* (soft), *harte* (hard), *holz-* (wooden-)

schmetternd (G.)—brassy

schütteln (G.)—shake

scordata (It.)—loosened, as a drumhead

scordatura (It.)—tuning the strings to different pitches than normal

sec (F.)—dry

secco (It.)—dry

secco recitative—see *recitativo secco*

secondo, II° (It.)—second player (winds)

section—a group of strings, as first violins, violas, etc.

semivowels—consonants pronounced with little obstruction of the air flow (l, m)

senze corde (It.)—without snares

senza sordino(i) (It.)—without mute(s)

senza vibrato (It.)—without vibrato

separate bows—not legato, change bows on each note

shake—in jazz terminology, a rough lip trill

Shastock mute—a wooden mute with a rough tone

shell—the body of a drum

short score—the original composer's sketches on a few staves; a four-stave score for conducting

slap tongue—in clarinet technique, the tongue being literally slapped against the reed for a percussive effect while playing

slur—to phrase two or more notes together; also the curved sign denoting such technique

smorzato (It.)—an intense vibrato in woodwind technique

snap pizzicato—a sharp pizzicato whereby the string rebounds against the fingerboard

soft pedal—the pedal on the piano which moves the action so that only some of the strings tuned to each note are struck by the hammers

solo—a passage for a single player on a particular line

Solotone mute—Latin mute with a nasal, echo-like tone

sonorants—see **semivowels**

sons d'onges (F.)—with the fingernail

sons étouffés (F.)—strings dampened with the palm while one is playing (on the harp)

sons soilés (F.)—covered

sordi (It.)—covered, muted

sordinato (It.)—muffling a stroke on a percussion instrument

sordino interno (It.)—see **Obertonkontrolle**

sospirando (It.)—a sigh

sostenete le taste taciamente (It.)—depress keys silently

sostenuto pedal—the pedal on some grands which enables certain notes which have just been played to resonate while the rest are dampened

sotto voce (It.)—in an undertone

soundpost—a peg which is set between the belly and back of a string instrument to transmit vibrations

sourdine (F.)—muted, covered

spazzole (metallica) di jazz (It.)—jazz brushes

speaker key—see **register key**

spiccato (It.)—the bow dropped on the strings and lifted after each note

spill—jazz term for a glissando down from a note

Sprechgesang (G.)—partially spoken song

Sprechstimme (G.)—music spoken on definite pitches

Springbogen (G.)—sautillé (q.v.)

staccato (It.)—short, detached notes

staccato volante (It.)—a "flying staccato," with a light, off-the-string bowing encompassing several notes on each bow

stage band—the small band used originally in vaudeville, later for dance music and galas

staggered bowing—half the section bowing at a different time from the other to obtain an overall effect of legato

stand—desk

staple—the tube connecting the reed to a woodwind

stimmen (G.)—tune; also orchestra parts

stock arrangement—in jazz, a two-stave arrangement from which can be derived an arrangement for any size ensemble

stopped—closed, as with a hand in the bell of a horn

straight mute—the standard orchestral mute

string orchestra—an orchestra comprised of string instruments only

string quartet—four solo string instruments, two violins, viola, and cello

strings—the orchestral string instruments

strisciato (It.)—brush the cymbals apart after crashing them together

study score—a small score reprinted from the full score

subtone—tone produced by pressing of the tongue against the reed of a clarinet or saxophone

sul bordo (It.)—on the rim or edge

sulla cassa (It.)—on the rim or body of the drum

sulla (la) corda (It.)—on the (A) string

sulla cupola (It.)—on the dome (of a cymbal)

sulle corde (It.)—on the strings

sul mezzo (It.)—in the middle

sul ponticello (It.)—at or near the bridge

sul tasto (It.)—on the fingerboard

sur (la) (F.)—on the (A string)

sur la protubérance (F.)—on the dome (of a cymbal)

sur la touche (F.)—on the fingerboard

sur le cadre (F.)—on the rim or body of a drum

sur les cordes (F.)—on the strings

sussurando (It.)—whispering

switches—a bunch of sticks used on the bass drum

symphonic band (winds)—a concert band

T

tacet—rest

tasten tonlos (stumm) niederdrücken (G.)—depress keys silently

tempered scale—the adjusted scale introduced in the eighteenth century so that all keys could be played equally in tune

texture—the density of an orchestration

throw-away note—jazz term for any of the half-valve embellishments

thumb roll—motion performed on the edge of the tambourine by a moistened thumb

timbre—tone color

tiré (F.)—downbow

ton de pédale (F.)—pedal tone

tone—a note; also the quality of a sound

tone clusters—several notes within a step or half step of each other

tone control—see *Obertonkontrolle*

tono di pedale (It.)—pedal tone

tous les deux baguettes (F.)—both sticks

transcribe—to transfer music written for one ensemble or instrument to another

traps—various noise-makers used by the drummer in a jazz ensemble

tremolo—the rapid alternation of notes

trémolo (F.)—tremolo

trill—the rapid alternation of two notes a step or half step apart

triple stop—a chord played on three adjacent strings

triple tonguing—type of tonguing used on wind instruments to play rapid passages in triplet rhythm

tutti—the full orchestra playing together

two-plate roll—two crash cymbals brushed together

U

umstimmen (G.)—retune

una corda (It.)—soft pedal

unison—two or more instruments playing the same line

unisono (It.)—unison

unmeasured tremolo—a tremolo performed as rapidly as possible

upbow—the bow stroke drawn from the tip to the frog

V

valves—the device by which extra lengths of tubing are added to the horn by depressing keys

vamp—a repeated accompaniment figure in popular music before the entrance of a singer

verge (It.)—switches

verges (F.)—switches

vergules—pairs of diagonal slashes used in jazz to indicate the repetition of a chord or accompaniment figure

verse—the initial part of a song which precedes the chorus; a song may have several verses

vibrato (It.)—rapid fluctuation of the pitch or intensity of a note

Viotti stroke—a short bow followed by a long bow on the beat

vocal cords—the pair of muscles in the larynx which produce the human voice

vocalize—to sing on a neutral vowel

voce bianco (It.)—pure, unchanged male child's voice

volta subito (V. S.) (It.)—turn quickly

vuota (It.)—empty; used to indicate a *Generalpause* (q.v.)

W

weicher Schlegel (G.)—soft sticks

whispa mute—a soft practice mute

wind ensemble—a group of winds specializing in concert music

wobble—a vocal defect created by bad technique or age

woodwind quintet—flute, oboe, clarinet, horn, and bassoon

woodwinds—keyed wind instruments played with a reed or air reed

wow—a jazz term for a rough lip trill; also an electronic malfunction

Y

yodel—rapid alternation of normal voice and falsetto

Index

1. Foreign terms of less than common usage will be found in the Glossary.
2. Proper names are to be found in the text and in association with the musical examples.
3. Names of standard orchestral instruments appear as chapter headings in the Table of Contents.
4. Twentieth century techniques and instruments are found in Chapters 36 and 37.
5. Obsolete and miscellaneous instruments are found in Appendix A.

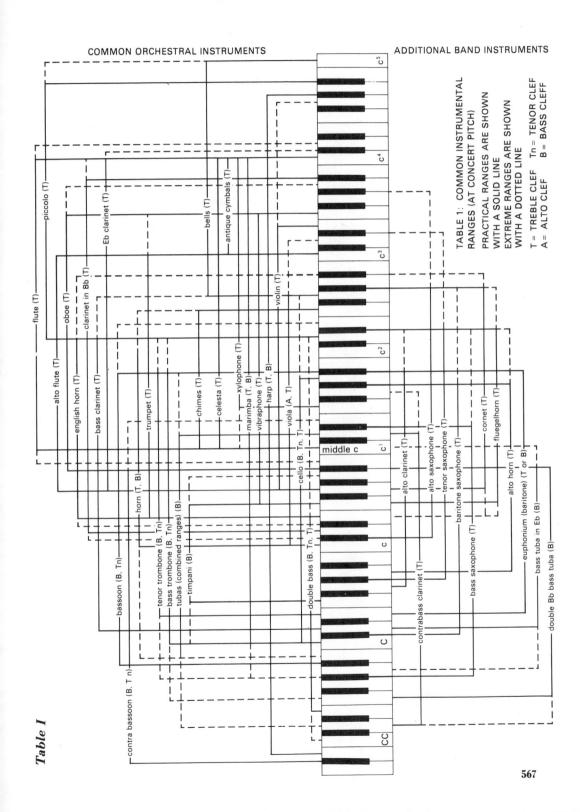

Table I

COMMON ORCHESTRAL INSTRUMENTS

ADDITIONAL BAND INSTRUMENTS

TABLE 1: COMMON INSTRUMENTAL
RANGES (AT CONCERT PITCH)
PRACTICAL RANGES ARE SHOWN
WITH A SOLID LINE
EXTREME RANGES ARE SHOWN
WITH A DOTTED LINE

T = TREBLE CLEF Tn = TENOR CLEF
A = ALTO CLEF B = BASS CLEF

567

Table II

Transposition Chart

The written note shows where 'middle' C (c′) would be written for the instrument, whether that note is encompassed by the range of the instrument or not.

Common Orchestral Instruments

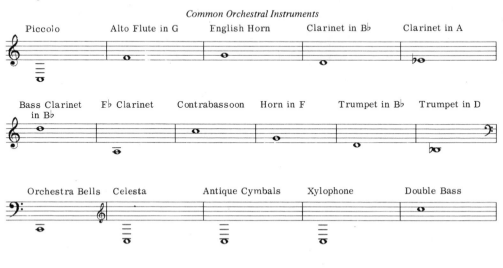

Common Band Instruments

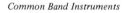

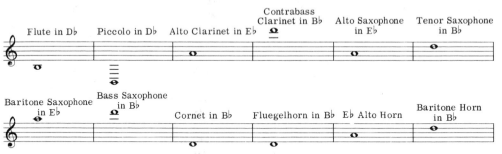